ANTHROPOLOGY CULTURE, SOCIETY, AND EVOLUTION

John J. Collins

Prentice-Hall, Inc., Englewood Cliffs, New Jersey

ANTHROPOLOGY
CULTURE, SOCIETY, AND EVOLUTION

Library of Congress Cataloging in Publication Data

COLLINS, JOHN J
   Anthropology: culture, society, and evolution.

   Includes bibliographical references.
   1. Anthropology.   I. Title.
GN24.C63   301.2   74–19399
ISBN 0–13–038596–4

ANTHROPOLOGY:
CULTURE, SOCIETY, AND EVOLUTION

John J. Collins

© 1975 by Prentice-Hall, Inc., Englewood Cliffs, New Jersey

Printed in the United States of America

10 9 8 7 6 5 4 3 2 1

Photo research by Gabriele Wunderlich

COVER PHOTO: © Philip Jones Griffiths/Magnum Photos

Prentice-Hall International, Inc., London
Prentice-Hall of Australia, Pty. Ltd., Sydney
Prentice-Hall of Canada, Ltd., Toronto
Prentice-Hall of India Private Limited, New Delhi
Prentice-Hall of Japan, Inc., Tokyo

CONTENTS

v

15
technology

16
economics

17
kinship
and marriage

PREFACE

This book is designed to be a very brief introduction to anthropology. It can be used as the sole text in a one-semester course or as the main text—to establish subject continuity—in a two-semester situation. Since most one-semester courses appear to emphasize aspects of culture, the bias of this book is also in that direction.

This book is written in as tight and organized a fashion as possible. Technical jargon has been kept to a minimum so as not to overburden the student who, after all, has to struggle with other courses and other terminology. It is a matter of some debate as to just what should be covered in an introductory course. To keep an introductory text small enough to be easily digested, not only must some topics be treated briefly, but others must be deleted entirely. How to do so becomes largely a matter of personal inclination. Although I have attempted to be as comprehensive as possible, three specific topics often covered in other introductory texts have been largely or wholly omitted. In the first portion of the text, I have made only brief reference to cultural evolution outside of Europe and the Near East. This is done, not only because separate chapters would add considerably to the length (and cost) of the book, but also because the aim is to present general stages of such development, for which limited examples can be considered sufficient. In the second half, there is no chapter on the history of anthropology as a discipline. It has been my experience in a variety of teaching situations that if one body of information is boring to students, this is it. Contemporary students are interested in "facts" of today, not who said what that was later rejected. I have also failed to insert a chapter on psychological anthropology. This is an important omission but justified somewhat by the notion that most students seem to receive much of the same material in introductory courses in psychology or sociology. So, in this attempt to present anthropology as a fresh and compelling subject matter, it has been deleted. Most other topics covered in general anthropology texts have been included.

What should the beginning student derive from an introductory text? Hopefully, an awareness of the approach of the field of study represented and a feeling for the quality of its results. To convey such information, I have constructed each chapter to be as independent of the others as possible while still maintaining a degree of integration. Hopefully, the casual reader, as well as our students dipping into the book, can derive some sense and satisfaction from it. I have also taken this approach as an expedient, since it would be difficult to present all these chapters in terms of a single organizing framework. From an inspection of the introduction, it will be seen that as a field of research, anthropology has yet to organize itself tightly into an overall framework. Perhaps this will be impossible due to its very nature. Any more limited approach in this direction—for example, seeing behavior in terms of its presumed functions for humans or in its relation to the environment (functionalist or ecological)—is also bound to have its critics. The present work, then, is an attempt at an anthropological "sampler" on the human species that can be used in any type of introductory course.

Moreover, the writing of an introductory text is a hazardous and presumptuous undertaking in a field as broad and comprehensive as anthropology. There are bound to be errors of commission as well as the problems described above. It is perhaps impossible for a single writer to synthesize even a portion of the basic knowledge in a given subject. On the other hand, many texts written by a "committee" of scholars also come out uneven and incomplete. At least here the level of complexity, even with the inevitable errors, is consistent. It is hoped that all the views and approaches of my colleagues and my own teachers in the past that are used in this book are fully documented. Often, however, this becomes impossible. One learns a bit of information and then incorporates it into one's own way of thinking and teaching. When one writes a book such as this, many such items are unconsciously included. If I have so sinned, I ask forgiveness. Along this line, I would like to take this opportunity to pay one intellectual debt. When I began teaching (and finding lecture materials), I used a book by John Honigmann, *The World of Man* (New York: Harper & Brothers, 1959). It became my "bible" even though I later discarded it as too lengthy. When I prepared for my doctoral examinations, it was again useful. If any single book shaped my own thinking, it was this text. I cite it often in this volume (probably not often enough), and would belatedly like to thank Dr. Honigmann. If students reading the present work can derive the same kind of satisfaction and part of the knowledge that I gained from his work, I will be satisfied.

I would like to express my gratitude to a number of people at Prentice-Hall: to Jim Morlock for original encouragement and interest; to Ed Stanford for continued support; and to Amy Midgley for sound advice and great patience. Thanks also to Lynn Winger who typed the manuscript with astonishing speed and good will, and to my family who always supplied moral support. I would like to dedicate this book to my parents who taught me the value of hard work.

introduction: anthropology's perspective on man

*A*nthropology, like most fields of study, is difficult to define prior to the exposure of the student to its data. If we examine the term linguistically, we can say that it is the study of man (from *Anthropos*, man; and *logia*, study). Usually, the anthropologist hastens to add that this study includes not only humans, the genus-species *Homo sapiens*, but the works of humans as well. By this, we generally mean the cultural creations of man: paper clips and pyramids, incest taboos and creator gods, languages and legal systems. It is perhaps this very lack of qualification relative to the study of man that gives anthropology its uniqueness and usefulness as a field of study. Anthropology is the comprehensive study of humans that views them as total beings. Other human-oriented studies seem primarily interested in more specialized approaches. So, for example, sociology is primarily interested in human social relations; economics in man's production and distribution of goods and services; and psychology in more individualistic human behavior, While these studies are interested in humans, they choose to emphasize a single major avenue as a way of collecting and analyzing such information.

Despite difficulties in drawing clear-cut distinctions, anthropology might be said to employ a more general approach that takes into account the dual nature of the human species. It accepts the fact that we are animals with biological behaviors and potentials, but also includes the study of our uniqueness as an animal: our highly developed learned social and cultural nature. Anthropology attempts to take both of these natures into account in the explanation of human behavior. To use a common analogy, it tries to see the whole forest in perspective rather than seeking to explain it by special analysis of particular types of trees. Thus, anthropologists study both physical and cultural natures of man, and they take a holistic approach. In addition, they limit themselves neither in time nor in space. They study the dual nature of humanity as far back as it can be traced and wherever it occurs. Hence,

Evolution of the human skull from fish to man.

anthropology goes beyond history, which deals with man subsequent to the development of written records, and beyond those disciplines primarily interested in human behavior in industrial societies.

The anthropologist, of course, is not an all-knowing scientist. Two facts must be taken into account at this point. First, because anthropology takes a comprehensive approach to the human species, we understand specific aspects of human behavior less well than do these disciplines that have staked out those aspects as their primary emphasis. The flag anthropology waves is one of extensive familiarity with humans rather than intensive understanding. Knowledge of the whole gives insights just as important as those provided by detailed understandings of the parts. Second, the mass of anthropological data, plus insights from specialized fields, necessitates specialization within the field for the individual anthropologist. Although anthropology is one field, there are many kinds of anthropologists. This is simply an acknowledgement of the limitations of time and energy. Nevertheless, although the anthropologist may have his or her own particular interests, there is the attempt to keep the total picture of the human species in mind.

Generally speaking, anthropological interests are divided into two main areas, each of which contains a number of subdivisions. One, *physical anthropology*, concerns itself with the physical nature of humans and the evolution of this nature. Some major emphases developed later in this text are:

1. The study of the animals most closely related to humans—primatology. This includes field and laboratory studies of monkeys and apes to ascertain how their behaviors compare with our own.

3

2. The development of the human organism—human paleontology. This includes the search for fossil forms leading up to Homo sapiens.
3. The structure and variations of the human organism—human biology. This includes the assessment of human physical differences and behavior as these exist today.

Two, *cultural anthropology,* concerns itself with the social-cultural nature of humans and the evolution of this nature. Some major emphases developed later in this text are:

1. The study of past cultural developments—archaeology. This includes the search for the tools and other evidences of culture of of past human groups.
2. The descriptive study of the structure and variations of existing cultural systems—ethnography. This emphasizes the cutural ways of life of given groups of people.
3. The study of the functioning of social-cultural behavior—ethnology. This includes, among other things, the comparison of major systems of behavior, such as religion, in various societies.

Perhaps the easiest way for the beginning student to grasp the kinds of interest areas and disciplines of anthropology is to view them not as specialities but as perspectives. One anthropologist (Hoebel, 1972: 8) has characterized these perspectives in diagrams which are reproduced below in simpler and somewhat altered form.

Physical Perspective

Past Perspective	Origin and evolution of man	Structure and function of man	Present Perspective
	Origin and evolution of society and culture	Structure and function of society culture	

Cultural Perspective

Each of these perspectives or emphases draws somewhat upon the others for data and understanding. It keeps the holistic nature of the human species in mind even while asking its own specific questions. It also employs contributions from more specifically oriented fields of study: from biology and physics, for example, for some dating procedures applied to human evolution. Anthropology is indeed a comprehensive study of human behavior, and it is the intention of the present volume to present information on ourselves from all of the above four perspectives. First, the origin and evolution of the human species, then of culture, followed by a discussion of the structure and function of humans today. The second part of the book deals with the structure and function of society and culture. Chapters are written simply and briefly, and at the end of each set of related chapters there is included a bibliographic essay on key selected readings.

ONE

HUMAN EVOLUTION

1

relations to the animal world

Through the years there have been differing views on how humans came into existence. At one time, largely as religious doctrine, it was believed that humans had acquired their physical nature both suddenly and recently: God placed the human species on earth with the same body and behavior as we possess now. This event was calculated to have occurred about 4004 B.C. Based on *Genesis,* this account is called the doctrine of **special creation** and was not seriously questioned in the Western world until surprisingly recently. The accumulation of fossils of forms of life and the increase in geological knowledge, coupled with the growth of skepticism, led to a questioning and revision of this view in the late eighteenth and early nineteenth centuries. The doctrine of **catastrophism** used such data to suggest that a number of violent cataclysms had occurred that extinguished old forms and necessitated new ones to replace them—the biblical flood epic being cited as the most recent example. Further developments in the understanding of time and nature, however, subsequently gave rise during the latter half of the nineteenth century to the doctrine of **evolution.** This view, simply stated, holds that our body and behavior result from an exceedingly long and slow process of change during which physical structures and associated behaviors were developed and passed on from one variety of organism to another until human forms emerged. It further holds that we too have undergone considerable change and may so continue. This does not assert that humans are the end product of this process.

We will presently discuss the mechanisms, principles, and evidences relative to the concept of evolution. First, however, it is necessary to spend some time on the supposition that follows from it, namely, that to understand the human species and our present behavior we must first understand what led up to us. There are two ways in which this might be accomplished. One way would be to use the data of paleontology—the fossil record—and survey the entire fossil record prior to the emergence of man. The easier way is to simply consider ourselves as a part of nature. We can accomplish this by discussing the taxonomic divisions of nature first suggested by Linnaeus (in 1737, although there are less well-known earlier attempts), taking into account the many revisions used by biologists to classify living things at the present time.

> This alone would be enough to please any scientist with a sense of order, and Linnaeus had his own sense of order developed to an almost pathological degree. For him, classification was an end in itself, and he sought for no higher meaning in what he had created. Not so for others. An orderly presentation was fine, but once the order was established, was there nothing more? Could there not be new truths, hitherto obscured by disorder, now emerging in full clarity? (Asimov, 1960: 28)

Although such a taxonomy is essentially a static classificatory device, progressing from general to increasingly specific categories, it does have developmental implications. It suggests to us that we as humans owe a great deal of our physical structure and behavior to the evolutionary histories of organisms other than ourselves. As one anthropologist (Kraus, 1964) has neatly put it, we are born with a number of "degrees" that we didn't have to earn prior to our own evolutionary "schooling." We are, for example, John Doe AK (animal kingdom), SPM (subphylum Vertebrata), and CM (class Mammalia). Hence, by briefly surveying our taxonomic position in nature, we can learn a great deal about ourselves.

Some examples of fossil records: a fossil lobster (top, left) and Sauropod dinosaur tracks, fore and hind foot (bottom, left). The reconstructed dinosaur illustrates the use of paleontological data in helping us visualize and classify the earliest forms of animal life.

American Museum of Natural History

First of all, of course, humans are living organisms, and as such, we have a certain fundamental structure as well as behaviors. We are composed of protoplasm organized into cells; we experience growth, reproduction, and death; we respond to outside stimuli and must adapt and adjust to our environment. Beyond this general nature, the human species is classified into a number of increasingly specific and circum-scribed levels and categories.

Kingdom

Since to be human is to be an animal rather than a plant, our kingdom is Animalia and we receive a fundamental inheritance. Among other things, animals acquire their food by eating other plants and animals, and they have degrees of mobility that do not characterize the sedentary plant forms.

> What are the characteristics of animals that distinguish them from plants? For one thing, animals are heterotrophic, that is, they must acquire the food they need by eating other organisms. Most plants can manufacture their essential food requirements from the elements. Plants never stop growing throughout their lifetime, but animals generally have a definite and limited period of growth ... Animals propel themselves through their environment while plants remain sedentary. Plants are dependent in part on the environment for successful reproduction and propagation, but animals are generally able to reproduce without significant assistance from environmental factors. (Kraus, 1964: 8)

Subkingdom

A human being is further classified as a *Metazoan*—a multicellular animal rather than a single-celled type. This provides us with some definite advantages. Being multicellular permits both larger body size and specialization of function. There appear to be definite limits on how big a single-celled creature can become, and, up to a point, larger size can confer survival chances on its possessor—if only that one becomes a bigger mouthful for some predator. In the single-celled animal, the cell has to perform all of the basic life functions, whereas in the multicelled animal, some cells can devote themselves to locomotion and others to digestion, and so forth, leading to the creation of greater organizational complexity. We have a "team of specialists" working for us. The larger size also takes longer to develop, thus requiring a longer life. Profit in terms of "life experience" can then be gained from this extra living time.

> Size alone does not afford protection, but other things being equal, it has proved advantageous to many different sorts of animals. Certain corollaries to size turn out to be useful as well. Large animals take longer than smaller ones to attain their full adult size, tending, as a result, to live longer. They have time to profit from experience if they are equipped to do so, and the lessons often prove useful to them. They are usually less prolific than small animals, so that each individual may receive more parental attention when young and inexperienced. The very fact that size imposes requirements of a more complex functional organization among their constituent cells permits the sharpening of many of the basic qualities of life. (Hulse, 1971: 26)

Phylum

Of the various types of Metazoa, humans are classified as *chordates*. These are characterized by a number of traits of importance. Some of these are: a complete digestive system for boosting the energy process, axial symmetry (both sides of the body alike), and an internal skeleton of bone or cartilage for greater structural support. This latter trait is a real aid in continued growth and body size. Unlike some crabs, we do not have to shed our support structure or, like caterpillars, wrap ourselves in cocoons in the process of reaching adult form. Chordates also have a dorsal central nervous system to improve behavorial control.

Subphylum

Among the various chordates, we are classified as a *vertebrate*. Here there are a number of definite advantages. Vertebrates have a vertebral column (backbone) of bone or cartilage that confers structural advantages in reaching larger size as well as serving as protection for the central nerve cord. Creatures in this category are also highly efficient

The following two pages illustrate the diversity among animals. *A* An amoeba (Eric V. Grave). *B* A sea anemone (Omikron). *C* Sea mammals (Omikron). *D* A ghost crab (Jack Dermid). *E* A Galapagos tortoise (Omikron). *F* A white-lipped garden snail (Leonard Lee Rue III). *G* A newly hatched Monarch butterfly (Omikron). *H* A phoebe on its nest (Leonard Lee Rue III). *I* A red-necked grebe on its nest (Leonard Lee Rue III). *J* A timber rattlesnake (Omikron). *K* A varying hare with its summer coat (Omikron). *L* A mother zebra with her young (Omikron).

at locomotion because of possession of a locomotor system consisting of appendages with attached muscles. In addition to many other traits is the existence of separate sexes (as we shall see later in chapter six), undoubtedly a factor in the development of human social evolution, if a problem today. Vertebrates also have better developed nervous systems. Such advantages are evident if we think of success of the various varieties of these creatures: birds, amphibians, reptiles, fish, and mammals.

Class

Of the various divisions of vertebrates, man is of the type called *mammal*. These forms of life first appeared in the fossil record some 160 million years ago. Most mammals, humans included, belong to a subclass, Eutheria, from which some real advantages have been gained: the possession of a four-chambered heart for efficient blood circulation; a layer of hair or fur as insulation; improved lungs and sweat glands to produce a constant body temperature. By acting like central heating, this gives mammals a greater independence from their environment and the ability to exploit diverse ecological niches. Cold-blooded reptiles, whose body temperature matches their environment, are at a distinct disadvantage in this regard. In addition, mammals have improved digestion by their possession of salivary glands to help speed up the process of energy conversion. The possession of specialized teeth of various sorts (biting versus chewing) is also a contribution.

Reproduction is also unique in eutherian mammals. The embryo remains within the mother's body for some time and is born in a rather helpless state, receiving nourishment (as well as antibodies to protect against disease) from the mother's breasts or mammary glands. This process not only leads to greater mother-infant dependency but also to the development of more complicated forms of social organization. This, in turn, gives young animals the opportunity to grow up and learn in the company of adults and with some degree of safety—a real competitive advantage. As one writer has so persuasively put it:

> Consider the virtues of this system. The warmth and protection it furnishes the unborn are useful, of course, but the birds attain the same ends in other ways. Mainly, there is a much higher limit both to the amount of nourishment this piratical proto-infant can requisition and to the time it takes in the process. In an egg it would eat and grow its way outward to the shell and then it must hatch or starve; and the size of an egg has practical bounds—ask a hen. Among mammals, on the

other hand, perhaps only human beings and a few of their relatives, with their overloaded heads, are putting the principle of live birth to any strain. The blank check on time and energy permits the unborn a gradual development to a high level, and a decent size, before it must face the harsh world. . . .

And provisions have also been made to extend the protected development for a relatively long time after birth. First are the mammary glands, which produce a concentrated food in the form of milk . . . Second are all the natural behavior and strong emotions which lead the mammal mother to care for her nurslings in the most devoted and unselfish manner through their infancy. Except for birds, most other animals never see their children. (Howell, 1967: 45)

Thus, the ability to write the above "degrees" behind our name gives us human beings some real, if unearned, advantages as well as explaining some of the basic aspects of our physical existence and behaviors. Another degree, OP (order Primates), is perhaps even more important. So important, in fact, that a separate chapter deserves to be devoted to it.

SUMMARY

1. Evolution represents the modern scientific view of human nature and development.
2. Evolution holds that human structure and human biological behaviors are the result of a long slow process of development and change.
3. A taxonomic scheme is one way to examine how humans fit into the natural world; it also suggests the path of human evolutionary development.
4. Humans are classified as an animal: metazoan, chordate, vertebrate, mammal, and primate.

REFERENCES FOR FURTHER READING

The placement of the human species in nature and the variety of living things is usually discussed thoroughly in any introductory biology text. Some specific references are *Man in Nature*, by Marston Bates (1965, Prentice-Hall); *Man in the Web of Life*, by John H. Storer (1968, New American Library); *The Basis of Human Evolution* by Bertram S. Kraus (1964, Harper & Row); *The Human Species*, by Frederick Hulse (1971, 2nd ed., Random House); and the delightful, if somewhat out of date, *Mankind in the Making*, by William Howells (1967, Double-day). For more specific information on the human species, see *The Body* by Anthony Smith (1968, Walker) and *The Study of Man* by E. J. Clegg (1970, American Elsevier). See also *Man* by Richard Harrison and William Montagna (1973, 2nd ed., Meredith). A beautifully written background to the nature of some of the topics covered in the present text is *The Wellsprings of Life*, by Isaac Asimov (1960, New American Library).

2
the
primates

The order Primates consists of a diverse and interesting array of life forms. Although basically mammalian in most of their behaviors, they demonstrate a number of more specialized characters, which result from a long involvement with life in the trees (such developments are discussed in chapter four). Since it was the evolution of these forms that led to the appearance of human forms, the behavior of living primates is of considerable relevance in the attempt to gain additional insight into our own ancestral, if not present-day behavior. In the following brief account of the primates as they are today, technical nomenclature will be held to a minimum (consult Table 2–1).

TYPES OF PRIMATES

There are two basic primate divisions: the *Prosimians*, or "lower" primates, and the *Simians,* or *Anthropoids*, the "higher" primates. This latter division is our own domain and also includes the apes and monkeys.

PROSIMIANS (LOWER PRIMATES)

The Prosimians consist of a number of relatively small creatures, most of which are little known to the general public. They do not immediately strike one as "typical" primates. The simplest form is the *Tree Shrew*.

Tree Shrew

This creature is often omitted from the order *Primates*. Included or not, it is certainly a transitional form between primates and insectivores. The tree shrew is usually described as small and squirrellike, spending

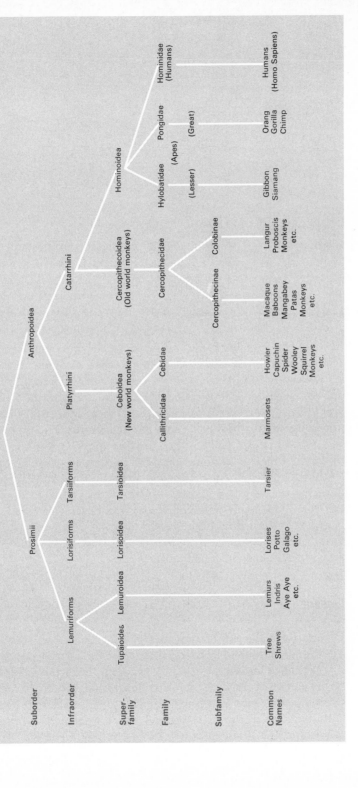

The tree shrew is thought to resemble the earliest phases of primate evolution. Note the pointed snout and the long claws.

Arthur W. Ambler, National Audubon Society

most of its time in lower branches of bushes and trees. They have pointed snouts and a well-developed sense of smell. They have claws on the digits that have poor grasping ability (prehensility). Their eyes are set on either side of the face so that they do not have the stereoscopic depth-perception vision advantage of most other primates. They are quite active, however, and are omnivorous in diet, eating seeds, insects, and fruits. The brain of the tree shrew is less complex than that of other primates but more advanced in comparison to insectivore forms. Most varieties are diurnal, being active during the day. One can say, perhaps, that the tree shrew is in the trees rather than of them. They are found today in parts of India, Southeast Asia, and Indonesia. It is generally agreed that the general structure of the tree shrew resembles fairly closely the earliest phases in the evolution of the primates from earlier generalized mammalian forms.

Lemurs

Lemurs form the most numerous varieties of "true" prosimians. They are catlike creatures, usually larger than the tree shrews but exhibiting a great range in body size. They generally have thick coats of hair and bushy tails. Larger types tend to be diurnal, whereas smaller ones are usually nocturnal (going around at night), enabling them to compete with monkeys in the same regions. Large eyes and ears are often adaptations to night-time activity. Most diurnal types are confined today to Madagascar, where no higher primates (save man) exist.

The hands and feet of lemurs are more prehensile than those of tree shrews and are characterized by flat nails rather than claws on some digits (fingers and toes). But, although they have good grasp, they have poor manipulation in comparison to higher primates. Although their eyes are also further forward toward the front of the face, many scholars believe that their depth perception is not fully developed. They are like tree shrews in using their tails as balancing organs. They have essentially the same diet and seem to divide their time between life on the ground and in trees. Most have relatively long snouts and a keen sense of smell. Types such as the ring-tailed lemur have scent glands for leaving messages behind (as a communication device). Some of these diverse forms have extra vertebrae for more flexibility in locomotion. Perhaps the strangest lemurlike form is the Aye Aye who has special front teeth for gnawing bark to get at wood-boring grubs. It has a long, slender middle finger with a sharp claw for skewering them. There appears to be a great degree of variety with respect to the social behavior of such forms. The lemurs of Madagascar alone can be divided into groups that live alone, those that live in "family" groups, and those that have more complex, trooplike social groupings. Because of great difficulty in observing the behavior of these creatures, we know much less about their behavior than that of higher primates. Somewhat confusingly, the term *lemuroid* is often used to refer to other prosimian types, such as lorises, pottos, and galagos. These, however,

The ring-tailed lemur is a "true" prosimian.

Arthur W. Ambler, National Audubon Society

have somewhat different structures and behaviors and wider geographic ranges, being found on the mainland of Africa and Asia.

Tarsiers

The remaining prosimian form is the tarsier, living today in the Malay Archipelago and in the Philippine Islands. They are about eight inches long and have long tufted tails. Their ears and eyes are quite large and the latter are set directly in front of the face for visual acuity in the trees. Most digits have nails rather than claws and round pads on the tips are an aid in grasping ability. The tarsier is so named because of the elongation of the tarsal bones of the foot, which, acting as a kind of third leg segment, enables it to leap great distances in the trees. The snout of the tarsier is reduced in comparison to other prosimians and its sense of smell is less well developed. Insects form the bulk of the diet, but these creatures also eat other small animals such as snails. Tarsiers are generally considered to be the link to the higher primates since in depth perception and grasping ability they display the beginnings of such higher exploitive developments. "In the structure of its nose and lips the tarsier resembles the monkeys and contrasts rather strongly with the lemurs. Other features in which it approximates to the monkeys include the structure of the brain (especially that part concerned

Tarsiers are generally considered to be the link to the higher primates; the long digits with round pads and flattened nails are an aid in grasping ability.

Arthur W. Ambler, National Audubon Society

with vision), the internal anatomy of the nose, and the details of the reproductive apparatus" (LeGros Clark, 1964: 66).

ANTHROPOIDS (HIGHER PRIMATES)

As previously stated, the **Anthropoid** primate division includes monkeys and apes as well as ourselves. *Monkeys*, both on structural and behavioral grounds and in terms of geography, are divided into two groups: monkeys of the New World (southern Mexico through South America) and the Old World (Africa and Asia). In general, monkeys are superior to prosimians in that they possess (with notable exceptions) the following characteristics:

1. nails, rather than claws, on the digits;
2. good prehensility, with an increase in manipulative ability;
3. stereoscopic, depth-perception vision with eyes in the front of the face;
4. color vision for locating fruit, etc.;
5. expansion in brain size;
6. ability to manipulate facial expressions as an aid in communication;
7. and, the capacity for more learned behaviors with less innate reflexes—thus giving monkeys greater adaptive potentials and leading to highly developed social behaviors in some groups.

New World Monkeys

These monkeys, the **Ceboidea**, are the furthest removed from man and include a variety of types: marmosets, capuchins, howler monkeys, wooly monkeys, squirrel monkeys, and spider monkeys. Most types have been much less well studied than the monkeys of the Old World. The first type of these (marmosets) are atypical in possessing claws, rather than nails, on most digits. They also differ dentally. All New World monkey types are strictly arboreal (tree living) and are rather flatfaced, lacking muzzles. Speaking of the howler monkeys of Barro Colorado Island Biological Laboratory in the Isthmus of Panama, it is said that:

> Howlers are well adapted for the arboreal life and the environment of tropical trees. They climb expertly up trees of small to moderate size and descend such trees and vines head foremost, constantly using their pre-

hensile tails. While moving from one tree to another over intersecting terminal branches they maintain contact with their tails and bridge spaces with a minimum of jumping. They are tree-bound and, in continuous stands of forests, range mainly through the mid-altitudes where the most continuous networks of intersecting branches are found. Howlers are strictly arboreal on Barro Colorado Island. (Carpenter, 1965: 276)

The nostrils of New World monkeys are separated by a broad nasal septum and face towards the side. This condition is called a *platyrrhine nose*. The *dental formula* of these monkeys expresses their possession of four more premolar teeth than other anthropoids have. Written I$\frac{2}{2}$ C$\frac{1}{1}$ P$\frac{3}{3}$ M$\frac{3}{3}$ x 2 = 36, this reflects that as one counts teeth from the middle around one half of an upper or lower jaw, one finds two incisors, one canine tooth, three premolars, and three molar teeth. The New World monkeys have very prehensile hands and feet, and some groups even possess prehensile tails that serve as a fifth hand for hanging on to branches. Such a tail is characterized by a calloused area near the top, which acts as a prehensile pad, an obvious advantage for life in the trees. One form, the spider monkey, also approaches some apes in its ability to swing overhand from branch to branch (*brachiation*). Generally, diet consists of fruits and leaves. In sum, the New World monkeys consist of a very interesting collection of types and demonstrate both parallelism to, and divergence from, those of Africa and Asia.

Old World Monkeys

These monkeys, the **Cercopithecoidea**, are taxonomically closer to humans and can be subdivided into two main types. One group consists of specialized leaf-eaters such as langurs, who are mostly arboreal. The other group, to which baboons belong, has a more varied diet and spends a considerable amount of time on the ground. The ground-living forms have more complicated social systems and display more aggressive behaviors (for survival there) than the more tree-living types. Old World monkeys have the same dental formula as apes and man, I$\frac{2}{2}$ C$\frac{1}{1}$ P$\frac{2}{2}$ M$\frac{3}{3}$ x 2 = 32, and also possess a *catarrhine nose* with the nostrils set close together and downward facing. Both of these traits place them closer to apes and humans than to New World monkeys. The monkeys of Asia and Africa also demonstrate great prehensility. Although they do not possess prehensile tails, they do have more fully opposable thumbs and greater locomotor variations. Another trait they possess is the presence of *ischial callosities*. These are regions of calloused skin in the buttock area that are presumed to aid in ground sitting and upright tree-sleeping. New World forms that lack these have greater sleeping difficulties, having to rest either hunched up or curled up on their sides. At any rate, such upright sitting is more a character of Old World monkeys and perhaps a precondition for the eventual uprightness of humans themselves.

Some of these monkeys also exhibit periodic swelling in the female external genitalia and surrounding area. This may also be highly colored at this time, signaling their coming into estrus, the period of sexual receptivity. This serves as a signal to the males of the species who, unlike humans, need not have our "will she—won't she" difficulties. Another trait possessed by ground-dwelling monkeys is the possession of cheek pouches. These act like a suitcase in that they can be packed with food at the source of supply, which can then be taken to a place of greater safety for consumption. It should again be mentioned that the diet of ground-living forms is tremendously varied. Of great importance is the fact of the occasional meat-eating activities of some species (hares, newborn gazelle, and other monkeys) even though this appears to be more accidental rather than planned. In any event, it is another suggestion of their closeness to ourselves. Considering the fact that the number of monkey species is large (in some areas they outnumber humans), one is tempted to consider them second only to man in the success of their existence.

The baboons of Africa have become the object of a number of ex-

Langurs are an arboreal, leaf-eating variety of Old World Monkey.

Irven DeVore/Anthro-Photo

As mainly ground-dwelling Old World monkeys, baboons display more aggressive behavior and have more complicated social systems than their arboreal counterparts. At left, a typical baboon threat gesture; at right, a family of baboons.

cellent field studies and appear to have made a highly successful adaptation to a terrestrial existence (although they sleep in the trees at night and retreat there in emergency situations). They exist in well-ordered social groups comprising some forty to eighty individuals ranging over up to six square miles of territory. The organization of these groups gives the members good protection from predators.

> As the troop moves the less dominant adult males and perhaps a large juvenile or two occupy the van. Females and more of the older juveniles follow and in the center of the troop are the females with infants, the young juveniles and the most dominant males. The back of the troop is a mirror image of the front, with less dominant males at the rear. Thus ... the arrangement of the troop is such that the females and young are protected at the center. No matter from what direction a predator approaches the troop, it must first encounter the adult males. (Washburn and DeVore, 1961: 3, 4)

The long, powerful canine teeth of the adult males and their cooperative activities are an adequate deterrent in most cases. Some baboon types (e.g., Hamadyras) organize somewhat differently from the above pattern. Adult males are the dominant members of such groups—based on strength and aggressiveness and, of course, on the effectiveness of the canine teeth. The dominance hierarchy is not a rigid pecking order, however, since the ability to enlist the support of other males is also important. Adult females are generally subordinate to adult males. Group ties are also reinforced by grooming behavior (removing dirt and parasites from the hair). Certainly, the terrestrial, open-ground adaptation of baboons and of some other types of Old World monkeys has similarity to developments in our own separate line of evolution.

The Apes

The apes, along with man, are classified as the Hominoidea. The living apes, with some exceptions, can be characterized as follows:

1. they are larger in body size than monkeys;
2. they are bigger brained (relatively);
3. they possess the same catahrrine type of nose and dental formula as man;
4. they have excellent manipulatory potential;
5. they possess long arms, and relatively shorter legs;
6. they possess free swinging arms, whereas monkeys, as quadrupeds, use their arms only in a forward and backward plane;
7. they are semierect in posture and occasionally go for short distances erect.

Lesser Apes.   There are two subdivisions of apes: the *lesser* apes and the *greater* apes. The lesser apes (Hylobatidae) include the *gibbon* and closely related *siamang.* The former is found in various areas of Asia and the latter is found today on the island of Sumatra. The gibbon is certainly the real swinger of the primate order. With tremendously long arms and narrow hooklike hands and fingers, it brachiates very successfully. In this, it is aided by a very lightweight size: about three feet and perhaps twenty pounds. Its feet are also extremely prehensile. It is characterized by a thick coat of hair and small ischial callosites. The latter are not possessed by other apes, who perhaps compensate by constructing sleeping nests of intertwined branches. The gibbon also lacks the ruggedness of skull possessed by the other apes.

Since gibbons, and apes in general, are close to man, it is worthwhile to mention brain sizes. The gibbon's is about 100 cubic centimeters of cranial capacity. Although gibbons have not seemed to perform well in tests devised by human experimenters, their brain, relative to body size, is large in comparison to those of most monkeys.

The long arms of the gibbon make him
the "swinger" of the primate order.

Leonard Lee Rue IV

It must be remembered, however, that

> Human beings, not animals, devise tests of animal intelligence, and in
> doing so we tend to test for the existence of capabilities upon which
> *we*, as a species, put high value ... Thus, looked at one way, human
> intelligence tests applied to apes have little meaning. For if the ape
> succeeds, this merely indicates that the capacity to respond adaptively
> in such a situation is one that has been important to both man and
> ape in their common evolution; if the ape fails, this does not necessarily
> indicate that it is stupid, but simply that such a way of responding has
> not been selected in the ape's forest life. (Reynolds, 1971: 195)

Finally, it may be added that gibbons display a restricted social unit,
consisting of mated pairs and young, and that their territory (30 to
100 acres) is defended against intrusion by other groups. This is
accomplished by bluff and by actual fighting. Their diet is chiefly fruit
and leaves.

Greater Apes. The so-called "greater" apes (**Pongidae**) include
the orangutan of southeast Asia (Borneo, Sumatra) and two African
representatives, the gorilla and chimpanzee. Of these, the *orangutan* is
perhaps the most distant to man. The adult male orang may weigh up
to about 165 pounds and is perhaps four to five feet high. They are
powerfully built. Females are much slighter in composition, weighing
half as much, being shorter and lacking the male flaps of cheek skin.
They have shaggy, reddish-brown hair and a cranial capacity of about
400 cubic centimeters. Orangs are almost exclusively arboreal. Despite
their larger size, orangs do brachiate; but unlike the bounding leaps
of the gibbon, their movements are, of course, more deliberate. They

seldom release more than one hand or foot at any one time (unless eating). As a result, somewhat unfairly, they have been designated as lazy or sluggish. Since they lack the ligament binding the femur (upper leg bone) to the hip socket, their legs are extremely mobile and can be stretched out like arms at right angles to the body. This permits orangs to proceed through the trees by upside-down movement. The diet of the orang is heavily vegetarian. Their social life has not been determined in any substantial way. They appear to go about in small familylike groups, often consisting of only a female and offspring. Males are often observed to live a separate existence, except when mating. In any event, establishment and/or defense of territory has not been demonstrated and they appear to be basically nonaggressive. We know less about this ape form than any of the others.

In terms of size at least, the *gorilla* is a primate's primate. Adult males in zoo environments reach over 600 pounds. They are somewhat less robust under natural conditions. Females are smaller. Gorilla height is about five and a half feet and their cranial capacity is about 550 cubic centimeters. They are far too heavy for brachiation, although juveniles exhibit vine swinging. They are primarily quadrupedal and terrestrial, even making their nests on the ground—perhaps a survival from a lighter, tree-living evolutionary past. They walk with the soles of the feet on the ground and with their huge upper body supported on the knuckles of the hands, a football lineman's stance but without the bent legs. Occasionally, they go upright for short distances.

The locomotion of orangutans.

Irven DeVore/Anthro-Photo

Gorillas are vegetarians and, because of their bulk prodigious eaters, often stripping the forest around them completely bare before moving on. It is estimated that an adult consumes up to thirty-five pounds of vegetation a day. They exploit a territory of some ten to fifteen square miles and exist in social groups ranging up to thirty individuals, with eight to sixteen members being most typical. The territory of adjacent groups overlap but contact is only occasional and apparently peaceful. The group is dominated by the largest male, with lesser males in a descending hierarchy. The dominant male generally directs group movements. Females outnumber males, and some males tend to remain peripheral, maintaining more isolated existences. Dominance is based upon size but competition for food, due to its abundance, is absent. Since sexual behavior is not prominent, one might say that their social behavior is independent, reserved, and lacking in conflict. Even juvenile play is more restricted than among most primates.

> The small number of overt social interactions was a most striking aspect of intragroup behavior. The most frequent noted interactions were dominance . . . mutual grooming . . . and social play. The relative infrequency of interaction can probably be attributed to the following circumstances. Competition for food and mates provided little basis for strife since forage was abundant and sexual behavior not prominent. The members of the group were alert to the possibility of aggressive encounters, and subordinate animals tended to circumvent issues before they materialized. And, finally, the gorillas gave one the impression of having an independent and self-dependent temperament, appearing stoic, aloof, and reserved in their affective behavior. (Schaller, 1965: 345, 346)

Although (contrary to myth) gorillas are seen as generally non-aggressive, they do display escalating patterns of hostility. These run from a brief unwavering stare and head jerks in the direction of the offender, to a forward lunge of the body, to bluff charges of about ten feet, and to actual physical contact in the form of biting and wrestling. In addition to these, there is the famous chestpounding display for attention and intimidation, which is apparently performed when tension rises above a certain level. It includes the emission of a number of hoots (often interrupted by symbolic feeding—touching vegetation to lips), rising up on hind legs while grabbing a handful of vegetation to throw, beating on the huge chest with cupped hands up to twenty times, running sideways while smashing vegetation, and, finally, thumping the ground. When such a display is in response to threat one suspects that such a view of a "berserk" gorilla would discourage even the most hardy of predators. Although gorillas are not as continually vocal as some of the other apes, they are said to possess the capacity to emit a number of separate low-pitch vocalizations. Most of the time, however, they live a quiet, food-oriented existence.

If the gorilla is independent and reserved, then the *chimpanzee* is the social mixer among apes and the closest of the primates to humans. It is also the most familiar of the primates because of its zoo and television exposure. Its numerous accomplishments in test situations have led perhaps to an overly high regard for its mental capacity, but it is clearly superior to the other apes under natural conditions as well. Male chimps weigh about 110 pounds, the female somewhat less. Brain volume is about 400 cubic centimeters. Chimps display a variety of locomotor possibilities. Both arboreal and terrestrial, they are fine, agile brachiators and spend about 70 percent of their time in trees. Long distances, however, seem to be traversed in a gorilla-quadrupedal fashion, and they often walk erect for short distances. Resting and sleeping occur in the safety of trees; nests made of pulled-in intertwined branches are often located sixty feet above the ground.

The normal territory of chimpanzees is about eight square miles and the size of the social unit often numbers in excess of sixty individuals. Such groups, however, do not appear to be closed units, but rather are constantly undergoing changes in membership because of available supplies of food and sexual requirements. Some scholars have reported the existence of four main types of groupings: adult bands, male bands, mother bands, and mixed bands. The first type consists of adults of both sexes and occasional adolescents but no dependent offspring. The second consists of only adult males and is the most far ranging. The third is composed of mothers with dependent young and, occasionally, other females. The last is a temporary aggregation of all the other types for purposes of sex and grooming and for feeding in some situations of abundance.

> To my knowledge, there is no other primate . . . among which the chief social distinction is between childless and child-rearing adults rather than between males and females. The pattern . . . may have grown out of the long and intensive care the animals give their young. Carrying a child around almost constantly for four or more years obviously tends to restrict the range of the mother's movements. (Kortlandt, 1962: 6,7)

Given the nature of such groups and their interplay, it is evident that chimps have a wider range of social relations than most primates.

There are numerous other points of interest in chimpanzee behavior. Dominance is not stable or well developed; there is little competition or exclusive sex rights or leaders. Group movement is initiated by numerous members of the unit and such "leadership" is of short duration.

A mother and infant chimp.

Irven DeVore/Anthro-Photo

Chimps display a great variety of communication techniques. These range from drumming on tree trunks to about twenty-three distinct calls to help keep subunits of the group in contact and to call attention to food. They also employ many gestures, postures, and facial expressions. For example, to signify threat, a chimp will move bipedally toward an offender and give high-pitched screams with the mouth half open and the lips drawn back. Shoulder, back, and arm hair will be erect, and the whole behavior is accompanied by the flapping of the forearms toward the object of the display. For submission, they use an appeasement gesture—a special grin—and reach out and touch the lips and scrotum of the other chimp.

Chimpanzees are primarily vegetarians and spend most of their time obtaining food. Those living in more open areas have also been observed eating meat on a number of occasions. They appear to do so in a more deliberate and planned fashion than do baboons. The food includes monkeys and young bushpigs.

> ...the prey...was sitting in a tree when an adolescent male chimpanzee climbed a neighboring tree, and remained very still as the monkey looked toward it. A second adolescent male chimpanzee then climbed the tree in which the colobus was sitting, ran quickly along the branch, leapt at the colobus and caught it with its hands, presumably breaking its neck...The other adolescent then leapt into the tree, and five other chimpanzees, including a mature male and a late infant, climbed up. The mature male pulled until he had half the carcass. Subsequently I observed that the mother of the infant had acquired a large piece of meat and afterwards the other chimpanzees...also managed to get small pieces of meat or scraps. (Goodall, 1965: 445)

34

Finally, chimpanzees are capable of employing rudimentary tools. Some have been observed using leaves as sponges to obtain water, using stones to break open nuts, and throwing sticks at predators. In addition, they appear to actually fashion tools; modifying a branch into a smooth stick to poke into termite nests; they then lick off the clinging termites. They have even been reported carrying such a tool for some distance in anticipation of such use. In sum, the communicational ability, meat-eating propensity, and tool-using capability bespeak a primate very close to humans. Some scholars even feel that prior to our own emergence as the dominant primate, chimps were even more capable in such endeavors but have since become "dehumanized."

Today, primates, in general, are less numerous than they were in the past. Decrease in the extent of typical environment and pressure by humans now threatens many varieties to the point of extinction. Their study substantiates the value of our primate "degree." Even this brief review suggests a basis for the genesis of much human behavior. Before specifically considering primate evolution, we must first generally discuss the mechanisms, principles, and evidences of evolution itself.

SUMMARY

1. The order Primates consists of two suborders or divisions: lower primates or Prosimians, and higher primates or Anthropoids.
2. Prosimians, a group of relatively small creatures with generally poor grasping ability, small brains, and minimal vision, include tree shrews, lemurs, lorises, and tarsiers.
3. The tarsier seems to have made the best arboreal adaptation of the Prosimians in terms of vision and grasping ability, and appears to be the link to higher primates.
4. Anthropoids include monkeys of the Old and New Worlds, apes, and human beings.
5. Old and New World monkeys generally have keener vision, better grasping ability, and larger brains than do prosimians; they differ from each other in terms of dental formula, nasal structure, grasping tails, as well as other traits.
6. The Hominoids include apes and humans and are divided into three groupings: lesser apes, such as the gibbon and siamang; greater apes, such as the orangutan, gorilla, and chimpanzee; and the Hominids, or humans.
7. Apes are generally larger in body size than monkeys, have rela-

tively larger brains, possess a humanlike nose and human dental formula, and have excellent manipulatory potential; they also show tendencies toward erectness in posture.

8. Chimpanzees are the closest of the apes to humans; they exhibit complex social behavior, communication potential, and rudimentary use of tools.

9. Humans are Primates, Anthropoids, Hominoids, and Hominids; the study of primate behavior and structure can tell us much about our own potentials.

REFERENCES FOR FURTHER READING

There exists an ever-increasing number of excellent books on primates and their behavior. Perhaps the best is J. and P. H. Napier, *Handbook of Living Primates* (1967, Academic Press), which is a sort of illustrated Who's Who! Other general texts are *The Life of Primates*, by Adolph Schultz (1969, Universe Books); *Social Groups of Monkeys, Apes and Men*, by Michael Chance and Clifford Jolly (1970, Dutton); *Primate Societies*, by Hans Kummer (1971, Aldine); *The Apes*, by Vernon Reynolds (1971, Harper & Row); and *The Primates*, by Sarel Eimerl and Irven DeVore (1965, Time). A popular discussion that includes many little tidbits of information is *Man and Apes*, by Ramona and Desmond Morris (1968, McGraw Hill). See also *History of the Primates*, by W. E. LeGros Clark (1964, 4th ed., University of Chicago Press). Two outstanding readers are *Primates*, edited by Phyllis C. Jay (1968, Holt, Rinehart and Winston) and *Primate Behavior*, edited by Irven DeVore (1965, Holt, Rinehart and Winston). The quotations from Shaller on gorillas, Goodall on chimps, and Carpenter on howler monkeys are taken from the latter text. Other chapter quotations are from S. L. Washburn and Irven DeVore, "The Social Life of Baboons," in *Scientific American*, June 1961 (reprint no. 614 by W. H. Freeman & Co.) and "Chimpanzees in the Wild," by Adrian Kortlandt, in *Scientific American*, May 1962 (reprint no. 463 as above). Finally, the most readable book on the closest primate relative—the chimpanzee—is Jane Lawick-Goodall, *In the Shadow of Man* (1971, Houghton-Mifflin).

3

evolution

The concept of evolution is ancient. Early Greek philosophers suggested the evolution of humans from lower forms of life. The impact of such thought, however, was not substantial until the nineteenth century even though isolated thinkers had continued to orient their thoughts in such a direction. Not only was the "mental climate" not sufficient until this time to accept such "heresy," but the mechanisms and evidences for such a process were also not discovered. In the nineteenth century, a number of thinkers devoted themselves to such endeavors. Among them, three names stand out: Jean Baptiste Lamarck, Charles Darwin, and Gregor Mendel.

LAMARCK: ENVIRONMENTAL STIMULATION

Although Lamarck's major contribution to evolutionary theory has now been discredited, it did have an effect on Darwin. It is the notion of evolution that lingers on in popular imagination and that is often rejected by laymen. Briefly, Lamarck felt (in *Zoological Philosophy*, 1809) that an organism is stimulated pleasurably or painfully by its environment. In response to furthering or avoiding such conditions, it acquires greater or lesser development of the organs and structures involved. This is the case of the ninety-eight-pound weakling building up his body into muscleman proportions or the classic example of neck stretching in the giraffe. As a result, changes occur in the individual that Lamarck then presumed to be passed on to the offspring. With the same stimuli in operation, the process is repeated from generation to generation until eventually new traits have developed and old ones disappear. The flaw in his theory was that such acquired characteristics are not inherited by offspring: the weightlifter's children do not inherit his bulging biceps and go on to superhuman developments.

Darwin advanced his theory in 1859 in *The Origin of Species*. Despite some revisions and significant additions, his theory remains the basis of our understanding of evolution. Although he too felt that organisms are stimulated by their environment, he stressed the fact that any population is characterized by a wide range of variation in its traits: some are taller, some faster, some larger. At any one time, such a varied population is adapted to its environment. There is, however, a struggle for survival inasmuch as more offspring are produced than can survive. Also, the environment is constantly changing, sometimes rapidly, sometimes extremely slowly. This places stresses on the populations involved and requires new adjustments. The process of adjustment he called **natural selection**. Those variations that by chance are best suited to the altered environment will have a greater opportunity to survive (to secure food and escape from predators) in the struggle for existence than those now at the less advantageous end of variation. As the environment continues to change in such a direction, there will be a definite shift towards the favored variation since its possessors will be the "fittest" that survive to produce offspring. The true gauge of fitness then is really the capacity to leave offspring even more than survival itself. If your parents don't have any children, chances are you won't have any either! Perhaps the best visible proof of such a process is indicated by the case of the peppered moth found in England. Until recently, dark-colored moths were rare. The typical moth of a century ago was characterized by light-color patterns that were "fit" to blend in with the tree trunks on which they rested. The industrial revolution altered their environment with soot and other industrial wastes. Trees and vegetation became covered and darkened. Dark color in moths was now a variation of distinct advantage as protective coloration against predators and now such darker varieties predominate. Lighter variants were selected out by their visibility. So,

> By Darwinian notions, the giraffe got its long neck not because it tried for one (as Lamarck had it), but because some giraffes were born with naturally longer necks and these got more leaves and lived better. In the long run they left more descendants. It was the forces of nature that lengthened the neck, and not an inner drive. This view explained the giraffe's blotched coat as well. The better the blotches, the less noticeable the giraffe was against a blotched background and the more likely it was to escape the eyes of a prowling lion. Consequently, the more descendants it left. (Asimov, 1960: 41)

Darwin himself was aware of some problems in his theory. He wondered what caused variations in the first place. He also wondered

what the mechanism of inheritance was, and, like many parents today, wondered why offspring do not closely resemble them. Ironically, as he pondered these questions, at least some of the answers were being developed by Gregor Mendel.

MENDEL: GENETICS

Mendel was an Augustinian priest who performed various experiments with garden plants. In so doing, in 1865, he developed many of the basic concepts of genetics. Unfortunately, his results were not "discovered" until about 1900, too late to give any satisfaction to Darwin. His concepts, however, with important recent additions, are highly significant contributions to the understanding of the evolutionary process.

ASPECTS OF GENETICS

The study of genetics has become a highly complex field. The discussion below is intended only as the briefest of nontechnical accounts. Basically, two aspects of any organism have to be considered: the phenotype— the observable physical characteristics, and the genotype—its total amount of hereditary potential. In the process of reproduction, we

40

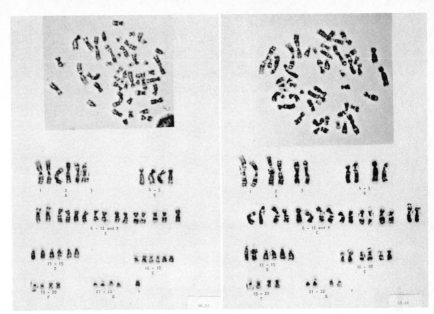

Normal human male (left) and female chromosomes.

receive half of our genotype from each parent. All the inherited genetic material is incorporated into sex cells, or *gametes*; the ovum of the female and the sperm of the male. The fusion of male and female gametes produces the *zygote*, or fertilized egg. Each has brought by reduction division, or meiosis, half of the normal amount of hereditary material, which then provides for the full amount in the embryo. Within the nucleus of the zygote are the hereditary materials, which consist of a definite number of *chromosomes* (rod-shaped bodies), positioned on which are the discrete units of heredity, the *genes*. These genes are now thought to be molecules of deoxyribonucleic acid (DNA). The traits themselves are determined by variations in this molecular structure.

A specific gene occupies a specific place (locus) on a pair of corresponding chromosomes, and paternal and maternal chromosomes are alike in having equivalent positions where there are genes determining the same traits. The genes can be the same or contrasting types— for example, blue or brown eye color. These variations are called *alleles*. When these alleles are of the same type the organism is said to be *homozygous*; when they are unlike, *heterozygous*. In this latter situation, one of the variations is said to be dominant over the other, which is recessive. This means that the possession of one of these gene variations is sufficient to make the trait appear in the phenotype while the other (recessive) is, so to speak, carried along for the ride in the genotype. If two recessive alleles are inherited, then the trait is expressed.

41

Not all traits, of course, are clearly dominant. An example can clarify these situations. The ability to taste a chemical substance called PTC (phenylthiocarbamide) is determined by a dominant "tasting" gene, T. We can code the possibilities of observable expression as follows with X, the "nontasting" variation.

genotype	phenotype
TT	taster
TX	taster
XX	nontaster

Hence, there are three genotypes but only two phenotypes. Genetic materials may be present that are not reflected in the observable characters. Furthermore, when heterozygotes mate, we can see why offspring do not always resemble their parents. Such taster parents on the average, have a 25 percent possibility of having nontasting offspring.

$$
\begin{array}{c|cc}
 & T & X \\
\hline
T & TT & TX \\
X & TX & \boxed{XX}
\end{array}
$$

So, there is more variation for natural selection to work on than meets the eye. In addition, we are multiallelic at many gene loci; we often possess more than a single pair of variations for a given trait. We are also polygenic for many traits, which are caused by the interaction of a number of genes. This adds to the fantastic number of genetic recombinations possible. Moreover, variation in chromosome material above the gene level exists. This is caused by deletion, duplication (material taken in from corresponding chromosomes), inversion (reversing the gene order), and translocation (exchanging segments between non corresponding chromosomes).

OTHER MECHANISMS OF EVOLUTION

It becomes clear, when thinking about all this genetic juggling, that the purpose of reproduction is not only to continue the group in question but also to insure continuing variability. One question, however, remains. Natural selection can only work on the existing variations possessed by a population. If the environment calls for more than what is possessed, demanding beyond the limits of response, extinction may result—as indeed it has for many forms of life. Where does fresh variation come from?

Mutation

The source for new traits is mutation—a change in the structure of genetic material, or, perhaps said better, a change in gene chemistry. These occur in the sex cells of the parent and may be passed on to the offspring. As yet, we are not completely sure of all of the causes of mutation or its mechanisms. We can, however, say the following. Different genes mutate at different rates and average mutation rates for different species vary as well. These are accidental changes. The genes of an individual do not mutate so his offspring can meet some environmental emergency. Most mutant genes are carried as recessives and the majority are detrimental, since an individual may be fairly well adapted at any one time and a change render his type less so. How many mutations are apt to confer advantages? This is obviously difficult to calculate. One scholar has suggested something on the order of one person out of ten thousand as carrying a potentially useful mutation.

> While rates of mutation vary enormously . . . a rate of one mutation per gene locus in every 100,000 sex cells is a conservative estimate. Because all higher organisms contain at least 10,000 gene loci . . . one individual out of ten carries a newly mutated gene at one of its loci . . . From various experimental studies we can arrive at a conservative estimate of the proportion of useful mutations as one in a thousand. On the basis of these estimates we can calculate that in any species about one in ten thousand individuals in each generation would carry a new mutation of potential value in evolution. Using conservative values of 100 million as the total number of generations in the evolutionary life of the species, we could expect that at least 500 million useful mutations would occur during this life span. (Ledyard Stebbins, 1966: 30)

The majority of mutant genes are detrimental to the species. This albino raccoon has no protective coloration.

Leonard Lee Rue III

Variations, then, are constantly, although accidentally, being altered by mutation, and there are so many of these that "the chief limiting factor on the supply of variability for the action of natural selection is not the availability or rate of occurrence of mutations, but the restrictions on gene exchange and recombination, which are imposed by the mating structure of populations, and the structural patterns of chromosomes" (Ledyard Stebbins, 1966: 31).

We must also realize that a mutant may be only partially "good or bad." A case in point is sickle-cell anemia—a human blood-cell disorder originally caused by a mutation. An individual homozygous for this trait usually dies before maturity. A person heterozygous for the trait apparently receives some sort of protection against types of malaria; at least, such people suffer less from them than those who are normal homozygotes. In any event, mutations are the raw materials for evolutionary change in that they supply fresh variations for natural selection to work on.

Genetic Drift

Although natural selection and mutation are the major mechanisms of evolution, in any given population there are two other mechanisms that can aid in changing their gene frequencies (the relative numbers of genes in a population). The first of these is **genetic drift.** This operates on the fact that in a small population the contribution of the individual to the next generation is relatively greater than in a big population. In a small population, it is easier for a trait to fail to be transmitted since fewer people may possess it to begin with. If, to give a hypothetical example, there is one red-haired person for every ten people, in a small population of only ten there will be only one possessor of this trait, whereas, in a population of a thousand, there will be one hundred. If the lone red-head accidentally breaks his neck before he reproduces himself, the variation may vanish. Such an accident would be negligible in the larger group. Such a genetic change is unrelated to factors of fitness or natural selection. It might be called nonadaptive evolution. Genetic drift is simply the gain or loss in the frequencies of genes due to the operations of chance on the reproductive mechanics in small populations.

Gene Flow

The other mechanism of evolution is **gene flow.** This is simply the interbreeding of organisms of one population with those of another. These must, of course, be of the same species to interbreed and produce fertile offspring. But where a number of breeding populations (within which mates are found) of the same species exists, there may be variations possessed by some that are absent in others, and swapping genes may result in the extension of the range of variation in one or both populations. As a possible source of gene frequency changes or new variations, gene flow certainly applies to the human species since most known human societies seek wives outside their own group (for such reasons as wife-capture customs and incest prohibitions). The term *gene flow* is sometimes used interchangeably with *hybridization*. This latter term, however, is best restricted to "gene-swapping" situations where the populations involved have different adaptive gene complexes; that is, they are fairly different. Here, hybrid sterility often occurs, or the offspring that do result may be less well adapted to the environment than either original population. Evolution by hybridization is probably rare.

Isolation

A fifth factor may be added to natural selection, mutation, genetic drift, and gene flow, although it is perhaps not a mechanism of evolution so much as a sufficient condition. This is isolation. In a sense, evolution is simply the change in gene frequencies from generation to generation. It means that "... all existing life forms, with their advanced and specialized organs, have grown out of preceding life forms through a natural process of modification" (Mckern and Mckern, 1969: 33). Sometimes this is a stabilizing event—a population keeps genetically constant or "average" because extreme variants have been eliminated by natural selection. It may also be a nonstabilizing or directional event when new forms develop in response to progressive environmental changes, migration to new environments, or different selective pressures. Such events may lead, over a long period of time, to the production of different species even though they begin with homogeneous or similar populations. Here isolation is important. The usual model for one such course of events runs about as follows. The original population represents stage one. In stage two, environmental factors split the population into two groups (some migrate, begin to exploit an environment differently, etc.). At this stage, they are isolated by geographic circumstances, but as time goes on and the mechanisms of change operate, they begin to diverge more and more from each other genetically until by stage three reproductive isolation occurs; they no longer are able to mate with other groups. They have diverged sufficiently with respect to genetic and chromosomal changes that, among other things, they may breed at different seasons, not be attracted to each other, be sexually incompatible, or at best produce infertile offspring. So much genetic distance has been created by now that even if they come to exist together again in the same region, they remain distinct.

The process of evolution behind such events, in terms of which of the mechanisms of evolution become effective, does require a tremendously long period of time. This is difficult to convey in numbers of years but one writer (Ledyard Stebbins) has analogized it as follows. All of the time since the death of Christ—1972 years (rounded off to 2000 years)—is equal to a one-hour television show. All previous time can be compressed into sixteen shows a day, seven days a week. In this sense:

Humans since 100,000 years ago:	3 days
Evolution of humans from prehuman forms:	10 months
Cat, dog, and horse evolution:	3½ to 5½ years
Entire fossil record:	60 years
Entire course of evolution of life:	250 to 400 years (of continuing viewing pleasure 16 hours a day).

The actual number of millions of years is certainly an ample amount of time for the working out of the above mechanisms of evolution.

OTHER ASPECTS OF EVOLUTION

Irreversibility

In addition to the mechanisms of evolution, several other aspects of this process must be mentioned. These closely follow the discussions of Betram Kraus (1964: chapter five). One is the concept of **irreversibility.** Simply put, this means that after a lengthy course of evolution has occurred the descendants of an original population cannot reverse the process and return to the ancestral state from which they have developed. As Thomas Wolfe once put it: "you can't go home again." This is a logical principle. Evolution obviously cannot run backwards since such a change in gene frequency would require step-by-step reversals in mutations, environmental changes, drift, and flow factors. This would appear to defy the laws of probability. However, should a new environment demand adaptations similar in kind to those of the past, "fresh" evolutionary changes have the potential to modify the organism to meet such conditions. This can result in a form coming to resemble its ancestral form, at least functionally. "Once a structure is lost in the course of evolution it can never be regained, but a different structure may arise to subserve the same function should the environmental situation demand it. There are numerous examples from the phylogenetic record of animals which have returned *functionally* but not *structurally* to an ancestral condition" (Kraus, 1964: 144). So you *can* go home again: by way of a different street. Except for short-term reversals of fairly minor characteristics, however, backwards evolution has not been demonstrated.

Convergence and Divergence

A second aspect of evolution is the idea of convergence and divergence developments. Convergence is the tendency of one group of organisms to develop superficial resemblances to another group of different ancestry because of response to the demands of similar environmental situations. The similar structures such creatures exhibit are called *analogues.* Perhaps the classic examples are the marsupials of Australia which include, among others, mice, anteaters, and wolflike forms. Such creatures are unrelated, however, at least in terms of sharing recent ancestors in common. This condition often makes for confusion in interpreting evolution since such analogues are not closely related even though they may appear to be so, whereas some structures (the arm of a bear and the flipper of a seal) that are related may appear on the surface to be different. Such structures are termed *homologues.* Such differences result from more recent divergence from a common ancestor. A closely related concept is *parallelism.* This refers to situations in which two organisms have also acquired similar characteristics independently of one another in relation to similar environmental conditions, but in this case they have stemmed from related ancestral stocks. Here a classic example would be the monkeys of the Old and New Worlds.

Adaptation

Another aspect of evolution that bears the refocusing of our attention is the principle of adaptation. Although in our discussion of natural selection we used the term in its general sense of adjusting to the environment, there are various ways adaptation can occur. *Specialization* refers to close adaptation to one environment or niche within it. This has usually occurred as a response to solving some immediate difficulty and leads to highly efficient exploitation of part of an environment at any one time. It's "going whole hog." It is, however, a solving of adaptive problems at the expense of adaptability. If the environment changes very much, the narrow range of variability resulting from such tight adaptedness may be insufficient to meet the challenge and extinction may result. The diets of the panda (bamboo shoots) and koala bear (eucalyptus leaves) are generally cited as examples of specialization.

> If, as often happened, animals had specialized to the extent that they had adapted themselves to particular conditions of temperature, humidity, and terrain, or to some very special food, they soon became extinct when their environment altered. . . .
>
> While selection is taking place, it is always advantageous to be better adapted than rival types to prevailing conditions. But for the future development of any line of descent it is better not to carry specialization too far. In case of change in environmental circumstances . . . it is possible for less specialized forms to undergo some phylogenetic alteration in structure and to adapt themselves anew on a basis of mutations, new gene combinations and selection. (Rensch, 1972: 21)

Generalization refers to adaptations that place the emphasis on the maintenance of variability and adaptiveness. Such organisms are less well adapted to any particular environment at any one time. They have not gone "whole hog" in environmental commitment and may be less successful than the more specialized types. Yet as environments change, these more generalized forms have a greater survival-development chance since their variability gives them more opportunism in natural selection. They are adaptable rather than adapted. Rats and humans, because they are able to survive under many conditions, are usually cited as examples of generalization.

EXTINCTION

Extinction is another evolutionary principle that requires fuller explication. In general, it refers to the dying out of some form of life. There is, however, more than a single sense in which organisms are no longer in existence. Extinction by *termination*, or *catastrophe*, is the process that is ordinarily associated with this principle. It refers to the complete disappearance of a particular line of development. No descendants remain. Extinction by *evolution*, or *speciation*, is another possibility. In essence, this refers to the development of one form from another. As gene frequencies change, this is reflected phenotypically. When a descendant no longer significantly overlaps with its ancestral form (has reached reproductive isolation, etc.), we can speak of the ancestral form as

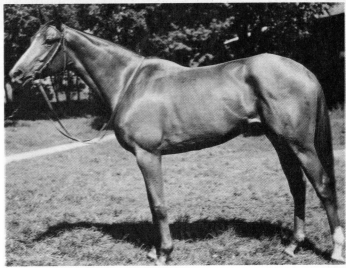

American Museum of Natural History

We can now say that small-sized horses with toes are extinct since the characteristics of the present-day horse no longer significantly overlap with its ancestor's. Compare the sizes of the two animals; eohippus was about the size of a fox.

being extinct (such as small-sized horses with toes) since a new species has developed. In this case, however, there has been no cessation of genetic transmission from one generation to another. Its children are different; not that it had no children at all. One of the intriguing puzzles concerning various fossil forms in our own line of development is whether they are extinct by termination or evolution. Are they a branch of humanity that failed to survive or our own ancestors?

EVIDENCES FOR EVOLUTION

A final aspect of evolution relates to the evidence we have for the principles related above. How do we know what we know about evolution? Selective-breeding experiments and natural developments taking place before our eyes, such as insects developing resistance to various pesticides, mostly confirm what we already know. The bulk of our evidence stems from paleontology (the study of fossil remains) and from observation of the living end products of evolution. Such evidence is of two types: direct and indirect.

Direct Evidence

Direct evidence is gained from the study of fossils (preserved parts or other indications of past life forms) whose recovery gives the scientist the actual remains of past organisms in the process of changing or

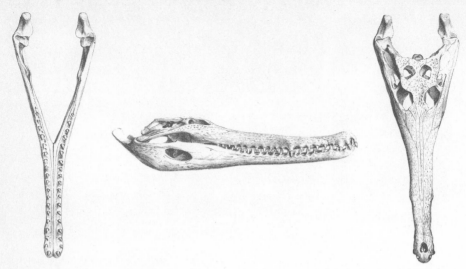

American Museum of Natural History

Fossils provide direct evidence of past forms of life; these are drawings of fossil crocodile mandibles.

becoming extinct. We find, for example, first ancestors, intermediate types, dead-end developments, and types grading into modern forms. These are located in different strata of the earth, which can be approximately dated by various techniques. Nor are we limited to bones and teeth alone, since paleontologists can learn much about the soft parts (shape, muscle structure, etc.) of an organism from the study of such hard remains. We now possess fairly good amounts of evidence for most major lines of development in the fossil record. We lack complete accounts, of course, since fossilization is an accidental process. While such remains are fairly resistant to decay, they must somehow be sealed off from depredations by predators or carrion eaters and from the effects of weathering.

Indirect Evidence

To the direct evidence we add *indirect evidence*. This is in the nature of a supplement to, rather than a substitute for, direct evidence. All indirect evidence is based on inferences of various sorts made on present rather than past data. Perhaps comparative anatomy is the most cited indirect evidence. Its data can be used in a variety of ways. We can note degrees of resemblance shared by the members of some group (for example, primates) and assume what they share in common they inherited from a common ancestral form that possessed these traits. "In so far as members of the same group possess certain anatomical features in common, a unity of design, it is reasonable to infer that they are genetically related ... and the closer the similarities, presumably the closer the relationship" (LeGros Clark, 1964: 9). We can also arrange the group into a graded series (in primates, from tree shrew to ourselves) that suggests complexity and sequence of development. Here we also assume the simpler form to have a nature similar to the common ancestor of the group. We can also look for the existence of vestigial organs and structures—for example, the toe remnants in horses. We can assume that these represent traits lost during the course of evolutionary development. Then, too, there is evidence deriving from embryological development, the development of the organism from the zygote.

> The embryos of all mammals (including Man) pass through a stage of development during which a foundation of gill arches is laid down in the neck region, precisely similar to that which, in fishes, finally leads to ... functional gills. But in the mammalian embryo, as development proceeds, the elements of these gill arches become completely re-arranged so as to form ... structures which are more suitable for animals which live on land.
>
> ... all these phenomena ... are quite meaningless unless they are simply due to the inheritance from ancestral forms of structures which have disappeared or undergone some modification as the result of a gradual evolutionary process. Their persistence in the embryo, even when they are no longer present in the adult, is an expression of the astonishing conservatism of anatomical structures ... (LeGros Clark, 1964: 12, 13).

It must again be emphasized, however, that indirect evidence must have some foundation in fact. Some direct evidence (finding horse remains with distinct toes) must confirm such speculations.

In sum, this chapter has surveyed some of the mechanisms and other aspects of evolution. There are additional principles but enough have been presented so we have a basic vocabulary to apply to the central issue of the next chapters, the evolution of the primates generally and of the human species specifically. The reconstructed story of the evolution of life up to the point of the rise of the primate order is too lengthy and too terminologically complicated a history to be discussed in the present volume.

SUMMARY

1. A number of early theories on evolution (such as Lamark's) are now at least partially discredited but influenced present day concepts.

2. Darwin's theory of natural selection is one of the major concepts in the theory of evolution. It states that some animals, by chance, are best suited for an altered environment, and therefore have greater opportunity to survive and pass on their traits to future generations. As time passes there will be a shift to the favored variations.

3. In understanding variations one must take into account both the phenotype—the observable physical characteristics of the organism—and the genotype—the organism's total amount of hereditary potential (genetic code). More variations exist genotypically than are exhibited in the phenotype.

4. Natural selection can only work on the existing variations possessed by a population. The source for new variations is mutation—an accidental change in the structure of genetic material.

5. Other mechanisms of evolution are genetic drift—a gain or loss in the frequencies of genes in small populations due to chance; and gene flow—the interbreeding of organisms of one population with those of another.

6. Adaptation, the "fitting in" of organisms to their environments, occurs as specialization (close adaptation to specific environmental features), or generalization (the maintenance of wider variability). If environments change, the generalized species have greater chances for survival.

7. Extinction is the dying out of a form of life. It can occur by termination, in which the entire line is no longer in existence and therefore produces no descendents; or by evolution, in which the descendants exist but no longer closely resemble the ancestral forms.

8. The evidence for evolution is from two sources: direct evidence comes from the recovery of fossilized bones and teeth—the actual remains of past forms of life; indirect evidence comes from inferences we make from living organisms—present rather than past data. To be acceptable, indirect evidence should have some confirmation in direct evidence.

REFERENCES FOR FURTHER READING

There are a number of outstanding texts on Evolution. Perhaps the classic work is by George Gaylord Simpson, *The Major Features of Evolution* (1955, Columbia University Press). Other useful texts include the following: *Evolution and Its Implications*, by Peter Kelly (1966, Hawthorn Books); *Understanding Evolution*, by Herbert H. Ross (1966,

Prentice-Hall); *Processes of Organic Evolution,* by G. Ledyard Stebbins (1966, Prentice-Hall); *Understanding Evolution,* by E. Peter Volpe (1968, Wm. C. Brown); and *Evolution,* by Ruth Moore (1964, Time). Two more specialized books are *Population, Species and Evolution,* by Ernst Mayr (1970, Belknap Press) and *Heredity, Evolution and Society* by I. Michael Lerner (1968, Freeman). The actual story of evolution is not taken up in the present text due to space limitations, but two excellent books on that subject are *The Vertebrate Story,* by A. S. Romer (1971, 4th ed., University of Chicago Press); and *Three Billion Years of Life,* by Andre De Cayeux (1969, Stein and Day). References in chapter three not covered by the above are *Homo Sapiens,* by Bernhard Rensch (1972, Columbia University Press); and *Human Origins,* by Thomas and Sharon McKern (1969, Prentice-Hall).

4

evolution of
the primates

The recovery of the nonhuman primate past is of importance, not only in formulating and understanding the trends of primate evolution, but also in understanding these forms at present. In addition, it can suggest the jumping-off point of man himself into his own unique evolutionary history. Despite such important interests in fossils of nonhuman primates, there are a number of obstacles to our understanding of them. They were never too numerous (not being herd animals) so their fossil remains are hard to find; fewer bones and teeth are available. Since most primates have been rather small forms their small remains do not attract easy notice either, even if they did escape predation. Finally, most have lived in tropic-semitropic areas where fossilization is poor anyway. Nevertheless, we have enough direct and indirect evidence to reconstruct their history. It is a complicated history, however, and is represented by various authors in varying ways. Moreover, there are many special taxonomic names applied to various fossil representatives and more accumulating all the time. To lead the student through such territory, this chapter will first list some of the major trends in primate evolution in general and then fill in the "story line." The latter account of events is brief, selective, and intended to give a general feeling for the events behind some of the trends.

GENERAL TRENDS

Some of the general trends in primate evolution are (following Napier, 1970):

1. Progressive development of grasping ability in fingers and toes and immobility of thumb and big toes. This is accompanied by the replacement of sharp claws by flattened nails. The earlier mammalian structure of limbs is retained.

55

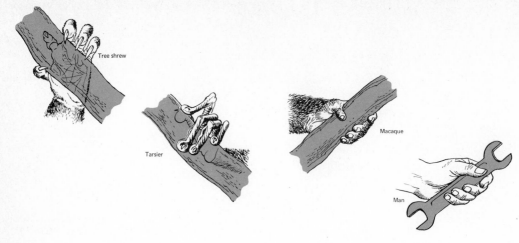

Pfeiffer, *The Emergence of Man*.

The grasping ability of various primates shows increasing opposability of thumb to index finger approaching man.

2. Increased frontality of eyes with the development of stereoscopic, depth-perception vision. This is accompanied by a progressive shortening of the snout and reduction in the apparatus and sense of smell.

3. Expansion and elaboration of the brain, especially areas concerned with vision, touch, and muscular coordination as well as with memory and learning.

4. Reduction in the number of teeth, loss of some early mammalian patterns, and preservation of a simple cusp pattern.

5. A greater dependency of locomotion on either the forelimbs or the hindlimbs at the expense of the others, accompanied by progressive development in truncal uprightness.

6. Prolongation of prenatal and postnatal life periods together with an increase in body size, accompanied by progressive development of gestational processes concerned with the nourishment of the fetus before birth.

7. Development of a complex social system, often hierarchical in organization, involving greater learned (as opposed to innate) responses and flexibility of behavior.

The story of primate evolution may be said to begin perhaps seventy million years ago with the beginning of the *Cenozoic Era* of geologic time (see Table 4–1). A major event beginning at this time was the rise to dominance of mammal forms, some of which were ancestral to primates.

56

TABLE 4-1

The Geological Record

Era, Period-epoch		Millions of Years Ago, When It Began	Characteristic Events On Life Forms
CENOZOIC ERA			
Quaternary:	Pleistocene	2,000,000	Ice ages; evolution of humans.
Tertiary:	Pliocene	12,000,000	Development of protohominids.
	Miocene	28,000,000	Development of pongids.
	Oligocene	40,000,000	Development of monkeys.
	Eocene	60,000,000	Monkey origins.
	Paleocene	70,000,000	Prosimian developments and origin of most modern mammal orders.
MESOZOIC ERA			
Cretaceous		130,000,000	Appearance of flowering plants, a few modern mammal orders, and extinction of dinosaurs.
Jurassic		170,000,000	Dominance of dinosaurs, origin of mammals and birds.
Triassic		190,000,000	Rise to prominence of reptiles.
PALEOZOIC ERA			
Permian		280,000,000	Decline of amphibians and rise of most modern orders of insects.
Pennsylvanian		310,000,000	Rise of amphibians and first reptiles; extensive tropical forests.
Mississippian		355,000,000	First amphibians.
Devonian		405,000,000	Dominance of fishes (rise of bony fish); earliest seed plants; winged insects.
Silurian		425,000,000	First forms of life on land.
Ordovician		500,000,000	First vertebrates.
Cambrian		600,000,000	Appearance of most invertebrates.
PROTEROZOIC ERA		900,000,000	Simple marine invertebrates.
ARCHEOZOIC ERA		1,500,000,000	Beginnings of unicellular life.

We will discuss developments correlated with subdivisions of the Cenozoic Era. The early *Paleocene* "primates" may not yet have been tree climbers in the strict sense; their fossil remains display no special primate skull-limb developments. Rather, they were generalized tree exploiters who may have spent more time on the forest floor. As time passed, some took to the trees more deliberately, although the sensory equipment for ground adaptation (smell and hearing) was still better developed than vision. We can only speculate as to why tree life would have become progressively appealing: greater abundance of food, freedom from predation, competitive pressure from rodents? Whatever the reason, life in the trees certainly led to "making" the primates. Soon there were various types of primates, all on a prosimian level of development.

> The oldest primates for which we know anything of the skeleton exhibit clear evidences of arboreal adaptations in their limb bone construction. The dentitions of many archaic prosimians, with their forward jutting and enlarged front teeth, may possibly have been adapted for husking seeds and fruits. The low-cusped cheek teeth suggest herbivorous habits. In the tropical forest, fruit, seed and leaf eating activities usually occur away from the ground. The basal radiation of the primates into the trees put a premium on visual acuity and locomotor agility, for which since then there has been strong selection. The ultimate resultant of arboreal survival is intense selection for greater intelligence as well. (Simons, 1972: 106, 108)

One such form was *Plesiadapis*, who is strikingly reminiscent of present-day tree shrews. Fossil forms related to and named after it are found in North America and Europe and range in body size from squirrel to domestic cat, with a "rodent" dentition of chiseling, gnawing teeth. Plesiadapis itself had a small brain, projecting snout, and long claws on the fingers and toes, which would have helped in climbing trees. Trees offered an adaptive niche and could be exploited by the simplest hanging on ability. The upper-central incisor teeth seem especially constructed for husking fruits and seeds. The heavy build of this creature has suggested to Simons that it was not yet very arboreally efficient.

By the middle of the *Eocene* period, many early primate experiments had become extinct, but a number of lemurlike types had developed: for example, *Smilodectes* and *Notharctus* in North America. These forms, and others, show improvement over earlier types. They display enlargement of the brain and a shifting of the eyes forward for better vision. Elongated hindlimbs may have permitted development of springing ability, and they are thought to have had greater prehensility. It is not likely, however, that either of these forms are directly ancestral to any types of lemurs living at the present time. Their ancestor is more likely some European form (for which we have inadequate evidence) living at the same Eocene time. In Europe, also at this time, there were some other somewhat similar forms; some of these, such as *Necrolemur*, had extended visual and prehensile abilities. Forms of early prosimians such as these may have ties to the tarsier. Certainly by the end of the Eocene, a variety of prosimianlike primates had staked a claim to successful exploitation of the arboreal environment. And evolution continued. Somewhere in the "mists" of the Eocene are to be found forms more directly ancestral to Anthropoids, although thus far, we have discovered no fossils clearly able to shoulder this distinction. One form from Burma, *Amphipithecus* (late Eocene) does appear to have a monkeylike jaw, but is dentally still a prosimian. Remains, however, are very fragmentary, and until further fossil evidence accrues, we shall have to wait to establish the Old World anthropoid links. As Simons has put it: "The evolutionary progress made by prosimians during the Eocene, both in North America and in Europe, is obvious. Yet not a single fossil primate of the Eocene epoch from either continent appears to be an acceptable ancestor for the great infra-order of the catarrhines, embracing all the living higher Old World primates, man included" (Simons, 1964: 6). Yet, even here we can safely assume some ancestors since by the next period, the *Oligocene*, there are a number of definite anthropoid types. Prosimians living today can be traced back to the prosimianlike forms of the Eocene period; they have survived to the present chiefly because many have lived in Madagascar, where there have been no higher nonhuman primates for competition and because elsewhere they have often been nocturnal, which has taken them out of competition with better-adapted diurnal anthropoids.

The monkeys of the Old and New World apparently have been separated since the late Eocene period, before the full level had been reached, and may have come from different prosimian ancestors. On the other hand, all anthropoids show biochemical similarities, in contrast to living prosimians; so monkeys of the Old and New World may ultimately be found to belong to some single past prosimian group not yet determined. We will focus attention on this stage in the Old World since in the New World at this time an "evolutionary ceiling" was hit, and with the exception of some later specializations, no higher forms developed. In addition, it should be mentioned that the fossil record of New World monkeys is rather restricted. Of the various forms that have been discovered (from the Miocene period on), none seem to have been directly ancestral to living species. The major differences between the Oligocene monkeylike fossils from the Old World and those found earlier is greater prehensility, accompanied by expanded brain size and stereoscopic, depth-perception vision. All this led to greater exploitation of their tree environment. Some forms may have expanded their diet. We find a number of forms existing in the Old World at this time: for example, *Parapithecus* (about the size of the smallest of modern African monkeys).

The next division of the Cenozoic is the *Miocene* period, at which time a number of hominoid forms appear in the fossil record. From this time on, Old World monkey types continue to the present relatively unchanged, save for the probability that greater numbers were adapting to at least part-time life in the expanding open grasslands. Because of the numbers, "it is odd that monkeys are not better known from Miocene localities in Africa, but the fact is that in these numerous sites fossil apes are about twenty times commoner than are monkeys. In an African forest today this proportion would be reversed" (Simons, 1972: 185). Simons concludes that the reason for this is that perhaps their major adaptive expansion had not yet occurred. Being small, they may also have fossilized less successfully or may have been searched for less effectively. Later on, many monkey forms appear in the fossil record, including one baboon form the size of a gorilla! The ape "level" of primate development was achieved in the Miocene period. It is characterized by developments such as some increase in brain and body size. Early forms are still somewhat monkeylike, however, and even later forms are the focal points of interpretational difficulties. Most of our earliest data on fossil apes comes from the Fayum, an area south of Cairo, Egypt. Today this area is desert but in Oligocene and later times it was a tropical area and hence an ideal territory for primates. The oldest candidate from this area during the Oligocene period is *Oligopithecus*, apparently small and generalized in form. Another form coming some four million years closer to us is *Aegyptopithecus*, about the size of the modern gibbon and quite possibly the ancestor of later Miocene ape forms. Although it had a tail, a "monkey" skull, and small brain, it had hominoid teeth. By the time the Miocene period had begun, a widespread ape type had appeared on the scene—**Dryopithecus**. This form, which is perhaps chiefly famous for its hominoid teeth, exhibits the five-cuspid lower-molar tooth pattern. These are separated by fissures generally shaped like a **Y** (y-5 pattern). This is a dental complex shared even by early man and is quite different from the four-cusp pattern of Old World monkeys.

Other series of forms are now being lumped together with this form as being generally similar although, in some cases, earlier: for example, *Proconsul*. This form, actually a series ranging greatly in size, includes skulls and long bones as well as teeth. These forms indicate that apes were not yet completely modern in appearance at this time. They were still comparatively light in build and not completely specialized for brachiation, although they were more "swinger" than quadruped. Their brains were still not much larger than those of monkeys, but they were certainly hominoid in terms of face, jaws, and teeth. Since forms of this sort are generally similar and are found in

Proconsul nyanzae may have looked like this.

Omikron

many Old World areas during Miocene and early Pliocene times, some writers have proposed that they all belong to the same "cosmopolitan" genus and call them Dryopithecines in general reference. It has also been suggested that they spent considerable amounts of time on the ground, possibly developing bipedalism. Certainly, they must have undertaken some terrestrial foraging for food; they were not specialized for arboreal life.

> The morphological variation characterizing the dryopithecines is important. Because of the morphological variation and because of the minor differences in living habits that the variation may have produced or reflected, the genus gradually differentiated ... Some members adapted to life in or near the trees and became the modern gorilla and chimpanzee and it has been suggested that others of them went a different path leading eventually to the hominid line. The group that led to the apes eventually died out in Europe ... Those in Africa survived.
>
> The argument for a dryopithecine ancestry of hominids suggests that the line leading to the hominids left the trees forever and moved into the savanna-grasslands fringing the forests ... The new econiche would have bombarded them with different and exciting stimuli forcing them to adapt to the new conditions. (Poirier, 1973: 45)

EARLY HUMAN ORIGINS

We can now ask the questions: what and when are the earliest hominid (human) origins, and what is the nature of our split away from our Miocene ancestors? Before pursuing possible answers, it is now necessary

61

to distinguish some anatomical and behavioral characters of modern apes and man. This will permit us to be more specific in assessing the position of such fossil forms—keeping in mind that the further back in time one explores, the more likely the degrees of similarity. As some writers have put it, we are less apelike, and the living apes less humanlike, than the earlier forms from which we both came. How do we differ from modern apes? We differ in many ways, and some of the most important that can also be discovered in fossil forms are listed below.

Human Differences from Modern Apes

1. Humans have erect posture and bipedal locomotion, which are reflected by:
   a. a foramen magnum under the center of the skull,
   b. an S-shaped spinal column,
   c. short and wide pelvic blades,
   d. legs longer than arms,
   e. feet arched and with heel and with big toe set close together to others and not opposable.
2. Humans have a different kind of skull and lower jaw. It
   a. lacks heavy brow ridges,
   b. lacks sagittal crest and occipital crest,
   c. has forehead and chin,
   d. has bony nose bridge,
   e. has evenly rounded dental arch,
   f. lacks the ape canine complex of projecting canine teeth, diastemas, and sectoral teeth;
   g. lacks a simian shelf on lower jaw,
   h. lacks facial prognathism.

Apes contrast with humans in these respects. They have a foramen magnum further to the back of the skull, a more bow-shaped spinal column, more narrow and elongated pelvic blades, arms longer than legs and different foot structures. Most have well-developed ridges and crests, a backward slope to the back of the head and bottom of the jaw, a U-shaped dental arch, a canine complex and simian shelf, and marked prognathism. Of course we differ from apes in many other respects as well. We have outrolled lips, sparse body hair, and year-round sexual receptivity. These are traits, however, not reflected in the fossil record.

We can now return to events in primate evolution. The generalized apes abounded during the Miocene period. Who are the earliest Hominids (our own ancestors)? From very scanty evidence, we come up with two late Miocene—early Pliocene forms that appear to be on our side of the fence: *Kenyapithecus* from Africa and *Ramapithecus* from India. Since a land bridge existed between these areas at this time, they may be varying species of the same form. At any rate, they do seem to be hominid because their teeth are set in a fairly evenly rounded dental arch, their incisors and canines are small, and their facial skeleton does not appear to be too projecting. Unfortunately, remains have not been forthcoming from the main part of the Pliocene period as yet, so there is a big interval between these forms and the next forms judged to be human that occur in the Pleistocene period. It is another of the gaps in the fossil record we hope will soon be remedied. The teeth of *Ramapithecus* show other interesting features. There is great wear between adjacent teeth, which is indicative of teeth crowded together. This (along with other dental features) suggests heavy chewing and abrasive foods—"adapting toward a diet different from that preferred by the typically forest-dwelling apes" (Simons, 1972: 274). It may also suggest the eruption sequence for molar teeth being extended over a longer period of time. This would indicate a longer overall growth period for Ramapithecus and the potential for ". . . a childhood learning period relatively longer than do the apes" (Simons, 1972: 273). Many scholars find no difficulty in assigning this form to the line of recent primate development leading up to ourselves; others believe it is merely an unusual sideline of ape evolution. This controversy is only with respect to anatomical features. Arguments are also couched in terms of overall interpretations of sequences of development, to which we can now briefly turn.

THEORIES OF APE-HUMAN DIVERGENCE

Given possible ancestors, the fascinating question to ask now concerns the nature of the splitting lines leading to modern apes and humans. Here major disagreements exist. We can, over-simply, discuss two points of view. One theory, the brachiator theory, holds that we came from apes of a "modern" type. In other words, our forerunners remained with the developing apes until after they had developed a specialization for brachiation. This "hanging posture" led to structural changes in the direction of uprightness that were prerequisites for erect posture later on in humans themselves. We came from apes who were already descending to the ground for some reason—perhaps because of increased

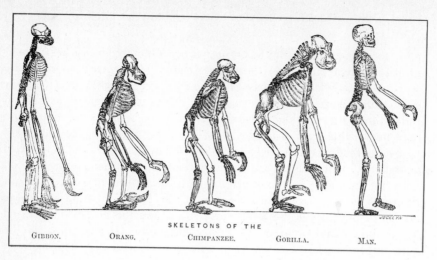

SKELETONS OF THE

GIBBON.   ORANG.   CHIMPANZEE.   GORILLA.   MAN.

American Museum of Natural History

weight and body size or because of competition for shrinking space in the tree environment. Our own emergence, then, would have occurred fairly recently; one guess is five million years ago. This theory derives our erectness from a brachiator ancestory and explains our present arm-swinging potential (seen in any gymnasium). One investigator (Sarich, 1971), using a biochemical time-scale system, has separated humans (immunologically) from chimpanzees and gorillas at about the time period demanded by this theory. Other scholars base their conclusions for recent separation in time more on the considerable anatomical similarities that exist between humans and modern apes in trunk and arm development. Some writers, as a refinement (Washburn, 1971), have postulated that human ancestors did not go directly from brachiation to bipedalism, but underwent an intermediate stage of "knuckle walking" as the gorilla does at the present time in its ground-dwelling existence. One writer observes that the structure of human hand bones do not support such a stage in human development. "Divergence of the hominid lineage from the lineage of the African apes probably occurred before the evolution of knuckle-walking" (Tuttle, 1969: 961). The primary objection to the brachiator theory in general is the evidence of *Ramapithecus* and *Kenyapithecus*, who are, at least in some known respects, apparently too modern too early in time (if they are hominids). Some writers have also suggested that this theory requires too many evolutionary reversals (gaining then losing brachiation) to make "logical" sense. We must remember, however, that evolution evolves what it evolves. We may well be redesigned apes.

The second theory can be called the **prebrachiator theory**. It suggests that human ancestors split off from those of the modern apes before arm swinging had fully developed. This would have occurred

64

perhaps twenty million years ago and thus would seem to fit the fossil record more closely as we now know it. Hominid types seem to have been present then, and apes were more generalized. The savannas of Africa were also spreading, offering a new potential niche for exploration (or at least a bigger area). Shrinking forests might have caused overcrowding for primate populations. In this theory, the apes go on to become efficient arm swingers and humans go out into the open, developing bipedalism as our locomotor specialty. Both adaptations require degrees of uprightness in posture and are departures from early primate quadrupedalism. Although it is difficult to poll the delegation of anthropologists, it can be suggested that many writers at least tacitly seem to defend some variation of this second theory. They differ mostly in the reasons our ancestors moved into the open areas. There also exist theories that push the diverging human line back to the Oligocene period or even earlier, although these views are not widely held.

Although it must be stressed that evolution is not usually explained by an either-this-or-that-way theory, and that we are certainly missing some key evidence, humans did become erect and bipedal and did forsake their primate heritage. Naturally, this did not occur as an abrupt process. It is impossible to quickly develop bipedalism, reliance upon new foods, and escape from predators that we now might come into contact with. Our ancestors must have spent a long apprenticeship in transitional environments—woodland savannas—where such locomotor

American Museum of Natural History

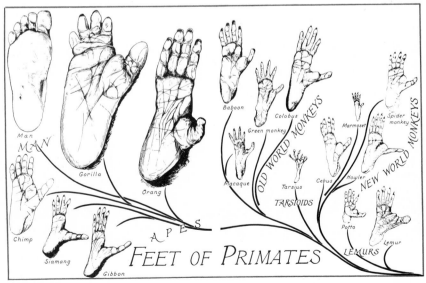

FEET OF PRIMATES

and other skills could be developed. Here, too, escape from predators (if really necessary) could still be facilitated by older "go-climb-a-tree" methods.

> The adoption of a ground-living way of life among the grasslands and savannas of Africa is generally accepted as the event which prodded man's ape-like ancestors up onto their two feet. In recent years, however, an increasing awareness of the impact of environment . . . has led us to question this assumption. Life in the savannas was no Elysium . . . Food would be less easy to come by than in the forest; predators would have abounded and escape would no longer be a matter of fleeing . . . through the security of treetops . . . If, in addition to these hazards, our early ancestors were in the process of adapting their gait from quadrupedalism to bipedalism, then it is difficult to see how they could have survived the transition. It seems plausible to suggest that man's ancestors did not start living in open grasslands until they were fully bipedal and were able to run and to carry weapons . . . During the dangerous transition periods it is improbable that the early hominids were inhabitants of woodland savanna . . . (It) . . . has enough trees to provide both forest foods and a ready escape from predators; and at the same time the open grassy spaces provide 'arenas' where new locomotor skills can be safely practiced and new food items sampled. (Napier, 1970: 172, 173)

Since the major structural departure during these times was the assumption of erect posture and bipedalism, it is perhaps instructive to suggest some of its advantages before returning to an inspection of the human fossil record.

ADVANTAGES OF BIPEDALISM

Bipedalism could have had at least three major interrelated advantages for a primate moving into open areas. First, it increases their range of vision. Chimpanzees out in the open stand erect to peer out in various directions. Some theorists even hold that such an activity was the original stimulus to erectness, although ground-living Old World monkeys seem to survive perfectly well on a quadrupedal plane. The other two major advantages have to do with the freeing of the hands in locomotion. This permits efficient carrying ability and the basis for continual tool use. Both of these would have been selectively advantageous. The tools (weapons) could help provide "the equalizer" against predators and the carrying ability could provide a way to bring food back to some place (home base?) of relative security. In fact, if early man was first a scavenger of the kills of other animals as some scholars would have it, the tools may have been used to beat off other scavengers. Developments such as the above would give populations with incipient bipedalism great adaptive advantages in early human populations. It would lead to greater perfection of and reliance upon such locomotor abilities and to more permanent exploitation of opening savanna areas. Some other advantages might have been gained as well: if, for example, predators are used to attacking four-footed types of prey, it might well be that the bipedal stance and unpredictable behaviors made early humans a less sought after target. Evidence from modern carnivore behavior suggests that this might have been true in the past. Waving sticks also would have made humans appear larger and more dangerous than other prey. Finally, a few writers (mostly non-anthropologists) see erectness of posture in early forms of man as resulting from foraging for sea food, as a response to wading activities. Many writers find this an extreme view, but that may be because anthropologists, for some reason, always seem to see postural erectness in response to flat-land activities. At any rate, in addition to vision, carrying ability, and potential for tool use, other useful side effects were undoubtedly gained by the development of new locomotor skills in early human ancestors. We can now turn to developments in human physical evolution for which greater fossil evidence is available.

SUMMARY

1. The evolution of nonhuman primates, even though incompletely known, suggests the departure point of the human line.
2. General trends in primate evolution include progressive development of grasping ability and flat fingernails, development of stereoscopic depth perception, reduction in the sense of smell, expansion of the brain, reduction in the number of teeth, and elaboration of learned behavior patterns.
3. Early primates were generalized tree exploiters that probably spent much time on the ground; their sense of smell and hearing were better developed than their vision.
4. By the Miocene period a widespread generalized series of ape forms appears in the evolutionary record. Called Dryopithecines, they probably served as ancestors to both modern apes and humans.
5. Two major theories exist relative to the split between apes and humans. The brachiator theory holds that humans came from apes of a modern type, that the human line did not split off until after brachiation had developed, and that the "hanging" posture led to human unrightness. The prebrachiation theory holds that human ancestors split off before such development occurred.

6. Bipedalism in early humans had a number of natural selective advantages: increase in the range of vision, and freeing of the hands for carrying things and for tool use.

REFERENCES FOR FURTHER READING

Scholarly writing on the evolution of the primates is extremely specialized. The best account of various fossil primates is in *Primate Evolution*, by Elwyn Simons (1972, Macmillan). See also his "The Early Relatives of Man," *Scientific American*, July 1964 (reprint no. 622, W. H. Freeman and Co.). A thoughtful discussion also occurs in *The Roots of Mankind*, by John Napier (1970, Smithsonian Institution Press). An account of primate evolution in terms of structural development is *The Antecedents of Man*, by W. E. LeGros Clark (1960, Quadrangle Books). See also *Fossil Man*, by Frank E. Poirier (1973, Mosby), for an account of fossil primates as well as an excellent account of human evolution. For perspectives on the pre-post brachiation controversy, there are the following: R. Tuttle, *Knuckle-Walking and the Problem of Human Origins*, in *Science* 166: 953–61; V. Sarich, "A Molecular Approach to the Question of Human Origins" and S. Washburn, "The Study of Human Evolution," both in Dolhinow and Sarich, *Background for Man* (1971, Little Brown, pp. 60–81, 82–117). See also Virginia Avis, "Brachiation: The Crucial Issue of Man's Ancestry," in *Southwest Journal of Anthropology* 18: 119–48.

5

major stages of physical evolution

There are four known stages or levels of development in human physical evolution that are recognized by anthropologists. These stages must be understood as points along a continuum of development where fossil evidence has accumulated to a degree facilitating generalization. Actual development moves imperceptibly; it does not jump from one stage to the next. In the absence of abundant fossil representatives from each time period, and because of the need to simplify, it is legitimate to deal with human development in this fashion. The four stages are the Australopithecine, Erectus, Neanderthal, and Sapiens. Each will be discussed in terms of the physical characters involved and the controversies associated with them. Most evidence for culture is reserved for later chapters. As in any "detective story," there is often a difference of opinion as to the "guilt or innocence" of a given form. Is you is, or is you ain't my ancestor?

STAGE ONE: AUSTRALOPITHECINES

Remains of the **australopithecine** forms were first unearthed in 1924, have been found off and on up to the present time, and now number parts of over one-hundred individuals. With one or two possible exceptions, the finds have been limited to southern and eastern Africa. The general time period assigned to these forms is the beginning of the Pleistocene period or perhaps the late Pliocene times. This era is sometimes referred to as the Villafranchian because of a collection of flora and fauna called by this name that were found at that time. Ignoring for the present variations among these australopithecines, we can generally characterize them as follows:

The brain is comparable in absolute size to that of some modern

70

apes, ranging from about 400 to 600 cubic centimeters; in relation to body size, however, it is relatively larger. This trait is suggestive of greater possible intelligence. The skulls themselves are rugged but brow and sagittal ridges are somewhat reduced in comparison to apes' or completely absent. Brow ridges are also rounded to follow the contour of the eye sockets rather than being a single bar of bone. There is no forehead. The jaws are fairly massive and projecting, and the lower jaw lacks a chin. These jaws, however, indicate some very human tooth developments. The dental arch is more evenly rounded than in the apes and there is no simian shelf (bridge of bone in lower jaw). The incisors and canines are not very large and are human shaped; the canines are not projecting and there is no diastema (gap for opposite canine teeth). Molar teeth are huge but with a human cusp pattern. The position of the foramen magnum is fairly far forward on the skull base, suggesting that the head was fairly well balanced over the spinal column. The upper part of the hips is also broad and flat in response to erectness of posture, although the lower part is somewhat less human. It has been suggested that although erect posture was present, long-distance bipedalism was not yet perfected. These creatures were certainly not as efficient as ourselves in this regard. Perhaps they were waddlers rather than good walkers or runners. Some writers have stated that running may have been easier than walking. "They may have walked with a sort of shuffling gait, but they were capable of an efficient running gait. The evidence . . . is based on the study of the foot skeleton and other bones of the hind limbs" (LeGros Clark, 1967: 111).

Reinforcing an interpretation of erect progression on two feet is the fact that upper limbs lack the muscular attachments that characterize the brachiating apes. The knee joint in the leg seems capable of being habitually flexed in the extended position for erect posture. Fragmentary foot-bone material appears hominid; there were no apelike diverging toes. In sum, we have in these forms creatures with a combination of low brain power, fairly rugged skulls and projecting jaws, along with essentially human posture and teeth.

> The best way to interpret the apparently "simian" characteristics of the australopithecine's skull, such as the small brain case and massive, projecting jaw, is to treat them as characters of common inheritance from a hominoid ancestry that also gave rise by divergent (branching) evolution to the modern anthropoid apes . . . These characteristics do not indicate a close taxonomic relationship with the pongids. On the other hand, the hominid characters are manifestations of independent acquisition clearly demonstrating that the australopithecines were representatives of the hominid evolutionary line. (Poirier, 1973 : 119)

Today, there are fewer and fewer scholars who would fail to place the australopithecines in the hominid category. If we recall the previous discussion concerning the adaptive significance of erect posture and bipedal locomotion, and think of these forms in this respect, we should expect natural selection to have encouraged further development along such lines. If such a trait has adaptive significance, it presumably should have significance for classification as well, outweighing other australopithecine traits in this regard. Even taking all traits into account, they seem closer to modern humans than modern apes.

The human status of these creatures could be aided by discovery of their capacity for making and using tools in a human fashion. Although many scholars have suggested that the survival of a slow creature on the ground without projecting canines is itself evidence of culture (tools and weapons), there is tool evidence of a more direct sort. First, however, we must make an attempt towards distinguishing between human and nonhuman use of tools. In thinking of rudimentary tools, this is difficult to accomplish, but one writer (White, 1949) has made the following distinction. The human species, he says, is characterized by symbolic and conceptual use of tools. Even when we are not using a tool, we are thinking of using them. We make them ahead of time, try to perfect them, etc. In essence, tool use is a continual unbroken experience. Other animals in this view have only temporary conceptual use of tools. For them, tool use is limited to a number of discrete, unconnected episodes in which a need arises, a tool is used, discarded and forgotten until such a situation occurs again. Here there is no continual mental relationship to them. In this sense, humans certainly are more continuous in their tool habits, although chimpanzees demonstrate certain advances in this direction. Is there evidence of conceptual use of tools by the australopithecines?

Two kinds of tool evidence have been uncovered in this connection. Simple stone-pebble tools as well as some more advanced types occur at some sites. Unless some advanced form of human was present—a distinct possibility, say some authors—it would seem that the australopithecines must have made them. Since the raw materials were brought to the sites, it is suggested that these are our kind of tools, made in advance and kept to be used later on repeated occasions. We also have evidence of bone tools found in the context of bone deposits in caves. These have, however, literally become bones of contention! The bone deposits consist of masses of bones, primarily of antelope, although other large animals are represented. According to one view, the australopithecines were scavenging or directly killing these animals and using some of the bones as "natural" tools: for example, heavy limb bones as clubs, jaws with teeth for cutting, and sharp bone fragments as daggerlike implements. Indeed, some skulls—both baboons and australopithecines—appear to have been smashed in by clubs. Although extremely rudimentary, such tools are conceptual if they were being horded up to use on some future occasion.

In opposition to such a view is the idea of some scholars that the bone accumulations are the work of scavengers and that the australopithecines' associations prove their being the hunted rather than the hunters. Perhaps they were killed by predators and dragged into the caves by hyenas. Still other writers have pointed out that such accumulations are not characteristic of hyenas or have been accumulated by purely natural means. Although this issue is certainly not yet fully resolved, there is a distinct possibility that at least some of the australopithecines may have been consciously collecting bones that had tool potential—possibly scavenging the kills of predators. It is hard to conceive of humans at this time as extremely efficient predators themselves. They may, however, have directly killed smaller animals, as well as their fellows, by using such tools. If so, such direct evidence of culture is another indication of the hominid status of these forms.

VARIETIES OF STAGE-ONE FORMS

Africanus and Robustus

As evidence has accumulated on these forms, scholars have come to recognize at least two basic types. With this distinction, however, has come further controversy. The two types are *A. Africanus (Australopithecus)* and *A. Robustus (Paranthropus)*. The first is rather small,

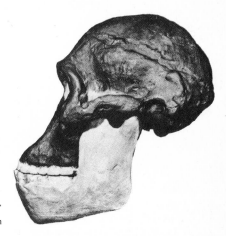

Skull of Plesianthropus (Australopithecus).

Fraser/Omikron

four feet high and weighing perhaps fifty to eighty pounds. It has a less rugged skull with mild brow ridges and no sagittal crest. It is usually characterized as *gracile* (slightly built) and from tooth-wear pattern, some scholars (Robinson, 1954, 1963) believe it was omnivorous in diet. The assertation that the little form is the earlier of the two in time is now suspect since earlier examples of both varieties have recently been found. *Robustus* was a larger form, about modern in size and weight. Its skull is more rugged, with larger brow ridges and a small sagittal crest. The teeth are said to show a vegetarian wear pattern and molars are larger. Conversely, however, the front teeth appear to be more human. Adding to problems of interpretations is the fact that the hips are sometimes characterized as being less human. Incidentally, a few people have suggested that the big australopithecines were males and the small ones females; in other words, that this species of early humans was characterized by great sexual dimorphism, not unlike some other primate groups. The distributional evidence, however, appears to negate this possibility since if this notion were correct, the populations at some areas would be mostly boys with the girls being elsewhere. This is highly unlikely. Although they may be uncertain as to their significance, most scholars accept the existence of at least two separate species of early hominid at this time.

The presence of these two forms of hominids raises interesting speculations. Did one evolve into the other, getting larger and more rugged to deal with predators? Is one generalized and the other specialized—the little generalized form moving into the open and the larger specialized variety remaining back in a forest habitat? Since they appear to have lived at the same time for at least part of their careers, did they compete? Which is our ancestor? Part of the answer may depend on still another hominid form recently found in east Africa.

Habilis

This form, presently consisting of rather fragmentary remains, has been designated **Homo habilis** by its discoverer (Leakey, 1966). Existing at approximately the same time as some of the australopithecines, it is said to be characterized by the following traits in comparison with the australopithecines: a more rounded braincase and a cranial capacity of 680 cubic centimeters, a less heavily muscled lower jaw, a more evenly rounded dental arch, somewhat smaller teeth, and a stature of about four and a half feet. It is asserted that hands and feet are also more human, but we lack clear evidence for these traits among the australopithecines. Finally, it has been asserted that this form is the real maker of the stone tools. This is based on distribution evidence of stone-tool associations with fossils where habilis and the australopithe-cines appear to occur together. Where the latter seem not to have company, only bone-tool possibilities exist. The presence of *Homo habilis* certainly adds further complexity to our interpretive problem. Is this form our ancestor—and not closely related to other forms—or simply another variety of australopithecine? Before attempting to answer these questions, it is instructive to move on to the second stage in human physical evolution. It is perhaps easier to make a decision when we know what later forms of humans were like. Before moving on, however, a further bit of information on the australopithecines is necessary. Until fairly recently the finds of these forms were limited to a number of sites in South Africa and to Olduvai Gorge in East Africa, with the earliest date being about 1.8 million years old—ob-viously giving these forms a considerable antiquity. Now a number of other East African sites have yielded remains. These finds include remains of both varieties of australopithecines. So, for example, from the Omo Valley in Ethiopia, dating back four million years

> ...the hominid samples from the Omo Beds would indicate the coexistence of (at least) two australopithecine taxa through much of the range of Pliocene/Pleistocene time. And this would have been the case not only in the Omo area, but even in broadly similar habitats, to judge from available palaeo-environmental data. The respective ecological niches of these creatures, however, remain essentially unknown. (Howell, 1969: 1239)

Fossil remains have also been uncovered from other areas, such as around Lake Rudolf, dated around two and a half million years in age. There, remains include not only evidence of a possibly super robust form but (recently) a super "modern" form as well; giving some support to the idea of a separate human (Habilis) line evolving independent from the australopithecines. Crude stone tools have also been recovered at some of these sites. Also recently discovered at the Baringo Basin in Kenya are fragments of hominid remains going back some nine million years, which may represent a link to the *Ramapithecus* forms. It has become apparent that many important clues for the "detective story" of human evolution will come in the next few years because of a concentration of work in key areas by physical anthropologists. We will return in chapter eight to the australopithecines.

STAGE TWO: ERECTUS

The second stage in human evolution is generally dated back to the early or early-middle Pleistocene period; perhaps back as far as a million years ago and lasting until 300,000 years ago. Fossil finds of

Erectus forms are wider in geographic distribution than are those of stage one. Three general developments have occurred by this stage. These forms had perfected erect posture and bipedalism; hips and limbs are like our own. This suggests the ability of these forms for long-distance walking and running. There has also been a substantial increase in brain size. Finally, the teeth, while still somewhat large, fall near the upper ranges of present-day human variation. In some other respects, however, the forms had not developed substantially beyond those of stage one.

Pithecanthropus

We have reconstructed this stage of human development from two main series of forms. In 1891, a form subsequently named *Pithecanthropus erectus* was found in Java. More recently (1930s) additional remains were discovered. These remains are characterized by the following traits: a cranial capacity ranging from 800 to 950 cubic centimeters housed in a rugged skull with no real forehead or chin. Large brow ridges are present and although there is no sagittal crest, there is greater midline ruggedness, which some writers refer to as a gabled effect. The jaws are still fairly prognathic. The limbs and posture are absolutely human, however, and the forms are reconstructed as having a height of five feet, eight inches and a weight of about 150 pounds. The teeth are human and smaller than those of stage one, although some forms are said, strangely enough, to possess small diastemas and slightly projecting canines.

No tools have been found in direct association with *Pithecanthropus*, but some types have been found in adjacent geological deposits,

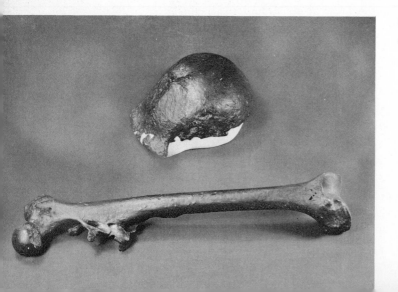

Skull of femur of Pithecanthropus.

American Museum of Natural History

and it is generally assumed that this form was their maker. Also, *Pithecanthropus* apparently had company. A lower jaw fragment substantially different from that of an erectus has been discovered in one of the earliest *Pithecanthropus* deposits and has been given the name *Meganthropus*. Although the status of this form was in limbo for some years, many scholars now classify it as a *Robustus (Paranthropus)* type of australopithecine. If it is really that, we may have the interesting case of the survival of an earlier form of man during a later stage of development. *Pithecanthropus* dates back to perhaps 700,000 years ago.

Sinanthropus

The second series of forms was first found in caves near Peking, China in the late 1920s and was originally assigned the name *Sinanthropus pekinensis*. This form is known from a fairly large sample of individual remains, is later in time than *Pithecanthropus* (360,000 years ago), and is also a slightly more evolved type. The *Sinanthropus* forms are characterized by the following traits: the skull is still rugged and has

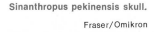

Sinanthropus pekinensis skull.

Fraser/Omikron

brow ridges, but the rear of the skull is perhaps somewhat less rugged than in *Pithecanthropus*. Jaws are still prognathic and the lower jaw lacks a chin, but the backward slope is less pronounced. The cranial capacity on the average is close to 1100 cubic centimeters. As a result of this brain expansion, a slight forehead begins to appear. Some of the skulls have been broken open from the bottom after death, suggesting brain cannibalism. Although some peoples in the "primitive world" of the recent past have done this for supernatural reasons, many scholars feel that pure dietary needs (waste not, want not?) might be involved in this case. Height is calculated as somewhat less than in *Pithecanthropus* but within the modern range. Teeth are still large but human and no diastema occurs.

Directly associated with *Sinanthropus* were slightly better tools, evidence of fire, and quantities of big-game animal bones. Although tools are crude, they include both stone and bone types and there is no doubt that *Sinanthropus* was their maker. The evidence of fire from charred hearths is extremely significant. Fire may have given protection at night to these cave dwellers, although some scholars feel this function to be greatly overrated. More important would be heating and lighting functions. Certainly, having an artificial, external sort of warmth permitted the humans of these times to live so far north, and the wider the geographic range, presumably the greater the survival chances. Artificial lighting would permit the extension of the working day. From this time on, we could "burn the midnight oil," planning and working on tools. Up to a point, one might say the greater the time to work at survival, the greater the chance of that survival. In addition to these functions, we can perhaps assume the use of fire for cooking food, as an aid in making tools (hardening wooden spears), and as a social center. The numbers and types of animal bones (especially of deer) is suggestive of the advent of big game hunting as the human way of life, made possible by long-distance locomotion. We will return to the possible effects of being such a hunter-predator in the next chapter.

Two final points may be mentioned in connection with *Sinanthropus*. First, although both physical and cultural improvements had taken place, life was evidently still a real struggle for existence. If the skeletal remains have been analyzed correctly, about 40 percent of the population died before maturity. Beyond the desire for sheer survival, the presence of old people in a population has distinct advantages; they not only can take over sedentary jobs and hence free younger, stronger group members for more active tasks, but as a repository of accumulated knowledge, they also have educational value. Secondly, there are a number of small physical traits (in tooth structure, etc.) found in Sinanthropus that are also characteristic of modern Asiatic peoples. Some authors have concluded on the basis of this an ancestral-descendant relationship and the beginnings of the formation of modern races. Most scholars, however, seem to feel that such developments came later in human evolution and that no one population at such an early point in time could be exclusively ancestral to later human groupings.

Other Erectus Forms

We might ask, at this point, about the rest of the Old World at this time period. We know of stage-two men in Asia and an earlier form in China (Lantian man) would have been a contemporary of *Pithecanthropus*. What do we know about such developments elsewhere? Curiously, we find a great many tool and other cultural remains but only a few fragmentary fossils of their makers. From the study of these, however, most scholars have concluded a significant overlap with the Asian forms. So now these forms are having their original names taken from them (for example, *Heidelberg* from Germany and *Telanthropus* from South Africa) and are simply being called *Homo erectus*, as are the Asiatic forms. Fragmentary remains are also found elsewhere in Africa as well as in Europe. Together they are now considered a single, if fairly widespread, Old World type of human at this general time period: not identical in form but appearing as only regionally differing populations.

> From this accumulation of finds, many of them made so recently, there emerges a picture of men with skeletons like ours but with brains much smaller, skulls much thicker and flatter and furnished with protruding brows in front and a marked angle in the rear, and with teeth somewhat larger and exhibiting a few slightly more primitive traits. This picture suggests an evolutionary level, or grade, occupying half a million years of human history and now seen to prevail all over the inhabited Old World. (Howells, 1966:8)

Thus, if our evidence reflects the actuality of the situation correctly, there was only one fairly similar type of stage-two hominid form.

Two questions relative to these forms remain to be asked. Where did *Homo erectus* come from (geographically) and who in stage one was his ancestor? Two major opinions have been advanced with respect to the first question. It can be held with some degree of logic that the stage-one ancestors first evolved into *Homo erectus* in Africa and then, with better locomotion, hunting ability, and bigger brains, slowly spread into other habitable portions of the Old World. This view suggests that our human ancestors were limited to Africa during stage one and did not spread until later in his evolutionary development. This view is, however, contradicted by the lone *Paranthropus* form (*Meganthropus*) in Java. If that designation is indeed the correct classification, it could also be held that stage-one humans existed in many Old World areas, either having spread there from an original "homeland" in Africa or having come from earlier hominid populations already present.

In any case, the advance to the *Erectus* stage is then seen to have taken place at approximately the same time across their entire range. This second theory also presupposes that repeated contacts between groups and exchange of genetic as well as cultural materials kept such populations essentially similar in biology and behavior. Although biologically acceptable, this is not entirely substantiated from cultural remains. We shall obviously have to await further accumulation of fossil evidence before either general view can be substantiated on other than logical grounds.

The question of ancestors for stage two is also a particularly thorny one at the present time. Before the discovery of *Homo habilis*, many scholars (such as John Robinson) were content to have the somewhat more "modern" smaller australopithecine evolve into *Erectus*, while the larger variety remained a plant-eater and eventually became extinct. It is, of course, not entirely impossible to maintain that the australopithecines were merely a highly variable population and that both types were involved in the transition to stage two.

Habilis adds to the confusion if its advanced hominid status is correct. Here some could argue that *habilis* is the real ancestor among the candidates in stage one: this form evolved to *Homo erectus*; *Australopithecus* became extinct because of ecological competition, followed much later in time by the extinction of *Paranthropus*. A counter proposal to this view is the assertion that Habilis is just another variety of australopithecine anyway! Robinson argues that the dental length/breadth index indicates only overlap between the varieties of these forms and with *Homo sapiens*. "It is not possible to distinguish taxonomically between these groups by means of this index if anything like adequate sample sizes are used" (Robinson, 1965: 122). He also sees substantial overlap in cranial capacity. Some scholars see differences between the *Habilis* remains themselves; assigning the earliest to the australopithecines and the later to an early *Erectus* stage. Clearly it is too early for a consensus to emerge. Many scholars have adopted a wait-and-see attitude with regard to this problem.

STAGE THREE: NEANDERTHALS

Certainly by the end of stage two, *Homo erectus* had become a widespread and eminently successful species. They were big game hunters and were beginning to make a real impact on their environment. But, although they were fully human in their posture and locomotion, evolution in other structural and behavioral features continued. The next

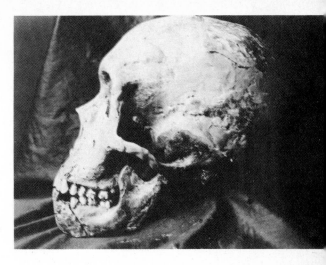

Reconstructed Neanderthal skull.

American Museum of Natural History

major stage of development is generally considered to be that of the
Neanderthals, thought to be roughly intermediate between *erectus* and
modern forms. Considerable evidence has accumulated concerning the
time of their appearance (near the onset of the Wurm Glaciation and
in Europe especially) 100,000 years ago. Although in most Old World
areas there is good evidence for cultural evolution *between* physical
stages two and three, there is a distinct gap in the fossil record of bones
and teeth. Further, the few remains available have been the focal point
of considerable differences in interpretation. We can discuss these first as
a lead into the Neanderthal forms themselves.

Early Forms

From near the end of the second interglacial period (250,000 years ago)
we have two finds. From Germany comes *Steinheim man*, represented
by a single skull crushed on the left side. The brow-ridges are large,
but the forehead is said to be expanded and the prognathism somewhat
reduced in contrast to *Homo erectus* forms. The back of the skull appears
somewhat more modern than in the *Erectus* forms. Brain size has been
variously estimated between 1150 and 1200 cubic centimeters. At the
same time period, we have *Swanscombe man* from England. This find
consists of the back and side bones of the skull, although the frontal
area is missing. The bones are said to reveal an essentially modern skull
conformation, and guesses as to cranial capacity run as high as 1325
cubic centimeters. We lack, of course, any direct evidence for the
presence of brow ridges, although some have claimed their existence by
logical implication. Skull bones are still thick, as in earlier forms. Recent
excavations in the Pyrenees Mountains in France have revealed frag-

81

ments of another form from this general time period (200,000 years ago). Although still incompletely reported on, the skull does have large brow ridges, lacks a real forehead, and in other ways seems only slightly improved over preceding forms. Another form, this one from the early part of the third interglacial period, is *Fontechevade man* from France. This find consists of fragmentary remains of two skulls. One is an almost complete skull cap, the second merely a small portion of the frontal bone. These appear to demonstrate a fairly modern forehead and reduced brow ridges, although they seem robust by modern standards. Estimated cranial capacity is about 1400 cubic centimeters. There is still a marked degree of thickness to skull bones. Other third-interglacial-period finds are from Ehringsdorf, Germany (rather modern cranial capacity with large brow ridges), Krapina, Yugoslavia (pronounced population variability), Saccopastore, Italy (with large brow ridges and a slightly smaller cranial capacity than other forms at the time), and many others of similar natures.

Considering these forms, the most logical assumption is that here is evidence of continuing evolution away from *Homo erectus* and toward *Homo sapiens*. We should expect the remains of the Neanderthals (forms dating from about 100,000 to 40,000 years ago and associated with the beginning of the Wurm Glaciations in Western Europe) to be a further step in this direction. Unfortunately, not all interpretations of these later remains have suggested that this, in fact, was the case.

Neanderthals

Although some of these forms are from times earlier and warmer than others, all of the Neanderthal remains show some common characteristics. They are as follows. The skull is rugged, with large brow ridges. These are curved, however, unlike the continuous bar of bone in *Erectus* forms. The vault of the skull is long and narrow and is made to appear more so perhaps by the drawing out of the back of the skull (occipital bun). The face projects forward and contains large, deeply set eye sockets. Jaws contain somewhat larger than modern teeth. The upper jaw is said to have an inflated appearance due to nasal prognathism. Cranial capacity is about the modern average or slightly higher in some forms. The body itself is rather compact (about five feet) with short, powerful arms and legs and strong neck muscles. It was originally believed that Neanderthal man slouched in posture and thrust his head forward—because of large neck vertebrae and the presence of curved leg bones in some specimens. Most scholars have now discarded this view as being generally applicable to forms of this time (not only were early reconstructions poor, but some specimens appear to have been diseased anyway). Forms of Neanderthal that date earliest in time differ in the degree that the above characteristics are fully present. At any rate, most scholars appear to feel uncomfortable when comparing these Neanderthal forms to the earlier types (Swanscombe, Steinheim, and Fontechevade), since they seem to point to a more "modern" successor than Neanderthal. The problem is increased by the fact that at least in western Europe, the Neanderthal remains seem to have been abruptly supplanted after the height of the Wurm Glaciation by forms of a definitely modern type (40,000 years ago). Due to the way evidence has accumulated this may be more apparent than real, but as more than one scholar in the past seems to suggest: Neanderthal goes into the ice and modern humans come out!

Theories on Neanderthal

How are we to interpret these fossil forms? Although there are numerous theories of the relationship between the Neanderthal stage and human evolution in general, they can be reduced (oversimply) to three basic formats or scenarios (shown in table 5-1): complete exclusion, partial inclusion, and total inclusion. The first possibility, complete exclusion, can be stated generally as follows: Steinheim, Swanscombe, and Fontechevade, plus the earlier, less rugged Neanderthals were evolving from *Homo erectus* toward *Homo sapiens*. As the Wurm Glaciation advanced, they remained in Western Europe and tried to adapt to increasing colder conditions. In this view, specialized, "cold-adapted" features developed (puffy cheeks, large nose to warm the air they breathed, compactness of body size for heat retention, etc.). These later forms are to be called *classic Neanderthals* in contrast to earlier forms. For any one of a number of reasons, such forms did not survive; they lacked sufficient genetic variability to survive or were killed off or genetically swamped by incoming *Homo sapiens*. In this view, *Homo sapiens* had evolved from *Homo erectus* separately, outside the European area. Hence, there is no Neanderthal stage in human evolution. It is a "dead-end" development. This is perhaps the oldest view of the situation and few modern scholars subscribe to it.

The second format, partial inclusion, has a variety of possibilities. One of these is argued as follows. Again, Steinheim, Swanscombe, and Fontechevade, and other early forms are evolving towards *Homo sapiens*. Again, the Wurm Glaciation advance begins. In this case, some forms evolve into the classic variety by virtue of remaining in "frozen" Europe, but others leave the scene and, in more equable clime, evolve

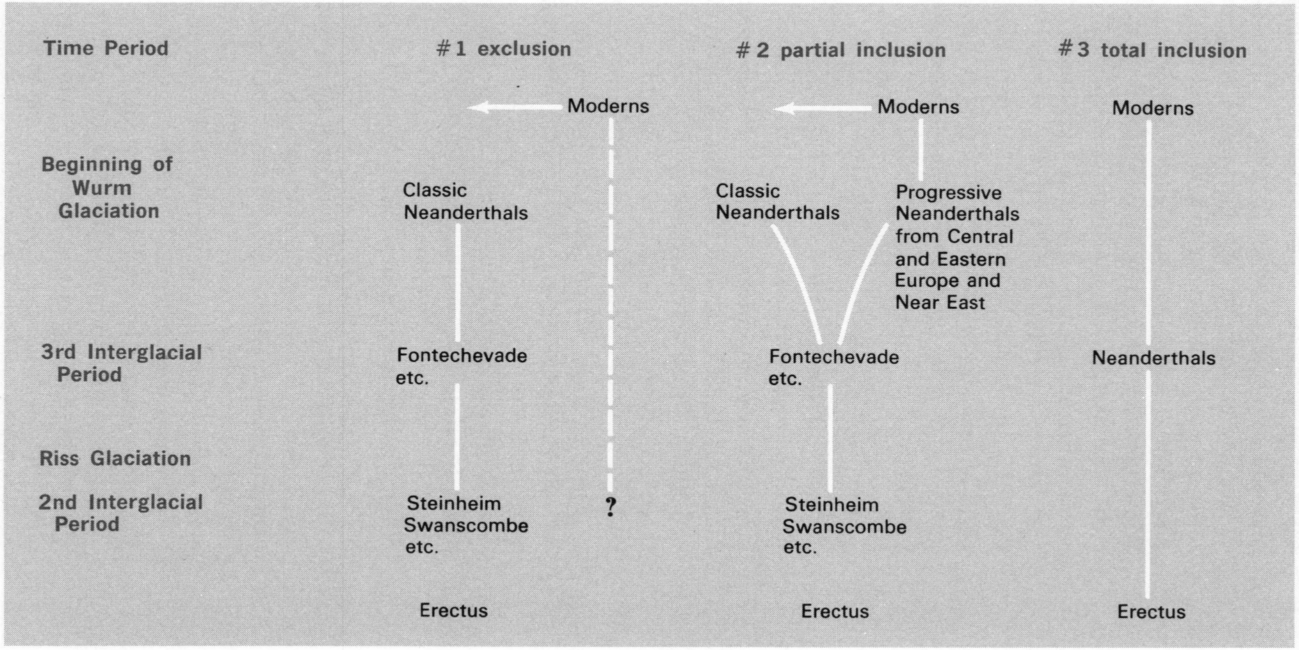

Time Period

Beginning of
Wurm
Glaciation

3rd Interglacial
Period

Riss Glaciation

2nd Interglacial
Period

1 exclusion

Moderns

Classic
Neanderthals

Fontechevade
etc.

Steinheim
Swanscombe
etc.

Erectus

?

2 partial inclusion

Moderns

Classic
Neanderthals

Progressive
Neanderthals
from Central
and Eastern
Europe and
Near East

Fontechevade
etc.

Steinheim
Swanscombe
etc.

Erectus

3 total inclusion

Moderns

Neanderthals

Erectus

into *Homo sapiens*. They then return to the scene and complete (if neces-
ary) the extinction of their classic cousins. Although there is no classic
Neanderthal stage between Erectus and modern humans, there is
a more general stage from which both arose. This is "having your
Neanderthal and leaving it too." A variant of this format is that the
early forms are already at the stage of *Homo sapiens*. Here again
some "stay and play"—becoming simply Neanderthal man (now
a sideline off the mainstream of human kind), whereas other sapiens
leave to return when climactic conditions or cultural abilities are better.
Here too, there are no classic Neanderthal ancestors but we can partly
include them since they too are an isolated sapiens form. There are
some real difficulties with this view. The fragmentary remains of Steinheim and Swanscombe and the lack of a good geologic context and
poor reconstruction of Fontechevade make the assertions of their
Homo sapiens status somewhat doubtful. Moreover, and this has a
bearing on any theory of rugged Neanderthals reflecting environmental
specialization and restriction, there are cave deposits in Palestine and the
Near East (at Shanidar in Iraq and Mt. Carmel in Palestine), outside the
range of inclement weather, containing skulls that exhibit "classic"
features. These, as time goes on, appear to be more modern. There also
exist a number of generally neglected forms of "Neanderthals" from
Central and Eastern Europe. These occupy the same general time period
and reflect the same cultural adaptations as the more classic forms in
Western Europe. They also appear to be evolving toward more modern
forms. As one recent writer, after surveying these other European finds,
put it:

> These Neanderthal forms display, to various degrees and in various
> frequencies, many of the characteristics that we find fully developed in
> H. *sapiens sapiens*.
>   These circumstances bear out the view that the appearance of H.
> *sapiens sapiens* in Central and Eastern Europe ... need not be explained
> in terms of a sudden migration from East to West, but rather in terms
> of local evolution in populations having basic morphological character-
> istics in common but differing in the intensity and frequency of others—
> a situation that would have permitted relatively rapid morphological
> change. (Jelinek, 1969 : 491, 492)

He would call the Neanderthals *H. sapiens neanderthalensis*.
    The third format is for total inclusion and posits a Neanderthal
stage (including rugged types) not only in Europe but elsewhere in the
Old World as well. This is the most recent view and appears to rapidly
be gaining adherents among some scholars interested in this problem.
Very briefly, this argument goes as follows. We have overdrawn the
modern nature of Steinheim and Swanscombe and made the Neanderthals more rugged than they actually were. They are really only slightly

less rugged than previous forms (if at all) and represent only fragmentary evidence anyway. Fontechevade is too suspicious to warrant any real appraisal. Other forms are fragmentary, so we really have to "toss these forms out" (suspend judgement). If we then place the Neaderthals between Erectus and Sapiens, the only significant differences between Neanderthal and Sapiens are in the structure of the face: bigger teeth, brow ridges, and prognathism. Brain size is modern and the body, except for some greater robustness, is hardly different. "Neanderthal man is the man of the Mousterian Culture prior to the reduction in form and dimension of the Middle Pleistocene face" (Brace, 1964: 18). Moreover, the Near Eastern cave finds and those from outside Western Europe can be interpreted as an evolving-population situation between Neanderthal and Sapiens at the correct time interval (when this would have had to happen). Some proponents of this theory also include forms outside of these areas from this general time period in the Neanderthal stage as well: *Solo man* from Java, *Rhodesian man* from Africa, and other forms with as yet no definite classification. So it is concluded that human evolution did pass through a Neanderthal stage of development (in many world areas), one that includes the European "classics" as well. Many scholars feel that this view makes the situation just a little too simple. We eagerly await the resolution of this problem.

STAGE FOUR: SAPIENS

In any event, definitely modern forms of humans appear on the scene in Europe and elsewhere after the height of the Wurm Glaciation, 40,000 years ago, and are associated with improved tool-making traditions. These early moderns are slightly more robust than modern Europeans; obviously, one still had to be somewhat rugged to survive. Stature is almost modern, although females are said to be fairly short. One of the first forms was discovered in southwest France and was called *Cro-Magnon man* after the site of its discovery. This form lacked the large brows of earlier forms and was nonprognathic, although jaws are slightly larger than in ourselves. There is a forehead and a chin and teeth are within the range of modern variation. Cranial capacity is about 1450 cubic centimeters. Other forms presumed to be living at the same time show some divergencies, and although considered full-blown, *Homo sapiens* are sometimes given separate designations: for example, *Predmost man* from a population in Czechoslovakia. Interestingly enough, one of these forms still overlaps with Neanderthal types. Most of these early forms have been recovered from Europe since most

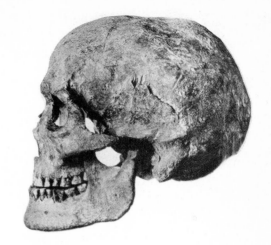

Cro-Magnon skull.

American Museum of Natural History

of the work has been done there. Fossil moderns have also been re-covered from Africa, Asia, (above the Erectus cave finds) and from the New World (although of lesser antiquity).

Only two real problems have emerged relative to these early modern representatives. The first is that many remains were uncovered by less than scientific techniques and so their precise dating is suspect, although their general age is confirmed. Some skulls also appear to suffer from poor reconstructions. This has not led to serious contro-versy. Second, some scholars have attempted to demonstrate affiliation of the European forms to various races of man existing at the present time. Since the concept of racial differences is a dubious one, since it is difficult to conceive of all modern races as originating in just one area of the world, and since some thousands of years have passed (would modern races really look like their ancestors?), these theories have not been generally accepted. We will return to the concept of race and such problems in chapter eleven. We can now turn to a brief summary of human physical evolution.

SUMMARY

1. There are four known stages of development in human physical evolution: Australopithecine, Erectus, Neanderthal, and Sapiens.
2. The characteristics of the Australopithecine stage are small brain size (400–600 cc), less rugged skulls than those of apes, generally human dental structure, basically erect posture, bipedal locomotion, and use of tools.

3. Varieties of Australopithecine include both smaller and larger, and more rugged types: for example, Africanus and Robustus. Habilis may represent a more advanced form at this time.

4. The characteristics of the Erectus stage include larger brain size (800–1200 cc), rugged skulls, human dental structure, erect posture, bipedal locomotion, and slightly improved cultural behaviors. Their geographic range apparently was wider than that of earlier forms.

5. The Neanderthal stage—still rugged forms but with expanded brain size—is subject to many interpretations, some of which do not consider the Neanderthals as direct ancestors of modern humans. Much of the controversy surrounds a rugged form possibly being preceded by more "modern" types.

6. By 40,000 years ago, forms hardly distinguishable from modern humans appeared in many Old World areas.

REFERENCES FOR FURTHER READING

There is a tremendous number of books and articles dealing with various aspects of human physical evolution. For information to expand the data given in the present text the following general accounts are valuable. *The Human Species*, by Frederick Hulse (1971, 2nd ed., Random House); *Human Evolution*, by J. B. Birdsell (1972, Rand McNally); *Physical Anthropology*, by Gabriel W. Lasker (1973, Holt, Rinehart & Winston); *Evolution and Human Origins*, by B. J. Williams (1973, Harper & Row); *The Ascent of Man,* by David Pilbeam (1972, Macmillan); *Physical Anthropology* by A. J. Kelso (1970, Lippincott); and *The Emergence of Man*, by John Pfeiffer (1969, Harper & Row). See also *Fossil Man*, by Frank Poirier (1973, Mosby); and *Guide to Fossil Man*, by Michael H. Day (1965, World), which neatly catalogues information on various fossil finds made before 1965.

Rather than citing numerous specialized articles (other than those referred to in the present text), I can offer the following readers that collectively have reprinted a veritable "orgy" of important contributions on human evolution. *Man in Evolutionary Perspective*, edited by C. Loring Brace and James Metress (1973, Wiley); *Human Evolution*, edited by Noel Korn (1973, Holt, Rinehart & Winston); *Human Variation*, edited by H. Bleibtreu and J. Downs (1971, Glenco Press); *Background for Man*, edited by Phyllis Dolhinow and Vincent Sarich (1971; Little, Brown); and *Evolutionary Anthropology*, edited by H. Bleibtreu (1969, Allyn & Bacon). Two thought-provoking collections are *Perspectives on Human Evolution* nos. 1 and 2, edited by S. L. Washburn and

Phyllis Jay, and S. L. Washburn and Phyllis Dolhinow respectively (1968 and 1972, Holt, Rinehart & Winston). Many of these readers also contain articles on the concept of race, primatology, and other related topics in physical anthropology.

Specific citations that are not covered above are: *Man-Apes or Ape-Men?*, by W. E. LeGros Clark (1967, Holt, Rinehart & Winston); *The Science of Culture*, by Leslie White (1949, Grove Press), tool-making abilities; "Remains of Hominidae from Pliocene/Pleistocene Formations in the Lower Omo Basin, Ethopia," by F. Clark Howell, in *Nature* 223 (1969): 1234–39; "Homo Erectus," by William W. Howells (1966, Freeman), *Scientific American* reprint no. 630; "Homo Habilis and the Australopithecines," by John Robinson, in *Nature* 205 (1965): 121–24; "Neanderthal Man and Homo Sapiens in Central and Eastern Europe," by Jan Jelinek, in *Current Anthropology* 10 (1969): 475–92; and "The Fate of the 'Classic' Neanderthals: A Consideration of Hominid Catastrophism," by C. Loring Brace, in *Current Anthropology* 5 (1964): 3–19.

6

summary of the
fossil record

It is now time to present a brief summary of the fossil record of human physical evolution and to speculate on the significance of some other possible developments. In accomplishing part of this, I am following very closely the summing up given in one recent text (Brace and Montagu, 1965). These scholars feel that one has to consider human physical development as a **mosaic evolution.**

MOSAIC EVOLUTION

By mosaic evolution Brace and Montagu mean that the human organism is a mosaic; it is made up of a number of different structures and behaviors that evolve somewhat separately. This is due to the different selective pressures working on different aspects of our biology at different rates and different times. In other words, we should not expect man to be 25 percent human, then 50 percent human, etc. in all respects. Some structures became modern earlier than others. Brace and Montagu recognize three main parts of the human mosaic: erect posture and bipedal locomotion, brain size, and tooth size. We can consider each of these with reference to the four sets (stages) of fossil forms we have previously discussed. This assumes we have some kind of ancestor at each developmental level and includes Habilis as an australopithecine variety.

Erect Posture and Bipedal Locomotion

Erect posture and bipedal locomotion already appear to have been well developed by the time of the australopithecines, although long-distance walking and running were perhaps not yet perfected. This suggests

91

previous development in even earlier forms, perhaps as far back as *Ramapithecus*. The fact that natural selection would have picked so early and completely on this human character should not surprise us in light of our previous discussion of the adaptiveness of freed hands. By the time our second major fossil series, *Homo erectus*, appears on the scene—perhaps a million years ago—this trait is fully modern. Even this postural change must be viewed as an improvement rather than a major development, given the occasional erectness of some other primates. This erectness also points to the use of tools.

> The evident bipedalism of the Australopithecines is one of the indications that points to their essential humanity, since a weaponless biped on the savannas of Eastern and Southern Africa could not have lasted a single generation. The success of the Australopithecines points to the likelihood of their use of culture as a major means of adaptation. (Brace and Montagu, 1965: 261).

Increase in Brain Size

The *increase in the size of the brain* took a longer period of time for completion. The australopithecine brain, relatively speaking, seems improved over those of living apes, but is still nowhere near that of humans at the present time. By the time of *Homo erectus*, brain size has about doubled. This suggests powerful evolutionary forces at work. By the time of the Neanderthals it has again increased, this time to its present dimensions. So modern brain size has been completed by about 100,000 years ago. Since that time, no significant brain-size changes have occurred, although culture at this point begins to accelerate in development at an ever increasing pace. Many scholars believe that brain size by this time had passed some "cerebral rubicon" beyond which further size increase conferred no particular adaptive benefit.

The increase in the size of the brain to its present dimensions (completed by about 100,000 years ago) suggests powerful evolutionary forces at work.

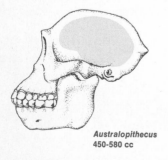

Australopithecus
450-580 cc

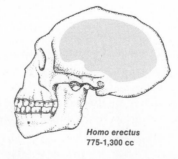

Homo erectus
775-1,300 cc

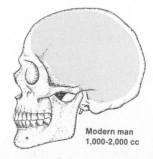

Modern man
1,000-2,000 cc

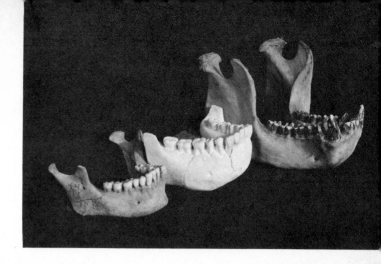

The lower jaws (from left to right) of modern man, Meganthropus, and a gorilla illustrate evolutionary reduction in tooth size.

American Museum of Natural History

Culture rather than biology at this point, became our primary adaptive commitment for survival, a trend that certainly continues at the present time. "We can only infer that some sort of threshold has been passed and that the efficiency of culture in transmitting information among individuals and across generational boundaries was sufficient so that beyond a certain point, marked increases in individual intelligence conferred no particular survival advantages upon the possessor" (Brace and Montagu, 1965: 261). We will consider the potential effects of such a commitment in a later chapter.

Reductions in Tooth Size

Finally, human mosaic evolution is evidenced by *reductions in the size of teeth.* Although australopithecine teeth are definitely outside the modern range of size, the nonprojection of the canines and lack of the canine complex display a definite trend away from other hominids. In the time between australopithecines and *Homo erectus*, molar teeth underwent rather dramatic reductions in size: down to the upper ranges of modern variation, although incisor teeth remained relatively larger. It has been suggested that decrease in molar-tooth size can be correlated with a shift to greater amounts of meat in the diet (requiring less mastication) and with the presence of fire (which makes food easier to chew). Even by the time of the Neanderthals, the incisors are large and remain so until modern forms of human beings appear on the scene. Until this time, and until the appearance of good cutting tools, the incisors appear to have been used as a kind of tool for holding and tearing meat and other things. When specialized tools for these purposes are developed, selective pressures are removed from the front teeth, which results in their final reduction. As a result of this, the supporting facial structures of large brow ridges and prognathism are also modified

93

to about present proportions. As the previously mentioned scholars have summed up this entire situation:

> Doubling the brain and reducing the molars changes the Australopithe-cines into . . . (*Homo erectus*). A further simple increase in brain size produces . . . the Neanderthals . . . and finally the reduction of the Nean-derthal dentition particularly at the forward end, and the accompanying adjustments by the supporting facial architecture accounts for the final development of modern form. Treated in this way, the changes which have taken place in man's physical form since the first record of his existence are actually less dramatic than they at first would appear. (Brace and Montagu, 1965: 264).

Two other ideas should be noted at this point. First, we must remember that some real basic changes—reduction in canines, loss of the canine complex, dental-arch modifications, and assumption of erect posture and bipedalism—were dramatic changes in human evolution but are almost completely undocumented changes for the period pre-ceeding the fossil record of the australopithecines (stage one). The above comments, then, apply only to known stages, occuring after the commitment to humanity seems to have taken place. Second, human physical evolution has continued beyond the early *Homo sapiens* times. We have not increased in brain size, but have decreased somewhat the robustness of our biology. Although not exactly ninety-eight-pound weaklings, we are less powerful creatures than even our immediate ancestors. In addition, dental evolution has continued with both the decrease in size and sometimes the absence of our third molars (wisdom teeth) as well as the development of an overbite (overlap of upper incisors in front of lower incisors). This is again generally ascribed to changes in food and tool developments. We will return to speculate on further human physical evolution in chapter twelve.

SPECULATIVE ASPECTS OF EARLY HUMAN EVOLUTION

The developments and summation of human physical evolution pre-sented in this and the preceeding chapter are based largely on direct fossil evidence. We can measure tooth-size reduction and estimate brain size. We can turn now to some traits and behaviors suggested in a very speculative fashion by utilizing, for the most part, indirect evidence. Certainly, the first real revolution for the human animal in-volved its initial penetration of open areas, its posture and locomotion, and its use of simple tools. These we have discussed in the previous chapter and will return to presently. The second revolution was the predatory revolution, the transition to big game hunting as opposed to small game hunting and perhaps scavenging. The role of meat in the diet itself may have been intensified by the first primates in the human line that moved out into the open: "... under changing ecological conditions, for example, if communities of higher primates were forced to occupy an open savannah type of country where vegetable food was scarce, normally vegetarian populations would develop their flesh-eating propensities to the extent that they would become predominantly carnivorous" (LeGros Clark, 1967: 121). A host of scholars have presented ideas as to what the physical and social consequences of this development might have been. They see the development as having been completed by the time of the *Homo erectus* forms. Some of these admittedly speculative possibilities can now briefly be discussed.

EFFECTS OF BIG-GAME HUNTING

It should first be mentioned that bipedalism gives humans one further advantage in addition to those mentioned in chapter four. By freeing the hands from locomotor responsibilities, it allows us to "eat on the run." This permits human beings, slow runners that we are, to move rather continually after our prey at a fairly steady pace. The prey, having no paws free from locomotion, eventually becomes seriously impaired in its ability to escape. If kept continually on the run, eating only small amounts of food (a task it must stop to accomplish), eventually it runs out of energy and can be brought to bay. Thus, although relatively weaker and slower, humans possess bipedalism, which permits them to develop big-game predation. One writer has called this *persistence hunting*: "... the game is finally taken primarily because the hunter has been able to persist in the chase for as long as one or two whole days" (Krantz, 1968: 450). This is a uniquely human type of hunting and permits a relative weakling (in contrast to most carnivores) to be a successful predator even in the absence of well-developed projectile weapons. Of course, persistence hunting would not have been the only available technique. As Poirier (1973) summarizes this situation, although actual hunting as described above is the most predictable way of getting meat, there also exist the possibilities of capturing such animals and their newborn, of scavenging animals already dead, as well as scavenging the kills of other predators by intimidating them to leave their kills. Certainly, the ability to make kills of active, healthy

In some areas of the world, hunting techniques have not evolved past their early printing stages. At left is a cave painting found in Paleolithic rockshelters in eastern Spain; at right, a "modern" bushman hunter.

game animals does not preclude other attempts at opportunism in the food quest. Nor would vegetable food resources have been neglected. Incidently, the hunter's heavy reliance on meat provided him with a good source of energy. Not only does hunting increase the total amount of food available but it is, in comparison to most vegetable foods, a highly concentrated form of nourishment. In fact, humans now were indirectly utilizing vegetable foods they were digestively unequipped to directly utilize by consuming animals that consumed the plants.

There are other factors involved here that have led to speculations as to the origins of some modern human traits that are unverifiable from the fossil record. Humans have a relatively hairless skin and well-developed sweat glands. These possessions give us further advantages in pursuing big-game animals. Hairy or furry animals being chased during the heat of the day would be severely impaired in any long-lasting attempt to flee from hunters. Hairlessness and sweat glands are heat-dissipating mechanisms that would thus aid the hunter in the chase. And, of course, lacking night adaptations such as excellent smell and hearing (already somewhat lost through primate evolution), humans do have to be active in the heat of the day. Lacking great speed, moreover, the chase is necessarily a long one. It is probably, then, a not unwarranted assumption that humans did, as some would have it, become "a naked ape" at this period (*Homo erectus*) in our evolution. One scholar has even postulated a further possible development. Commenting on a naked hunter pursuing game in the heat of the day, he suggests that dark skin pigmentation would have been of prime advantage in screening out the harmful rays of the sun—a task hitherto performed by the hairy primate covering. Did humans become sweaty, hairless and darkly pigmented?

> It would appear that the development of human predation long ago capitalized on the limitations which a coat of fur has placed upon mammalian activity during the heat of the tropical day, and one can suspect that the perfection of the hominid pelvis for long-distance walking was accompanied by the effective loss of human body hair. At the same time, the intensity of ultraviolet radiation poses something of a problem to the hairless tropic-dweller, since it greatly increases the chances of developing skin cancer. The solution is the development of a concentration of the protective pigment *melanin* ... it is possible to postulate that with the development of effective hunting techniques, somewhere between the Australopithecine and the (*Homo erectus*) stages, man became hairless and black. (Brace, 1967: 75)

In future time, clothing would come to perform such screening functions. It has also been suggested that the human development of a "sweating capacity" would have come as a compensatory mechanism after the loss of body hair. Exposure out in open areas with a naked skin would have increased the heat load. "This must have constituted a disadvantage ... in man it has taken the form of dependence on thermal sweating for heat dissipation to the point where *Homo sapiens* have the greatest sweating capacity for a given surface area of any known animal" (Newman, 1970: 25).

There must also have been many other (unverifiable) changes, some of the more intriguing of these possibilities can now be discussed. Some writers have postulated that big-game hunting would have radically altered the relationship between the sexes. This would have a number of potential aspects. Certainly, some physical separation must have taken place. Males necessarily would have had to "commute" long distances in running down or even finding their prey. Females, one suspects, would be more limited because of their problems with pregnancy and child care. Such would reduce, somewhat at least, their biped hunting advantages and restrict them to a more home-base vegetable collecting existence. Such range difficulties are even foreshadowed by chimpanzee social organization discussed in chapter two. We might even infer the development of a base camp, a place to which the hunters could, in time, return. Did the use of fire during *Homo erectus* times begin as a signal device for such a practice? Also involved here is the possible development of a sense of dependence between the sexes through food-sharing activities. Other primates usually secure all

Males going hunting together. With the advent of organized hunting came the separation of male and female duties.

Irven DeVore/Anthro-Photo

of their own food. It would have been of distinct advantage for returning hunters, tired and empty-handed, to have some female-collected foods waiting for them. And, of course, if females who didn't hunt were to obtain meat, sharing would have to go in the other direction as well. Of some interest in this connection is the general fact that most carnivorous animals do share their food. It is not altogether unlikely, then, that the creation of a sexual division of labor between males and females had developed by the time of Erectus as well as the creation of a home base for operations; perhaps similar to behaviors among some modern hunting peoples of whom we do have knowledge. Possession of a more or less fixed home base would also give sick or injured members of the group a greater chance for survival, unlike other primates who, for the most part, must keep up or die.

Moreover, because of their activities, males would have an unparalled opportunity (for primates) to gain a variety of new experiences. They would get to know (by having to cope with it) a wider world. Also, hunting itself requires the development of many new possible courses of action since it is a more unpredictable activity than gathering plant foods. Hence, the psychological and behavioral horizons of the males must have undergone tremendous increases at a time when these were increasing for humankind generally. Further, as a few writers have suggested, the greater cooperative nature of male activities at this time possibly led to a greater associative bond between them. Certainly modern hunting societies are characterized by male groups. Did male chauvinism develop with big game hunting?

So here was another heightening of the differences between the sexes. The gathering of plant foods could usually be conducted in the general vicinity of the home base, but hunting could not. Men went away in groups, ranged widely and stayed away, perhaps all night and perhaps

98

for several nights on occasion. They began forming the all-male associations which more recently have led to such things as clubs, lodges, athletic competitions, secret initiations, and a variety of stag institutions. Women were in the process of becoming the "other sex" in a sense that is true for no other primate, the first females to be left behind and to fear being abandoned. (Pfeiffer, 1969: 140, 141)

And we may safely assume that males were hunting collectively by these times, at least on occasion, since the social behavior of most carnivores appears to capitalize on such a potential. A recent study summarizes the many advantages of such cooperative activity, perhaps the greatest of which is that "Several individuals hunting together tend to be more successful than a lone animal . . . (and) . . . A group of carnivores hunting together can kill larger prey than can a single individual" (Schaller and Lowther, 1969: 314).

All of the above kinds of activities would require better communication potential than that possessed by any nonhuman primate. Certainly, gestures and facial expressions (like those exhibited by many higher primates) were retained from previous times, but the vocal-call systems must have been somewhat elaborated upon and expanded. At this time, one would need a better device for coordinating the chase and kill of game and to pass on the accumulating store of knowledge and behavioral experience. The development of a human kind of language (see chapter twenty-four), plus the necessity for participation in some very nonprimate behaviors, in turn, made tremendous demands on the children. In order to learn to talk, to use and make tools according to standardized traditions, to engage in the new social relations, an extra premium was being placed on the capacity for thinking and learning, and on the capacity for memory and recall. They had to possess bigger brains. It is obvious why the brain had doubled in size by the end of the Erectus stage in human physical evolution: those less capable of handling the above would have been weeded out.

Females, however, were presented with a new problem. They were giving birth to bigger-brained offspring, but bipedalism places limits on delivery. Females could widen their hips somewhat (via evolution) and apparently did, but this places further limitations on their mobility; they could run less ably. Apparently this obstetrical dilemma was solved by earlier delivery; infants were born at an earlier stage of development than among other primates. The brain size of modern human infants is only about 25 percent of its modern adult size, that of apes over 50 percent. Such a delayed maturity was made possible by life on the ground, which does not require the newborn to cling to the mother to survive (as well as by the general primate tendency for single births). The emerging interdependent social life would also help in the protective sense to insure survival. And, of course, delaying maturity gives the offspring a longer period of potential learning—just what would be required at this time of exploding human knowledge! And all this would further rearrange social behaviors.

> The differences between the sexes were steadily increasing. The widening of the hips to permit the delivery of infants with larger brains was one step in this direction. Far more significant was prolonged infant dependency, which meant prolonged female dependence and helped decrease female mobility to a much greater extent than changes in pelvic structure. The longer and more intensely an infant needs its mother, the longer and more intensely the mother needs a reliable adult male. Circumstances called for the formation of new and stronger male-female bonds . . . (Pfeiffer, 1969: 140)

Another interesting possible development at this general time is a modification in sexual behavior. Humans are perhaps the only primates apparently fully free from biological controls in regulating sexual behavior, although some others have made gains in this direction. Human females are characterized by year-round sexual receptivity, as opposed to periodic receptivity (periods of heat or estrus). Biological controls have been replaced by those of a cultural sort. This has tempted a number of scholars to "pin the rap" for this development too on big-game-hunting arrangements. Although none of their explanations seem totally sufficient, we can briefly examine two of them, both related to hunting but approached from different perspectives. The first is argued somewhat as follows. Sex can be disruptive among aggressive animals that live together in groups, especially if survival by cooperatively killing big-game animals is necessary. If female receptivity were restricted to brief periods, competition and conflict would develop over gaining access to them. In this view, permanent receptivity would insure that there would be less to fight about and would promote cooperation. It might be objected that a stable dominance hierarchy might accomplish the same thing; but this might weaken cooperative hunting arrangements. Certainly, other predators have handled the problem differently. The other view is that permanent receptivity was a development to insure that the males would return to base camp and share food in the first place. Certainly, having this as an on-going enticement might have led to more continual male-female interaction. In either case the end result would tend to stabilize permanency in social relationships.

Finally, mention may be made of one further possible development connected with big-game hunting. At least a few writers have suggested a real breakthrough in primate aggressiveness at this point, seeing at least males as having become a "killer ape." The argument for this

Prolonged dependence of infants on their mothers greatly decreased female mobility. They became limited to a smaller geographical area and tended to the gathering while the men were away on hunting expeditions.

Irven DeVore/Anthro-Photo

suggestion runs something as follows. *Erectus* males must have become more aggressive than the other primates in the effort to kill the game animals. Other primates generally keep their aggressive levels at the bluff stage in territoriality or in maintaining dominance hierarchies. Not only would evolution select the most aggressive males for hunting endeavors, but by pursuing game, a group of hunters could wind up in the home territory of some adjacent group. This is another nonprimate pattern that could cause aggression, leading to conflict situations. Such a thesis is sometimes extended to hypothesize that humans still have some "biologically ordained" aggressiveness in their present-day nature, retaining this long after its usefulness has passed. Such a proposal is generally countered by the assumption that aggression is a learned phenomenon (see chapter twenty-two).

Nonetheless, aggressive or not, stage-two societies, via their hunting activities, could have been brought into contact with other groups in a way uncharacteristic of other primates. Such contacts may not have generated conflict, however. Intergroup cooperation is a possibility too, perhaps fostered by the development of woman exchange to make allies out of potential enemies. In addition, such contacts between different *Erectus* groups could lead to gene flow, planned or not, which could help homogenize human differences. Further, such groups could pool their developing knowledge which could stimulate cultural progress.

In any event, although nonaggressive males might fare poorly under the condition of securing game food, the extent and nature of that aggression is very much an open and unresolved question at the present

101

time. Despite this and the lack of verification for the other developments postulated at this time, the shift to big-game hunting (predation) indeed must have wrought a profound revolution in the way of life of the human species. We can now turn to evidence of a direct sort again, this time to the remains of tools, and attempt to reconstruct human cultural evolution. Prior to doing so, however, we must provide a minimal background and discuss the work of the archaeologist, the specialist who works to recover such materials.

SUMMARY

1. Human physical evolution is best understood as mosaic evolution which theorizes that different structures such as posture, locomotion, brain size, and tooth size evolved somewhat separately in response to different environmental pressures.

2. Posture evolved earliest to its present day form due to the human necessity to adapt to open areas. This was followed by increased brain size and, finally, smaller physical stature (the latter being a response to the development of sophisticated stone tools).

3. The big game hunting way of life during Erectus times, brought about a real "revolution" in human behavior. It not only stimulated human intelligence and aggression, but possibly helped form new human relationships (for example, cooperation among males) in addition to delaying the maturity of offspring.

REFERENCES FOR FURTHER READING

Specific references for chapter six include *Man's Evolution: An Introduction to Physical Anthropology* by C. Loring Brace and M. F. Ashley Montagu (1965, Macmillan); "Brain Size and Hunting Ability in Earliest Man," by Grover Krantz, in *Current Anthropology* 9 (1968): 450–51; *The Stages of Human Evolution*, by C. Loring Brace (1967, Prentice-Hall); "Why Man is Such A Sweaty and Thirsty Naked Animal: A Speculative Review," by R. W. Newman, in *Human Biology* 42 (1970): 12–27; and "The Relevance of Carnivore Behavior to the Study of Early Hominids," by George B. Schaller and Gordon R. Lowther, in *Southwestern Journal of Anthropology* 25 (1969): 307–41.

7

archaeology
and its
techniques

*A*rchaeology is the study of the past of the human species. Unlike the physical anthropologist who attempts to recover and interpret evidence of human physical evolution, the archaeologist is primarily interested in cultural remains and cultural evolution. Many recovery techniques, however, are similar. Unlike the physical anthropologist, the scholar attempting to recreate and understand our cultural past usually has a better and more complete record. Tools and objects of stone and other materials fossilize better than human physical remains. And there are more of them to recover in the first place. Hence, there are perhaps fewer major controversies and gaps in interpreting human cultural evolution than physical evolution.

SOME TYPES OF ARCHAEOLOGY

In the age of the specialist, of course, there are different kinds of archaeologists. Although the techniques they use are basically similar, the scope of their interests both in time and subject matter have led to a general division of this field along the following lines.

Prehistoric

Prehistoric archaeology deals with the period of prehistoric human cultural development; with peoples who had no written records (existing "before history") or who, even after the invention of writing, did not themselves possess it. This covers most human developments and most world peoples and, so, most working archaeologists as well. This thropology since the remains discovered have perhaps their closest interest area also leans heavily on the findings of other areas of an-

104

Classical archaeology deals with Mediterranean and Middle East civilizations. This excavation is in Phaestos, Greece.

Peter Buckley

counterparts in existing primitive societies. One major drawback in working on prehistory is that, lacking written records, one has to lean more heavily on interpretation of the data. An excavated pot does not say, "Made in Japan, 1950 B.C." A compromise field of archaeological interest in this respect is sometimes called *parahistoric* archaeology. Here one deals with a society that itself was prehistoric, lacking written records, but that is mentioned by a historic people. The writings of the Greek historian Herodotus are filled with references to nonliterate neighboring peoples. Here the archaeologist may get a little aid in his endeavors. The Sythians of South Russia are a good example of such a parahistoric people. Many New World societies described by early Spanish Conquistadores would also fit into this category.

Classical

Classical archaeology deals primarily with the classical civilizations of the Mediterranean and the Middle East (for example, Greece, Rome, and Egypt) and ancient civilizations in some other areas—societies that did possess writing systems. Not only does their possession of this trait often make interpretations easier, but such groups are usually also characterized by more striking cultural remains; there is more to recover and interpret in the first place. As a matter of fact, many such objects, because of wealth or craftsmanship, are often recovered for their own sake. Many of the first diggers into our cultural past were more

105

grave robbers than scholars interested in reconstructing man's past. As a result, much valuable data was not recorded. As it has been suggested:

> The foundations of classical archaeology were thus established in the study of objects or buildings for their own sake. Moreover, literary sources provided the historical, chronological and cultural background against which such things could be studied. It follows that classical archaeology has been much less dependent upon scientific excavation than the newer branches, and has concentrated more on stylistic studies. Comparatively recently, excavations have begun to add to the facts available for these stylistic studies by providing chronological evidence for developments, and have also brought to light new information about the history of sites. (Kenyon, 1968: 43)

Today's classical archaeologists are often trained in humanities rather than anthropology (unlike the prehistoric archaeologist); studying art, architecture, ancient history, and languages. Unlike the historian, however, the archaeologist still has a bias towards material culture.

Specialized Types

While prehistoric and classical archaeology are the two general fields of interests, differing perhaps more in degree than kind, there are some other types that deserve brief mention. *Biblical* archaeology deals with any type of culture from so-called biblical areas of the ancient Near East. It is an area of specific subject interest and its practitioners have occasionally been accused of selecting their data to substantiate or detract from the authority of biblical accounts. What is often called *historical* archaeology seems to be a developing specialty in our own country because of the interest in colonial history. It refers to such activities as the excavation and reconstruction of an early village or perhaps a tavern site. Of course, recourse can be made to written documents of the time. Finally, among other specialties, there is *salvage* archaeology, which is the attempt to rescue archaeological sites of any type deemed important from destruction by natural or human sources. This is a situation generally calling for suspension of precise techniques. With imminent destruction, the rationale is that it is better to gain some understanding than none at all. Many areas in Egypt were the objects of salvage work prior to their flooding by the Aswan Dam. This is not to be confused with "pot hunting," generally an activity of amateurs who often plunder any site by unsystematic techniques for the sole purpose of building up a collection of artifacts. Such activities are a "pet peeve" of the archaeologist.

Basically, scientific archaeologists employ the following four techniques: excavation, classification, interpretation, and dating—although not always in such a strict order. We can discuss each of these in turn.

Excavation

Excavation is digging up the remains at a site. Before mention of such techniques, we must first discuss how one finds such a site and something of the nature of such locations. Certainly, the type and location will somewhat determine the exact nature of the techniques utilized. Finding the site is often a problem. Sometimes a site is visible. It is large enough to draw attention from a distance: for example, a burial mound in the eastern United States or a ruined city of the ancient Near East. Most sites, however, are less obtrusive and are found either by sheer luck or by deliberate search attempts. The latter is accomplished in a number of ways: by knowing where to look on the basis of prior knowledge of a particular time period or place (in caves, along rivers) and by a more general attempt (simply looking for unusual features in a given area). Site discovery has been facilitated in recent years by the development of new scientific devices and aids. These include aerial photography, magnetic devices to detect metal and other objects, and electrical resistivity (in which electrical current is run through the ground between two electrodes to probe for solid structures). In all events, however, much site discovery remains a task involving lots of good leg work, tramping through the fields, plus luck!

Types of Sites. Basically, a site can be characterized as either *open-air* or *buried*. In the former case, the cultural remains are on the surface of the ground, although they may once have been buried—their present condition a result of redeposition. In the buried site, of course, they are still in the ground. The majority of sites, perhaps, are of this latter sort, and with their context still secure, interpretation and dating are greatly aided. It is to such sites that the excavational techniques produce the best data. Somewhat along the same lines is the distinction sometimes made between primary and secondary sites. "Sites may be either *primary*, if a people has deposited its own remains there, or *secondary*, if the remains have been redeposited by another people or by a natural agency" (Rouse, 1972: 33). Sites are also classified according to the content of the materials recovered (or their nature). Here a great many types are recognized. *Habitation* sites are places where people centered their daily activities, seasonally or on a year-round basis. Such sites generally yield a varied set of materials and often contain such a diversity so as to lead to interpretations of the quality of the life of the people involved. *Kill* sites are locations where animals were killed by hunters. Remains are usually limited to bones, killing and butchering objects, and campfires. Since such remains are important in assessing technology, they may present valuable information; they may be the only remains left behind by nomadic peoples. These are found in some areas more than others.

> It is common in the United States to find *kill sites*, places where one or more animals were killed by hunters, some of whom may have had no permanent dwellings. At kill sites archaeologists find the bones of the animals, projectile points used for killing them, and the tools for butchering . . . Outside the Americas it is less common to find kill sites . . . We should remember, however, that hunters usually have a home base from which they wander in pursuit of game and often bring back only the edible portions of butchered animals. The amount of bone and stone tools in these sites suggests seasonal, or perhaps year-round camps. Archaeologists usually call these sites "living floors." (Hole and Heizer, 1969: 61–63)

Ceremonial sites are places where supernatural activities were conducted. They range from inner areas of caves to special buildings to whole centers (clusters of buildings all dedicated to such activities). Such sites

This excavation site is at Catal Hüyük, a Neolithic settlement in southern Turkey.

Ralph S. Solecki

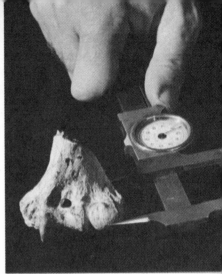

Excavation and identification procedures. The man at left is reliefing fossil dinosaur bones; at right, a 2.5-million-year-old Pleistocene upper arm bone is measured.

help the archaeologists reconstruct the development of human concern with the world of religion. *Burial* sites, places for disposal of the dead, also range widely; from single pits to elaborate stone tombs containing many human and other remains. These sites often yield "mint-condition" tools and other artifacts and goods placed with dead and, of course, provide data for the physical anthropologists. There are, in addition, many other kinds of sites: areas of art work on rock walls, quarrys, or workshops, and remains of no real definable sort. If one wishes to excavate, perhaps a buried habitation site gives the archaeologist the most general materials for his time and energy.

Excavation Procedures. How does the archaeologist actually excavate? Very carefully, since he or she is, in effect, destroying the context of the site as it is excavated. If elaborate precautions and careful records are not kept, when one is finished, one has many piles of remains but no way to reconstruct and interpret the results. You can dig a site only once. As one writer puts it: " . . . indeed the director of an excavation spends more time writing and drawing than he does digging" (Fagan, 1972: 92). Before actual excavation, the archaeologist surveys the entire locality, mapping its major features. This helps in obtaining a feel for the area in general. The archaeologist then establishes a *datum point*, some fixed position that serves as a reference marker for all subsequent measurement and excavation. He or she then maps out a *grid* over the presumed or actual area of the site itself. This divides up the area horizontally into a number of squares. The size of each square depends on the extent of the site and ambitions or purpose of the excavators. In the events of a building or house, the interior rooms or units

109

can serve in place of the artificial squares. These units serve as devices for keeping the excavated remains separate as they are removed from the ground. Of course, not everything is removed. *Artifacts* (man-made objects) and things like bones are taken from the site, but *features* such as house remains, pits for storage, and fireplace rings are not. Moreover, part of the site may be left unexcavated so that later archaeologists with new and better techniques can work on it and test or expand conclusions. Then, too, a site may be so large that time and monetary considerations may preclude total excavation. Sometimes, before actual excavation, an exploratory pit or trench is dug to get an indication of the possible content and the stratified layers and depth of cultural materials. Objects are not removed rapidly; one digs slowly and carefully to avoid missing any smaller objects. Remains of bones and vegetation, often miniscule, may aid in establishing diet, climate, and time period. Even the dirt removed may be sifted for data a second time. Drawings and photographs of the objects, as they are exposed and after removal, help to preserve their context and aid in interpretation later on. As excavation proceeds, the archaeologist may also divide the site vertically, identifying successive layers of depth. Sometimes such a division is made artificially, each layer being a certain equivalent distance apart (every foot or yard of depth, for example) from the others; often the natural stratigraphy itself serves this end, data being identified with the different geological strata or soil types in which it was found. This helps in ordering the data in chronological terms and can serve as a recording device in the same manner as the surface grid itself. Finally comes the arduous jobs of sorting, preserving, cataloging, storing, and interpreting —activities that go on long after the work in the field is completed.

Classification

Classification is a second major archaeological technique, occuring both in field and laboratory situations. Basically, the archaeologist classifies artifacts by placing them into groupings and categories. This not only helps in storing them, but can be an aid in interpretation and reporting as well. Although in theory there are many ways to group such objects together, in practice three main types of classification are used, often in combination. A *convenient* classification has as its goal, making placement easy. It involves placing things together by some convenient criterion: for example, by material, technique of manufacture, or decoration. So, all stone objects might go in one class, all wood in another; or the catagories may reflect artifacts that are decorated versus those with no decoration. Such placement can be accomplished rapidly since

Classification of archaelogical artifacts by grouping them into categories.

little thought is required. However, these categories may not be very helpful for later interpretation. A *functional* classification has as its goal some preliminary interpretation of supposed use. It involves placing together of objects whose function was the same or similar, regardless of materials and decorations involved. So, for example, a clay pot, woven basket, animal skin bag, and wooden jar could be included together since at least potentially, they functioned as containers. This sort of greater thoughtfulness may aid in quicker analysis of cultural behaviors later on. Besides the drawback of requiring greater initial expenditure of time, not all artifacts have a readily perceptible use.

> Archaeologists find it easy to classify a bow and arrow if they are lucky enough to find them preserved. They are able to recognize and know their use because they know that similar tools are used by living peoples. However, if they should find several variations of bows and arrows at one site, they will have a hard time trying to decide whether they should take notice of the differences. In short, once archaeologists get beyond very gross classification of material or known use, they run into difficulty. (Hole and Heizer, 1969: 169)

A *cultural* classification involves placing objects together the way the archaeologist (using intuition and expertise) believes the makers/users themselves would have categorized them. In other words, it can be the attempt to recognize broad cultural categories, such as religion. Since it represents a considerable amount of time and energy, it is often reserved for later phases of study. In the religion category, for example, one might place a sacrificial knife, a wooden altar, the clothing of the

111

priest, and a clay pot for collecting the blood of the victim. All of these elements are of different function and material, but all represent a united segment of behavior. The term *cultural classification* is also used to refer to categories that include the "ideal types" of artifacts that the people themselves were thinking of during the act of production: " . . . archaeologists try to find the ideal to which a series of artifacts conforms" (Hole and Heizer, 1969: 171). They try to discover by visual inspection or statistical analysis of a series of spearheads, for example, the standard the makers were intending to achieve.

Interpretation

Interpretation, or reconstruction, is the third major technique of the archaeologist and refers to the attempt to penetrate beyond the understanding of the objects themselves in order to infer something deeper about the quality of the life of the times. In other words, having found a clay pot, we know the users had containers; what we want to know is what uses they were put to, whether decorated types had different functions, and what the decorations mean. In this latter sense, one is reminded of the Greek urn immortalized in poetry by John Keats—"What men or gods are these." This may be the exciting part of archaeology. Again, when we find a burial site we know people died and were subsequently disposed of; what we want to know is if this represents a belief in a life after death or what this might have been. If there are differences in the amount of grave goods, does this reflect social inequality beyond the grave as in daily life? Because such beliefs and behaviors do not fossilize directly, we have to interpret their existence. We have to go beyond the material remains themselves. And, of course, the job of the archaeologist goes far beyond such concerns and becomes the attempt to delineate (on the basis of recovered data) one social-cultural group from another.

> Indeed one of the prehistorian's first tasks is to define the social units of his study. In practice his concern will chiefly lie in distinguishing the main groups through and by which culture is shared and transmitted from one generation to another. It is not merely that such groups have been the most influential: they provide a frame of reference by which other categories and classes can be detected; and they form units by comparing which prehistorians are able to detect the major changes of cultural history . . . A main test and one of the most important tools used in defining such entities is the distribution map, showing the occurance of diagnostic traits and making clear the spatial limits of individual cultures at any particular period. (Clark, 1967: 169)

Since much interpretation is given in the chapters that follow, we can leave further examples until that point.

Dating

The last major archaeological technique is **dating**: the placement of an object or site in time. It is somewhat traditional for the numerous dating techniques to be placed in two categories: *relative* dating, which places things relative to one another in time (as older or younger than something else) and *absolute* dating, which works in terms of actual chronological dates. Absolute dating allows the placement of archaeological data with reference to a scale of universal time applicable anywhere in the world. "It follows . . . that all events that are given the same absolute date will actually be contemporaneous regardless of the parts of the world in which they took place" (Rouse, 1972: 105). Relative dating, obviously, cannot be employed on a world-wide basis, and does not yield actual dates for comparative purposes. In practice the archaeologist uses a combination of such methods. We can briefly mention a few such techniques of each dating category.

Absolute Techniques.   Of the absolute-dating techniques, *radiocarbon* dating is perhaps the most popularly known. It is based on the fact that living organisms contain radioactive carbon (Carbon 14) produced as a reaction to cosmic radiation. This remains at a constant level during the life of the organism. After death, the carbon 14 begins to disintegrate by one half every 5,730 years. Hence, by measuring the amount left in an archaeological sample (bone, wood, etc.) one can establish within reasonable limits when the plant or animal died and date the object or site in association. One measures by counting the number of *beta* radiations given off per gram of material per minute.

Radio-carbon dating of an archaeological sample.

American Museum of Natural History

Carbon 14 that is in an object 5,730 years old should emit half the number of that of a living object. Although this is an often-used dating technique, there are some drawbacks. Contamination of the sample is possible both before and after discovery. Dates are expressed with a margin of error (standard deviation) given as plus or minus as many years, which is confusing if two dates have overlapping ranges (2000 ± 150 versus 1900 ± 150). Finally, this technique is only work-able with ages going back to about 50,000 years ago. A relatively newer dating technique, *potassium-argon* dating, reaches further back in time. This is also a disintegration technique, measuring the decay of radioactive potassium relative to argon gas in some minerals (K40 to A40). By measuring the ratio between these, one can calculate the age of the rocks involved (by use of a mass spectrometer). Unfortunately, this technique does not always yield very accurate results.

Another variety of absolute dating is *dendrochronology*. This is dating by the use of tree-ring analysis and hence is limited in time as well as geographically. It is based on the fact that trees (especially conifers) in some regions have well-defined annual rings of growth: thin in a dry year, relatively thicker in one with greater moisture. These are perceived as a concentric series of rings of growth of different width that form a unique pattern for the life of the tree. To establish the date the tree was cut, one matches its pattern to a master chart of tree-ring growth for a particular region, determining its chronological position. "Where a sufficient number of overlapping sequences is avail-able it is possible to work back from modern timber to the beams incorporated in old structures and so to work out the pattern of minor climatic fluctuation over long periods. Ancient beams and timbers can then be dated, by seeing into which phase of the full sequence the pattern revealed by their growth-rings will fit" (de Paor, 1969: 64). Difficulties also exist with this method. It works best only in arid climates where wood is preserved. One must use trees that have not had contact with underground water (which changes their growth patterns) and great care must be exercised to assess that a log used in a site actually represents the time it was cut. Otherwise the date assumed for the associated site will be incorrect. It may have been used later or more than once. At any rate, although other absolute-dating techniques exist and more are currently being developed, the above give some ideas of the methods involved. Such techniques, incidentally, are usually beyond the competency of the archaeologist; they are farmed out to other specialists.

Relative Techniques.   Relative-dating techniques are used more often by field archaeologists themselves and can sometimes be correlated with or substantiated by those of the absolute type. Each such method, however, has severe limitations or margins of error. A few relative-dating techniques can be mentioned. *Stratification* is perhaps the simplest and most continually used method. It assumes that objects found in deeper stratigraphic layers are older than those nearer the top. In this appraisal, one has to be aware of possible redisposition of cultural material and changes in these levels themselves.

> Geologists originated the stratigraphic method and prehistorians have adopted it from them. If an assemblage deposited by People A is found overlying an assemblage deposited by People B, then it may be concluded that People A was later than People B—unless, of course, the stratigraphy has been reversed by subsequent disturbance of the site or there is reason to believe that two peoples lived side by side, alternating at the site. The method works best if assemblages of all the peoples under study can be found in a single stratigraphic column ... This configuration happens only among peoples who were permanently attached to their sites or kept coming back to them ... Once one has determined the stratigraphic sequence of peoples (in one site) ... one can use this sequence to date the other remains in the local area. One need only identify the people that produced each assemblage and arrange the assemblages in order of the sequence of their peoples that has been stratigraphically demonstrated at the master site. (Rouse, 1972: 122, 123)

Chemical analysis of bone materials is also a possibility. For example, buried bones and teeth gradually absorb fluorine and other substances from ground water, which can be measured. For some materials like fluorine, the amount increases with age; hence, the greater the amount that the bones contain, the greater their age. While such analysis can be applied only to a restricted locale, it can help order the relative sequence of such buried materials or establish contemporaneity for them—for example, of humans and the animals they may have hunted. Materials such as nitrogen decrease relative to the amount of time spent in the ground and can be used in reverse: the less contained, the older.

A different variety of relative dating is *patination*. Here, it is assumed that rock surfaces undergo chemical alteration when exposed to the atmosphere: they develop a patina. All other things being equal, stone tools that are older should have relatively larger amounts of patina. This technique, of course, is most dependable when the relative ages of the tools in question can also be correlated to stratigraphic differences. "In sites where there is a long sequence, the flints in the bottom levels of a site may have more patina than those found in the upper levels. This difference is especially common in river gravels and terraces of rivers or lakes. When one has a large series of tools from several levels, it is sometimes possible to see clear-cut differences in the relative amounts of patina" (Hole and Heizer, 1969: 231–32). A somewhat different method is that of *refuse accumulation*. This is employed with reference mainly to habitation sites and is based on an estimation of the length of time a site was occupied as reflected in the accumulated debris (garbage), sometimes even being worked out and expressed in feet of accumulation per generation. This technique, however, involves a number of unknowns: population fluctuation, multiple debris areas, and possibly the general untidiness or neatness of the residents. Nonetheless, in some situations, for restricted dating problems, the technique has proven useful; the more the debris, the longer the occupation.

Finally, as a last varied example, we can mention *sequence* dating. This involves using some of the cultural materials themselves and works on the following assumption. If tool types or pottery change over time so that sequences of development can be established (say from square-short to round-tall pots) one can take such objects from elsewhere and fit them into the sequence in a given area. This is a kind of "cultural stratigraphy." A difficulty here, of course, is that many types of things may be used at the same time by the same people; we don't always throw out the old when accepting the new. And cultural lag may occur between different groups; some living "primitives" (e.g. Australian aborigines) are still using tools long since rejected by industrial societies. We will see such problems emerge in the following chapters. This technique is widely used, however, and the major traditional periods of cultural development for humankind in general have been formulated in terms of its general application.

Other Techniques

In sum, the archaeologist uses four main techniques in pursuing his cultural records of man: excavation, classification, interpretation, and dating. A brief flavor of these techniques has been simply suggested in this brief chapter. Many methods or special techniques are utilized in addition to those discussed, and sources for discussion of these are to be found in the next set of references for further reading.

Stone Tools.   One special facet of prehistoric archaeology does require brief mention here, however. This is the knowledge of various stone-tool manufacturing possibilities and variations. This is as important to this type of archaeologist as language study is to the classical type, since stone tools are the earliest and most consistently recovered cultural evidence of prehistoric peoples; stone provided the sharp edges and points early humans could apply to most activities. Preservation, of course, is also good. Often, with little other evidence to pursue, archaeologists have naturally attempted to exploit stone tools and the techniques of their manufacture in order to be able to speculate on the presence of different peoples (by their techniques) and to analyze rates of cultural progress.

Although the earliest humans used stone tools that were probably previously and naturally broken, a tool a little more effective in terms of size and shape could have been achieved by one of two basic methods. In the first, the maker removes flakes from a lump of stone according to what he wants the final desired shape of the tool to be. The maker trims the core into that shape, treating the flakes struck off primarily as waste material (*debitage*). Many such flakes also must have been utilized as tools. The tools made from the stone's core have been called, logically, **core tools.** They are generally fairly large implements with cutting edges meeting along the sides (*bifaces*) or along the bottom (*choppers*). In the second technique, the intent is to obtain flakes that can be used after being struck off the core (*parent lump*) or then finished (*retouched*) into special shapes. In this case, the core is utilized primarily as a source of raw materials. Such implements are called **flake tools.**

> The making of flake tools ... has definite advantages over the bifaces. For one thing, their manufacture is not so wasteful of flint as the shaping of a biface which requires the removal of a great deal of material from the flint core, with only a few usable flakes resulting. For another, a flake tool's cutting edge is obtained by a single blow on the flint nucleus, while the production of a similar thin, straight edge by alternate flaking of a biface requires much more time and skill. Finally, the cutting edge of the best possible biface is never so sharp and smooth as that of a flake. (Bordaz, 1970: 30)

In either case, the technique of manufacture, called **flaking** or knapping, is the same. There are various methods of such flaking, some crude, some extremely sophisticated. Archaeologists recognize three basic types.

1. **Direct percussion** applies the force for removing flakes by directly banging one object on another. Here, there are two basic varieties.
   a. *Block-on-block,* in which the lump is hit upon a larger anvil stone, resulting in the detaching of rather thick irregular flakes (and occasionally fingers!).
   b. *Hammerstone,* in which a smaller stone or baton of softer material is hit against the lump to be flaked. Here, one has greater control over the direction of the blow, and the detached flakes are generally smaller and more symmetrical.

2. **Indirect percussion** applies the force for removing flakes indirectly, mostly by placing a shaft of material (punch) between the hammer and the core and then striking this. By such a method, the force of the blow is more precisely concentrated and look-alike flakes can be detached.

3. **Pressure** techniques apply the force by placing a small, hard, pointed object against the stone or edge to be flaked and "pressing" off a small flake. This gives the knapper excellent precision control over the intended result. Used chiefly for converting small pieces into special shapes or for working the edges of larger tools, it is inappropriate for creating a large tool in the first place.

The type of stone materials to which these techniques may be applied with best results are siliceous minerals and rocks that are hard enough to perform their intended functions but that fracture easily in the process of their manufacture. Flint and chert were most often used. So-called coarse-grained rocks work less well for such methods because of their tendency to crumble when flaked. Such materials are very hard, however, and when prepared by different techniques (grinding and polishing) make very durable tools. These do not appear until relatively late in human prehistory.

The results of stone-tool manufacturing will vary depending upon the type of support used in the flaking process. "Results will depend on whether the hand holding of the stone is unsupported or whether the hand or arm rests or leans against some part of the knapper's body. If an anvil is used to support the stone, the resilience of the anvil's material is also a contributing factor" (Bordaz, 1970: 13). With some idea of archaeological techniques and some knowledge of stone-tool manufacturing methods, we can now turn to the cultural record of our earliest and longest period of cultural development.

SUMMARY

1. Among the various types of archaeology, prehistoric archaeology is probably the most common. It deals with peoples who existed before history and who had no written records.

2. Basic archaeological techniques are excavation, classification, interpretation, and dating. Excavation must be done carefully since the content is destroyed in the process.

3. Archaeological sites are classified as open-air or buried, and as to content, habitation, types of burials, and types of ceremonies.

4. Dating procedures are of two types: *relative*, which places things as older or younger than others; and *absolute*, which works in terms of actual chronological dates.

5. Knowledge of techniques for manufacturing stone tools is especially useful to the prehistoric archaeologist since it supplies the primary data in his field. There is a basic distinction between core and flake tools as well as between methods of flaking (for example, direct and indirect percussion, pressure and grinding, and polishing techniques).

REFERENCES FOR FURTHER READING

There are a number of excellent specialized texts that comprehensively review and expand the topics covered in chapter seven. Among the best are *An Introduction to Prehistoric Archaeology*, by Frank Hole and Robert F. Heizer (1969, 2nd ed., Holt, Rinehart & Winston); *In the Beginning*, by Brian Fagan (1972; Little, Brown); *Introduction to Prehistory*, by Irving Rouse (1972, McGraw-Hill); *Introduction to Archaeology*, by James Deetz (1967, Natural History Press); *Archaeology and Society*, by Grahame Clark (1967, Barnes & Noble); *Beginning in Archaeology*, by Kathleen M. Kenyon (1968, Praeger); and a very useful readings book edited by Brian Fagan, *Introductory Readings in Archaeology* (1970, Little, Brown). A very useful small volume is *Archaeology: An Illustrated Introduction*, by Liam de Paor (1969, Penguin Books); and an encyclopedic inventory is *Science in Archaeology: A Comprehensive Survey of Progress on Research*, edited by Don Brothwell and Eric Higgs (1963, Basic Books). For stone tools the best introduction (also well illustrated) is *Tools of the Old and New Stone Age*, by Jacques Bordaz (1970, Natural History Press). See also *Man the Toolmaker*, by Kenneth P. Oakley (1957, 3rd ed., University of Chicago Press). A magnificent volume containing many articles on prehistoric toolmaking and related activities from early time to the fall of ancient empires is *A History of Technology, Vol. I*, edited by Charles Singer, E. J. Holmyord and A. R. Hall (1954, Oxford University Press). Two popularized books dealing with the "romance" of archaeological endeavors are *Gods, Graves and Scholars*, by C. W. Ceram (1951, Knopf); and *The Testimony of the Spade* by Geoffrey Bibby (1956, Knopf). A somewhat more professional work is *The World of the Past* (2 vols.), edited by Jacquetta Hawkes (1963, Knopf). This includes selections by archaeologists describing their own activities.

8

the paleolithic and mesolithic periods

For most of their existence, humans have been hunters of game animals and gatherers of wild plant foods. This chapter covers the time and cultural developments of the heyday of these activities. The major cultural period involved is the *Old Stone Age* or *Paleolithic* period. This is named after developments in stone-tool technology as is the *Mesolithic* period or *Middle Stone Age* and the *Neolithic* or *New Stone Age* (the subject of part of the next chapter). Such a way of classifying periods of cultural development is no longer accepted as completely valid since it suggests that the only important developments were in stone-tool technology. It remains, however, widely in use, so we will employ it in this text. Because of the extreme length of time involved in the Paleolithic period, it has been subdivided into early (lower), middle, and late (upper) stages, succeeding one another in time.

The sequence of Old Stone Age culture can really be said to start with protoculture, probably at the time when our ancestors first began moving into the open, the time of the ecological revolution. At this time, they must have made use of sticks, stones, and bones in an unaltered kind of way and when the need arose. These are generally referred to as *tools of occasion* and such use would not really have differed in kind from some other animal behaviors in this respect. The difficulty is that there is no way of knowing how early any intensification of such behavior took place. Disputed tools of this type, sometimes called *dawn stones* or *eoliths*, are generally discredited, but humankind certainly must have begun its tool career in this manner.

OLDOWAN TRADITION

By early lower Pleistocene times, however, beginning perhaps 1.8 million years ago (and with recent discoveries, even earlier) and persisting to perhaps 700,000 years ago, we do find a single, fairly wide-

121

From left to right: a section of Olduvai Gorge where remnants of the earliest and most continuous tool tradition of man have been found; a pebble tool typical of those found at Olduvai; grasping a pebble tool in the way in which it was probably used by early man.

spread tool-making (as opposed to just using) tradition. This at present is claimed to be the earliest and certainly the most continuous tool tradition of man. It is referred to as the oldowan or *pebble-tool tradition*, although some scholars name it more technically as the *chopper* and *flake tradition* since tools were made from raw materials other than river pebbles, and we may someday find examples in which pebbles are entirely absent. The early sites of this culture are mostly confined to East Africa, where Olduvai Gorge is certainly the most famous location. Some have been found elsewhere, however: Vallonet cave in France, for example, and at Tell Ubeidiya in the Near East.

The most typical tools of this tradition are chopping tools made from river pebbles (simple core tools) up to four inches in length, probably mostly manufactured by the block-on-block technique. Few show any signs of further finishing. Such pebbles, of course, must be altered for most tool uses. At some sites, these simple choppers take a variety of different forms, but some standardization is evident; their makers knew what they had in mind, even if their technique was crude. It is probable that such tools were used for a variety of tasks; they were *general purpose tools*. In addition, there are, at least at some sites, a number of artificially made ball-shaped stones that may have been missile weapons. There are flakes of quartzite, the edges of which show wear patterns from use (probably as scraping devices). Bone tools may also have been used as weapons. We can perhaps infer the use of wood for simple spears or for digging roots. One scholar (Chard, 1969) feels that the manufacture of wood tools required stone-cutting tools in the first place, although most writers suggest the latter as necessary for butchering animals and for breaking bones to extract the marrow.

122

Most of the sites appear to be campsite locations (along lake fringes, etc.), where butchering indeed may have been the primary tool behavior.

> The living floors consist of concentrations of stones and bones; many of the latter are artificially broken to extract the marrow, and the fractures resemble similar remains left by later and even by modern hunters. Many of the stones have been intentionally flaked, and even those with no trace of working have been brought to the sites deliberately ... The stone tools consist of choppers, cores, pounding stones, and flakes ... The raw material for these tools was primarily pebbles. (Chard, 1969: 83)

Since this is the time of stage one, in physical evolution, the human species had yet to become an efficient hunter: bone remains are mostly of smaller animals and immature young of larger forms. One site suggests that the hunter-scavengers may have first skinned and butchered their prey and then moved a short distance to eat and break up the bones for marrow. Certainly, the size of these early populations was small, and their geographic range of activity was probably quite restricted.

LOWER PALEOLITHIC

Eventually, groups in some world areas began developing their tool industries. Some cores began to be flaked on both faces (bifaces) and became what archaeologists call **handaxe traditions**. The time period is from about 700,000 to 150,000 years ago, and the culture is generally called the *Lower Paleolithic*. Many scholars would also include the Oldowan culture in this culture designation. The makers of the tools of these times are the varieties of *Homo erectus* and later forms such as Steinheim and Swanscombe. The idea of making handaxes seems to have occured earliest in Africa and may have spread from there to parts of Europe, the Near East, and India.

> The most significant development of the Middle Pleistocene was without doubt the emergence of the hand-axe ... This was made by thinning down a nodule or thick flake on two faces to form an edge that was usually confined to one end but might in highly evolved specimens run all the way around. The assumption is that hand-axes were probably grasped directly in the hand ... and used for such purposes as grubbing up roots, cutting up game and even shaping wood. They were made from a wide range of raw materials, from flint and obsidian to the more difficult quartzes, quartzites, lavas, and even granites; yet the degree of standardization is often remarkable. (Clark, 1967: 33, 34)

A chopper tool (left), two flake tools (middle), and a handaxe.

In other parts of Europe and in Central and Southeast Asia, evolved chopper and flake traditions continue. Why these areas remained conservative is still one of the enigmas of prehistory.

Chopper and Flake Traditions

European chopper and flake traditions are well represented at Vertesszollos in Hungary and at Clacton-on-Sea in England. These tools are somewhat better made than before, probably due to the use of coarse hammerstone retouch. Most tools are choppers and flake tools made on thick flakes. The latter include side scrapers, flakes with a notch on the bottom (perhaps for shaving spear shafts), and denticulates (having a series of small notches along one side). A few backed knives (with a dull side opposite the cutting edge) have been found as a more specialized cutting tool.

Hand-axe Traditions

The European hand-axes evolved naturally from choppers, simply by completing the flaking process. They are generally pear-shaped but vary from more circular to triangular types. They are usually flaked over most of their surface and average perhaps five inches in length. Most have a point on the bottom in addition to the two side cutting edges. Like choppers, they were probably all-purpose tools. As time passed, these handaxes improved. The earliest are designated *Abbevillean* (*Chellean*) after the original site of discovery in France. These are quite unsymmetrical with rather poor cutting edges and with part of the original core remaining unflaked. They appear to have been made by the stone-hammer technique. Later and better types are generally called *Acheulean* and are smaller and possess more even, more efficient cutting edges. They were made by more carefully preparing the edges for trimming off the flakes and perhaps also by using a hammer consisting of a baton of wood or bone. A few handaxe sites (mostly outside of Europe) also contain cleavers (tools with a cutting edge only along the bottom) as another major tool. At many *Acheulean* sites, there are also considerable numbers of flake tools similar to the chopper-flake varieties. Early handaxe finds are generally of a re-deposited nature or were dug before procedures of scientific excavation were developed, so we are actually unsure as to what other kinds of tools are involved.

Prepared-core Technique. The makers of Acheulean core hand-axes also invented a new way of making flake tools prior to the end of the Lower Paleolithic period, and these flake tools seem to have soon caught on, becoming eventually more important and widespread than the core varieties themselves. This new technique is called the *Levalloisian* and involves the careful preparation of a core (prefabrication). The type of flake tool derived is shaped on the core and then dislodged ready to use or needing only minor retouch. Whereas early flake tools could be made from the debris of core-tool manufacture, here the entire core is intended to be used up. The technique is perhaps a recognition on the part of stage-two toolmakers that flake tools are less wasteful of raw materials and time than core tools and that they are more efficient for most tasks anyway. It should be mentioned that the Levalloisian technique did not spread to some of the nonhandaxe cultures in areas of Europe until the next cultural period.

Aspects of Lower Paleolithic Life

What else can be said of the nature of life at this time? The evidence of animal bones suggests that hunting had become progressively more efficient. Large types of animals regularly appear, as do greater numbers of truly large game such as elephant and rhinoceros. Remembering evidence of skulls broken open from the bottom in *Homo erectus* forms outside of Europe, some scholars conclude that one's neighbors may have received some attention as food. Certainly vegetable species con-tributed to their diet. At some sites, such as Torralba in Spain, there is evidence that bands of humans seasonally burned grass to drive ele-phants into a swampy area and then either killed them or waited for them to die. Similar evidence of such activities comes from Africa. So, at least on occasions, these early populations ate "high off the elephant." Some scholars have suggested such periodic activities would have re-quired cooperation between a number of bands. This may be so, but a small group could have let the fire do the work of many people; certainly, for most of their existence, human groupings must still have been small and their territory still restricted, although greater movement may have occurred than previously.

The site of Terra Amata along the coast of southern France suggests the return of one group to the area eleven consecutive spring seasons for a few days each time. Here, they hunted a great variety of game animals, took some sea food, and made new tools. These people (an early Acheulean level of culture, 300,000 years ago) also erected crude oval wooden huts, made fire hearths with wind breaks. Their tools included *choppers*, a variety of bone tools and well-made flakes.

> How did the visitors occupy themselves during their stay? The evidence shows that they gathered a little seafood, manufactured stone tools and hunted in the nearby countryside. The animal bones unearthed at Terra Amata include the remains of birds, turtles, and at least eight species of mammals. Although the visitors did not ignore small game such as rabbits and rodents, the majority of the bones represent larger animals ... Although the hunters showed a preference for big game, they generally selected as prey not the adults but the young of each species, doubtlessly because they were easier to bring down. (De Lumley, 1969: 45)

At the site of Torralba, we also find dwellings: elephant tusks being used to support a hide shelter, held down and supported at the bottom by a ring of stones. Such recently (and scientifically) excavated sites are beginning to suggest a greater richness for the Lower Paleolithic than had hitherto been suspected.

At Olorgesailie in Kenya, there is even evidence that a band of *Homo erectus* forms occupied a series of camp sites—some by a few families and others apparently by the whole group—and the remains suggest a fairly typical hunting existence. At one site, these humans apparently massacred a troop of baboons (Isaac, 1968), perhaps surrounding them at night when they were sleeping. Additional evidence of hunting skill comes, as indicated earlier, from the caves of Sinanthropus in China.

Nonetheless, human progress was still very slow at this time, and this has been a matter of much speculation to scholars. Some have suggested the less-than-modern brain size of the people of this time as being responsible. Others explain it with reference to the small inventory of tools and techniques they had available to work with, the isolation of human groups (reducing borrowing), and sheer feelings of complacency: who desires something new when his or her stomach is full of elephant? Also unexplained, of course, is why handaxes never really spread to all parts of Europe or to the Far East.

So far as we can tell, the Lower Paleolithic peoples used hand tools requiring some degree of physical power; especially the chopper and handaxes. Hence, biological selection would still have been important; culture could not afford to produce ninety-eight pound weaklings yet! Finally, there are differences in craftsmanship in the mode of manufacture of these tools, which has suggested to many writers that each user still made his (or her?) own, was still self-sufficient—or as much so as an omnivorous primate could be; at least, a man and his family were jacks-of-all-trades and masters of them if they were to survive.

MIDDLE PALEOLITHIC

The Lower Paleolithic is succeeded by the *Middle Paleolithic*, lasting from about 150,000 to 35,000 years ago. Most of it is the handiwork of stage-three human beings, or at least those forms living at the time of the Neanderthals. The kinds of tools and general way of life of these times represent no real break in continuity with earlier developments.

Variety of Tool Traditions

Existing traditions have become elaborated, however, and there are more varieties of tool traditions and a greater number of specialized tools. In western Europe, most of the tools are made of flakes. In the preparation of these the Levalloisian technique was widely used but in a slightly different manner. Middle Paleolithic toolmakers apparently tried to obtain a greater number of usable flakes from their prepared cores and hence employed more retouch finishing than previously. Such prepared cores are not found in central or eastern Europe, however, even though human groups were spreading through here and out into the vast plains of Eurasia. No real cultural uniformity exists other than that of a general level of development. In western Europe, the Acheulean evolved into the *Micoquoian*, with many lanceolate handaxes, and diverse new traditions have developed. Some scholars now call these Mousteroid since they are generally similar to one culture (Mousterian) first well-defined for France. Even here, however, one writer (Bordes, 1968) has suggested the presence of at least four varieties. These include a "typical" expression consisting of almost all flakes on prepared cores, with points and scrapers being most common tool types; another variety that has many rare scraper forms and notched flakes by non-Levalloisian technique, one comprising many denticulate tools but few points and scrapers; and still others characterized by numerous triangular handaxes. These are not generally thought to represent seasonal or functional aspects of the same culture, although some scholars (Binford and Binford, 1966) disagree. Elsewhere, still other varieties occur. So, certainly for the student, the term *Mousteroid* for the general culture of the time is a comfort.

> Since it seems desirable to have a broad term comparable to our usage of Acheulean to designate the flake industries of the Neanderthaloid phase in the stretch of contiguous territory ... from western Europe to Mongolia and south to the Near East and North Africa, which all share certain common features in greater or lesser degree while retaining their individuality, the label "Mousteroid" ... would probably be acceptable and convey the right idea. We must emphasize that Mousteroid is not synonymous with the culture of Neanderthaloid man: Neanderthaloid populations over large areas ... isolated from the Mousteroid world, had industries sufficiently different that the term cannot be applied ... (Chard, 1969: 114)

Some scholars recognize, in the European area, a difference between peoples living in caves and reflecting a somewhat conservative culture, more like the Lower Paleolithic, and people living more out in the open in artificial housing, the remains of which occur, for example, at the site of Molodova—a hut with walls made of elephant bones and tusks, probably covered with skin, and enclosing an area about 20 by 26 feet. It contained remains of numerous fireplaces and evidences (flint and debris) of human activity. All groups, of course, possessed fire as a heritage from earlier times, and the numbers of scrapers and other skin-working implements suggests fairly well-made clothing. Variations in culture also characterize human societies elsewhere in the world during Middle Paleolithic times. In Africa and the Near East, peoples who were living in open areas developed traditions that were very Mousteroid in their compositions. Other African peoples were moving back into forested areas and went against the general trend towards smaller and lighter tool kits (away from big core tools) by manufacturing many large pick and handax types. Evidence from the Far East for this period is somewhat inconclusive. Some very evolved Mousteroid types have been found at the site of Shui-tung-kou, but they may be somewhat later in time. It is hard to generalize given our present state of knowledge, but the consensus appears that there were still areas of cultural conservatism at this time, precisely those that were most remote from the areas of Mousteroid originations. Of course, in light of the distribution of technology in the modern world, we should not expect even development at any time in human development.

What can be said about the quality of life during Middle Paleolithic times? Certainly, in the major Mousteroid area the improved tools and other cultural additions suggest that cultural efficiency is beginning to supplement biology. The projectile points suggest the development of the true spear as a more effective killing device for bigger game animals, and remains of these are quite frequent. Some round balls have been found at some sites and may represent the use of bolas: a very effective instrument for killing small game and one that requires less precise accuracy than a single thrown stone. Most tools are still stone; the use of bone and antler does not seem to progress substantially. There are some bone splinters that may have been used as awls for punching holes through various materials (or possibly as spear points?). Perhaps some pieces were used as flaking hammers. As yet, humans apparently did not realize the potential of this raw material or (more likely) they lacked the proper tools for utilizing it.

Aspects of Middle Paleolithic Life

Life must have been somewhat easier for the people of these times, although direct evidence for such an assertion is meager. In the Near East at Shanidar Cave, the remains of a man have been found who had been a cripple from birth and yet who had survived until his accidental death at the ripe old age of forty. To be able to afford maintaining such a person suggests a relaxation of some of the previous rigors of human existence. As in Lower Paleolithic times, however, life had not lost all its harshness. Wounds and evidence of hostility and cannibalism still occur, and at one site, Krapina in Yugoslavia, the remains of perhaps twenty humans are mixed in with animal bones and have been broken open for marrow and brains. As some have put it, charity certainly remained at home, and humans of other groups may still have been looked upon as an attractive supply of food, at least in emergencies.

Despite such "brutality," the people of the Middle Paleolithic period left behind the first reasonable evidence for supernatural activity. This takes two forms. Most convincing is the fact that human burials occur, often in a flexed position in pits, along with a few grave goods thrown in for good measure. Sometimes heads were buried separately. This is certainly suggestive of some kind of ritualistic endeavor, probably of a life-after-death sort. Might it have started by trying to avoid cannibalization of one's departed by other groups? At Shanidar, pollen analysis suggests that a body was put down on a layer of pine boughs and was surrounded by brightly colored flowers. At the site of Teshik-tash in Uzbeckistan, a child's grave was surrounded by a ring of ibex horns. Whatever the precise beliefs must have been, the general supernatural motivation seems evident. The other evidence concerns the burial, or walling up in caves, of the skulls of cave bears. This is generally cited as evidence of some variety of animal ceremonialism, a practice still undertaken in recent times by many primitive peoples. The suggestion is that the fear-awe generated by this powerful competitor (eight feet long and 1500 pounds) gave rise to veneration of it. In any event, it seems highly unlikely that peoples of the Middle Paleolithic would have taken so much trouble, just as a way of disposal, without some ritual intentions. So, from this period, and increasingly so thereafter, we see evidence for human development and concern with the supernatural to go along with their elaboration of technology and science. Speaking of the finds at Shanidar, one scholar has been moved to write:

> From archaeological findings elsewhere, we already know that Neanderthal man seems to have 'had a spiritual concept, since he evidently practiced funerary rites over his dead . . . With the finding of flowers . . . we are brought suddenly to the realization that the universality of mankind and the love of beauty go beyond the boundary of our own species. No longer can we deny the early men the full range of human feelings and experience. (Solecki, 1971: 250)

UPPER PALEOLITHIC

The Middle Paleolithic is succeeded by the *Upper Paleolithic*, lasting from about 35,000 to 12,000 years ago. This is the cultural record of the first representatives of stage-four human beings. In contrast to earlier divisions of the Old Stone Age, the Upper Paleolithic is characterized by many local traditions, a more rapid pace of cultural development, and many specialized and standardized tools that were probably made by specialists. Many Mousteroid-type tools continue to be made, however—evidence that the break between Middle and Upper Paleolithic culture and physical type has been greatly exaggerated. And the number of tool types, overall, continues to increase. "We have seen that during the Middle Paleolithic there came a widespread diversification of industries . . . the evolution of the Upper Paleolithic was a continuation of this process under somewhat altered conditions" (Valoch, 1968: 358).

Blade Tools

The most typical stone tools of these times are varieties of what archaeologists have called **blade tools**, a few of which types are occasionally found earlier.

To manufacture a blade tool, the maker first prepares a core so that it resembles a pyramidal or cylindrical shape with a more or less flat surface toward the top. Blades are then detached by a series of blows directed successively along the edges and continuing in a spiral fashion until the center is reached. These blows were probably accomplished by indirect percussion. The blades struck off were then retouched,

American Museum of Natural History

Left, a blade tool; right, implements and ornaments typical of the late Paleolithic period.

by percussion or pressure techniques, into numerous varieties of quite specialized tools. Some of these are:

Backed blades:	with one sharp edge and a blunted back opposite for applying pressure (a few may be spear points).
End scrapers:	end of blade is sharp and rounded.
Notched blades:	somewhat like a backed blade but with a concave notch for shaving down shafts of wood.
Drills:	for boring and perhaps for working skin.
Tanged points:	blades with a sharp point and with a projection at the rear to facilitate hafting.
Burins:	perhaps the most characteristic blade tool, used for engraving and chiseling functions.

Two main types of burins with countless variations exist:

1. *Truncated:*	like a modern chisel with transverse edge.
2. *Dihedral:*	like a prow of a ship.

Such tools obviously represent a very sophisticated level of stone-tool development. Although most of the better-known sites of the past have come from western Europe, scholars are beginning to recognize that at least the original emphasis for this progress came from the peoples living out in the open-tundra areas of Eurasia. Here is a description of one of these more eastern cultures, the eastern Gravettian (now called Pavlovian):

Extensive and sometimes thick middens in close association with settlements both in south Russia and central Europe, reinforce the impressions
that the eastern Gravettians lived mainly by hunting mammoths, the
young animals in particular. On the other hand, remains of such animals
as reindeer, horse, arctic fox, arctic hare and wolverine, as well as of
arctic grouse, show that they were by no means restricted to a single
species ... A telling sign that plant food was also gathered is the presence, for instance at Kostienki IV, of stone pestle-rubbers and grinding
slabs. In western and parts of central Europe the Gravettians were able
to occupy caves and rock shelters, but over most of south Russia these
were not available and they had to camp in the open. (Clark and
Piggott, 1967: 74, 75)

Certainly, the sequence of traditions from France that used to be text-
book citations for this period are no longer regarded as typical. Further,
there are some local developments that appear quite unrepresentative,
for example the Solutrean industry of southwest France, containing
some long, thin points or knives (*laurel leaf*) that were sharp on all
sides and that are often regarded as supreme examples of the art of
flaking stone tools. At least one scholar (Chard, 1969) has suggested that
the term **Aurignacoid** be applied to all blade-tool traditions that display
general similarity (like *Mousteroid*, the term is taken from a former
distinct industry.) This tradition was geographically distributed over
most of Europe, North Africa, North Asia, and the Near East.

In addition to the characteristic stone tools, the Aurignacoid is also
known for numerous varieties of bone tools and objects of antler,
ivory, and horn. Some groups even preferred these raw materials over
stone, especially for making projectile points. Burins made it possible
to utilize such materials, mostly by the groove and splinter method.
This involves carving parallel grooves in the bone surface, prying off
the splinters in between, and finishing these by scraping, grinding, and
polishing them into the desired shape. Many varieties of such projectile
points occur: bevelled, tanged or split-on-the-base types as well as
harpoon heads, needles, awls, and other smaller objects. Also appearing
for the first time was the spear thrower which greatly aided human
hunting abilities.

Relatively late in the Upper Paleolithic, in some areas, *microliths*
(tiny blade fragments) came into general use. These small bits of stone
were retouched into geometrical shapes and hafted into handles of bone
and perhaps wood to serve as composite tools for cutting operations. It
is also possible that bows and arrows had been invented by this time—
perhaps originally developed by peoples in North Africa, where they
appear earliest. Outside the Aurignacoid area, predominately nonblade-
tool cultures continue. In Africa, many local industries exist, some retaining bifacial handaxes and lanceolate spear heads, others with many

Levalloisian flake tools. In central and southern Asia, the chopper tradition appears to continue but our data are still very incomplete. Human beings had also reached the Americas as well as Australia before the end of the Upper Paleolithic. Apparently, the major population control device (in addition to infant mortality) was migration, and with the exception of islands that required sea transportation to reach, all the habitable world areas were now occupied.

Aspects of Upper Paleolithic Life

What can be said of the quality of life in Upper Paleolithic times? Certainly, in the Aurignacoid areas many peoples were living out in the open. We find a number of semisubterranean pit houses with bone and brush walls roofed over with skins and perhaps dirt. When available, caves were still being used and also rock shelters: overhangs fronted by artificial windbreaks. In cold areas, clothing is perhaps better than before, since we have discovered eyed bone needles used for sewing well-tailored garments. Although advances in hunting technology had occurred for single animals (harpoons, points, and spear throwers), the practice of mass kills (driving herds over cliffs or into blind canyons) continued. Some writers have suggested that separate groups were selectively hunting particular species. We can guess, however, that most groups exploited most available food resources, and we have evidence of smaller game being taken as well as fish—the latter apparently for the first time in inland areas. In a few areas (as previously mentioned) we even find food-grinding equipment, a remarkable discovery since this only becomes common in future times. Certainly, given the increase in cultural "ability" to secure food, human groups became somewhat larger, and the amount of leisure time for other activities perhaps also increased. This is represented by musical instruments, bone flutes and whistles, and by various types of ornaments. Some necklaces even contain sea shells the acquisition of which probably required trade relations with coastal people. A final indication of greater leisure being devoted to other pursuits is the occurrence of the first art tradition in human existence.

Upper Paleolithic Art

The distribution of this art tradition generally correlates with the Aurignacoid of Eurasia, but its highest developments appear to be limited to southwest France and northern Spain, where it is generally called the

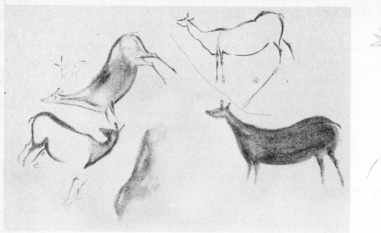

Some examples of Franco-Cantabrian paintings. The panel from the Cavern of La Pasiega in Spain (left) depicts big-game animals of the time; the highly complex "Sorcerer" (right) is from Les Trois Freres, France.

Franco-Cantabrian Tradition. The art took many forms: modeling in relief and in the round, engraving and carving, and paintings—all from miniature to larger-than-life size representations of the subject depicted, and on rock walls, or in stone, ivory, antler, or bone. The paintings, which are the most spectacular of the art forms, must have involved great skill and considerable expenditure of time and energy. The paint pigments consisted of ochres and burnt bone and wood, which were ground up in hollow rocks and stored for future use. The artists in some cases seem to have made preliminary sketches on small flat rocks. Application was accomplished by fingers, crayons, brushes of hair; by blowing through tubes, and with pliable pieces of wood. It is essentially an art depicting the big-game animals of the times, generally in a realistic fashion (although, in many cases, to capture the animals' most characteristic features rather than achieve complete fidelity was the goal of the artist). Humans are less often depicted and have been traditionally interpreted as not an important component of this art. There are also a number of signs and geometric figures, the significance of some of which is open to question. Most experts consider that the art was in the hands of specialists.

The major representations of the art are difficult to date because of their lack of association to stratigraphy, but one writer (Leroi-Gourhan, 1968) has suggested an evolution through three periods and four styles:

Style one   is represented by crude representations of animals, many carved on portable objects and with realistic symbols of males and females.

Style two   begins about 25,000 years ago and has the first real cave-wall art (in areas of easy access); it is widespread but still fairly crude (sloppy fill-in between the outlines). Some small sculptures and realistic signs occur.

Style three   begins about 18,000 years ago and demonstrates great detail and use of color. Sculpture technique is good but signs are few. Many animals and human figures occur in some areas.

Style four   begins about 13,000 years ago and ends the tradition. It is mostly confined to western Europe. Wall and portable representations are rich and well done, with body hair and other details represented. The best known examples come from this "classic" style.

The major argument relative to this art revolves around its purpose. Because of the presumed ease of existence, it was originally explained as art for the sake of art. Later, scholars saw a magic intent (see chapter twenty-three) because of the preponderance of food animals represented and the deep-cave locations of some of the art. On the basis of parallels among modern primitives, they saw the aim as an attempt to increase the number of these animals or to gain supernatural control over them. Still later, writers saw religious possibilities: the art was believed to be located in areas sacred to the initiation of young boys. Discovery of sex signs and apparently pregnant human figurines also suggested attempts to manipulate human fertility. Clay animals displaying evidence of countless punctures were also interpreted as hunting magic. Some geometric signs were interpreted as traps. The most recent scholars seem to be taking two approaches. They reject interpretations based upon an analysis of the content of the art and they stress analysis of the distribution of the art itself (within the caves), which they feel to be less random than traditionalists have suggested.

Some writers have pointed out content differences between that art which is deep in caves and that which is within reach of daylight as at least partly representing sacred/profane differences in functions. Other scholars have indicated (fairly convincingly) two patterns of groupings: a female series in the central parts of large galleries, with bison representing females as the central figures, and a male series (primarily horses) either peripheral to the female series or remaining by itself. Leroi-Gourham interprets sex signs in the same fashion and sees the intent of the art to make ideal compositions based upon metaphysical opposition/complementarity between the sexes—human fertility in abstract form! Obviously, much of the older magic interpretation is dismissed by such interpretations and some of the art for art's sake creeps back in. It should be obvious also that we are a long way from a true understanding of this art. However, the deep, difficult-to-reach locations of at least some representations, and the selective content and nature of the motifs themselves, does suggest some deeper significance than a simple urge to beautify one's surroundings. As a last word, it is probably true that different instances of the art will be demonstrated to have different motivations. It is a single tradition only in content and technique.

> It seems, therefore, that if any of the suggested interpretations have any real validity ... each of them is likely to apply to only certain works. There is nothing against assuming that Paleolithic art, as is also the art of many living "primitives," is the result of many different interests. Within any one cave, therefore, it is possible to imagine that many of the possibilities ... apply: that some representations were the work of children ... that some were used in acts of sympathetic magic ... that some were placed in particular situations in order to please ... and that some were illustrations of myths and traditions ... It is very possible, however, that some and perhaps many Paleolithic representations were made for reasons which still totally escape the modern observer. (Ucko and Rosenfeld, 1967: 239)

In fact, a recent writer (Marshak, 1972) considers some of the art as involving astronomical notations. In any event, the major thrust of art generally disappears with the close of Upper Paleolithic times.

MESOLITHIC PERIOD

We now arrive at the last part of human existence revolving around a hunting existence—the Mesolithic period. Where isolation from later developments or poor environments existed, this stage of development (sometimes called *terminal food collecting*) persisted. Most people, however, went on to food production or benefited from its development. The Mesolithic period in Europe began with the close of the Pleistocene geologic period, roughly 12,000 years ago, and persisted a varying amount of time depending on the area in question, perhaps longest in the far north. In some world areas, this stage was of very short duration or was perhaps omitted altogether. In Europe especially, it was a time of readjustment after the finish of the Wurm Glaciation. Water levels were rising, and many cold-adapted big game animals (Mammoth) were becoming extinct (possibly helped by overhunting). A number of general responses occurred: reliance upon small game animals and greater ingenuity in taking them, extensive utilization of fish and marine resources, and in some areas the increasing reliance upon wild plant foods in the diet. There was an increasing use of microlith composite types of tools as well as the introduction of some new types.

> Changes in the environment on the scale indicated for northern Europe must have affected profoundly the conditions of life of the hunting peoples of the Advanced Paleolithic world and not least in what is now Temperate Europe . . . The indigenous peoples had . . . to adapt themselves to hunting, fishing and gathering in a predominantly forested environment. In so doing, they had to face harder conditions. The spread of forests reduced drastically the area available to grazing animals, the main source of food and even raw materials . . .
> Early man responded in two ways; he had . . . to adapt his hunting methods to the pursuit of individual animals rather than herds and to this end he made much greater use of the bow . . . Secondly, he had no choice but to widen the range of his quest for food. (Clark, 1967: 92, 93)

In an attempt to make some sense out of the variety of localized adaptations, one scholar (Chard, 1969) has suggested that the period is best understood in terms of three adaptive categories, each of which was characterized by a different subsistence orientation. The first of these he calls *Pleistocene survivals*. These groups were located in areas where disruptive postglacial changes were not as rapid and/or complete and where the people in question continued the older Paleolithic way of life. Such opportunities were apparently short-lived. As environmental changes occurred or new ideas reached them, most such groups became at least culturally extinct. The Tasmanians prior to modern extinction, and the ancestors of the Bushmen of South Africa, are cited as the most recent examples. Discovery of a "Stone Age" tribe in the Philippine Islands recently shows how long this way of life lingered on!

Chard calls the second of these orientations *postglacial adaptations*. These groups represent enriched cultures that dealt with the altered conditions. They represent " . . . adaptations to changed conditions or else increased complexity and enrichment over their Pleistocene counterparts, often as the result of borrowings." (Chard, 1969: 175) At the beginning of the time period in question, most Eurasian cultures were probably of this sort. These, too, were eventually mostly extinct by the spread of food production, although a few survived into recent times, the Eskimo being cited as an example. The best known culture at the time in question was the *Maglemosian* of northern Europe (Denmark). These peoples hunted birds and game animals with bows and arrows, took fish with nets and floats, spears, harpoons, and extensive traps, and collected edible plants and shellfish. They were more totally exploitative of the wild food resources of their environment. These, or related peoples, invented and used dugout canoes and skin-covered boats, sleds for use during winters; and reinvented the core axe, now made out of stone by the ground-and-polished manner and hafted to handles. These were excellent woodworking tools. They also inserted chipped axe heads into sleeves of antler to use as adzes for the same purpose.

The third orientation Chard calls **incipient cultures.** These were peoples living in areas where the accessibility of wild plants and potentially domesticatable animals was more promising. Although they remained hunters and gatherers, these people, because of the greater environmental promise available to them, played the central roles in the early shifts to food production: the domestication of plants and animals that characterize the next period of development (Neolithic period). In the following chapter, we shall examine the transition to Neolithic culture and the characteristics of the Urban culture that followed it.

SUMMARY

1. Human use of tools began with tools of occasion (proto-culture) at the time of the first human open area experimentations. The earliest actual stone tool tradition is the Oldowan, mostly limited to Africa. Most Oldowan tools are general purpose and reflect the culture of Australopithecines.

2. The lower Paleolithic period begins by 700,000 years ago and is characterized in many Old World areas by handaxe traditions which became more sophisticated over time. In some areas, chopper and flake traditions lack the handaxes. Near the end of the period prepared core flake tools became important and widespread. Remains of big game are common and indicate cooperative hunting; there is evidence of shelters but cultural progress is slow. This is the culture of Erectus.

3. The middle Paleolithic begins about 150,000 years ago and a variety of tool traditions occur, most of which can collectively be called Mousteroid. Evidence of religion is documented as well as human aggression against other humans. This is the culture of Neanderthal.

4. The late Paleolithic begins about 40,000 years ago and is the culture of the first modern humans. Blade tools are common in a number of regional traditions and are made in many specialized shapes. Tools of bone, antler, ivory, and horn also occur. There is evidence of shelters and, in some regions, art reaches a high level of development (possibly having supernatural significance).

5. In many areas, the Mesolithic period was a time of readjustment to altered ecological conditions. New types of tools became common (microliths and ground stone types) and different adaptations occurred (Pliestocene survivals, post glacial adaptations, and incipient cultures.

REFERENCES FOR FURTHER READING

The best coverage of the Paleolithic and Mesolithic periods is given in *Man in Prehistory*, by Chester S. Chard (1969, McGraw-Hill). See also, *Prehistoric Societies*, by Graham Clark and Stuart Piggott (1967, Knopf); and *The Stone Age Hunters*, by Grahame Clark (1967, McGraw-Hill). The latter text contains excellent illustrations of tools, as does *Tools of the Old and New Stone Age*, by Jacques Bordaz (1970, Natural History Press). Two other general surveys are valuable: *The Old Stone Age*, by Francois Bordes (1968, McGraw-Hill); and the first part of *Prehistory and the Beginnings of Civilization*, by Jacquetta Hawkes and Leonard Woolley (1963, Harper & Row). *The Emergence of Man*, by John E. Pfeiffer (1969, Harper & Row) is also useful. Any number of books on cave art can be found in most libraries. The most thoughtful discussion appears in *Paleolithic Cave Art*, by Peter J. Ucko and Andree Rosenfeld (1967, McGraw-Hill). Another useful text is *The Art of the Stone Age*, by Hans-Georg Bandi et al. (1961, Crown). A new approach is given in *The Roots of Civilization*, by Alexander Marshack (1972, McGraw-Hill).

More specific studies include "Recent Studies in Paleoanthropology," edited by J. Desmond Clark and F. Clark Howell, in *American Anthropologist* 68, no. 2 (1966). The statement by the Binfords occurs in this study, plus useful reviews of Lower Paleolithic sites. For tools and sites, see also, "Early Upper Paleolithic Man and Late Middle Paleolithic Tools," by David Brose and Milford Wolpoff, in *American Anthropologist* 73 (1971): 1156–88; "Evolution of the Paleolithic in Central and Eastern Europe," by Karel Valoch, in *Current Anthropology* 9 (1968): 351–68; "The Evolution of Paleolithic Art," by Andre Leroi-Gourhan, in *Scientific American* 218: 59–70; "A Paleolithic Camp at Nice," by Henry Delumley, in *Scientific American* 220 (1969): 42–50; and *Traces of Pleistocene Hunters: An East African Example*, by Glynn Isaac, in R. Lee and I. Devore, eds., *Man The Hunter*, pp. 253–61 (1968, Aldine).

9

the neolithic
and
urban periods

The shift to food production with domesticated plants and animals during the Neolithic period represents a basic change in human behavior. Some scholars equate its effects to those of the Industrial Revolution of later times. Certainly, the character of human existence, not only technologically but socially as well, underwent alteration. Some writers even feel that only after this transition occurred can human beings be truly characterized as distinct sorts of creatures. This stage of food production is conventionally believed to have begun about ten thousand years ago. It is traditionally thought to be earliest in the Near East, but this basic revolution also occurred somewhat later in India and China, perhaps as early in Southeast Asia, and much later (but apparently independently) in various locations in the New World. Each Old World area may have been partially stimulated by others at some time, although special plants and animals were also locally developed. The Neolithic revolution spread rapidly to still other areas where most existing populations were converted and absorbed or extincted. Partially this spread was due to the great rise in population (facilitated by food production) at this time; one estimate puts eighty-six million in the Old World as compared to three million during the Paleolithic.

THEORIES OF FOOD PRODUCTION

Because of the importance of this transition, great energy has been expended by scholars in the attempt to locate its precise geographic origins and to explain why this technological shift occurred. Perhaps most effort has been expended in studying areas of the Near East: Anatolia, the Levant, and the areas adjacent to the Tigris and Euphrates rivers (i.e., Zagros mountains). Because of archaeological preoccupation with more monumental remains from these more restricted areas of later stages of development, however, our data as yet are rather scanty

141

and incomplete. The task of explaining reasons for this shift has also been a problem. An early theory explained the shift as a response to rapid changes (*dessiccation*) in the environment that forced humans, other animals, and plants together at places of permanent water. In this *oasis theory*, by intensive interaction a symbiotic sort of relationship emerged, eventually leading to fuller human exploitation. We now recognize, on the basis of paleobotanical studies, that such changes after glacial times were much less profound, and that they had occurred in earlier times without resulting in food production. Another theory, the nuclear area approach, saw parts of this area as a natural habitat zone, where varieties of plants and animals existed that were potentially capable of being domesticated, and where climate conditions were "perfect" for facilitating early experiments in this direction. To exploit such a zone, the right human "psychology" would be necessary; a shift from the short-term outlook of hunters to the longer-term deferred-gratification view of the herder and farmer. The general assumption was that some Mesolithic peoples with a more settled-in wild-plant orientation

Ancient wheat gathered at an archaeological site in Iraq.

Field Museum of Natural History

would meet this incipient cultures criterion. When such peoples found themselves in such a nuclear area, the result would be food production. The most recent theories stress the ecologic balance between technology and environment. Some scholars now hold that as early as 20,000 years ago in this area, there was a shift from hunting to a more total exploitation of environmental resources (including indigenous wild grasses). Most groups didn't settle in, however, but rather pursued a seasonal-shift type of existence, moving from place to place as wild resources became obtainable. As populations grew larger, groups of people had to move away towards more marginal areas, where they attempted to continue this way of life. Climate changes (documented for these times) would have made this endeavor somewhat more difficult. Consequently cultivation, so says this theory, began as a conservative attempt to preserve an older way of life:

> . . . a change in the demographic structure of certain areas of south-
> western Asia caused impingement of groups of hunters and gatherers
> upon other groups. Population growth increased population densities
> beyond the carrying capacities of the environment. Specifically, pressure
> was applied around the margins of the optimal habitats, for it was within
> these zones that population densities were the highest. These population
> increases resulted in the splitting off of daughter populations into the
> more marginal areas. Disequilibrium, then, occurred in the tension zones
> between the optimal and marginal areas, and it was here that an
> adaptive shift became necessary. (Wright, 1971: 460)

In any event, we as yet lack enough evidence to solve this complex
problem; likely, more than a single explanation is needed, and, of
course, no one suspects one group to have been responsible for all
plant and animal domestications.

Recent evidence, incidentally, indicates a strong possibility that
the earliest agricultural development took place in Southeast Asia,
where some of the foregoing theories are clearly inapplicable. Before
going on to present some traditional (and better documented) examples
of the process from the Near East, we can briefly examine the nature of
this new evidence. Two sites in Thailand have yielded interesting remains. Non Nok Tha has revealed bronze and pottery, rice, and humped-
back cattle dating between 3000 and 4000 B.C., with origins going back
perhaps to 5000 B.C. At Spirit Cave, the earliest site of which goes back
to 10,000 B.C., were found the remains of ten plant genera including
many different types of nuts, pepper, cucumber, bean types, and water
chestnuts. Some of these appear to have been cultivated. Other Neolithic
traits appear by 6800 B.C. Their level of development suggests considerable development (and antiquity) elsewhere. Those who have worked
with this material feel that the "revolution" to food production may have
begun some thousands of years earlier here than in the Near East areas.

> The fact that some of the most technologically advanced cultures in
> the world in the period from about 13,000 B.C. to 4000 B.C. flourished
> not in the Middle East or the adjacent Mediterranean but in the northern
> reaches of mainland Southeast Asia is not easy to accept. Nontheless,
> recent excavations in Thailand have convinced my colleagues and me
> that somewhere among the forest-clad mountains of the region man's
> first tentative efforts to exploit wild plants and animals opened the way
> first to horticulture and then to full-scale agriculture and animal hus-
> bandry. (Solheim, 1972: 34)

We can look forward to further enlightenment on human cultural development to originate from this area, just as physical evolution is now
being "rewritten" in East Africa.

EARLY FOOD-PRODUCTION EXPERIMENTS

One early experiment in food production occurred in the Near Eastern area of the Levant and is called the **Natufian culture**. It is dated about 10,000 B.C. These people occupied caves as well as sites in more open areas. They were still hunters, fishermen, and gatherers, with deer and gazelle the major animal foods. However, wild cattle, goats, and pigs were among the hunted species. We find flint sickle blades (with a harvesting sheen and wear pattern) and many grinding stones for vegetable preparation. Such foods as wild wheat and barley, legumes, and nuts were exploited. They were not a major part of the economy, although a few scholars feel the first one might have been partially domesticated. At one open-area site, archaeologists have uncovered the remains of fifty, round semi-subterranean houses roofed over the top with reeds and matting. Population estimates run to about 300 people, far more than existed in that area during Paleolithic times. Another site (culture?), in the Tigris-Euphrates highland area, is Zwai-Chemi, dated to approximately 9000 B.C. As among the Natufians, wide exploitative activities are indicated. This was apparently a seasonal occupation, but storage pits have been found. Tools include sickle blades and grinders, so these people, too, were somewhat reliant upon vegetable foods in the diet. Because of the high proportion of immature sheep bones (in contrast to the number of young sheep in wild herds), some authorities feel that this animal was being kept and was perhaps in the process of being domesticated. Still another more recently discovered site, Ali Kosh (more than 9,000 years old) displays charred kernals of two early forms of wheat and domesticated barley. So, whatever the specific reason, in various parts of the Near East, some peoples were displaying connections to the origins of food production.

NEOLITHIC CHARACTERISTICS

Before mention of a few sites where the Neolithic boundary had been securely passed, it is instructive to make mention of the several traits that in general characterize the Neolithic period.

Agriculture

This aspect of food production is an obvious trait. Cultivated plants gave Neolithic peoples permanent settlement and led to further population increases since humans could now grow as much as they wanted and to some extent where they wanted. Such crops, of course, came to

Representation of a Neolithic village in Denmark about 2700 B.C.

American Museum of Natural History

differ significantly from their wild ancestors in terms of size, seed retention, and resistance to climate. Exactly how early farmers accomplished this is an open question at present. At any rate, they would have had to learn the importance of retaining seeds of valued types, weeding out competing growth, and other gardening techniques. Such would have demanded new outlooks toward plants: how to nurture and perfect them. Their perfection, in turn, would have led to a surplus and longer periods of leisure time, facilitating other developments as well. In the Near East area, wheat and barley appear to be the earliest cereal grains, with oats and rye being developed later. Other cultivated crops were apparently developed in other areas of early food production: for example, peas, cucumbers, and rice in Southeast Asia; millet and rice in China; and corn, beans, squash and a host of other food crops in the New World. In any area, early Neolithic farming was certainly a relatively simple affair of hoes and digging sticks. Plows and irrigation came later on in human development.

Animal Husbandry

The domestication of animals is the other half of food production and presents a somewhat different mental outlook. Domesticated animals (tame and able to breed in captivity—reproduction controlled by humans) require a new animal orientation: not killing the tamest and youngest, protection against predators, and provision of a food supply or access to one. The earliest domestic animals were probably regarded as a convenient supply of meat. Since wild sheep have little wool and wild cows give little extra milk, other uses would have been later in development. The earliest Near Eastern domesticates were sheep and goats, followed by pigs and cattle. Dogs were not domesticated as early in this area as in Europe and may also have been considered as

145

a food resource. Again, we are ignorant of both the precise reasons for and the steps involved in the domestication of each animal. Given a fair amount of cow-religion symbolism at some Neolithic sites, it is entirely possible that a ritual motivation for domestication preceded a food motivation. But whatever the specific motivation, "Apparently farming and a settled community life were cultural prerequisites for the domestication of animals ... animal domestication first occurred in this area, because wild goats, sheep, cattle, pigs, horses, asses and dogs were all present there, and settled agricultural communities had already been established" (Braidwood, 1960: 9). Outside this early domestication area other animals eventually appear. Chickens and silk-worms appear in China along with most Near Eastern domesticated animals. In Southeast Asia are found pigs, chickens, humped-back cattle, and dogs, and, of course, later on in the New World, llamas and alpacas, guinea pigs, and turkeys.

Pottery

During the Neolithic, some peoples also invented or discovered the principle of forming and baking some kinds of clay into vessels of various sorts. This was certainly a great scientific breakthrough since it involves many not-always-obvious steps, the knowledge of which must have been gained by considerable trial-and-error activity. The potter must find a suitable deposit of clay, mix it with water to form a paste, add temper materials for strength and to allow gasses to escape when heating, shape the vessel (coiling and modeling), let dry, and then heat to bake into a solid. Once developed, however, pottery became a great aid in cooking and provided storage that was not only cool and waterproof but that discouraged rats and other pests as well. Although pottery is a characteristic hallmark of the Neolithic, it, nevertheless, came in only after the Neolithic had developed in the Near East, and it did predate this period in Southern Japan. So, it is not an absolute characteristic.

Spinning and Weaving

This, too, is a scientific breakthrough, one that seemingly had its origins in earlier basketry techniques. These could be applied to textiles once the right fibers existed: flax, and then, later on, wool and cotton. Basically, it involves spinning a thread, twisting fibers together, and connecting them into a long skein with the help of a *spindle* (thin stick) and *whorl* (weight). Once spun, some of the thread material (*warp*) is hung on a frame or simple loom with a bar in the horizontal position, and other thread material (*weft*) is then passed through it. The advantage of even simple weaving is that it permits the created product to be of any shape, size, or weight—certainly a boost for the covering-clothing industry.

Tool Types

Traditionally, the Neolithic was defined by the presence of ground and polished stone tools. This is, of course, a misnomer since these types did appear in the Mesolithic. Those of the Neolithic are perhaps on the average smaller, better made, and in a greater variety of shapes. Perhaps the most typical type is an axe shape called a *celt*. Generally, these tools were hafted into handles rather than the handles being inserted into the stone—a development requiring greater drilling skill. In some areas, antler sockets served as shock absorbers between stone and wood. Other ground and polished tools include grinders, stone bowls, and dishes. Some cutting tools were still made by older knapping techniques: not only the sickle blades, but arrow heads, and many extremely specialized shapes, some of which may have been pure prestige items. Trade existed for obsidian and in Europe unflaked pieces of flint were traded great distances. Neolithic peoples in some areas (Belgium and England) also began to mine flint, sinking shafts as deep as fifty feet connected by radial galleries. Perhaps more flint was needed in Europe for woodworking or forest adaptations.

In addition to these technological developments, a host of other things characterize the Neolithic period. Settled village life begins, and with its increased population, some scholars have suggested come also health hazards caused by sanitation problems and the potential proliferation of disease. It has also been proposed that the consequent shift to a heavier diet of cereal grains might also have led to diet-deficiency diseases. Each of these villages was probably basically self-sufficient even though trade was becoming more of a necessity. Not all raw materials would have been locally available. Certainly, individual self-sufficiency if it ever existed, had disappeared by these times. It is possible that emerging crafts such as weaving and pottery may have been in the hands of specialist craftsmen, although such specialization is not definitely ascertained until the next period. We may also speculate that changes occurred socially and religiously. If modern preliterate societies are any indication, food production requires greater sustained cooperation and organization by community members. This may have been reflected in the Neolithic by some political office of a more permanent and powerful sort than the respected elder type commonly found among hunters and gatherers. Some more effective social control or arbitration would also have been necessitated by the greater population numbers themselves. The community rather than the kinship group was probably becoming the focus for loyalty. So, too, religious concepts and behavior are thought to have changed. Most food producers take a definite interest in the soil and weather as well as the crops themselves and tend to deify these things. The most commonly occurring Near Eastern representation seems to be *mother-goddess* figurines. Of course, some practices such as burial of the dead continue from earlier times.

NEOLITHIC SITES

Jarmo

One of the most famous early Neolithic farming villages is Jarmo (6750 B.C.), found in the foothills of northern Iraq. It covers about four acres on a high, natural promontory serviced by a perennial spring and consists of a series of mud walls suggesting not only houses (twenty to twenty-five) but internal rooms with clay-lined basins as well. These dwellings were roofed over with reeds and perhaps also clay and were all adjoining each other. Over time, they become larger and more complex. The economy demonstrates that agriculture has arrived. Emmer and barley were domesticated, as evidenced by carbonized kernels. Dogs and goats were also domesticates, and sheep, pigs, cows, and gazelle were hunted. Wild peas, lentils, nuts, and land snails rounded out the diet. Ground and polished stone tools are numerous: grinders, axes, adzes, and cups and bowls as well as jewelry.

Archaeological site of Jarmo, one of the most famous early Neolithic farming villages.

Courtesy of Robert J. Braidwood, The Oriental Institute, University of Chicago

On the other hand, the old tradition of making flint blades and micro-lithic tools was still very strong at Jarmo. The sickle-blade was made in quantities, but so also were many of the much older tool types. Strangely enough, it is within this age-old category of chipped stone tools that we see one of the clearest pointers to a newer age. Many of the Jarmo chipped stone tools—microliths—were made of obsidian, a black vol-canic natural glass. The obsidian beds nearest to Jarmo are over three hundred miles to the north. Already a bulk carrying trade had been established—the forerunner of commerce—and the routes were set by which, in later times, the metal trade was to move. (Braidwood, 1967: 120)

There are also many unbaked clay figurines of animals and mother god-desses. Pottery itself is absent until the later history of the site (upper levels) and seemingly represents an introduction from the outside.

Nea Nikomedia

Another such site, outside the traditional Near East area, is Nea Niko-media in northern Greece, dated at 6220 B.C. House remains here, in contrast to the Near Eastern style, consisted of detached individual buildings. These were made on a pole frame perhaps twenty-five feet square covered by reeds and plastered with mud. The village itself was surrounded by walls. One larger building contained a collection of unfired clay mother-goddess statues and is assumed to have been intended for ritual use. Some Near Eastern sites also contain rooms of this sort. The economy of Nea Nikomedia included wheat, barley, and lentils, and domesticated goats and sheep. Pigs and cattle may have been in the process of experimentation. Small game, fish, and wild fowl rounded out the diet. Pottery is present and of good quality and loom weights and spindle whorls indicate the presence of a textile industry.

Khirokita

Another variation is provided by Khirokita, a site on the island of Cyprus, dated about 5900 B.C. Here, a further variation in building style occurs. Up to 1000 round "beehive" houses of mud brick and stone occur, with larger types having a second story.

Several compounds were found consisting of one large beehive house and several others used as kitchens, workshops for grinding corn, etc. Courtyards were often paved with flat stones and circular tables show where the food was eaten. Some corridors appear to have been roofed and access to the courtyards was gained by ramps leading from the central street. The general impression is one of great efficiency and good organization. (Mellaart, 1965: 54)

Pigs, sheep, and goats appear to have been domesticated. Although no cereal remains have yet been found, it is apparent that they provided a considerable portion of the diet. This and other sites outside the focal areas of the Near East suggest that the primacy of that area in the transition to food production may not be as central as hitherto suspected.

THE URBAN PERIOD AND CIVILIZATION: TRAITS

The stage of Neolithic village farming, beginning in the Near East about 8000 B.C. represents the pattern of life basic to most humans subsequent to the spread of this revolution. Many tribal and peasant groups continue at this general agricultural level today. Despite its obvious security as a way of life and its advances in technology relative to earlier developmental periods, the Neolithic revolution was not yet at the level of cultural complexity that scholars designate as **civilization.** In some Old World areas, beginning about 4000 B.C., new economic and social patterns arose, and the level of civilization developed. Archaeologists and other scholars are not in complete agreement as to what traits characterize the level of cultural development that they call civilization. Most, however, seem to include the following:

1. **An urbanized society** concentrating great numbers of people. This is not only the setting for civilization but apparently generates a host of social developments as well, involving concepts of power, wealth, and social inequality.

2. **A territorially based state** that retains political and military authority. Legal codes are developed in more formal manners—laws imposed from above in most cases—to regulate the affairs of the larger populations. The political controls first take the form of the *city state*—a city and the surrounding rural country side. These grow in time, and wars with neighboring societies occur over markets and raw materials. War now takes the form of conquest and subjugation, with special practitioners, technology, and the development of the institution of slavery.

3. **A symbiotic economy** based on a centralized accumulation and distribution of surplus. Since the urban center cannot feed itself, it re-

mains dependent upon surrounding producers (peasants) for its existence. Tribute and taxation support these town dwellers, who are characterized by craft specialization; the city becomes a market for goods and services produced by a complex nonsubsistence division of labor. Cities become dependent upon trade to secure raw materials and markets, and lose self-sufficiency, which is at this time at best only regional.

4. Great advances in scientific knowledge—for elaboration of technology, provisioning of greater numbers of people, keeping track of people and things, and for building the cities themselves. Part of this is also a pursuit of knowledge for its own sake.

5. Impressive public works and monumental architecture are built to house and serve the social, political, religious, and economic needs of urban man. We now find temples, palaces, fortifications, storage areas, and the like, which not only reflect the technological abilities of the times but the political development necessary to secure execution of their construction as well.

Although there are many other hallmarks of civilizations, some of which we are about to turn to, the above perhaps best characterize the nature of civilization and what some have called the *urban revolution*. Certainly, by this time human beings have become heavily dependent upon a social/cultural environment—perhaps as much as hunters on their physical surroundings. If anything, the dependency of humans on an artificial, complex, social-political-economic order is more difficult than having to come to terms with nature itself. In retrospect, the farm-village way of life may have been an ideal compromise: not complete dependency upon nature but not yet at the mercy of artificial social relations. We will return to this idea in the next chapter.

What are the other developments of the urban period in the Near East?

1. Metallurgy. So important is this that the period was originally designated the *Copper-Bronze Age*. Metallurgy seems to have begun as a rural craft: working copper, silver, and gold. It really developed, however, in an urban setting about 4000 B.C., with the invention of bronze (copper and tin). The basic technique of metallurgy is casting: melting metals into a liquified state and pouring the molten materials into a mold and then allowing them to harden in this desired shape. Perhaps the most exciting part of this process is its reversibility; you can reuse raw material to change a shape (sword to plowshare) or repair a broken object (by recasting it). Plus, of course, there is little

waste of raw material in the first place. In addition, the use of metallurgical techniques leads to great standardization as well as permitting mass production. Thus, industry began to assume a modern character.

> Metal working involved two groups or complexes of discoveries: (1) that copper, when hot, melts and can be cast into any desired shape, but on cooling becomes as hard and will take on as good an edge as stone, and (2) that the tough, trenchant, reddish metal can be produced by heating certain crystalline stones or earths in contact with charcoal . . .
> The real superiority of metal is that it is fusible and can be cast. Fusibility confers upon copper some of the merits of potter's clay. In working it the intelligent artificer is freed from the restrictions of size and shape imposed by bone or stone. A stone axe-head, a flint spear point, or a bone harpoon can only be made by grinding, chipping, or cutting bits *off* the original piece. Molton copper is completely plastic and will adapt itself to fill any desired form . . . The only limit to size is the capacity of the mold . . . (Childe, 1958: 95, 96)

It should be noted, however, that most of these first metal products were of a luxury nature or were intended for military use; the common man and woman for the most part, had to make do with Neolithic types until about 1500 B.C. in the Near East, when the "poor man's metal," iron, came into general use. Perhaps the most important effects of the development of metallurgy was the stimulus it gave to trade and travel for raw materials and markets, to the emerging division of labor (miners, metallurgists, merchants, etc.), and to social inequality; wealth is required to own molds and places of production, and power is required to control sources of supply.

In addition to metallurgy, a number of other developments characterize the urban age of the Near East.

2. New Farming Techniques.   Use of the ox-drawn plow permitted greater-sized fields to be brought and kept under cultivation. In some areas, irrigation also came into general use—reflecting, perhaps, greater political control and coordination, as does the existence of public store houses for surplus to support other technological activities.

3. The Development of the Wheel.   The wheel was developed to fill the need for an aid in transportation. The first wheels were of three parts fit together and were pulled by oxen. Later with the advent of better axles and spoked wheels, transportation was upgraded; and with the introduction of the horse as a fast power source, war chariots changed warfare tactics and mobility. At this time, too, barges came into use for floating goods down rivers as well as being pulled along the banks by men and animals. Sailboats were developed for long-distance travel, spreading this new way of life.

4. The General Development of Trade and Travel.   To aid in the development of commercialism in these times, there were roads, coinage or standards of value, and a host of related modern elements: inns, prostitutes, and highwaymen, adding still more specialists to society. Other more scientific developments necessitated by this and the other urban traits were a knowledge of geography and astronomy, calendars and mathematics, and tables of weights and measures. It should be recognized even today that new cultural-social behaviors have the effect of creating others, whether desirable or not.

5. The Development of Other Specialties.   Certainly, by these times, pot-making had become a craft for the most part divorced from home industry. The potters wheel for "thrown" pottery had developed and with it the capacity not only for mass production, but for better pots and vessels as well. Pot-making thus became a real outlet for artistic expression. Weaving had also become a speciality by now, joined by barbering, brickmaking, carpentry, and medicine, among others. Clearly social life in urban areas had become exceedingly complex and interdependent, although life "down on the farm" was still conservative and more self-supporting.

6. Religious Development.   Some scholars see this as the catalyst in many early civilizations. In the Near East at least, the city God and his temple personnel stood at the center of many things; the priests themselves were either the center of power or an aspect of it, forming a ruling class that held a monopoly over skills and wealth. As time went on, this power tended to become more secular, but religion still played a heavy role in organizing and maintaining behavior.

7. The Development of Writing.   Finally, with the advent of such "modern" forms of behavior, came the need for records, culminating in the development of writing systems. The earliest attempts are called *pictographs*, in which pictures stand for various concepts of things: for example, a picture of a cow representing a cow or some stalks of wheat representing grain. Because such a system is susceptible to interpretation difficulties, and because it lacks real facility for abstraction, phonetics elements soon were introduced: symbols standing for actual objects or words as well as concepts (for example, in English, a symbol to represent both the insect, *bee*, and the fact of existence, *be*). Eventually more purely phonetic systems were developed. *Phonetic cuneiform* (wedge-shaped) writing on clay tablets was developed by the Sumarians by about 3000 B.C. This, of course, added still more specialists to society—the scribes.

Apart from records of political leaders, of commercial transactions and religious accounts and myths, the content of some of these early documents is of extreme interest in that they record a number of "firsts" in human history. Scholars have translated and/or compiled tablets dealing, among other things, with the following motifs: proverbs and sayings, animal fables, biblical parallels, social reforms, juvenile delinquency, epic literature, love songs, and moral ideas. Clearly, by this period of cultural development, the foundations had been set for a great deal of later human behavior.

We will turn to a more descriptive account of the first Near Eastern civilization in the next chapter as well as some brief comment on the spread of this way of life and of the earlier Neolithic culture. First, however, we must very briefly survey general developments leading up to the urban stage in *Mesopotamia*—the area between the Tigris and Euphrates rivers where these early civilizations developed. What happened after the advent of the Neolithic way of life?

TRANSITION FROM THE NEOLITHIC PERIOD
TO THE URBAN PERIOD

By about 6000 B.C., *Hassuna* culture had developed beyond the earlier stages of food production. Sites of this culture suggest that hunting activities still played a role in the food supply. Material culture is like that previously described for the Neolithic. As time went on, decorated pottery originated (Samarra ware); houses became somewhat more complex, villages larger, and trade more apparent. Religious behavior is reflected not only in mother-goddess figurines but by burials of children in jars and the placement of pottery vessels in graves. "An important feature of the Hassuna and Samarra period is the establishment of settlements in areas where the annual rainfall is insufficient to practice dry farming. We must therefore infer that irrigation methods were used" (Mellaart, 1965: 66). By about 5000 B.C., the *Halafian* culture had developed, characterized by a new pottery style and a wider range of cereals and domesticated animals. The presence of kilns suggests that the making of pottery may have become a specialist's operation. A textile industry is well represented. There is also evidence for wheeled vehicles of a simple sort. The settlements consisted of houses along cobbled streets and some special (religious?) buildings occurred: for example, a circular dome structure with an attached long, rectangular chamber. At this general time period more people than before were occupying the more southern areas of Mesopotamia; areas of marshland where inadequate rainfall precluded early agriculture. The earliest site

Early Neolithic religious beliefs are evidenced, in part, by mother-goddess figurines.

here is a settlement at *Eridu,* whose early inhabitants had to begin drainage operations and make canals and irrigation ditches. The necessary cooperation involved (says one disputed theory) required larger population units and political control and helped pave the way for later urban developments. The presence of a shrine/temple of unbaked brick suggests control may have been of a religious nature. By about 4000 B.C., progress had continued, and the result is termed the *Ubiad* culture by archaeologists. We see a well-developed farming culture based upon irrigation spreading out of the south and into the north, outnumbering the Halafian Cultures there. At Eridu, we see an intensification of religious development, reflected in the temple now being raised up on a platform and with many rooms off each side of the central portion. Figurines of various types exist, some of which are grotesque.

> Nothing . . . more clearly demonstrates the change in culture than the monumental temples which were now built in the cities. Built of mud brick, which makes its first appearance, and sometimes on stone foundations they dominated the cities from the top of ancient mounds. At Eridu they were set on mud-brick platforms, the origin of the temple tower or *ziggurat*, made by filling in earlier buildings, and a long flight

155

of steps gave access to a door in the long side of the building. This consisted of a long central room ... with a broad platform at one end and
an offering table at the other. The main room was surrounded on both
sides by smaller rooms from which ladders led to an upper story and
the roof. The central part of the building was probably higher ... and
lit by triangular windows. The outside of the building was ornamented
with elaborate projections and recesses which remained a characteristic
of all later sacred buildings in Mesopotamia. (Mellaart, 1965: 132)

Although towns are still fairly small, we can see in the central
temple and irrigation farming the groundwork for later developments.
By about 3500 B.C., we see in *Uruk* culture in the south, at sites such
as *Warka*, the creation of true cities and indications of truly revolutionary changes; new pottery shapes made on the wheel, pictographic
beginnings of writing (sometimes these times are called the *Proto-literate*
period), extremely elaborate temple constructions, and the beginnings of
metallurgy. We have now arrived at the time when the Sumerians
were coming to power in a number of early city states; we have reached
the level of early civilization. Despite gaps, then, there is a continuum of
cultural development out of the early Neolithic and culminating in the
level of civilization in the area of Mesopotamia in the Near East.

SUMMARY

1. The shift to food production, completed by the Neolithic period,
   represents a basic change in human behavior. Many theories of
   causation have been advanced, some stressing this shift as a conservative attempt to preserve older ways of life. Only some regions
   of the world had the potential for the first steps in this direction.
2. Some of the general characteristics of the Neolithic are agriculture,
   animal husbandry, pottery, spinning and weaving, and large numbers of ground and polished stone tools. Settled village life begins
   as well as social and religious changes.
3. The Urban period is represented by the stage of cultural development called civilization. In addition to the concentration of great
   numbers of people, it is represented by the territorially based state,
   a symbiotic economy, great advances in scientific knowledge, and
   impressive public works and buildings.
4. Metallurgy is an outstanding feature of Near Eastern civilizations
   along with new farming techniques, development of the wheel,
   trade and travel, and specialization in most areas of life. Religion
   emerges as a major focal point of life and writing systems develop.

REFERENCES FOR FURTHER READING

For information on the Neolithic period and the development to levels of civilization, some of the following are valuable: *Prehistory and the Beginnings of Civilization*; *Man in Prehistory*; and *Prehistoric Societies* (cited at the end of chapter eight). The following are also worth serious attention by the student interested in early food production: *The Neolithic Revolution* by Sonia Cole (1963, 3rd ed., British Museum); "The Ecology of Early Food Production in Mesopotamia," by Kent V. Flannery, in *Science* 147 (1965): 1247–56; "Origins of Food Production in Southwestern Asia: A Survey of Ideas," by Gary A. Wright, in *Current Anthropology* 12 (1971): 447–70; and "An Earlier Agricultural Revolution," by Wilhelm S. Solheim, in *Scientific American* 226 (1972): 34–40; and "The Agricultural Revolution," by Robert J. Braidwood (Freeman), reprinted from *Scientific American* (September 1960), reprint no. 605. See also, *Post Pleistocene Adaptations*, by Lewis R. Binford, in S. R. and L. R. Binford, eds., *New Perspectives in Archaeology*, pp. 313–41 (1968, Aldine). On animal domestication, there is the classic, *A History of Domesticated Animals*, by Frederick E. Zeuner (1963, Harper & Row). *Prehistoric Men*, by Robert J. Braidwood (1967, 7th ed., Scott, Foresman) also deals with early farming-village developments. For a somewhat out of date but still meaningful and delightful-to-read contribution, see *Man Makes Himself*, by V. Gordon Childe (1958, New American Library).

Two excellently illustrated volumes on the rise of civilization are *Early Mesopotamia and Iran*, by M. E. L. Mallowan (1965, McGraw-Hill); and *Earliest Civilizations of the Near East*, by James Mellaart (1966, New American Library). See also, *The Beginnings of Civilization,* by Leonard Wooley (1965, New American Library). An excellent reader is *Courses Toward Urban Life*, edited by Robert J. Braidwood and Gordon Willey (1962, Aldine). It is more world-wide in scope than most of the above texts. An excellent discussion involving the irrigation-civilization controversy is to be found in *The Evolution of Urban Society*, by Robert M. Adams (1966, Aldine).

10
sumerian culture

We can now briefly summarize the culture of the Sumerians, the first civilization, as a way of adding additional data on this stage of cultural development. By the third millenium B.C., the area of Sumer consisted of perhaps a dozen city states. Each of these consisted of many farming villages and a central walled city. So although essentially urban, it still rested on an agricultural base.

TEMPLE

In addition to the wall itself, the main feature of monumental architecture is still the temple complex, now consisting basically of a large tower building (*ziggurat*) composed of a number of levels. The main shrine was inside the tower building and was surrounded by rooms for priests and storage of ritual paraphernalia. In the central shrine stood an offering table and a statue of the main city God. Other similar but smaller accommodations were made for lesser deities.

> The [main] temple was the largest, tallest, and most important building in the city, in accordance with the theory accepted by the Sumerian religious leaders and going back no doubt to very early times that the entire city belonged to its main god, to whom it had been assigned on the day the world was created. (Kramer, 1970: 74)

Work by recent writers suggests, however, that although temple estates were large, there were various other state and even private properties, some in the hands of free commoners. Temple lands themselves were divided into various categories: some functioned to support the upkeep of the temple, some to serve as compensation for workers in the temple, and some as a supplement to the income of temple personnel.

159

This exceptionally well preserved ziggurat gives a good indication of their size and complexity.

The University Museum, Philadelphia

POLITICS

Political organization is imperfectly understood. In early Sumerian society, political power apparently was held by an assembly of free citizens, which may have been split into two divisions (elders and "men") headed up by a governor (*ensi*) who appears as simply a first among equals. Such a structure seems likely enough in terms of what Neolithic governmental procedures may have been like. However, as city states competed, and as they resisted incursions by less civilized peoples, it has been suggested that political control began to centralize until a kingly type of leader ("big man") came to hold most of the power, and the office came to involve hereditary privilege. These "kings" seem to have developed the military, the first so organized in human history, with chariots and more organized military formations (with a front row of shield bearers backed by rows of spearmen). With the army to back up their power, these rulers soon came to equal the religious establishment in power and wealth. Some scholars have suggested that the high priest and priestess were, in fact, relatives of the king. So, power may have been even more consolidated. Whatever the case, it should be pointed out that most people by this time were not members of either power base; they were craftsmen and specialists of various sorts and herders and farmers, the latter of which were apparently organized in large patriarchally organized extended families.

CLASSES

Representing the overall class structure is at best hazardous, but most writers have indicated its dimensions along the following lines.

Nobles: The ruler, wealthy landowners, higher priests, and military officers and their families.

Commoners: Those who owned their own land, plus the various craftsmen attached to one or another institution.

Clients: Those who labored on the fields of the ruler, the nobility, and the temple.

Slaves: Mostly captives of war. Debtors also could be enslaved and, in necessity, an entire family could be substituted for payment of debts, although only for three years. Although slaves were property, their lives were less harsh than might be suspected; they had rights under law, could engage in business and buy their freedom, and their children, apparently, were born free.

LAW

Legal rights were generally on a high level of development. About 2350 B.C., one leader had undertaken reform of past abuses (as a way of strengthening his own power?), and in 2050 B.C., at the beginning of the third dynasty, in the city of Ur, the first such recorded document existed: the *Ur-Nammu law code.* Courts existed, made up of judges who appear to have been city elders, temple administrators, scribes, etc., and who appear to have functioned in a "modern" fashion. Cases could be initiated by private individuals or the state; testimony was taken from witnesses and past precedent cited. Many of the early written tablets are contracts of various sorts.

EDUCATION

With writing and records, as previously mentioned, came the need for scribes; and with the developing sciences, other learned individuals. Education as a formal institution developed perhaps as early as 3000 B.C., and actual schools existed—the *Edubba* or "tablet house." A hierarchy of school officials existed: from a director ("expert") to instructors ("big brothers") and disciplinarians! "In the matter of discipline . . . there was no sparing of the rod. While the teachers no doubt encouraged their students to do good work by means of praise and commendation, they depended primarily on the cane for correcting the student's faults and inadequacies." (Kramer, 1970: 235, 236). Also, school apparently met on a dawn to dusk basis. Most students appear to have come from the wealthier families, education apparently being as expensive then as

Stages in the development of cuneiform writing. From the simple pictograph (left) man progressed to more sophisticated writing systems.

The University Museum, Philadelphia

now. The beginning student started with elementary exercises and progressed from "sorry scratches to elegantly made signs." Eventually, advanced students were given assignments more practical than simply copying of old contracts or religious documents.

RELIGION

By all accounts, religious life seems to have been the most complex social institution, although this may reflect the writing bias of the times and/or sampling error by archaeologists. Most of Sumerian religious belief and behavior appears to have served as the foundation for much of ancient Near Eastern religion. They postulated a pantheon of deities behind the operation of the universe, regulating it in terms of supernatural laws as binding as those of the city state itself. Rulers existed to make sure that all things conformed to the plan of creation. Each god controlled some aspect of existence. They were arranged in a hierarchical manner and consisted of creator types as well as simple "controllers" of things. Three deities stand out. *Enlil*, the air god, was the major creator deity and the father of the other gods. Although he carried out punishments desired by the other gods, he seems generally well disposed towards man. *Enki*, a water deity, seems to have put the world in shape for Enlil and was also the god of wisdom. *Ninhursag* was a mother-goddess (earth) type and was regarded as the mother of all living things, including, apparently, man himself. Among other deities were *Sin*, the moon god; *Utu*, the sun god; *Inanna*, a fertility goddess; and *Ereshkigal*, the god of the dead. Such gods were necessary

162

not only to order and control the universe but also to aid humans who had no power in such matters.

Certainly, the center of religious activities was the temple itself. Daily sacrifices were offered to various deities, one of which, the city god, was preeminent. There were also a number of public annual festivals. The most important of these was a new year's festival, the high point of which was a symbolic marriage between the king and a high priestess, which represented the coupling of the fertility goddess and her spiritual husband (*Dumuzi*). The purpose of this rite was to ensure the fertility and prosperity of the city state: a kind of world-renewal ceremony. Most rites, however, took place within the confines of the temple and were done by various priests on behalf of the common people. A great number of different types of priests served the gods and led the rites in their honor. The *Sanga* was the chief administrator of the temple and the *En*, the spiritual head who especially related to the city god. Beneath these were many types arranged hierarchially with respect to rank and function: diviners, singers and musicians, lesser administrators, and temple prostitutes (whose earnings, apparently, were income for the temple).

OTHER ASPECTS OF LIFE

The more mundane aspects of life, at least for the nobility, kept pace with the above developments. Population of cities had, of course, exploded; by 2000 B.C., Ur contained about 200,000 individuals. Except for the ziggurat complex, the cities of that time were not very pleasing architecturally; streets were narrow and winding, many areas of residence were slums, and shopping areas were crowded. The "average" house was simply a number of mud-brick rooms surrounding a central court. As always, the nobility lived better. Their dwellings were of two stories and consisted of numerous rooms of plastered and whitewashed brick. Fairly decent wooden furniture existed and walls and floors were covered by mats and rugs. Wealthy individuals often owned a number of such houses and apparently entertained lavishly, with musicians and dancing girls for diversion. Tablets recording dining arrangements for such affairs list the following as a menu: an appetizer of garlic in sour cream, barley soup and unleavened bread, tigris salmon, dates, pomegranates and goat cheese, roast pigs and lambs, both wine and beer; and a good time, presumably, was had by all.

Such was the life of the Sumerians. The general impression it leaves is of the profound unity of all its forms, under the dominant force

Golden head of a bull found at the Sumerian city of Ur.

The University Museum, Philadelphia

of religion. Every human activity, whether of peaceful works or warlike enterprise, was performed for the benefit of the gods; man's every step depended on the gods, not only those activities connected with the cult but those of economic and commercial life which we regard as quite remote from religion. This harmony within the faith, characteristic of the Sumerian conception of all the universe, remains a potent and typical feature of all the civilizations which succeed them in the ancient Orient. (Moscati, 1962: 31)

DEVELOPMENTS IN OTHER WORLD AREAS

While the Sumerians were flourishing (and the nobility feasting), what about the rest of the world? Prior to the development of civilization in the city states of Mesopotamia, the Neolithic ideas of food production, pottery, weaving, and settled life had spread into other areas. Sometimes this occurred by actual migration of peoples, sometimes just by the spread of these ideas themselves. Certainly, independent invention played a role, especially in the New World. In any event, Neolithic ideas were reshaped to meet local ideas and necessities. In northwest India (Baluchistan) by about 4000 B.C., we find early farming village communities displaying the tools, crops, and animals occurring in the Near East. By approximately 2500 B.C., civilization had developed in the valley of the Indus river. This is represented by the large cities of *Harrapa* and *Moheno-Daro* as well as others less famous. This culture level had a wide geographic distribution but, because of ecological circumstances and/or invasion, apparently lasted for a shorter duration than other early civilizations. There were similarities as well as differences in comparison to the Near East variety of civilization. City development, in terms of planning, sanitation, and standardized construction, seems advanced, whereas workmanship in metallurgy, art, and some other elements seem less developed. Political organization was probably comparable, as were differences in class and status. Warfare must have been present also, as evidenced by the presence of fortified locations.

By one or another means, the Neolithic had also developed in China, although archaeologists have difficulties in dating early sites. At first it seems to have been localized in northern China along the Huang Ho or Yellow River. Then, in later stages, it expanded out from this "nuclear area." Cultural developments are later but generally equivalent to those found in the Near East. Prior to 1500 B.C., the *Shang* civilization had developed and with it most of the technology and other aspects of culture found elsewhere: urban areas, social inequality, writing, warfare and religious development. Some of these assumed typically Chinese formats, others were remarkably similar to the Near Eastern types. As yet, scholars have not satisfied themselves as to the relative outside influence on the Neolithic and urban ages of China.

The development of the Near Eastern Neolithic had also spread closer to home, to Egypt, where comparable sites occurred along the Nile River shortly after 6000 B.C. By about 3300 B.C., advanced Mesopotamian traits began to occur as evidence of further influence; and after a period of time, communities became larger and joined into confederations, followed by the unification of Egypt under Menes in 3200 B.C. This is the beginning of the dynastic period. Egyptian civilization was also a variation of the Near Eastern theme. Perhaps its outstanding differences were its longer continuous time span, its god-king (*Pharoah*) political leadership, its writing system, its religion-death connections (pyramids, rock tombs, and mummification), and its inherent conservatism over time. This last was perhaps due to a lack of outside ideas stemming from its more isolated geographic position. Of all the early civilizations, that of Egypt seems to have captured the place of preeminence in movies and in the popular imagination.

Modern pottery techniques reflect those developed in ancient Sumeria and related areas.

A similar pattern of development characterized progress in the New World. In certain favorable areas, perhaps earliest in parts of Mexico, a transition to agricultural food production from the hunting and gathering way of life occurred, introduced by migrants from Asia in Upper Paleolithic times. It soon spread to many other areas. Subsequently, in the original areas and a few others, the level of civilization was reached during the first thousand years A.D. Civilization here was also marked by similarities in political, social, religious, and architectural and technological developments. New World varieties, however, did lack the wheel, writing systems like those of the Near East, and many domestic animals. On the other hand, the range of cultivated crops was wide and mostly different from Old World types, and developments in pottery and weaving in some areas were outstanding. Because of the great similarity to Old World civilizations, a raging debate has for years occupied scholars over whether such developments were truly the result of independent invention, or if subsequent sea-borne contacts with Old World areas was responsible. This is still an unresolved problem. Proponents of the isolation-of-the-New-World viewpoint have generally prevailed, citing limitations-of-possibilities and "psychic-unity"-of-humankind arguments to explain away many isolated similarities in material or social culture; (such as pyramids). Recent work on the genetics and history of some cultivated crops, and the discovery of a few sites containing a number of interrelated traits, however, now suggests that perhaps at least some contact must have taken place. Future evidence relative to

166

this controversy promises to be exciting since at stake is not simply the inventiveness of American Indians but whether civilization itself was invented more than once.

The food-producing revolution, of course, also made its way into Europe. A village-farming way of life was present in southeast Europe by 6000 B.C., if not earlier. Somewhat later, we also find Neolithic sites in central Europe in the Danube basin and on the islands and costal areas of the central and western Mediterranean, the latter spread having been accomplished by sea migration. Following this initial spread, many diversified local cultures came into existence, some emphasizing domesticated animals more than others. Prior to 2500 B.C., some areas of northern Europe had been reached and many groups there were converted to the new way of life. Bronze Age developments also filtered into European areas. Many of the trappings of civilization, however, did not spread or develop. Although metallurgical techniques were excellent, social, religious, and political developments remained on essentially Neolithic levels until much later times. One of the most outstanding developments was the spread of a religious cult (*megalithic* religion) consisting of burials in tombs (for example in Spain) made of large rocks, along with worship of mother goddesses and possibly ancestors. In parts of the Aegean area, on Crete and parts of mainland Greece, eventually the higher levels of Bronze Age civilization did appear (the Minoan and Mycenean cultures).

TRENDS IN CULTURAL DEVELOPMENT

So, by the time of recorded history, human beings had developed their culture to the point of great complexity and adaptive value. Is it possible to summarize stages or trends of cultural development in the same kind of simple terms as we did for physical evolution in chapter six? One scholar (Titiev, 1963) has suggested that despite the varieties of cultural progress in world areas, as we look back we can recognize some general "laws" of cultural development. We must keep in mind, however, that these laws are not of the same degree of inflexibility as natural laws. Although they seem to have operated in the past and may reasonably be expected to continue to do so in the future, being cultural (learned), they can be altered if such development, or "progress," no longer fits or serves human needs.

> Today it can be shown that from the beginning a number of consistent trends have been operating along regular and, therefore, predictable lines. Once the existence of these trends has been recognized, their past

courses can be charted, and if they show steady movement in a given direction it may be forecast that they will, until diverted, continue to go in the same direction in the future. Archaeology makes one of its major contributions when it provides the data from which trends may be charted. It is convenient to talk of trends as moving consistently in one direction, but trends generally move in zigzag fashion. (Titiev, 1963: 370).

Four such "laws," or general trends in human cultural development are recognized.

1.   *The law of increasing reliance upon culture* suggests that as time went on, human beings increasingly made their adaptations in terms of cultural adjustments to their environment. In a sense, cultural fitness replaced biological fitness. Of course, we can never reach a 100 percent replacement; to exist is to retain at least minimal biological functioning. This explosion of culture can be said to have begun in the Upper Paleolithic and to have intensified at ever-increasing speed ever since. So, for example, we go from hand-to-hand combat to heavy and awkward hand axes or wooden spears (placing great demands on biology), to the potential of pressing a button with one arthritic finger and launching missiles to wipe out half a continent! There are obvious problems with this trend—apart from the motives behind that finger. First, culture has obviously become *the* human specialization, and some scholars would say the overspecialization. We remember with more than a little concern the possible fate of overspecialization by other creatures in nature. Second, much of culture is now coming to be recognized as potentially or actually harmful to our biology—not just bombs, but pollution, drugs, and alcohol, for example. We must remember that we are still a part of nature even if our culture shields us from its grossest disadvantages.

2.   *The law of expanding utilization of natural resources* suggests that as time went on, to create and supply our ever-increasing degree of cultural adaptation, humans had to use more and more natural resources. Most of material culture is the alteration and utilization of these. Again, this trend really got off the ground in Upper Paleolithic times by adding substantial amounts of bone, antler, ivory, and horn to stone materials. Of course, as with trend number one, we can never reach 100 percent utilization because as needs and desires change, the uses of some raw materials become obsolete: little desire exists for stone tools these days! Perhaps the greatest problem connected with the second trend is that due to the accelerated development of modern culture, we are rapidly exhausting our supplies of many of the most important natural resources. Ours has become, in the words of one writer, a "plundered planet." The ultimate consequence of such exploitation and depletion would seemingly be a lessening in the level of cultural development, one that

some scholars see as an impossibility for "soft" modern humans. Few writers predict a rosy future for us when our natural resources run out.

3.   *The law of declining relative individual knowledge* suggests that as the first two trends develop, the stockpile of human knowledge becomes too great for any one individual to encompass or comprehend. The more there is to know, the less any one individual can know of it; although in terms of the totality of personal knowledge, we do know more all the time. It is the percentage of the sum total of knowledge that can be encompassed by a single person that goes down. Again, it is tempting to see this trend begin in the Upper Paleolithic period with new tool types and art. Certainly by Neolithic times, the range of activities was too great for any one individual to accomplish. Today, of course, a trip through even a small library quickly convinces one of his almost total ignorance. It is argued by Titiev that there are two other trends that go hand in glove, so to speak, with a decline in individual knowledge relative to what is known. First would be *the law of increasing specialization.* Because of knowledge limitations, individuals have to concentrate their activities over knowable ranges. "Whenever a stage is reached . . . the only way its culture can be maintained is by a process of compartmentalization, which means that its stockpile of knowledge is divided up, with particular subgroups or specialists assuming responsibility for particular fractions of the total" (Titiev, 1963: 377). In modern society this leads to very narrow sectors of expertise indeed: for example, being able to write advertising copy for only corktip, mentholated, king-size cigarettes—perhaps a joke, but uncomfortably to the point. Certainly, place-kickers in football are a real example. Second, this increasing specialization leads to the absolute *necessity for increasing cooperation* between specialists (by exchanging the results of their activities) to ensure survival. No longer is "man an island unto himself." One breakdown in the scheme of things, one uncooperative group (note the effects of labor strikes or slowdowns) and everyone suffers. Perhaps it would be better to be at the mercy of nature alone!

4.   *The law of increasing efficiency* suggests that none of the first three trends were random developments. It is suggested that whether consciously prompted or not, they developed in the interest of greater efficiency by human beings wanting to save either *time* or *energy* or both. A quick look at present behavior confirms this attitude. Even programs of exercise designed to reverse the deteriorative effects on the body by saving time and energy, now stress that they are quicker to accomplish than before and with less sweat: "Running five minutes on our executive jogger is better than five miles of roadwork." We seem trapped!

The major question to ask about these trends is not if they characterize our past, which in general it can be demonstrated that they do, but if we want them to continue on into the future. Given the eventual lack of raw materials, should we not consciously limit, or even cut back, our species' involvement with cultural adaptations? Have we overspecialized? Moreover, is it not psychologically debilitating to recognize that human ignorance, relatively speaking, is continuing to increase? In such terms, can any group of political directors ever hope to solve human problems, problems they can comprehend less of every year? Can one be too efficient for one's own good? Granted this is the age of the panic button; granted that technology (culture) itself may ultimately be able to solve some of its own difficulties. All this considered, many scholars are now rationally suggesting that the human species may have come too far too fast. Warning: too much culture may be hazardous for your health!

It must always be kept in mind that human beings have spent the vast majority of their evolutionary history, both physically and culturally, making hunting and gathering adaptations. Since the time of the Neolithic revolution we have entered into a world where there are little opportunities for such behavior. Many recent writers, however, have suggested that the mentality of the big-game hunter lingers on in the human species and that many of our problems at the present time relate to this fact. Has our psychology not yet caught up with our accelerated rate of cultural progress? Answers to questions such as these—indeed, research on the very possibility—is sorely needed.

> The problem of the future is whether there will be a future fit for human beings to live in. The question arises now after more than twenty million years of evolution in the hominid line, after the transformation of a clever ape into a creature with unprecedented and increasing powers to create and to destroy. The crisis man faces is the first of its kind on earth, the first involving the entire species. As the only remaining members of the family of man, we may or may not survive. The issue will almost certainly be decided within the next hundred years. (Pfeiffer, 1969: 436)

We will examine related problems and possibilities in chapter twelve. We can turn now to a brief discussion of the varieties of the human species that exist at the present time: the concept of race.

SUMMARY

1. The Sumerians were the first Near Eastern civilization. They had perhaps a dozen city states which consisted of farming villages and a central walled city.

2. Political control was eventually held by a king type of leader who developed military power and undertook conquest warfare against neighboring states. The temple complex also had political power.

3. A class system was comprised of nobles, commoners, clients, and slaves (the last mostly war captives).

4. Many cultural developments seem "modern" in their expression: for example, law codes, courts, schools, and the lavish entertainments of wealthy people.

5. Religious life, revolving around the Ziggurat (or temple) and the chief city god, was highly organized and served as a basis for much of later Near Eastern belief. An air god, a water god, and an earth goddess seem the most important early deities. Most rituals were held within the temple by a large and hierarchically organized priesthood.

6. Developments comparable to the Neolithic and Urban periods of the Near East occurred in India, China, Egypt, and parts of the Americas. Subsequently the food producing revolution diffused into Europe.

7. A consideration of world cultural development allows a summation to be made in terms of general trends: increasing reliance upon culture and expanding utilization of natural resources leads to declining relative individual knowledge and increasing efficiency. These trends may ultimately be responsible for the destruction of the human species.

REFERENCES FOR FURTHER READING

The best writings on the Sumerians are by Samuel Noah Kramer. See, especially, his *The Sumerians: Their History, Culture and Character* (1970, University of Chicago Press) and *History Begins at Sumer* (1959, Doubleday). For books on other (later) civilizations in this geographic area, the student can consult *Ancient Mesopotamia*, by A. Leo Oppenheim (1964, University of Chicago Press); and *The Greatness that was Babylon* by H. W. F. Saggs (1968, New American Library.) For wider coverage, see *The Face of the Ancient Orient*, by Sabatino Moscati (1962, Doubleday); and *The Anvil of Civilization*, by Leonard Cottrell (1957, New American Library). The literature dealing with other early centers of civilization is enormous. Since there is no space in the present text to deal with these, a brief mention of some of the best works can be cited here. For Egypt, see *The Ancient Kingdoms of the Nile*, by Walter Fairservis, Jr. (1962, New American Library); and *Egypt to the End of the Old Kingdom*, by Cyril Aldred (1965, McGraw-Hill). For India, see *The Roots of Ancient India*, by Walter Fairservis, Jr. (1971, Macmillan); *The Birth of Indian Civilization*, by Bridget and Raymond Allchin (1968, Penguin Books); and for Southeast Asia, *The Ancient Civilization of Angkor*, by Christopher Pym (1968, New American Library). For China, see *The Archaeology of Ancient China*, by Kwang-Chih Chang (1963, Yale University Press); *The Birth of China*, by H. G. Creel (1964, Ungar); and *The Prehistory of China*, by Judith Triestman (1972, Doubleday). The standard for texts on the entire prehistory of the New World is by Gordon R. Willey, *An Introduction to American Archaeology*, 2 vols. (1966, 1971, Prentice-Hall). They ought to satisfy the most curious student. For Africa, see *The Prehistory of Africa*, by J. Desmond Clark (1970, Praeger). This is in a multivolume series, *Ancient Peoples and Places*, that covers just about every world area. There is also *The Great Ages of Man* series, published for Time-Life books, which also contains beautifully illustrated volumes on most world areas.

For the spread of the Neolithic way of life into Europe, and for later developments there, the most simplified approach is found in chapter twenty-two of *Man in Prehistory*, by Chester S. Chard (1969, McGraw-Hill). For more specialized approaches, consult *Ancient Europe*, by Stuart Piggott (1965, Aldine); and *Prehistoric Europe*, by J. D. G. Clark (1966, Stanford University Press). For various points of view on human cultural evolution, see *The Science of Man*, by Mischa Titiev (1963; Holt, Rinehart & Winston); *The Emergence of Man*, by John E. Pfeiffer (1969, Harper & Row); *The Imperial Animal*, by Lionel Tiger and Robin Fox (1972, Dell); and *The Human Imperative*, by Alexander Alland, Jr. (1972, Columbia University Press).

11

present
human diversity

At least for the last 40,000 years human beings have belonged to a single species capable of interbreeding and producing fertile offspring. Because of such a similar identity, we share the vast number of our physical traits in common.

EARLY CLASSIFICATIONS OF HUMAN BEINGS

The recognition that humankind is a unity goes back a considerable amount of time. In 1738, Linnaeus (cited for his taxonomic scheme in chapter one) assigned all world populations to the *Homo sapiens* category. He did, however, see fit to recognize also some differences below the species level. Hence, he divided man up into four varieties:

Americus	which he categorized as tenacious, contented, free, and ruled by custom. They were the red-skinned people of America.
Europaeus	which he categorized as lively, inventive, and ruled by rites. They were the white-skinned people of Europe.
Asiaticus	which he categorized as stern, haughty, stingy, and ruled by opinion. They were the yellow-skinned people of Asia.
Afer	which he categorized as cunning but slow and negligent and ruled by caprice. They were the black-skinned people of Africa.

Many scholars in his own time objected to the use by Linnaeus of mental rather than purely physical traits at this level of his taxonomy. They

174

did not, however, throw out the concept of differences, even though they
had dismissed some of his criteria. In a sense, we have been attempting
to rationalize such possible differences ever since. As many writers have
taken pains to point out, the idea of race begins by stating definitions
before any real research has been undertaken that could allow us to see
if a valid definition is really possible. We have assumed such differences
to exist and then have attempted to substantiate them, rather than first
looking for them. All race classifiers since Linnaeus have taken for
granted what remains to this day to be proven: that there are such differences. "In fact, what the anthropologist has done has been to take a
very crude eighteenth-century notion which was originally offered as no
more than an arbitrary convenience, and having erected a tremendous
terminology and methodology about it, has deceived himself in the belief that he was dealing with an objective reality" (Montagu, 1941: 246).
We shall return to this point presently.

By 1775, physical traits have become the basis for such classification, and the word *race* had been substituted for *variety.* In that year,
Blumenbach divided the human species up according to "skin color."
His grouping, with some recasting, curiously remains with us (at least
in popular imagination) at the present time. His groupings were:

Caucasian:	White
Mongolian:	Yellow
Ethiopian:	Black
American:	Red
Malayan:	Brown

If he was applauded for turning to physical traits (he included other
features as well), Blumenbach was assailed for having stressed only one
variation—and a highly variable one at that, as members of populations
are not homogeneous in this respect. Since his time, scholars have used
a great number of different physical traits, although no two classifications necessarily emphasize the same set. Hence, there has been a real
multiplication of race classifications. Some scholars have emphasized
measurements of the human skull, ascertaining the length and breadth
and converting this into a cephalic index—long, medium, and broad-
headed. This, too, like skin color, was found to differ within, as well as
between, populations. Other writers stressed such racial "criteria" as
nose width and hair form. Some writers have pointed out that even if
there are human physical differences, such differences are expressions of
many independent traits; that there are no races, only distributions of
traits that cross one another in their geographies. The more one selects
to base a classification upon, the harder the problem of delimitation be-

comes, since these traits do not associate themselves together neatly. A group set apart from another on the basis of one trait may be allied with it in terms of some other trait. At this point, scholars disagree as to whether to throw out the race concept altogether. "If one genetic character is used, it is possible to divide a species into a subspecies according to this character. If two characters are used, it may still be possible but there will be some problem populations, which . . . will be labelled composite or mixed. As the number of characters increases it becomes more nearly impossible to determine what the 'actual races really are' " (Livingstone, 1962: 279).

TRAITS COMMONLY UTILIZED IN RACE CLASSIFICATIONS

If one searches back over the various race classifications for the types of traits employed, it soon becomes apparent that three kinds of differences are represented in them (as many anthropologists have pointed out). First, many of the older classifications as well as the more recent types of racist slants have utilized learned differences such as language or religion: for example, erroneously, the French and Jewish races. Certainly, cultural differences can lead to isolation, which may enhance physical differences. And one can discriminate on such bases. But since these differences are not themselves biological, they are inappropriate for a biological taxonomy of subspecies differences. They belong only within the realm of cultural classifications.

> Race and culture act as independent variables—that is, the fact that a particular human racial type is associated with a particular kind of culture is a consequence of history rather than biology. Our culture . . . has dominated the world for nearly 500 years, and we are apt to think that "Westernized" and "civilized" mean the same thing. The Chinese emperors of the past had quite different ideas . . . Highly complex cultures . . . have been developed more or less independently by Mongoloid peoples in China, Caucasoid peoples in India and the Near East, Negroid peoples in various parts of Africa, and American Indians in Central America and Peru. (Bates, 1965: 46)

Recognition of the learned nature of these cultural differences has sometimes led to using them at least to substantiate unseen biological differences. Writers of this persuasion infer a biological basis for "inferior" cultural patterns. Not only is it dubious to rank expressions of culture, but anthropologists overwhelmingly deny any connection of this sort between culture and biology. Hence, from any view, such cultural differences should play no role in any attempt to classify mankind into races.

Besides learned differences, a second kind of character used in such attempts is a difference that is biological but very susceptible to environmental influences of various sorts: from simple exposure to the sun creating darker "skin color," to poor diet suppressing expression of "normal" body build and height. Here, problems in separating the influence of the environment on the phenotype by "guessing" the genotypic nature are often insolvable—resulting in great inexactness when such traits are used in classificatory schemes of race. This problem, in its larger scientific connection, is the nature-nurture controversy. For the "production" of phenotypes, are genes more important than the environment in which they are expressed, or vice versa?

Clearly, what is needed is a third kind of trait, one that is biological but apparently free from significant manipulation by the environment. Very few such supposed traits were employed in the past, but today, they are being used increasingly since they should reflect actual innate genetic differences, and could ultimately substantiate the validity of the concept of race. However, with these traits, too, there are difficulties. Most such variations are trivial (if real) differences and as some scholars have pointed out, it is dubious if they are entirely unrelated (uneffected) by the environment. Indeed, there may be no nonadaptive traits. It may be that we have not as yet discovered the connections.

SPECIFIC HUMAN DIFFERENCES

In order to get a better feeling for the kinds of traits employed in attempts at race classification, we can now turn to a brief examination of some specific biological traits as discussed above. In so doing, this account follows closely the presentation of a physical anthropologist (Garn, 1968) cited in the bibliographic essay at the end of the chapter.

Biological Traits

Pigmentation.   "Skin color" is due primarily to the existence of dark melanin (pigment) in various amounts in the lower layers of the skin. Only albinos lack such pigmentation, lacking the genes that produce it. The apparent skin color is mostly a result of reflections from the skin surface and from blood pigments showing through. Tanning capac-

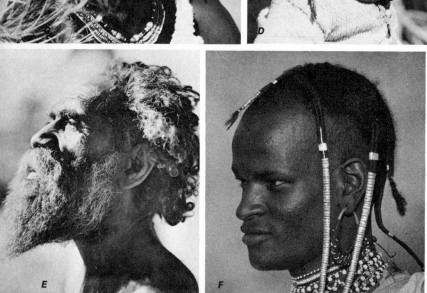

ity, as previously mentioned is also a factor. There is a great overlap between human populations with this trait, and much discussion has ensued over its adaptive value: protection against ultraviolet radiation from the sun. Skin cancer does appear more frequently in less pigmented peoples.

> Where the ultraviolet component of solar radiation is strong, as it is in the tropics, the possibility of damage to the living cells in the dermis of the human skin is always present. Melanin in the outer layer of skin absorbs the harmful ultraviolet radiation and does not allow it to penetrate the living skin. As a result, physicians have long noted the much higher frequency of tissue injury and resultant skin cancer in relatively depigmented as opposed to relatively heavily pigmented peoples . . . (Brace, 1969: 110, 111)

Today's distribution for this trait seems skewed geographically by the movement of lighter peoples caused by Neolithic and later developments as well as by the development of protective clothing.

Hair. Hair is extremely variable in the human species, differing in terms of head hair (color, form, and balding patterns) and body hair (mostly in terms of amounts). In the latter case, humans differ from very heavy among the Ainu of northern Japan to relatively little among Asiatics and American Indians. There appears to be some correspondence between hair color and skin pigmentation since the skin base is related to both—lighter pigmented peoples having brown to blond hair. The forms of head hair are highly variable, ranging from straight to curly and from coarse to thin and tuftlike. "Unlike hair color, hair form apparently has had definite adaptive significance . . . A good hair covering can serve as protection against mechanical injury to bone and that rather vital organ, the brain" (Brace, 1969: 122). Hair is also assumed to have a general sun-protective adaptive significance. Culture practices can mask one's genetic potential for this trait; only your hairdresser or roommate may know for sure!

Bones. Bones differ among human populations in terms of their relative proportions, absolute size, and mineral contents. Many of these differences appear to be a result of nurture ("you are what you eat") and

The preceding two pages illustrate diversity among humans. *A* Old woman from Tessin area (Media Features). *B* Women of Morocco (United Nations). *C* A young Swazi man (Satour). *D* Peruvian Indian mother and child (Omikron). *E* An Arunta tribesman of central Australia (Australia News and Information Bureau). *F* A Fulani man of Nigeria (Peter Buckley). *G* A Zulu matron (Satour). *H* An American girl (Omikron). *I* An elderly Mexican man (Media Features). *J* A Swiss couple (Omikron). *K* Pondo women of the Eastern Cape Province (Satour). *L* A group of Eskimos (Omikron).

are results of adaptations to differing environments. For example, long and slender arms and legs are said to occur more in desert areas, shortness in cold areas such as the Arctic. Most scholars presume this aids in the creation of body builds for heat loss or retention. The presence of extra (*Wormian*) bones along the suture lines of the skull and some variation in the construction of the hip area, are perhaps the best-documented bone traits characteristic of specific populations. Then, there are also other aspects of body build in general. Alice Brues (1959) has speculatively argued for a correlation between body type and weapons. The habitual use of a spear and its thrusting action is maximized by a long forearm and rangy body for leverage and running ability. Use of a bow and arrow, on the other hand, utilizes energy supplied almost exclusively by the arms—requiring short forearms and broad, well-muscled shoulders. Here again, we must be aware of the role of cultural modification of our biology.

Teeth.   Here, there are a great number of recognized differences. These variations occur in terms of size, form, and occasional congenital absence. For example, Asiatic populations have a higher degree of incidence of "shovel-shaped" incisors, fused third-molar roots, etc., than other world populations.

Growth Patterns. Patterns of growth and development (*maturation*) also differ among human populations: for example, age of calsification of wrist bones, suture closure in the skull, and eruption of the permanent teeth. Although some of these traits seem quite clearly the result of genetics, others are probably influenced a good deal by dietary differences in environment.

Intelligence.   This has been a supposed trait of human variation over which great concern and controversy has developed—today as in the past. Most of the more recent declarations have their genesis in "intelligence" test-score differences, which rather consistently have put the averages of some groups above or below "standard" ranges. Generally speaking, in the past, American Negro children and those of some other minorities have fared poorly. Most social scientists have pointed out a number of objections that they feel invalidate such test results. Such tests essentially measure academic performance in terms of middle-class values (book learning); they place a stress on enriched early socialization patterns not available to minorities, so they not really test innate intelligence—only what should have been learned at a given point in time. "Such tests do not purport to measure many of the skills and abilities that the term intelligence commonly suggests. Intelligence tests, moreover, are never culture-free. They measure in relation to a particular cultural background . . ." (Garn, 1968: 114). For example, how does one measure the kind of intelligence demanded for street-corner survival in a black ghetto? Still other scholars have determined that the attitudes of tester and test taker, too, have real influences on the results. Evidence has demonstrated that blacks perform more poorly under white stimulus, and that the attitude of the teacher can also change the results. And, of course, in application to humankind as a whole, such tests are "culture bound"; they are not instruments capable of meaningful cross-cultural applications. How does one devise a fair test for both Bushmen and Bostonian? If based upon recognition of edible foods in one's environment, the former would easily score highest. So, it has generally been the consensus that there is no way to equitably test intelligence, especially since it is hard to agree on a definition of this concept in the first place. "Conclusions attributing a genetic basis to intelligence differences between groups are, to say the least, premature" (Alland, 1971: 195).

Other Traits

In addition to traits such as the above, which are old standbys in attempts at race classification, newer traits in either discovery or implementation are now becoming common. Among these are such traits as the ability to taste PTC (cited in chapter three), the excretion of chemical substances (such as beta-amino-isobutyric acid in the urine of some Asiatics), and blood types.

Blood Type.   Blood type is often basic to attempts at race classification. The four basic blood types (factors) A, B, AB, and O generally have some possessors in all populations and are of simple known inheritance, being governed by three genetic variations. Hence, by sampling, we can discover proportion differences. For example, some Amerindian populations are about 90 percent type O, whereas in parts of Africa, the proportion falls to about 30 percent. Type B is high in Asia and Africa, but infrequent among Amerindians. There are also other blood factors (e.g., the Rh factor) which help anthropologists to assess the distribution of such human variations.

Diseases.   Finally, among other characters, is the relation between populations and the incidence of certain diseases presumed to be hereditary. Some such diseases are very common among some peoples: for example, sickle-cell anemia among blacks, as previously cited. Perhaps the classic example is kuru, a disease apparently limited to restricted

Australian Information Service   E. Baitel/Omikron

How does one devise a fair intelligence test which can be applied from culture to culture?

areas of New Guinea among the Fore people. It appears to be a hereditary neurological disorder, the gene responsible being kept proportionate to normal genes by the execution of sorcerers blamed for the death of the afflicted individual. So, each time a carrier dies, a noncarrier leaves the gene pool as well. Since at least one scholar has suggested the possibility that this disease may in fact be a virus passed on by brain cannibalism, we should remember that even in the case of disease distributions, cultural influences may still be involved.

DEFINITION OF RACE

Given the history of the concept of race, problems with the notion itself, and with the traits commonly associated with it, is there any safe approach to such a concept? Clearly, none of the existing classifications are worth memorization by beginning students in anthropology. Is there a workable definition that does not presuppose what it attempts to examine? One approach is to simply state the limiting features of an operational concept of race. It presupposes a human population. It also

183

presupposes some degree of inbreeding or common genetic history that is manifested—even if with less than complete fidelity—in the phenotypes of that population. If race is anything, it would seem to have to conform to the above restrictions. The last part of the definition reminds us of the genotype-phenotype relationship. If there are human differences, they must be considered in genotypic terms, as innate genetic variations. Unfortunately, we are generally limited at present to discovery of these on the phenotype level, with all its problems of nurture. So, if differences do exist, it is in this difficult context that we must seek for them.

The middle part of the "definition" reminds us again of our previous discussion of isolation in fostering change. A population becomes distinctive over time in comparison to others by such isolation, either geographic and/or social, which causes inbreeding—"keeping your genes to home." If sufficient isolation and inbreeding occur, some genetic distinctiveness may come to characterize such a population. Finally, the first concept in the "definition," that of population, can mean a number of things and we must be careful how we use it. In one sense, it can refer to *microraces*, relatively small and tightly inbred populations that do exhibit (potentially) a fair amount of genetic distinctiveness: for example, the Polar Eskimos who were extremely isolated from other Eskimo groups. It can be used to designate *local races*, larger but localized populations or ethnic groups, which show less "uniqueness" but are readily perceptible from other such groups: for example, the Navaho Indians. Finally, this concept may refer to *geographical races*, rather abstract aggregations of populations inhabiting (now or in the recent past) major world areas and having superficial similarities within themselves as opposed to similarly grouped populations: for example, American Indians in general. "For a geographical race is by definition, a geographically-delimited collection of similar races . . . . Within each geographical race the individual populations resemble each other more or less. In the aggregate, resemblances within geographical races are far greater than those between them" (Garn, 1968: 14, 15). This biggest unit derives its isolation mostly from major geographic barriers, whereas smaller populations are isolated by either geography or more social causes—language or religion or even simple biological distance ("marrying the girl next door"). Moreover, each sized population (race) is a construct designed to relate to different problems relative to humankind—the larger grouping perhaps for gross evolutionary history, the smaller more for the investigation of the mechanisms of differentiation. Certainly, if the concept of race does have validity, the differences it suggests will be discovered on the level of the micro-race population.

SUMMARY .

1. The concept that groups of human beings differ from one another goes back a considerable amount of time. Linnaeus postulated four major groupings of humans and in 1775, Blumenbach suggested five human races which he based upon skin color. Little agreement has existed ever since on the exact number of races and their determining criteria.

2. Three types of racial traits have historically been recognized: that based, inappropriately, on nonbiological learned characteristics; that based on biological traits that are greatly susceptible to environmental influences of various sorts; and that based on the few, if any, biological traits completely free from such manipulations. The last would be the best to employ in ascertaining the validity of the concept of race.

3. Traits commonly employed in race classifications are skin pigmentation, color of hair, bone and dental structure, growth patterns, level of intelligence, and variations in blood type.

4. If significant human differences exist, they are based on genotypic variations brought about by isolation (caused by physical and/or cultural barriers). Variations may be considered on a number of levels: geographical, local, and microgeographical (the latter being the most significant for the race concept).

REFERENCES FOR FURTHER READING

There are a number of reading options on race open to the beginning student. One might first consult any of the general texts and readers on physical anthropology previously cited. Then, one can turn to more specialized volumes. Out of these, I have found the following most instructive: *Human Races*, by Stanley M. Garn (1968, Thomas); *Human Diversity*, by Alexander Alland, Jr. (1971, Columbia University Press); *The Kinds of Mankind*, by Morton Klass and Hal Hellman (1971, Lippincott); and *Man's Most Dangerous Myth. The Fallacy of Race*, by Ashley Montagu (1964, World). Three excellent readers are *The Concept of Race*, edited by Ashley Montagu, (1969, Collier-Macmillan)—the quotes from Brace are from this text; *The Biological and Social Meaning of Race*, edited by Richard Osborne (1971, Freeman); and *Science and the Concept of Race*, edited by Margaret Mead and others (1968, Columbia University Press). For a view on the evolution of separate racial lines of humanity—one that has been hotly contested in some of the works cited above—see *The Origin of Races* and *The Living Races of Man*, both by Carleton S. Coon (1962, 1965, Knopf). References in chapter eleven not covered above are *Man in Nature*, by Marston Bates (1965, Prentice-Hall); "The Spearman and the Archer," by Alice Brues in *American Anthropologist* 61 (1959): 457–69; "On the Non-Existence of Human Races," by Frank B. Livingstone, in *Current Anthropology* 3 (1962): 279; and "The Concept of Race in the Human Species in the Light of Genetics," by Ashley Montagu, in *The Journal of Heredity* 23 (1941): 243–47.

12

the future
of the human
species

The human species has come a long way during the course of our more than two million years of physical and cultural evolution, and yet such a time span is very much shorter than that of many other creatures, many of which are now extinct. Where are we to go from here? How many millenia do we have remaining as a species? What kind of creatures are we apt to become? An overwhelming number of scientists from many diverse fields of study are now warning us that the future of humankind may be measured in centuries or perhaps even decades. And they are arguing that we must reorient our thinking.

> The earth is a spaceship. We should have known this for the past two thousand years, and in a sense we have—in a coldly intellectual sense, as a mere fact of physics, the human implications of which almost completely eluded us. Before we can make "decisions for survival" wisely we must see these implications clearly. We must feel in our bones the inescapable truth that we live on a spaceship. From now on no major political decision can safely be made without taking into consideration this basic fact. (Hardin, 1972: 16)

In "leaving" nature and subjecting it to our will, we have in their estimation set certain processes into being that, ultimately, may cause our own extinction. Nature always gets even.[1] In chapter ten, we discussed our increasing reliance upon culture and natural resources. It is the purpose of this brief section to suggest other difficulties in the areas of overpopulation, unrestrained technology, and genetic change.

[1]If we destroy ecological balance, nature will strive to restore it. And since the "concern" of nature is the totality of things, humans may well be the "losers" in the process.

188

In subjecting nature to his will, man may be causing his own extinction.

POPULATION

World population today has become an ever-increasing problem. In the past, human beings were not very numerous. Estimates by one scholar (Deevy, 1960) suggest only one million people in Middle Paleolithic times, perhaps three and a half million in the Upper Paleolithic, and, with geographic expansion opportunities, about five and a half million in the Mesolithic. With the food producing revolution, however, by the time of Christ, we are estimated to number about one-hundred and thirty-three million—a geometric jump forward that in intensified form plagues us today. Simply put, world population doubles every so many years and the time necessary to accomplish this is rapidly decreasing. Today every eight seconds, a new American is born, and people are living longer all the time, as well as having longer periods of childbearing potential. As numerous writers have put it, it took until 1850 to have one billion people in the world, then one hundred years for the second billion, and thirty-one years for the third (reached by 1981). By the year 2000, the estimates exceed six billion people, with a population density of forty-six per square kilometer (as opposed to about one per square kilometer at the time of Christ). Such figures, however, inexact as they may be, put the problem of overpopulation in perspective. We will soon have too many people, and they will be hungry. After all, people consume things. Our one-every-eight-seconds American, among other things in his lifetime, requires over 10,000 pounds of meat, 56 million gallons of water, and 9,000 pounds of wheat. So it is not simply the number of people or their density and overcrowding that is the

189

problem, but the tremendous strain they place on resources. It is not just culture but ultimately humans themselves that use them up. And we humans seem difficult to convince of the dangers of overpopulation; we seem reluctant to curb our expanding populations. In fact, modern medical practices and other developments have even contributed to the population explosion by prolonging life.

CONSUMPTION

As pointed out, the more people, the faster the consumption of remaining resources and the less of them available for each individual. To avoid this, we place even heavier emphasis on technology, with potentially disastrous results. In agriculture, we go from mixed crops to mono-culture, a single crop over a large area to increase returns. This delights insect pests and results in the use of chlorinated hydrocarbons like DDT to control them and chemical additives to increase fertility (but not to re-store the productivity of the soil). All these either pollute the environment and/or end up as harmful residues in man himself at the end of the food chain. Again, some writers claim that the teeming numbers of the human species are using up oxygen faster than it is being produced in the air, especially since whole areas of the world are being stripped of

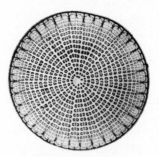

The diatom, a microscopic form of algae and an important source of food for all marine life, is in danger of being killed by various types of water pollution.

Omikron

their forests. The rest of our oxygen is produced by microscopic or-ganisms floating in the oceans, which may be in danger from various types of water pollution. Industrial air pollution itself, of course, also helps use up oxygen. Indeed, there seems to be very little in modern technology that does not pollute the environment in some fashion. So we have air, water, and food pollution, and we are rapidly using up some natural resources and contaminating others. We are overbreeding and overtechnologizing, and if the ecologists are right, we will soon pay for it. We are grossly negligent in our use of such natural resources that are (temporarily) in rather plentiful supply, treating them with a cavalier attitude that seems to say we can never run out of these things. Take, for example, our wasteful and unreflective use of water.

The flush of a toilet costs three to four gallons.
A shower bath uses ten to twenty gallons.
A washing machine cycle consumes between twenty and thirty gallons.
A leak in a toilet bowl wastes thirty-five gallons a day.
Sprinkling an 8,000-square-foot lawn accounts for 30,000 gallons a year . . .
It takes twenty-five gallons of water to make you one gallon of beer . . .
And 75,000 gallons of water to make a ton of steel.
Every ton of newsprint takes 188,500 gallons. (Rienow, 1970: 64)

Lacking many natural checks on population, such as predation by another species, and up to now possessing the technology to overcome others, such as starvation and weather, we have indeed overbred as a species. However, every population increase eventually gets curbed or leveled out; when humans have run out of living space, food and raw materials, when our overdeveloped technology creeps to a halt and we have poisoned the air, waters, and ourselves, we will be checked indeed —by our own stupidity and shortsightedness. No wonder many biologists today are pressing for birth control and population-regulation programs. Many admit, however, that we may be too late to save some world areas.

POSSIBLE GENETIC DIFFICULTIES

In addition to the strains and stresses caused our environment by the population and accompanying technological expansion, there are also genetic difficulties that may impair the continuing process of human evolution. Researchers have abundantly demonstrated that radiation striking a chemical molecule can alter it from its original condition to a different (abnormal) state. Hence, radiation and many other modern "benefits" or substances can affect our sex cells and genetic code, given the chemical nature of the gene. In other words, these things possess mutagenic qualities and can alter our heredity. Since radiation is perhaps the most obvious of these, our discussion here will focus solely upon it but modern drugs (LSD) and other comforts (caffeine in coffee) are thought to possess similar potentialities.

Radiation has a number of sources. Some of these are natural: in cosmic rays which reach the earth from space and in substances in rocks and soils. We also take in minute quantities with our food and water. These radiation sources have always been with us; it is sources of the man-made variety that pose the real threat to our genetic future. These include atomic fallout (some from actually breathing of the particles but most in contaminated foods, etc.) from bomb testing, from waste disposal of nuclear power plants (a great threat in the future since we may have to turn to these to service the power needs of expanding populations and industry), and X-ray radiation (chiefly from medical and industrial sources). Although this last source is perhaps the most terrifying, it seems to be the least objected to in the current ecological literature. That X-ray sources can cause mutation has been demonstrated over and over again by geneticists working with fruit flies. In one case, using comparable-sized groups, one population receiving a brief exposure recorded 143 lethal mutations as opposed to only 5 in the "normal" control group. Other studies reflect similar results. We are not insects but heredity is heredity. Some such results must occur in ourselves. We are not some chosen species that is chemically immune! What is frightening here is that there is no safe dosage for radiation; no matter how small the amount one is exposed to, some mutation could result. Apparently the sex cells are less resistant to damage than body cells, which do require a given amount (about 500 roentgens) for radiation illness to occur. Further, radiation in the sex cells is a cumulative process, building up over time like cigarette tars on lung tissue. So small doses over time can build up to the level of a single but more intensive exposure. It goes without saying, of course, that all this genetic damage is unseen and may be transmitted to offspring. Being unseen, it is difficult to gauge the present levels of our genetic difficulties, but some writers have proposed that perhaps 42 percent of the population of the United States carries defective genes that render their possessors less fit. And, our exposure to such radiation sources is just beginning: they are so useful! Numerical estimates credit 4,000 to 400,000 infant and fetal deaths in the United States to fallout alone (Commoner, 1971).

So we have, potentially, an ever-increasing rate of mutation. In addition, natural selection, which preserved those that were beneficial and culled out those that were not, no longer operates as fully upon man as in the past. Ethics of mercy and advances in medicine and in public health preserve genetic types that formerly would not have survived to reproduce themselves. Thus, human developments alter still another natural process. Some scientists have estimated that up to 90 percent of the individuals who would not have survived during Paleolithic times, now survive to pass on their genes.

It is probably a considerable under-estimate to say that half of the detrimental genes which under primitive conditions would have met genetic extinction, today survive and are passed on. On the basis of this conservative estimate we can calculate that in some 10 generations, or 250 to 300 years, the accumulated genetic effect would be much like that from exposure of a population to a sudden heavy dose of 200 to 400 roentgens, such as was received by the most heavily exposed survivors of Hiroshima. If the techniques of saving life in our civilization continue to advance, the accumulation of mutant genes will rise to ever higher levels. (Muller, 1955: 9)

To make such a point concrete, some scholars discuss the case of retinoblastoma (eye cancer of children). This disease, without treatment, is generally fatal prior to the opportunity for genetic transmission. With medical technology existing today, about 70 percent of the possessors of this trait survive and hence have the possibility to pass this defect on to their offspring. Therefore, there is an ever-increasing number of mutant genes and less and less are being culled out by natural selection. It is a situation one scholar (Muller) has called our genetic load: a load of defective and disadvantageous genes of ever greater number and seriousness that is being successively bequeathed to each human generation.

As stated above, we can't see what damage we carry. Moreover, such mutants are mostly carried as recessives and may not actually appear in the phenotypes for many generations. When they do appear, some writers feel they may represent a level of species damage that is beyond repair. Scholars have suggested that this making of our genetic load is made even more complete due to the modern decrease in isolating mechanisms. Our more random mating procedures may make all recessives more rare in the phenotype. But when population eventually stabilizes, as the initial part of this chapter suggests it must, they will again start coming to the level of surface recognition. What an irony if we were to finally recognize the dangers of population, limit it, and then discover that we are beyond hope anyway. Will we have to spend most of our time, energy, and effort in the future just attempting to perpetuate our species? One final point may be suggested. As stated in the chapter on evolution, a broad range of variation is valuable. During the course of the spread of modern technology and its possessors, there has been a trend toward greater outgroup mating, towards "homogenizing" world population. At the same time, many small primitive groupings have been, or are in the process of being, extinguished. A few writers have suggested that this has narrowed the range of human variation to its tightest dimensions in our evolutionary history; certainly, the range is narrower than at the time of our beginnings. They go on to suggest that this makes our future possible ranges of adaptability overly slim, and if we ever have to depend more on biology and less on culture, we may be doomed as a species. "No one knows if a more heterozygous human population would in fact be 'better' in some sense, but any other kind of solution would literally paint us into an evolutionary corner" (Wills, 1970: 107).

POSSIBLE SOLUTIONS

What are we to do in the face of these genetic difficulties? Possibly nothing. Yet humankind is the one species that does know of its evolutionary past and can think of its future. So it is certain that sooner or later we will make some attempts in this direction. In fact, some solutions have already been proposed or discussed as future possibilities. Three major types of these exist, and in concluding this chapter, we can briefly take note of them.

Euthenics

Euthenics proposes working with our genetic heritage as is, by creating environments in which its best potentials can be realized. This means working with the nurture aspects involved in phenotype creation—nutrition, sanitation, health practices, education, etc. Certainly it is difficult to deny the morality of this view, but it is no solution to the genetic problems. Not only is it a cover-up, one we (regrettably) can ill afford if we are to deal realistically with our "bad genes" but as previously explained, it can even lead to an increase of the problem; more people will be enabled to pass on such traits.

Eugenics

Eugenics is the attempt to work with and alter the gene frequencies themselves. It can be applied two ways:

1. Positive—urging persons judged to be sound genetically to reproduce.
2. Negative—stopping persons judged to be unsound genetically from reproducing.

Eugenical measures may be positive or negative. Positive eugenics programs urge people who are regarded as carriers of desirable gene combinations to undertake the responsibilities of parenthood. Apart

from propaganda designed to influence public opinion in desirable
directions, positive eugenics favors economic measures which would
ease the burdens of maternity and child care ... More enthusiasm has
been shown in many places for negative eugenics, which urges elimi-
nation of undesirable genes by discouraging or making it impossible
for persons who show the effects of such genes to have children. Since
voluntary abstention from parenthood may be difficult, "sterilization"
for individuals who are likely to have severe hereditary defects is
recommended. (Dunn and Dobzhansky, 1960: 85, 86)

In either case, the idea is to eliminate the unsound genes by selective
genetic transmission: swamping out the bad genes or actually removing
them. There are numerous difficulties with programs of this sort for
humans even though they have worked well in selective breeding experiments with plants and other animals. What are the criteria and who
determines them? History (in Nazi Germany) has already provided one
tragic example of negative eugenics. Recessives are difficult to weed
out (since they can't be seen or their occurrence always predicted),
so the qualities objected to would not be completely eliminated. Even
negative eugenics is basically a one-generation proposition. Moreover,
what if someone has both "good and bad" traits? Even some dominant
traits that are bad (i.e., diabetes) require just the right environment in
which to develop and might be passed over by the "board of genetic
control."

Biological Engineering

This as yet remains a solution of the future. Biological engineering
basically refers to the presumed eventual ability of human beings to
interfere directly in the hereditary process; to change and remake their
own genetic potential. It is the logical outcome of our feelings that the
first two solutions are of no real help as much as an expression of our
confidence in the growth of biological knowledge. In a kind of science-
fiction way, it is suggested, among other things, that we will be able
to insert genetic material into the sex cells, direct radiation to a mutant
gene to restore it back to normal, and perhaps synthesize our own
molecules to DNA to create any desired result. Although this all sounds
like something out of *Brave New World,* it is apparently closer to becoming a reality than most people think. A recent book (Taylor, 1968)
clearly points this out. And, it will be remembered, we humans have
seldom failed in the past to use a new bit of technology after it became
available. Is this the ultimate answer? It certainly answers the problem
the way we humans of late have always answered our problems: using
technology to solve the problems created by technology. But there

Lorraine Mullaney

An archaeological site in the making?

remain significant questions of ethics here, as with regular eugenics. A recent article dealing with genetic engineering lists ten ethical considerations, the first of which bears repeating.

> The ethical questions raised by the possibilities implicit in genetic engineering are no less fundamental than the issues of free choice, the quality of life, the community of man, and the future of man himself . . .
> . . . if we are to engage in any eugenics . . . we must confront three vital questions that pervade this entire subject: what traits are to be considered desirable? Who is to make that determination? When in the course of human development will the choice be made? These questions cannot be underestimated in their importance to the future of man, particularly when we are considering biological alternatives that might not be reversible. (Tunny and Levine, 1972: 24)

Our species has come a long way during the course of its evolutionary history. It has conquered nature, expanded its numbers, and developed a fantastic technology. In the process, it may have conquered itself, sown the seeds for its own destruction along with those of agriculture in the Neolithic period. Maybe we should have remained a hunter-gatherer, remained a part of nature. Early humans came out of the woods, so to speak, but we are back there again. Can humans, with like determination and resourcefulness, do so a second time? Time will tell, but it may well be running out for humans as a living species. As a recent author brilliantly summarizes this situation:

> Yet man is the only product of biological evolution who knows that he has evolved and is evolving further. He should be able to replace the blind force of natural selection by conscious direction . . . It is as certain that such direction will be needed as it is questionable whether

196

man is ready to provide it. He is unready because his knowledge of his own nature and its evolution is insufficient; because a vast majority of people are unaware of the necessity of facing the problem; and because there is so wide a gap between the way people actually live and the values and ideals to which they pay lip service. (Dobzhansky, 1960: 7)

We shall see.

SUMMARY

1. The human species has made incredible "progress" as a form of living creature, but in subjecting nature to our will we may have limited our own species' future in terms of overpopulation, unrestrained technology, expenditure of resources, and pollution.

2. In addition, radiation and other mutagenic agents pose a hazard to our genetic constitutions. The rate of mutation and the number of disadvantageous genes has increased while the operation of natural selection to counter these has diminished. The result is genetic load—our ever increasing number of dubious genes is bequeathed to successive generations.

3. Solutions to such difficulties are not completely effective and are productive of problems in their own right; these solutions include euthenics, eugenics, and biological engineering (the last being only in its preliminary developmental stages).

REFERENCES FOR FURTHER READING

The number of excellent books on ecological topics and the future of the human species has grown enormously in the past decade—and continues to increase at a rate that precludes anyone but a specialist in this area keeping up. Any brief bibliography is highly selective, but a few volumes I have personally found useful include the following: *Population, Resources, Environment*, by Paul and Anne Ehrlich (1970, Freeman); *The Population Bomb*, by Paul Ehrlich (1968, Ballantine); *The Closing Circle*, by Barry Commoner (1971, Bantam Books); *Science and Survival*, by Barry Commoner (1966, Viking Books); and perhaps the best quick introduction of all, *Man Against His Environment*, by Robert Rienow (1970, Ballantine Books). Two volumes written by Garrett Hardin are must reading inasmuch as he writes so beautifully— *Nature and Man's Fate* (1959, New American Library) and *Exploring*

New Ethics for Survival (1972, Viking Press). Three general texts dealing with future possibilities from a wide series of perspectives are *The Unheavenly City*, by Edward Banfield (1968: Little, Brown); *The Crisis of Survival*, by the editors of *The Progressive* and others (1970, Morrow); and *The Futurists*, edited by Alvin Toffler (1972, Random House).

For the problem of "bad genes" in our future, see *Heredity, Race and Society*, by L. C. Dunn and T. Dobzhansky (1960, New American Library); "Radiation and Human Mutation," by H. J. Muller (1955, Freeman), *Scientific American* reprint no. 29; "Genetic Load," by Christopher Wills, *Scientific American*, March (1970): 98–107; "The Present Evolution of Man," by T. Dobzhansky (1960, Freeman), *Scientific American* reprint no. 609; "Genetic Engineering," by John Tunney and Meldon Levine, in *Saturday Review of Science* (1972): pp. 23–28; and *Genetic Load*, by Bruce Wallace (1970, Prentice-Hall). Two excellent sources on the guidance of future human evolution are *The Biological Time Bomb*, by Gordon Rattray Taylor (1968, World); and "Man Into Superman," *Time*, April (1971). A useful paper dealing with population growth is "The Human Population," by Edward S. Deevy, Jr. (1960, Freeman), *Scientific American* reprint no. 608.

TWO
CULTURAL DIVERSITY

13

the nature of
cultural
behavior

The term culture has appeared in many chapters in the first part of this book. Before passing on to the variety of cultural behaviors exhibited by humankind it is first necessary to attempt serious definition of this concept. It is also valuable to suggest the various dimensions of such behavior and to show why and how it is that the anthropologist generally selects primitive societies for such information. It is the task of the present chapter to define and discuss the concept of culture.

THE CONCEPT OF CULTURE

On first hearing the word culture many students feel already aware of its significance. Culture is a set of refined behaviors, a case of having acquired the right tastes in books, food, and music: it is being cultured. In this popular sense, culture refers to behaviors that not everyone has but that, in a value-laden sense, they ought to strive towards. In such a usage, there are those who are cultured and those who are culturally deprived. Although it is possible to consider certain behaviors as "better or higher" than others—especially if they are your behaviors—the concept of culture in this narrow sense (encompassing only certain behaviors) is not grounds for the more formal anthropological conception. For anthropologists, the term *culture* includes behaviors shared in general— in light of the above, all books, food, habits, and music (from the Beatles to Brahms). In this sense, all humans have culture by fact of their very existence as part of humanity.

Although anthropologists are in agreement as to the universality of culture in this sense, we are not all in agreement as to how best it ought to be defined. This failure is typical of social scientists in general; the more overreaching and important concepts are the most difficult to define to everyone's satisfaction. Ask a sociologist to define society or

202

a psychologist, the term personality. Not that we haven't tried. Hundreds of formal anthropological definitions of the term *culture* exist. Before attempting to add to the confusion with a compromise definition, perhaps a brief presentation of a few others would be valuable as a background.

DEFINITIONS OF CULTURE

One of the earliest definitions was by E. B. Tylor (a founding father in anthropology) who is often quoted in this connection. He stated that "Culture . . . is that complex whole which includes knowledge, belief, art, morals, law, custom, and any other capabilities and habits acquired by man as a member of society" (Tylor, 1958: 1). This "laundry list" of behaviors and the fact that we are characterized by them by virtue of being born as human beings again suggests the universal nature of the concept. They are behaviors that we possess and that other primates do not. Listing such traits, however, does not really give us a feeling for their unique qualities. A second definition stresses that culture could be equated with all those human behaviors that are transmitted from generation to generation by learning. This suggests the non-biological nature of much of human behavior as that which makes us humans unique. It also suggests, as many different writers have pointed out, that such behaviors are super-organic; that is, they exist over and above any single human being. They are passed on as though they had a separate existence (like the English language), even though they are ex-

Although we tend to think of culture as something to acquire and to strive toward (left), to anthropologists, culture is a universal concept which includes all shared behaviors.

United Nations   American Museum of Natural History

pressed by and through human beings. One generation of humans is gone but the "cultural melody" lingers on in the next.

Still another definition of culture has been advanced by a sociologist, Talcott Parsons, who (with the perspective of his discipline) suggests that culture is all a part of a system of action. For him, culture results from social interaction in the past, and as it proves useful or necessary, it becomes a guide for further human behavior. This indicates the conception of culture as a normative system, the system of agreements we humans have built up and validated.

ASPECTS OF CULTURE

Components

Such definitions of culture could be repeated almost endlessly. Yet if one compares any great number of them, it is possible to arrive at a compromise in terms of what sort of behaviors are included as culture and as to what qualities are connected to them. As John Honigmann has pointed out (1959), three components go into making up culture: ideas, activities, and artifacts. *Ideas* are thoughts, beliefs, feelings, and rules: for example, aversion to incest, the Holy Ghost, and food-sharing desires among relatives. These may be directly a part of some behavior, the underlying cause, or even by-products of it. *Activities* are the dynamic component of culture: what people do as opposed to what they believe or feel. Such might include the act of punishing incestuous behavior, sacrifice in religion, and the celebration of Christmas. Finally the *artifacts* are the man-made products of the ideas and activities: the knife that kills the incestuous pair, the altar for sacrifice, the pot that contains the meat for the feast, and even the meat if taken from a domestic animal.

Now, of course, there are activities, ideas, and artifacts that are not culture. Put crudely, not all of human "feces behavior" is culture; some is purely physiological in cause, act, and result. And yet since this is not normally accomplished in public, it does involve some aspects of culture.

Qualities

So we have to say that culture comprises ideas, activities, and artifacts that have certain qualities. At least five such qualities have been emphasized in anthropological definitions. One quality of culture is that it is *learned.* Ideas, activities, and artifacts are not acquired by genetic hereditary processes; they are not like brown eyes, five fingers and toes, or the capacity for brachiation. Culture is not part of our innate bio-logical equipment, but is learned in the process of growing up and takes the form of extragenetic behavior. As we saw in the first half of this book, it has become the most important part of our total behavior even though some of our behavior is not cultural or is only partly so.

> We are, in sum, incomplete or unfinished animals who complete or finish ourselves through culture ... Beavers build dams, birds build nests ... on the basis of forms of learning that rest predominantly on the instructions encoded in their genes and evoked by appropriate patterns of external stimuli ... But men build dams or shelters ... under the guidance of instructions encoded in flow charts and blueprints ... conceptual structures molding formless talents.
>
> The boundary between what is inately controlled and what is cul-turally controlled in human behavior is an ill-defined and wavering one. Some things are ... entirely controlled intrinsically: we need no more cultural guidance to learn how to breathe than a fish needs to learn how to swim. Others are ... largely cultural ... why some men put their trust in centralized planning and others in the free market ... Almost all complex human behavior is, of course, the vector outcome of the two. Our capacity to speak is surely innate; our capacity to speak English is surely cultural. (Geertz, 1968: 27)

So if ideas, activities, and artifacts are cultural, they must be learned behaviors or at least partly conditioned by learning.

A second quality of culture is that it is *transmitted*. Being ac-quired by learning, cultural ideas, activities, and artifacts do pass from generation to generation as a super-organic inheritance. Some of this is accomplished by social learning—by imitating the acts of others—but most of it is transmitted more directly by human language, which is itself a part of culture and seemingly the most important part. Because humans possess language, we can be told what to do and when and where, words becoming for us genelike in producing behavior: "This is how to make a stone tool, this is why we avoid close relatives in marriage." Not only are we given our social heritage through such transmissions, but unlike that of our biology, this heritage is bestowed in a cumulative fashion. There are more ideas, activities, and artifacts added to culture behavior each generation (although more in some societies than in others). The sum total of such behaviors, then, tends to increase over time. This, at least potentially, increases the cultural behavioral repertoire of a human group. As one writer has aptly sum-marized this transmitted quality:

> Since culture is not innate, it must be acquired anew by each individual and transmitted from generation to generation. It is this transmission which insures the continuity of culture in spite of the impermanence of the individual.

The continuity of human culture is insured by its transmission from generation to generation.

United Nations

But culture is not only continuous; it is also cumulative. New inventions and acculturations from without are added to the stream of culture in each generation, and in most cases the new does not displace the old. Thus we still retain wine in spite of the later invention of distilled spirits, and both in spite of Prohibition. The stream of culture, the social heritage, thus shows a definite tendency to grow richer and fuller with the passage of time. (Murdock, 1969: 13A)

A third quality of culture is that it is *social*. This means that the ideas, activities, and artifacts are shared in common by the members of a society or group. They have become socially standardized. If such behaviors are to be useful and gratifying, if they are to help humans in gaining ends and satisfying needs, then it becomes obvious that at least in general we must be parties to the same cultural ways. In the absence of such agreements (everyone speaking his own language), our extragenetic behaviors would be of dubious value in taking us away from a purely organic level of existence. In this sense, then, cultural behaviors are a "team-player" phenomenon creating shared expectations and results. It should also be pointed out, to give the sociologist his due, that we come not only to share our culture in common, but we also validate it as we behave it. Since culture is extragenetic, its transmission is not automatic but depends on the willingness of humans to give and receive it. We can, at least potentially, alter ideas, activities, and artifacts if they no longer give us satisfaction. We can "mutate" them prior to their transmission and can reject them afterwards. We may dislike aspects of our biology but are rather powerless to alter much of it. There is no "generation gap" for our biological behaviors. So cultural behaviors are shared by groups of people and depend on those groups for validity and transmission, even if we don't always exercise that privilege.

A fourth quality of culture is that it is *adaptive*. Cultural behaviors permit humans to fit into and adjust to their environments; for example, by clothing. In our own society, culture has even developed to the point where it permits us to fit the environment to ourselves: to air-condition the desert and heat the arctic. As was pointed out in chapter three, the more generalized and variable the organism, the greater the survival chances over the long run. As has also been pointed out, biologically we are very generalized organisms. The fact that we have cultural behaviors to add to our biology gives us further advantages in adaptation. The cumulative and social nature of our ideas, activities, and artifacts gives us a tremendous potential source of variability in adaptation, permitting us to specialize for the short run as well as maintain generalization. We can also borrow such potential from different groups if their cultural behaviors are found to have survival value: sort of a hyperdeveloped gene flow but with tremendously magnified results. This does not mean that all human societies have opted to employ the flexibility of cultural behavior or have even been aware of its potential. Culture for humans is rather like water for fish, so omnipresent and important that we are hardly aware of its significance. Yet consciously or not, humans more and more have adapted to their environments in cultural ways rather

Cultural behaviors permit humans to fit into and adjust to their environments. Shown here are a New England seaside village and a Moslem castle in the Jordan Desert.

Gabriele Wunderlich   United Press International

than biologically and, in so doing, have gained a maneuverability and plasticity in adaptation unchallenged by other forms of life.

The last quality of cultural behavior to be discussed here is *integration*. For any one society or group, the various ideas, activities, and artifacts are not only shared, but the arrangements of these more or less fit together and interlock to form a consistent whole: for example, the technology with social and political patterns. Certainly, the various behaviors we observe are different kinds of cultural expressions and are behaved for different reasons and purposes. Nonetheless, they can be viewed as a rather patterned general response to the problem of existence. In other words, the tools available, the social behaviors associated with their use, concepts of ownership, concepts of leadership, and even religion must in some degree be interrelated if the whole culture is to be effective. It seems a truism that a society cannot possess a set of tools if it lacks the social system to properly manipulate them and vice versa. Although integration is never anywhere near complete (culture is not a closed system), changes in some aspects of culture generally necessitate changes in other areas. This consideration is explored further in the last chapter of this book. In any event, viewing the totality of cultural behavior of any human society suggests that such behaviors do form a more or less discernable and integrated whole. There is a "fit" between the various aspects of their culture.

A COMPROMISE DEFINITION OF CULTURE

We have seen that culture is composed of three basic phenomena and these are seen by most writers to have (among others) five basic qualities. In this sense, a short compromise definition of culture can be offered as follows. *Culture* is the learned, transmitted, and integrated ideas, activities, and artifacts that are adaptive and that depend upon human social interaction for their existence. Such a definition is as good and as bad as other such definitions but it does have the value of rather comprehensively reminding us of the "guts" of anthropological employment of this term.

Before passing on to various other aspects of cultural behavior, there is one remaining general notion of importance. One of the most persistent arguments that preoccupy anthropologists is whether our culture concept represents reality or if it is merely the abstraction we have made of it: a way of thinking about and categorizing behavior. If the latter case is true, then culture is not behavior but merely a way to understand and describe it. Certainly, a stone axe or a book is real enough, but what about a marriage rule, a kinship status, or a belief in witches?

In this sense, perhaps culture can be considered both abstraction and behavior. Possibly, it is simply a difference in the context in which culture is viewed. As we have defined culture, all human nonbiological behaviors are cultural behaviors, and a belief in witches can become terribly real, as we shall see later. Yet, in a different sense, culture can become an abstraction as well. As the anthropologist sees behavior and recognizes the impossibility of describing it in its entirety, he begins to lump amounts of it into behavioral categories. He begins to abstract commonly repeated behaviors into a kind of "shorthand" description or construct of the behaviors of that particular group. So, in this sense, culture is dual; it is the actual ongoing behavior and our categorical description of it. The only real difficulty arises when we become so enamoured of our abstract categories that we come to think of them as a separate reality.

CATEGORIES OF CULTURE

We can now begin to examine some of the constructs that have been created to aid anthropologists in their descriptive and ultimately analytical endeavors. These are categories we use to help us structure the cultural behaviors we observe. It is somewhat traditional to represent ideas, activities, and artifacts as falling into three basic areas of cultural behavior: those relating humans to the environment, those relating them to their fellow humans, and those relating us to the world beyond both our physical and social reality, the world of ideology and the supernatural. This first area of culture consists generally of technological and economic behaviors, the second of social organization and its control, and the last of philosophy and religion. Many text books, including the present volume, are oriented along these lines. Of course, all of these areas of culture are linked together and interrelated as a result of the integration of culture in any one society. For practical purposes this means that even if an anthropologist is interested in only one area he will be led inevitably into the others. For example, if he is interested in examining religious sacrifices, he might begin by describing the ideas, activities and artifacts involved in the sacrifice of pigs to some diety. This will lead to securing information on the role of the priest or sacrificer and his relation to his fellow worshippers and their social relationships. Finally, it will involve such technological items as how one raises pigs in the first place, or which pigs are set apart for sacrificing. This interconnection again reminds us that our abstract categories are just that—divisions we make up out of the actual flow of observed behavior.

In order to discuss these basic areas of culture in sharper detail, anthropologists have devised a host of technical terms to describe on different levels the forms, frequency, and amounts of such behaviors. The *forms* of cultural behavior are generally categorized into contrasting pairs of terms and refer basically to how such behaviors impress themselves on the observer. We can briefly discuss three such pairs. The first is represented by the terms overt and covert culture. *Overt* forms of culture are those ideas, activities, and artifacts that the anthropologist can observe directly. Certainly, one can most easily perceive the artifacts of a society—for example, house types and blowguns. Many activities can also be observed—house-warming parties and hunting techniques. Often we can directly perceive an idea in bold relief as well—rules of avoidance in communal housing and respect for hunting ability and its results in prestige. Often, however, the beliefs of a society, its values, sentiments and feelings cannot be observed directly. Such are the *covert* forms of their culture: for example, why people favor communal houses over single dwellings, and why a blowgun may be valued over a bow and arrow in hunting. These answers are inferred from the overt forms of behavior and, as such, are more difficult to describe and analyze since they may not always be reflected in that observable behavior as adequately as we might desire. They may not be suggested at all. Many descriptive accounts of life in primitive societies are, for the most part, presentations of the overt cultural behaviors of those groups. And, of course, when we do attempt description of covert culture we often present it inadequately and incorrectly.

A second and somewhat different pair of contrasting terms are real and ideal culture forms. *Real* culture refers to actual behavior, those things and events that really exist or occur in the life of a society. In this sense, real culture is somewhat similar to our concept of overt culture. *Ideal* culture represents what people say they do or say they ought to do. Real or actual behaviors may or may not conform to such expectations or descriptions. So, for example, the Ten Commandments are one of our statements of ideal culture but one beset by behavioral discrepancies; stealing and coveting our neighbor's wife are perhaps commonplace in our society. These terms suggest a real difficulty for the anthropologist. We cannot observe all the actual behavior manifested by the members of even a small society whose culture we wish to study. So we ask our informants to tell us about behaviors we can't observe and to explain for us many covert or even secret items. In response they may describe behaviors that do not really occur or indicate their hope

210

rather than the actuality. Of course, how people think they behave, as opposed to how they really behave, is itself valuable covert behavioral data, if one can come to recognize it as such. Many published accounts may contain more ideal behaviors than their authors would like to admit.

A final set of terms is the distinction drawn between explicit and implicit forms of culture. *Explicit* (conscious) culture refers to those ideas, activities, and artifacts that people are aware of in their own behavior and can talk about in a critical or rationalizing way. This may not be to the satisfaction of the anthropologist who wants the "real" reason for things, but at least some useful explanations can be obtained. For example, they know that they sacrifice pigs to the gods and that otherwise there may be misfortunes. They may even feel the gods are too demanding. *Implicit* (unconscious) forms of culture, on the other hand, are those behaviors that people do that they are largely unaware of or, if known, that they have difficulty rationalizing for the anthropologist. In the latter case, their usual explanation runs something like "because that's the right way to do it." Such an answer is very frustrating for the explanation-minded social scientist. Of course, the anthropologist himself is surely guilty of many such implicit behaviors in his own social milieu. I don't eat cold potato salad in the winter or hot salads in the summer, but I drink cold beer on both occasions. How come? Why do women's and men's coats button differently? Why do the subject words in these sentences precede the verbs? Obviously, because that's the right way to do it.

FREQUENCY OF CULTURE

In addition to the forms that culture may take, such behaviors also differ in the *frequency* with which they are expressed: for the most part, frequency not in numbers but in possibility. Here again anthropologists have devised a number of terms to categorize this cultural dimension. In all societies, some behaviors are compulsory. These are situations in which if one wishes to behave, to do, believe, or make something, there is only one acceptable way to do it. For example, in our society one doesn't have to get married but if one does, monogamy is the only legally acceptable possibility. Compulsory behaviors in societies, channeling behavior as they do, are a good index of the covert concerns of the membership of those societies. This suggests that such behaviors are also very highly valued. Such behaviors also often stand out and are easy to discern from on-going behavior since they are not masked amidst the welter of numerous behavioral patterns. Preferred culture refers to situations in which there are several possibilities for behavior but one of these becomes expressed much more often than the others: for example, in our society the habit of marrying someone of the same general age. Since such behaviors are generally chosen over the others, one suspects that the value attached to the behavior is correspondingly higher. Certainly, the pressure to conform to expectations is not as crucial as in the compulsory situation. Alternative behaviors are those situations in which a number of possibilities exist and each appears to be expressed about as often as the others. This suggests that they may be valued equally, although the precise choice of behavior may be limited by the context of the choice situation. For example, in disciplining my children I may equally display spanking, scolding, threatening to withdraw my love from them, or shutting them up in their room. Which one I choose and value at any given time may depend upon my frustration level at that moment.

It should be noted that there are other terms like those described above that attempt to define the frequency of behavior; the three presented are only a sample. There is, however, one further frequency concept that is important to mention: the frequency of behavior in terms of the number of people in the society involved. Here, it is usual to talk about restricted behaviors. This is culture that is valued and expressed by only some members in a given society as opposed to behavioral possibilities that apply generally to all members. Restricted behaviors often highlight special social concerns or status positions in such societies. For example, in many religious systems the priestly leaders are restricted from marriage altogether, the medicine men in others can indulge in physiological and psychological expressions not condoned in "normal" people. Like compulsory behaviors, restricted behaviors are often the first that intrude on the attentions of the observing anthropologist.

AMOUNT OF CULTURE

A final approach taken by anthropologists in categorizing cultural behavior is the attempt to ascertain what might be called the *amount* of culture. This refers to how much of the sum total of the cultural repertoire of a society a particular expression may be said to represent. We have traditionally employed a number of descriptive terms here, but these have often become confusing in application. In presenting a few of these, the present volume generally follows the list given by John Honigmann (1959). A trait is the smallest significant unit of cultural behavior, whether idea, activity, or artifact—monogamy in marriage, the wedding, the wedding ring. Naturally, the scope of the particular study will determine exactly how much or what kind of behavior is being considered minimally significant. If the study is a fairly restricted one, say Eskimo hunting technology, then the traits are apt to be small behaviors: a spear and its throwing technique for one seal species and a net and its means of placement for one kind of fish becoming separate trait items. If, however, the study is to encompass all of their technology, then the trait may include all seal-hunting techniques or even hunting itself, as opposed to other major technological operations. In any event, since the trait is the smallest element or amount of behavior that is significant in a given study, one has to be aware of the baseline of size: one man's cat is another man's feline.

Many anthropologists, as they see various traits fitting together, call the resulting merger a pattern. They define this as a significantly interrelated series of traits, behaviors that go together in bigger packages. Again, the size of the pattern varies in behavioral scope as do its constituent traits. "Pattern designates the regularities derived by a field-worker when he observes several people acting or examines a series of . . . artifacts. A trait denotes the parts . . . from an already formulated system of patterns. Pattern construction is the process of formulating a way of life. Element analysis enumerates the constituent items of that configuration" (Honigmann, 1959: 126). This sugests that in actual practice (and for convenience) the anthropologist first notices larger patterns of behavior that "hang together" and then works them down to the smaller building blocks of behavior appropriate for his particular study.

In actual behavior, of course, traits and patterns often combine into larger behavioral units that probably stand out for the observing field-worker regardless of his particular research interests, although he may scale them down to fit his own size categories. Such generally larger groups of interrelated behaviors have persistency and interdependency as a unit and may be called a complex. So, for example, many writers have discussed "the cattle complex" of East African peoples. This consists of interrelated behaviors in technology (herding of cattle and dependency on their products), social life (cattle as wealth and status and means of obtaining wives), and religion (for ritual and sacrificial purposes). The size of the study will still to some extent determine the inclusiveness of the behaviors comprising the postulated complex, although less so than for the constituent traits and patterns.

Another way to ascertain larger amounts of culture is to observe which behaviors are made objects of great concern by the people themselves in a society. Knowledge of these behaviors, then, is gained more by a psychological than a culturological inspection. Such a perspective is derived from the conversation, time, and energy of the people involved and is often called a focus by anthropologists. "A focus consists of an area of behavior about which the members of a community show much concern" (Herskovits, 1948: 544). Since we usually arrive at the foci of culture in this more interpretative manner, anthropologists have often disagreed as to the amount of behavior represented. Generally, it appears we are dealing with fairly large amounts of behavior. In reality, of course, people can and often do display concern over small and isolated behaviors.

As if scholars had not already reached a level of sufficient confusion, some scholars have indulged in even more abstract attempts to categorize culture. In a sense, they have tried to combine the major foci into one all-embracing view of the major thrust of a society's way of being human. This has resulted in the portrayal of an entire cultural system in terms of the emotional quality consistently revealed in its major behaviors. The term ethos has arisen to cover such a possibility. The major and always-cited work in this direction is by Ruth Benedict in her book *Patterns of Culture.* As she suggests: "Anthropological work has been overwhelmingly devoted to analysis of culture traits . . . rather than to the study of cultures as articulated wholes . . . If we are interested in cultural processes, the only way we can know the significance of the selected detail of behavior is against the background of the motives and emotions and values that are institutionalized in that culture" (1959: 54–55).

Briefly stated, she compares a number of societies in terms of the major dominating emotional tone that ran through their cultural behaviors. Perhaps her most famous contrast was drawn between the Plains and Pueblo Indians of North America. Here she categorized (in terms drawn from Greek religion) the former as *excessive (Dionysian* ethos) and the latter as *restrained (Apollonian* ethos). Some of the behaviors suggesting these different ethos designations of Benedict have been summarized by Honigmann (1959: Table 4, p. 130). A slightly abbreviated form is represented below.

Plains Indians (Dionysian)	*Pueblo Indians* (Apollonian)
Fasting is a way to obtain visions.	Fasting is a means to prepare for ritual activity.
Self-torture is used for visions and protection.	Self-torture is absent.
Dancing is employed to induce ecstatic states and is often "wild."	Dancing is monotonous and is intended to promote crop growth.

Value is placed on the self-reliant man of initiative who wins honor and prestige.	The ideal man is mild-mannered and tries not to stand out from his fellows.
Death promotes uninhibited grief and mourning is prolonged and involves self-torture.	Death promotes sorrow but little is made of the event.
The war hero is honored and envied.	The war hero must be purified of the impurities brought about by killing.
Men often vow suicide if they have been failures or shamed.	Tales about suicide cannot be taken seriously.

Despite criticisms to the effect that a culture cannot be characterized in terms of one major emotional theme (there being themes and counter-themes), Benedict's attempt is a reminder to us that culture is, nevertheless, an integrated phenomenon. It also suggests that we must not lose sight of the whole general culture in our pursuit of the particular—a warning that anthropologists especially should not need to be reminded of.

CULTURAL RELATIVISM

In sum, then, anthropologists have tended to describe and analyze culture in terms of its forms, the frequency of such behavioral expressions, and by the amounts of such ideas, activities, and artifacts. Before turning to how we pursue such tasks, one major series of points about culture in general remains to be mentioned. It is probably reasonable to assume that many anthropologists, as a result of their careful consideration of various cultural alternatives for being human, have adopted a kind of live-and-let-live philosophy ("different strokes for different folks"). This is dignified by the term cultural relativism and holds that criticism of particular behaviors (especially outside of their integrated contexts) is an inadmissible activity. Furthermore, in a more extreme sense, it holds that different cultural alternatives are not really amenable to comparison in terms of qualities of effectiveness and satisfaction. In this sense, Bushman culture and American culture are equally relevant as extragenetic solutions to the problems of being human. As is perhaps understandable, other scholars have resisted a pure relativism, although their criticisms are still generally not couched in directly comparative terms. So, for example, Edward Sapir draws a distinction between what he calls genuine and spurious culture.

The genuine culture is not of necessity either high or low; it is merely inherently harmonious, balanced, self-satisfactory. It is the expression of a richly varied and yet somehow unified and consistent attitude toward life, an attitude which sees the significance of any one element of civilization in its relation to all others. It is, ideally speaking, a culture in which nothing is spiritually meaningless, in which no important part of the general functioning brings with it a sense of frustration, or misdirected or unsympathetic effort. It is not a spiritual hybrid of contradictory patches, of water-tight compartments of consciousness that avoid participation in a harmonious synthesis. (Sapir, 1962: 90)

FUNCTIONAL PREREQUISITES

A somewhat more ambitious attempt to assess the "quality" of culture in any given society has been to list the **functional prerequisites** or cultural imperatives that require satisfaction in any society for that way of being human to retain its adaptive qualities. "Functional prerequisites refer broadly to the things that must get done in any society if it is to continue as a going concern . . . " (Aberle et al., 1950: 100). The solutions, of course, will differ among societies and even from time to time within a single society. Although it is difficult to compare different societies in terms of how well these functions are met, one can perhaps agree (up to a certain point) that "One measure of the efficiency of a solution is the extent to which the solution is satisfactory to a large . . . number of the members of a society," and that "The more rationally efficient the solutions, the more adequate the chance of survival and continuity . . . " (Bennett and Tumin, 1964: 11).

A combined and shortened list of these prerequisites/imperatives includes the six following crucial areas, all of which overlap and interconnect with each other.

1. Maintain the biological functioning of the members of the group. This is necessary to keep the membership of the society "alive and well," and is accomplished by the sexual reproduction of new members or their recruitment from outside the group. It also involves their provision with the basics of life such as food, clothing, and shelter; and the enhancement of other needs such as health and security.

2. The production and distribution of goods and services. Like the first area, this involves technoeconomics and includes dividing up production and distribution and other important social tasks by the assignment of roles to the members of society.

> In any society there are activities which must be regularly performed if the society is to persist. If they are to be done dependably, these extensive and varied activities must be broken down and assigned to capable individuals trained and motivated to carry them out. Otherwise everyone would be doing everything or nothing—a state of indeterminacy ... which precludes getting essential activities carried out. (Aberle et al., 1950 : 105)

3. The sharing of common goals to insure that the necessary activities of the second function will indeed be accomplished. This includes mechanisms to insure that the means for attaining these goals exist. Group members must be made aware of how such goals can be attained and then motivated to achieve them. On a higher level, societies must also define the meaning of life in order to motivate a desire for existence in the first place.

> Perhaps the major task for any society ... is to provide new members with a patterned set of life conditions which will make them want to continue to live in the first place ... In the second place it must provide them with a patterned set of explanations of the "purpose of it all," in short, a sense of worthwhileness of the whole human venture. Or it must attempt to reduce this question to an unimportant status ... (Bennett and Tumin, 1964 : 19)

4. There must also be shared cognitive orientations to make behavior predictable. If social interaction in pursuit of the first three functions is to achieve any degree of harmonious cooperation, then the "actors" must interact in terms of shared behavioral expectations. It is suggested that these are generally attained by means of learned and shared symbolic modes of communication, especially that of language.

5. The accomplishment of all of the above goals and behaviors in a continuous ongoing fashion requires socialization. This includes the passing of culture across generational lines as well as the assumption of new behavioral responses from time to time within generations: for example learning new roles. Because culture is a learned, extragenetic phenomenon, its transmission is as vital to the survival of a society as is their biological well-being and continuity.

> A society cannot persist unless it perpetuates a self-sufficient system of action—whether in changed or traditional form—through the socialization of new members, drawn, in part, from the maturing generation. Whatever the defects of any particular mode of socialization, a universal failure of socialization means the extinction of the society ... (Aberle et al., 1950: 109)

6. Finally, there must be maintenance of order. This is necessary to insure that disruptive behaviors will not halt or impede the proper execution of the first five functions. Hence, societies must not only instill some drives and motivations but actively retard the expression of others.

In most of the chapters that follow we will examine the structure of many of the behaviors that function to secure most of the above necessities for human survival. We will also compare various cultural responses from different societies in a nonevaluative way.

SUMMARY

1. Definitions of culture are not unusually agreed upon by anthropologists. A useful definition considers culture as learned, transmitted, and integrated ideas, activities, and artifacts which are adaptive and which depend upon human social interactions for their existence.
2. Cultural behavior may be considered as overt and covert, real and ideal, explicit and implicit. Some of these behaviors are more difficult for the anthropologist to record and understand.
3. Cultural behaviors differ in the frequency with which they are expressed. They may be compulsory, preferred, alternative, and restricted.
4. Behaviors studied and described by anthropologists differ in terms of how much of the total cultural system (or part under study) they represent. These behaviors run from the smallest significant unit of behavior—the trait—through patterns, complexes, and foci, to the ethos behind a whole cultural system.
5. Although many anthropologists espouse cultural relativism, attempts to compare the efficiency with which cultural systems solve common problems do exist. This is generally done in terms of functional prerequisites such as maintenance of biological functioning; production and distribution of goods and services; sharing of common goals and cognitive orientations; socialization; and the maintenance of order.

REFERENCES FOR FURTHER READING

Every introductory text dealing with cultural anthropology attempts to define the concept of culture. The one general work I have found valuable in many ways is *The World of Man* by John Honigmann

(1959, Harper & Row). It is jam-packed with information and can be best used, perhaps, as a reference work. Another general text that raises many issues is *The Science of Man* by Mischa Titiev (1963, Holt, Rinehart & Winston). The best all around survey limited just to culture is *Culture, A Critical Review of Concepts and Definitions*, by A. L. Kroeber and Cylde Kluckohn (1963, Random House); there is enough material here for a course on definitional problems alone. Two more limited approaches cited in chapter thirteen are Clifford Geertz, "The impact of the Concept of Culture on the Concept of Man," in the *Cultural Present*, edited by Yehudi Cohen (1968, Aldine); and G. P. Murdock, "The Science of Culture," quoted from Collins, *Readings in Social and Cultural Anthropology* (1969, Simon & Schuster) and originally published in the *American Anthropologist* 34: 200–15. The classic statement on culture by Edward Tylor is from *The Origins of Culture* (1958, Harper & Row; first published in 1871). A good overview of anthropology and its problems is supplied by Morton Fried in *The Study of Anthropology* (1972, Thomas Crowell and Co.) The idea of amounts of culture is portrayed in the classic work of Ruth Benedict, *Patterns of Culture* (1959, New American Library). The issue of the genuineness of culture is discussed by Edward Sapir in *Culture, Language and Personality* (1962, University of California Press). The two articles that deal with behaviors necessary for societal survival are David Aberle et al, "The Functional Prerequisites of Society," in *Ethics* 60 (1950): 100–111; and John Bennett and Melvin Tumin, "Some Cultural Imperatives," in Hammond, ed., *Cultural and Social Anthropology*, pp. 9–21 (1964, Macmillan). A different perspective on cultural behavior in general and examination of its varieties is provided by Edward T. Hall in *The Silent Language* (1959, Doubleday).

14

the study
of culture

We have seen some of the aspects and dimensions of cultural behavior. Before we become involved with the variety of such behaviors in areas such as technology, social life, and religion, it is first necessary to briefly discuss why the anthropologist chooses primitive peoples of the world as main subjects for such studies. It is also important to know how we go about accomplishing such studies. Anthropologists have pursued their study of culture mostly in primitive societies. As a result, anthropology has become a "field" discipline more than the other social sciences. At least in cultural anthropology, laboratory work is distinctly limited; we have to go to where the culture is being behaved if we are to study it (correctly) in its natural setting and we generally do not pick our own society. This is, as we shall see, inconvenient and often a threatening experience. It would be much easier to administer a questionnaire on drinking behavior to my students (a sociological technique) than to go to the jungles of Brazil and observe drinking behavior in some society at first hand. Hence, there must be some compelling reasons for the traditional preoccupation of the anthropologist with primitive societies.

REASONS FOR STUDYING PRIMITIVE PEOPLES

The reasons are compelling and they are very much related to the nature of primitive societies themselves. Typically small in population as well as in geographic territory, primitive societies (in the past, at least) were relatively isolated from other groups; many are still located in more remote world areas. As a result, physically and linguistically, their members tend to be alike and, in general, there are fewer alternatives for behavior. Much behavior appears to be traditional, automatic, and unquestioned; hence, there is considerable similarity in what people do

Primitive societies provide valuable opportunities for the study of cultures. Many anthropologists begin their study by simple observation of behavior and the settings in which it occurs.

and say. Finally, among other things, such societies are relatively slow to change their behaviors. In this sense, the term *primitive* (anthropologists have not agreed on a single definition) simply refers to a set of life conditions different and generally opposite from ours. The term, then, does not imply that they are less worthy than "modern" societies or that they are backward savages.

This behavioral context makes primitive societies attractive for study for a number of reasons, of which the following are perhaps most important.

One reason is that their size and range of behaviors makes them a kind of microcosm of bigger and more varied societies. This permits the anthropologist to at least attempt to make integrated, holistic studies of their behaviors. It becomes possible to understand the interworkings of a whole way of being human. If I am interested in the religious life of a group of people and how it fits into the social life and technological concerns of their society, it is easier for me as an individual or member of a small research team to apprehend this in a primitive society than in a more complex and varied culture. Not only are there millions of believers in our society but hundreds of different religious alternatives, far too many, as the poet has put it, to allow me to "grasp this sorry scheme of things entire." It is perhaps beyond the capabilities of an entire discipline to do so. A related idea here is the belief that not only do these primitive societies offer better opportunities for general cultural understanding, but that studies ought to proceed from the simple to the complex anyway. This is to say that if we seek to understand some behavior, we ought to attempt to sketch its more restricted and homogeneous expressions first.

The anthropologist wants to understand both simple and elaborate ways of life. Preparation for the latter is sought by working with communities which contain few people, a limited number of alternative

forms of behavior, simpler forms of organization, and hardly any conflicting values or beliefs. Such communities probably are easier to
understand at the present stage of knowledge than those at the opposite
end of the continuum. (Honigmann, 1959: 71)

A second and closely related motive involves the concept of objectivity. It is extremely difficult, even for a trained social scientist, to look
at his or her own cultural behaviors from a purely detached perspective,
to be objective in our analysis of our own way of life. After all we
have a big emotional investment in ourselves, and we are so involved
in our way of being human that we can easily miss important aspects of
it. Fieldwork in some other society can help rectify this situation in at
least two ways. First, it is easier to be objective when the way of life
you have selected for study is different from your own. The "cultural
blinders" have been removed, and you are detached from the witnessed
behaviors whether you want to be or not. Even little details, being so
foreign, may be presented in bold relief.

Perhaps the most important benefit derived from fieldwork in an exotic
locale is the sense of perspective it develops in the fieldworker. At
first, this is manifested in the ability to look at the host culture more
objectively than he regards his own. . . .
The trouble about working in the culture in which one grew up is that
almost everything is taken for granted . . . A field trip in an alien culture
can produce results greater than this imagined trip in a time machine.
Even the simplest assumptions of the fieldworker about what he sees
and must do to conform to . . . may be in error . . . One of the great
benefits of this kind of shock to the anthropologist is that it makes him
sentiently aware of culture, alert to the minutest variations and to
subtle links between newly experienced institutions and freshly observed behavior. (Fried, 1972: 123–24)

In addition, such an experience enhances the ability of the anthropologist to be more objective about his own society. Not only does the
actual behavior of primitive peoples give us insights into our own behavior (why don't we do it that way?), but the exposure gives us a more
sophisticated posture from which generally to examine that behavior.
A third value derived from the study of primitive peoples is in
acquiring broader comparative knowledge about human behavior. There
are at least three aspects of significance here. Perhaps the most theoretical value lies along the following lines. Social scientists as they
study behavior wish to generalize about that behavior. For example,
they want to discover what the functions and significance of the family
are for the human species. If we study the family only with reference to
our own society or in Western-oriented societies, then we will be able
to state only some generalities: it plays a role in the initial socialization

of the children, for example. This is, however, a biased sample. The family in primitive societies often structures itself differently and has many additional functions not reflected in the "modern" form. And some families may not be the socializing unit. Until we collect data on the family from all human societies, all generalizations are bound to be narrow and restricted or in error. In this sense, broader comparative knowledge gives us a more scientific base from which to talk about human behavior.

Second, by gaining more universal knowledge from the study of primitive societies, anthropologists are in a better position to attempt to distinguish those behaviors that are cultural (extragenetic) from those that are biological. By not remembering that humans are dual in their behavior, it is easy, without wide behavioral comparisons, to assume that some particular behavior is either innate or heavily conditioned by genetic sources. Human aggression, for example, seems so common in occurrence and distribution that it is tempting to conceive of it as at least partly due to our genetic past. If we can search widely and discover societies in which aggression seems not to be present, then the issue is much less clear cut. The implications of gaining enough comparative knowledge to differentiate between innate and acquired behaviors are obvious: not only to clearly understand behavior but to use that understanding in a practical manner to alleviate undesirable behavior.

Finally, comparative knowledge gained by the study of many diverse ways of being human can help free us in general from the problems derived from ethnocentrism. This is the view that one's own way of life is either the only way of human behavior or, if admitting the possibility of others, the best. Such a view leads to many misunderstandings when people from different cultures come in contact. In a world that is ever "shrinking" because of improved communication and transportation techniques, in a world that will ultimately survive or fail (spaceship earth) depending on how well we humans can pull together, we need to be freed from the view that only one way of behaving is natural or correct. That the anthropologist, with his comparative perspective, has much to contribute to such an end by alleviating misunderstandings is incontrovertible.

So anthropologists focus on primitive societies because they offer opportunities for holistic studies, they help promote objectivity, and offer comparative knowledge. In their various senses, these are a few valid reasons for such a preoccupation. Certainly, there are other, perhaps more restricted motivations as well. Studying such societies can help us fill in gaps in the archaeological record. We can, for example (with certain reservations), suggest what the behaviors of Stone Age people might have been like by examining hunting peoples still in existence in the present. Then again, such societies are rewarding to study in the purely personal sense; their exotic behaviors—initiation rites and witchdoctors—are behavioral exhibitions outside the range of our own activities. One hopes that few anthropologists are motivated by this reason alone! Finally, it is possible to suggest that at least cultural anthropology began as a modern field of inquiry because no other social science at the time was utilizing the resource of primitive society.

TECHNIQUES FOR STUDYING PRIMITIVE PEOPLES

It has been seen that the anthropologist studies primitive peoples for various and justifiable reasons. How do we set about such a study? After selecting a problem and a society that can help us in its solution (or a society about which little is known), the anthropologist prepares for the field situation. This is done by talking with people who are familiar with the group and/or area, reading previously published materials on the problem and people, and, if possible, learning the language of the people with whom fieldwork will be done. Of course, one does not accept all verbal or written information at face value. One should be aware of the possibility of taking the biases of others into the field. If the language has no writing system, it may be impossible to learn anything about it in advance. Unless interpreters are available, this may retard the progress of investigation until you learn enough of the language in the field.

Having thoroughly prepared oneself in advance and presumably having gained financial support, the next problem is reaching the area in question and establishing contact with the people to be studied. Unquestionably, the problems of contact and of establishing rapport—getting people to accept you and your goals—are among the greatest difficulties that the anthropologist may have to face. These people did not ask you to visit them and they are usually resistant (aren't we all?) about being made the objects of questions and study. Moreover they may be an actively hostile group and deeply suspicious of the real motives of the anthropologist. In many cases, the fieldworker even becomes the scapegoat for any ills that have beset the community; you become responsible. Obviously, many a field experience is abruptly terminated! Thus, establishing rapport is highly important, yet there is no course (rapport 101) that can train the anthropologist in advance. All one can take to the field is a sense of determination, hope, and a lot of sensitivity. Often the crux of getting people to accept you is simply to prove your essential humanity—not an easy task since it may have to be accomplished on their terms. One fieldworker known to the writer had to fall out of a canoe before his "powerful outsider" image was tarnished enough to make him acceptable. Such experiences are legion. In addition, one must be careful of who the first contacts are. If the first people whose trust you gain are not themselves respected in their own society—and it is often such marginals who gravitate to the anthropologist—serious fieldwork may become an impossibility: you are identified with low-status individuals, and hence you and your goals are unacceptable.

Making the problems of contact and rapport even more difficult is the situation of culture shock, a "malady" often encountered by anthropologists. This is the sense of strangeness and alienation one feels as one becomes enmeshed in a foreign society.

> Culture shock is precipitated by the anxiety that results from losing all our familiar signs and symbols of social intercourse. These signs and cues include the thousand and one ways in which we orient ourselves to the situations of daily life . . . Now these cues . . . are acquired by all of us in the course of growing up and are as much a part of our culture as the language we speak or the beliefs we accept. All of us depend for our peace of mind and our efficiency on hundreds of these cues, most of which we do not carry on the level of conscious awareness. Now when an individual enters a strange culture, all or most of these familiar cues are removed. (This is) . . . followed by a feeling of frustration and anxiety. (Oberg, 1954: 1, 2)

These feelings may lead to others of helplessness and loneliness and may lead to rejection of the field situation and a great longing to be back home where behavior is more comprehensible. Many an anthropological career may have been ended at this point. If one is aware of the difficulties, however, and works hard at surmounting them, then one does eventually come to adjust. The anthropologist comes to accept " . . . the customs . . . as just another way of living. You operate within the new milieu without a feeling of anxiety, although there are moments of strain" (Oberg, 1954: 5). We will return to this point at the end of this chapter.

Specific Techniques

If one survives culture shock and gains rapport, he or she is now ready to apply the specific techniques of the anthropological fieldworker. There are a great number of these and, of course, the problem and circumstances partially dictate which ones will be employed. Basically, however, three major activities are the general techniques usually employed, although they are not unique to anthropology. These are sampling, observation, and interviewing. "Sampling consists essentially of finding members of the population who are representative of the community as a whole and from whose behavior one can validly predict for the entire population" (Honigmann, 1954: 110). This reflects the fact that even in a small primitive society the anthropologist still cannot construct a cultural shorthand based on the behavior of all group members. He must still pick and choose in terms of his own limited time and energy. Here is still another way in which anthropological culture description is an abstraction of behavior.

Basically, there are two kinds of *sampling* procedures. If one is interested in all kinds of behavior—as a background for a specific study or to gain a basic description if none is available—then the sampling procedures will tend to be of a random sort. This means that we assume a casually selected number of people will probably adequately represent a reflection of cultural behavior. If the society is varied in its composition, then the random sample may have to be somewhat more structured to be a useful cross section device. If, however, one's interests lie in a more specific problem, for example the area of religious sacrifices, then the individuals are selected to assure maximum information on that topic. Some people will be more valuable than others in such an effort, and a purely random effort at sampling will not suffice. Such a "biased" sample might select all of the priests connected with the sacrifice (who can best supply the belief system behind it) and only a few of the laymen. Obviously, one selects those who can tell you the most about your particular interests. A purely random sample would turn up informants who might have nothing to contribute. In most cases, sampling consists of a mixture of these two techniques.

Observation refers to looking at behavior as it goes on around the anthropologist. This simple and obvious technique is the first method employed in the field situation. Even while waiting to establish rapport the field worker can observe behavior and the settings in which it occurs. This doesn't mean that one's observations in the beginning are going to reflect items of profound importance. Often, while in the grip of culture shock and the fear of failure, the first impressions are trivial. One anthropologist's first impression was that "the feet of the natives are large." Nonetheless, first observations can suggest features of interest and lines of questioning to be followed up at the first opportunity. For example, if one observes that housing takes the form of communal arrangements, then one can wonder if special social devices might not occur to ensure the harmony of the domiciled group, to keep them apart. If the houses are individual and widely separated, are they social devices to promote the cohesiveness of the group, to bring them to-

gether? What do different decorations and body ornaments mean? In some cases, simple observations can yield basic data: you observe, for who go into the fields for agricultural pursuits.
example, that it is the men who go off hunting each day and the women

Simple observations, however, only go so far. The real guts of the anthropological use of this technique is to get involved in the patterns of behavior that are observed—to do participant observation. This is based on the assumption that if one learns about a behavior while doing it, one will understand that behavior in a much better fashion. "Walk a mile in their moccasins and see how they really fit." Although this gives the fieldworker a more firsthand knowledge, participant observation cannot be undertaken until a fair degree of rapport has been established. Moreover it cannot be undertaken lightly. With such involvement can come a loss of objectivity. Although one is aware of one's own cultural background and how it may alter one's interpretations, one tends to forget that if one gets enmeshed in their way of life too deeply the same loss of objectivity can occur. Many are the warnings given to the novice fieldworker about the dangers of "going native." In addition, if one slips too deeply into the native way of being human, the anthropologist may lose the "outsider" status and his or her own behaviors and mistakes, once overlooked, may be treated harshly.

The third major field technique is that of *interviewing*, also shared with other social sciences. It is not enough to find the right informants and observe and participate in their behaviors. One has also to ask questions to enable perception of all of the ramifications of the behavioral situation. This is accomplished in the interview technique, which also requires a high degree of rapport. Most early interviews are of a passive nature in which the conversation is of an undirected nature. You get the informant to start talking and hope the conversation will cover topics you are personally interested in. At this point any direct question probably would

Interviewing is an important field technique in studying a society.

American Museum of Natural History

ruin the relationship. Generally, the topics covered are those that the informant does not feel to be threatening, even if only the weather. Even here, the successful fieldworker may have to learn when to steer the conversation into more acceptable channels. Later on, as trust in the anthropologist builds up, the interview situation may proceed into more active forms. These may range from the "let's talk about religion today" to point-blank questions about specific behaviors: "why are dead people buried facing east?" If trust is very high, the informant may even do some anthropology on his own by asking questions of other people for you or even gathering helpful information on his own initiative. Needless to say, this is an ideal situation that does not always occur.

There are other difficulties in interviewing. Among these, two problems stand out. First, as good as informants may become, they are only as good as "their" anthropologist. This means that in all but exceptional cases they can only respond to the questions asked. In practice this results in many important aspects of behavior not being recorded. I suspect that every fieldworker at some time in his or her career has engaged in the following exchange: "But why didn't you tell me about that custom?" "Because you didn't ask me." And the sad thing is that we often don't think to ask even some obvious questions until after we have left the field situation. Certainly, much of any social science is asking the right questions. A second difficulty is that of recording the information gained from interviews as well as observations. How do you remember it? At least during the early part of fieldwork, there may be a resistance to the anthropologist actually writing down information in the presence of the informant or the behavior. This means that one has to trust to memory and later recall; "you go back to your hut and write like hell!" The advent of tape recording devices suitable for use in the field has helped this problem but has not completely alleviated it. After a time, the anthropologist generally is able to record information on the spot, solving his difficulty, but in a "delicate" field situation this may never be possible.

Other Techniques

The techniques discussed above and their variations are the major techniques employed by the anthropologist in the fieldwork situation. Other devices, such as recording life histories and analyzing art and literature, are used as supplemental techniques towards gaining an understanding of the behaviors of some groups of people. In addition to methods such as these, there are also some very general procedures that can make for the success of such pursuits. All of these are employed with the aim of helping to ensure the accuracy of the results of anthropological investigation. These have been nicely summarized by Mischa Titiev (1963). One is to question a number of informants on the same topic or to observe different individuals in the same behavior. This is a check on how representative one's sample really is. If there is a high degree of agreement or duplication, the fieldworker can be reasonably certain that the data is valid. A second technique is to attempt to remain in the field situation for a sufficiently long period of time to witness the "yearly round" of activities. This is to take into account the fact that people engage in different things and events at different times of the year. Remaining in the field for less than one calendar year may give a distorted picture of behavior. Just after you leave, they sacrificed four hundred virgins to the moon goddess and you missed it!

Another general technique is that of checking from time to time the internal consistency of one's own data. "If . . . an anthropologist discovers that his informants insist that their society never indulges in violence, yet finds in his notes frequent instances of assault and murder, he is faced with a marked lack of internal consistency and must seek its explanation" (Titiev, 1963: 392). Finally, it has been suggested that the fieldworker attempt to make a divided field trip; to return on a second visit to the same people. This not only permits checking out theories based on the initial data and overcoming any of the deficiencies of the first visit but makes contact and rapport establishment much easier (if you left good feelings behind).

PERSONAL CONSIDERATIONS

So the anthropologist has a number of specific and general fieldwork techniques at his or her disposal. The use of such techniques may be affected, moreover, by certain personal considerations, such as attitudes and ethics, which perhaps add a more psychological dimension to our attempts to study culture. For example, it is impossible for the anthropologist pursuing fieldwork to be completely objective. He or she may like or dislike the field situation itself: either the people or the geographical circumstances of the study. One writer, who studied the Siriono of Eastern Bolivia, can be quoted in this connection:

> Once having established contact with such a group, I had intended to settle down or wander with them for several months, or until I could

complete my studies. I was forced, however, to abandon this plan when, after being with them for a day or two, I came down with an infection in my eyes of such gravity that I was almost blinded.

[later] No Siriono was a willing informant; little information was volunteered and some was consciously withheld. Had it not been for the fact that I possessed a shotgun and medicines, life with the Indians would have been impossible. By contributing to the food supply and curing the sick, I became enough of an asset to them to be tolerated for the period of my residence.

. . . the time spent in satisfying my own basic needs—acquiring enough food to eat, avoiding the omnipresent insect pests, trying to keep a fresh shift of clothes . . . and obtaining sufficient rest in a fatiguing climate where one is active most of the day—often physically prevented me from keeping a full record of native life. (Holmberg, 1969: xxi, xxiv)

In addition to such difficulties, the fieldworker is often struck with the truthfulness or morality of the behaviors he or she observes; and, as in the above case, it is difficult not to let such personal impressions influence the account or assessment of such behaviors and one's relation to informants. You can't really cure the sick by bringing their souls back from the underworld. Is it right to leave an elderly woman behind to die when she can no longer keep up with the group? Should one introduce modern medical practices? Such problems often weigh heavily on the anthropological fieldworker.

Finally, there is another ethical problem, that of publishing fieldwork studies: how much of your hard-won information (for example, about cannibalism and head-hunting) can you publish without compromising your informants? Although some anthropologists deal with this difficulty by adopting a "sanctity of the confessional" approach, most recast such information in such a manner as to render it useful for other social scientists but not harmful to those who trusted them. This problem has been exaggerated in recent years by demands by the United States government wishing to use such information for international purposes. Shouldn't you aid your own government? A bitter debate rages over this problem at present.

We have now examined the nature of cultural behavior and have suggested why anthropology studies the primitive peoples of the world. In addition, we have discussed how such studies are accomplished and the particular problems that result in and from them. Perhaps it can now be understood why such studies are less than satisfactory or complete in many cases. We can now examine the first major dimension of cultural behavior: how the human species adjusts to the physical environment and the associated technological and economic activities.

SUMMARY

1. Anthropologists have traditionally studied primitive societies to learn a number of things including size, alternatives for behavior, and conservatism with regard to change. More holistic studies of their behavior are possible which help to promote objectivity and to offer comparative knowledge.

2. In doing field work, anthropologists must establish rapport and overcome culture shock. Techniques include sampling, participant observation, and interviewing.

REFERENCES FOR FURTHER READING

There are a number of excellent accounts that communicate the joy and despair of anthropological fieldwork. Three of the best are *Being an Anthropologist,* edited by George Spindler (1970, Holt, Rinehart & Winston), which deals with fieldwork in eleven different societies; *In the Company of Man,* edited by Joseph Casagrande (1960, Harper & Row), which portrays the lives of twenty informants; and *Stranger and Friend,* by Hortense Powdermaker (1966, Norton & Co.), which discusses her activities in four different research situations. A first book to read on the nature of primitive society in general is Robert Redfield's *The Little Community and Peasant Society and Culture* (1960, University of Chicago Press). The problems of alienation during field study are discussed by Kalervo Oberg in *Culture Shock* (1954, Bobbs-Merrill). A specific account of fieldwork is given in *Nomads of the Longbow,* by Alan Holmberg (1969, Natural History Press). A fine introduction to field techniques is supplied by John Honigmann, *Culture and Personality* (1954, Harper & Row); and more specifically by Benjamin Paul, "Interview Techniques and Field Relationships," in *Anthropology Today,* pp. 430–51 (1953, University of Chicago Press). The classic manual for the anthropologist preparing for fieldwork is *Notes and Queries on Anthropology* (1951, Routledge & Kegan Paul). A more recent work by G. P. Murdock et al. is the *Outline of Cultural Materials* (1961, Human Relations Area Files Press). A book with an excellent bibliography on various aspects of fieldwork is by L. L. Langness: *The Life History in Anthropological Science* (1965, Holt, Rinehart & Winston). Although this book does not deal with the history of anthropological theory or its current varieties, the interested student will find H. R. Hayes, *From Ape to Angel* (1958, Knopf), a most interesting review of the life and times of some of the best-known anthropologists. It gives a feeling of the excitement of anthropology itself.

15 technology

Technology is one of the fundamental dimensions in the relationship between human beings and their environments. In this book, technology is taken especially to encompass the tools in the possession of some group and the techniques associated with their use. These can range from a computer and the special "language" used to program it down to a fishing spear and its customary manner of employment. Of course, technology has a broader range of application than merely to human concerns relative to the physical environment. There are tools and techniques for relating to our own bodies (in medicine), to other people (in warfare), and to the world beyond (in religion). In this chapter, however, the term is restricted in use to refer to those tools and associated techniques that are employed in adaptation and adjustment just to the physical environment itself. This includes the basics of making a living in that environment in terms of food, clothing, shelter, and related activities. Since culture is an extragenetic mechanism to aid in human survival, then, in contrast to other forms of life, the forms of such technology will presumably reflect real advantages in this regard as well as our great variability. And in truth, no other species enjoys such freedoms in coping with its environment.

THE COMPLEXITY OF PRIMITIVE TECHNOLOGY

So we survive in our environmental settings largely through such technology, following out one of the functional prerequisites discussed in chapter thirteen. It has often been maintained, however, that societies differ in the levels of complexity with which such pursuits are followed —some groups being better fed, clothed, and sheltered than others. It is hard not to agree, if only partially, with such a statement. Some societies do possess greater controls over their food supplies, even if to the point of conspicuous waste. And, in general, it is the primitive societies that are placed on the lower end of this scale. We are less dependent upon the uncertainties of nature, even if we are destroying it in the process. We also have central heating and air conditioning in our cultural bag of tricks.

Such a range in technological adaptations does not imply, however, that primitive societies are mentally backward, that they do not realize the potentials of their environments or understand how to cope effectively with them. Given the general level of technology available, they do adapt to and manipulate their environment in a sophisticated and understanding manner. Countless examples can be cited to illustrate this point. Among some Eskimo groups, wolves are a menace—a dangerous environmental feature that must be dealt with. They could perhaps be hunted down and killed, but this involves danger as well as considerable expenditure in time and energy. So a simple yet ingenious device is employed. A sharp sliver of bone is curled into a springlike shape, and seal blubber is molded around it and permitted to freeze. This is then placed where it can be discovered by a hungry wolf, which, living up to its reputation, "wolfs it down." Later, as this "time bomb" is digested and the blubber disappears, the bone uncurls and its sharp ends pierce the stomach of the wolf, causing internal bleeding and death. The job gets done! It is a simple yet fairly secure technique that involves an appreciation of the environment as well as wolf psychology and habits.

In the Marquesas Islands of the Pacific a similar knowledge of animal behavior is applied in catching parrots for flesh and feathers. Here the problem is how to kill them since, unlike many birds, they don't land on the ground, and how to preserve the feathers from destruction in the process. The islanders build a blind in a clearing and lean a pole against one side. An open window faces the pole. A domestic parrot is tied to the bottom of the pole—hopefully a noisy one. One waits quietly. Along comes a flock of parrots. The leader sees the bait and circles to investigate. Seeing no humans, it lands on the top of the pole and marches down. When it is opposite the window, the hunter grabs it, twists off the head, and hangs it upside down to allow the blood to drain without ruining the feathers. By this time, the second parrot—playing follow the leader—is on the way down, and the process is repeated until the desired number of parrots has been secured. Again, this is a simple technique yet in tune with an expert knowledge of parrot behavior (of the environment).

A final example will suffice. The maguey cactus (century plant) of Mexico would hardly strike the modern tourist as displaying much in the way of potential; there isn't even any fruit. Yet in the past the Aztec used it for a variety of purposes. They used the grubs that live around the plant for food and made a drink (pulque) out of the sap. They employed the fibres of the plant for clothing and rope and the thorns at the tips of its leaves as sewing needles. Other juicy substances were used as a kind of soap, and paper was manufactured from its inner lining. Simple primitives you say? Less developed in general technology perhaps but certainly well aware of the potential to be discovered in their environments.

SUBSISTENCE TECHNOLOGY

As mentioned previously, there are many forms of technology. The most basic forms, however, are in subsistence technology, the specifics of how a society goes about exploiting the potential of its environment for food purposes. Since humans, like other organisms, have to eat to live, such activities obviously form their most basic concern, around which many other aspects of cultural behavior come to revolve. Indeed, the food technology of a society greatly influences (but does not determine) many of the forms that these other behaviors may take, and such technology may limit other developments or facilitate them. This is so related that often societies on the same level of subsistence will develop comparable religious needs, values, and expressions. This is perhaps even more true for primitive peoples. "Food, and the few devices employed in obtaining it, is the focus of economic life among primitive bands in a more fundamental sense than it is in more complicated economies. Food getting is the major enterprise . . . but more than that, it is a direct confrontation of man with nature" (Service, 1966: 9). It has been traditional in anthropology to divide subsistence technology into two basic categories: food collection and food production. Food collection refers to techniques that gather those food items from the environment that are of natural occurrence. This includes wild vegetable products (fruits, berries, roots, nuts, seeds, etc.), insects, fish, and various game animals. Techniques for such collecting activities assume a passive stance relative to the environment. For the most part, societies of this subsistence category make no attempts to alter or increase such food supplies, apart from some attempts at conservation. As such, they are totally dependent upon the uncertainties of the environment. Food production refers to techniques in which humans have intervened in nature to promote the development of domesticated plants and animals. As a result, such subsistence efforts reflect a more active interplay with the environments; they make attempts to increase its potential. They represent attempts to free humans from limitations and assume greater control

Food production involves active participation with the environment and represents greater human control over nature.

United Press International

over the factors of uncertainty. Of course, food collection and food production are not exclusive categories. Agriculturalists still hunt and may
gather wild-plant products.

COMPARISONS OF SUBSISTENCE TECHNOLOGIES

Before discussing the varieties of subsistence technology of these two
basic types, it is perhaps useful to indicate some of the ways anthropologists have attempted to make meaningful their comparisons of these
various activities. Comparison in terms of population numbers is one
possibility. Generally speaking the more people that a subsistence technique can support in one area (density per square mile), the more
valuable that technique would seem to be. Although one can argue the
fact that a subsistence technique that produces overpopulation is not
necessarily as good as one that keeps it in some natural balance, nonetheless population is a device that promotes useful comparison and
evaluation. Density of population does speak to the ability of a people
to control and secure their food supply. A second factor to observe is
the amount of surplus. This is defined here as the amount of food left
over after consumption demands have been met. Generally speaking,
the more valuable the technique, the larger the surplus of food. In
comparing surplus, however, it should be understood that perhaps few
societies lack it even if subsistence is limited. People will often go hungry in order to set aside food for nonconsumptive purposes in social (in
food displays) or religious (for sacrifices) life. There are, however, great
differences in the absolute surplus of foodstuffs generated by the varying
subsistence techniques. A factor definitely related to surplus, of course,
is the ability of a society to store food in the first place. Lacking sufficient preservation mechanisms, a society may have to pass up accumulating a surplus even if the procuring techniques are sufficient to obtain it.

A third factor useful in comparisons is the degree of **dependability**. This refers to whether the pursuit of food-gaining activities is successful in a high percentage of cases or whether it is subject to more than occasional failure. Again, it is valuable to engage in food-getting activities that reach the goal in at least a satisfactory number of cases. Such dependability is often closely related to the ability to control other environmental factors such as water supplies as well as the actual food resources themselves. You may have excellent agricultural techniques, but the technique may ultimately fail because of lack of rain. Finally, there is the concept of **energy**. In pursuing any livelihood, people must expend energy—in chasing an antelope, hoeing corn, or herding sheep, for example. One does this in the expectation or hope that the energy returned from the food itself (expressed in calories, etc.) will be greater than that expended. If not, starvation soon results. In general terms, then, and ideally, one can measure outgo-income ratios of energy, and compare subsistence techniques in this respect as well. Since few specific studies of this sort have been attempted, we will have to deal in generalities in this case.

Factors of population, surplus, dependability, and energy can be used for comparative purposes in the analysis of subsistence technology systems. Although population numbers are more a result of these than a variable factor, such can still be used as a success indicator. Certainly, if the other factors are well in hand in a society, such a group may be said to be "better off" than peoples having difficulties with respect to one or all of them. In the former type of society, fewer people need be involved in basic food-getting activities and, thus freed, can pour their energies into nonsubsistence activities that can lead to cultural elaboration and development. With the above factors in mind, we can return now to a consideration of the varieties of subsistence technologies.

FOOD COLLECTION

Most textbooks subdivide food-collecting techniques into one major type, hunting and gathering, and two minor types, intensive fishing and foraging or gleaning. In each case it is generally the proportion of components of the food supply that has been the decisive classifying factor: game animals, fish, and wild-plant foods. We are now beginning to realize that this classification in fact may be misleading. A recent study (Lee and Devore, 1968) gives a sample of societies revealing twenty-nine societies emphasizing gathering, eighteen emphasizing fishing, and only eleven gaining most of their food supply from hunting. Moreover, even many hunters may depend more on vegetable materials for their day-today requirements. This suggests that, at least recently, heavy reliance on game animals is not the major lifeway we have pictured it as being.

Hunting, Gathering, and Fishing

The position taken in this text is that in reality only one food-collecting subsistence technology may be said to exist, that called *hunting, gathering, and fishing,* and that, except in a few societies, hunting may actually always be of less importance. Speaking of the bushmen of Africa, who have always been considered a prime example of the hunting way of life, it has been said that they "eat as much vegetable food as they need, and as much meat as they can" (Lee, 1968: 41). Certainly, the fact of the adaptation of such peoples to a broad range of environments and the variability of their basic techniques should make us aware of the fact that they are not going to fit into ideal anthropological classification very easily. "On the contrary, they display great diversity and in some instances a remarkable specialization. So wide are the varieties . . . that it is hard to find a term which will embrace these hunters, fishers and collectors of wild seeds, roots and fruits" (Forde, 1957: 371).

What we can agree upon is the antiquity and adaptability of this way of life.

> Of the estimated (people) who have ever lived out a life span on earth, over 90 per cent have lived as hunters and gatherers; about 6 per cent have lived by agriculture and the remaining few per cent have lived in industrial societies. To date, the hunting way of life has been the most successful and persistent adaptation man has ever achieved . . . . It is still an open question whether man will be able to survive the exceedingly complex and unstable ecological conditions he has created for himself. (Lee and Devore, 1968: 3)

It is also important to realize as we discuss the hunting, gathering, and fishing way of life that the modern representatives are not typical food collectors. They do not occupy the environments where this lifeway was so successful in prehistoric times. Since the Neolithic period, hunters have been pushed by expanding food producers into less rewarding ecological niches: areas posing greater problems for their survival. In the following pages, three specific varieties of such peoples will be discussed in the attempt to represent the full range of adaptations engendered by this way of life. We will then attempt a summary statement relative to the general quality of life on this subsistence level.

The Eskimo.   The first variety is the Eskimo culture of the North American Arctic, where, because of the environment, hunting and fishing

The Eskimos are mainly a hunting and fishing society. These Eskimo hunters are hauling a freshly killed walrus onto the ice.

United Press International

were employed almost to the exclusion of gathering activities. Although there is perhaps no "typical" Eskimo group, the Netsilik Eskimo of the Arctic coast west of Hudson Bay are taken as fairly representative. A brief description of their yearly round of subsistence activities indicates much about this variety of collecting technology. Their yearly round can be seen to be tied to the problems engendered by a mobile and irregular game supply and to differences in summer and winter conditions.

At about the beginning of July, the Netsilik begin to move from winter camps on the sea ice to the land for their first summer camp. At this time, they subsist on leftover seal meat and on lake trout and salmon trout migrating downstream to the sea. They spear the lake trout and erect a weir or fish dam for the migrating variety. These stone basins concentrate the fish for better spearing opportunities. This is also a time for making repairs on summer equipment. At the beginning of August, the Netsilik move inland. Now, stone-weir fishing commences in earnest, with greater catches; caches are constructed for storing surplus fish. Ptarmigan (a partridge like bird) may also add to the diet at this time. In September, they begin to hunt caribou. Here, a variety of techniques are possible. Sometimes two men can stalk them or wait in concealment in a narrow valley for the caribou to pass by. A more active possibility is to employ a number of people as beaters who by noise-making can drive the beasts to the waiting hunters. Caribou are also taken by driving them into a lake or intercepting them as they naturally crossed and spearing them from kayaks (skin boats). Of course, caribou are not only a source of meat but of hides and bone to make into tools. The ripening of wild berries is also a food resource at this time of year.

The late fall season was primarily a transitional period between the autumn caribou hunts and the winter sealing activities ... The marshy tundra became hard from the frost but there was still not very much

240

> snow on the ground. For subsistence during this period, the Netsilik
> depended primarily on their cached fish and caribou meat, on river or
> lake fishing and occasionally on musk-ox hunting. In general it was only
> when the summer caches were emptied, or nearly so, that seal hunting
> would begin. (Balikci, 1970: 47, 48)

This is also a time for women to make new clothing and for repair of
winter equipment.

The movement back to the sea ice can begin any time from Novem-
ber to January and lasts until the necessity to move again in summer.
Now seals are the staple food and are taken mainly by the breathing-hole
technique. Seals make holes in the ice for breathing (they are mammals)
and numbers of these air-filled domes are kept open. The Netsilik join
together in larger groups to increase discovery chances and move frequently after seal resources become exhausted in any one area. The
actual technique of hunting is complicated and involves examining the
contours of the hole to determine the likely path of the seal, enlarging
an area to permit harpooning, placing an indicator to warn of the presence of the seal, and waiting and watching. The wait may be long and
unrewarding. Balikci quotes a case in which fifteen hunters watched their
holes for eleven hours and caught just one seal! Polar bears may also be
taken at this time. As the ice melts in spring, seal hunting becomes more
productive, holes are visible, and seals basking in the sun may be
stalked. Sea gulls and their eggs also relieve the monotony of the diet.
Then, in July, summer fishing commences once again. Some other
Eskimo groups have a greater range of game (walrus and whale, for
example), but still the Netsilik, with a simple technology, are able to
adapt these techniques for survival in a very difficult environment.

The Washo.   Clearly, however, such reliance upon meat is not
universal among food collectors. Speaking of the Bushmen of Africa, Lee
(1968) suggests that despite the prestige of and energy expended on
hunting, it is wild-plant foods that supply 60 to 80 percent of the annual
diet. For them, meat is a special treat, a break from the regular diet. As
an example of such a more typical collecting life-style, we can examine
the Washo of the Great Basin area (Utah and Nevada) of North America,
as they formerly existed.

> The Washo obtained food by three means: gathering, fishing, and hunt-
> ing. Each of these activities required knowledge and skills and could be
> most successfully carried out by groups composed in a certain way. No
> single means of livelihood could provide a year-round supply of food
> for these people.... no matter how plentiful any given source of food

> might be it would not support a population for an entire year. (Downs, 1966: 12)

In the spring, wild lettuce, spinach, and potatoes were utilized although these did not yield substantial amounts. They broke the winter camp to move to Lake Tahoe to fish for whitefish, accomplishing this journey by June. At this time too, cattails yielded quantities of roots, seeds, and fresh shoots. Soon, other lake fish began to migrate up streams in considerable numbers. Trout and suckers were scooped up in baskets and furnished the Washo with a time of relative plenty. Later, some groups went higher into the mountains for wild strawberries and rhubarb and to spear or net other fish in streams and pools. Eventually, everyone headed back down into the lowlands. At this point, except for scooping minnows out of shallow pools, the fishing year had ended and the diet was maintained basically by gathering quantities of chokecherries and grass seeds. In the fall, the tempo of gathering increased with the ripening of tremendous quantities of pinon nuts, the large meaty seeds on the pine cone. At this time, from two weeks to a month of steady collecting permitted the Washo to lay away a winter's supply of this basic food, although it would have to be supplemented by supplies of meat from game animals.

Hunting was chiefly a fall activity. Rabbits were taken by the hundreds by being driven into nets. Deer were taken by individual stalking techniques utilizing a deerskin disguise or by waiting in a blind. Occasionally, they were hunted by a drive technique similar to that of the Eskimo for caribou. Antelope were usually obtained by stampeding a herd into a brush corral, closing it, and then slaughtering the animals caught inside. Mountain sheep were occasionally taken by stalking techniques. Rounding out the diet were wild fowl and quantities of insects such as locusts, which were collected in baskets or driven into a ditch by fire for easier collecting.

Like the Bushmen, the Washo are perhaps typical of food collectors in the plant orientation of their technology. In this regard, it is sometimes maintained that hunters such as the Eskimo require greater ingenuity and technology in making their living than do simpler gatherers like the Washo. This is not entirely true.

> The gatherer requires only a digging stick to probe for roots and bulbs and baskets in which to carry the harvest. And once learned, the skills of harvesting are relatively simple. But to be an efficient gatherer requires a vast fund of knowledge about the growth cycle of dozens of plant species, an understanding of the effect of weather on growth and knowledge of soils and growing conditions. These mental skills can be taught in part. Many of them required learning through experience, so it was

the oldest of the Washo women who were the most expert gatherers. (Downs, 1966: 21)

In addition, wild plant foods often require special treatment before they are palatable or even digestible. The skills probably even out in the long run.

Indians of the Pacific Northwest. As a final example of the food-collecting way of life, mention can be made of those Indians who lived in the Pacific Northwest of North America. Here, ideal ecological conditions permitted a level of ease in passive subsistence perhaps not matched elsewhere for peoples on this subsistence level. Most of these environmental blessings were due to exceptionally varied and numerous fish varieties. Fish were so important that many texts classify these groups (the Kwakiutl, for example) as intensive fishing societies to distinguish them from more generalized collectors. Such fish supplies included five species of salmon, smelt, cod, herring, and halibut. Techniques for taking these varied enormously. As salmon migrated up the streams to spawn they were taken by the thousands in dip nets, by spearing, and in highly ingenious wooden and stone fish weir and traps. Fish were taken in the ocean by spears, rakelike devices, and by the hook-and-line method. Other trap types were placed along the beaches. A great variety of shellfish species and crabs also contributed to the diet.

Many types of marine game animals occurred. Whales, seals, sea otters, and sea lions were taken by harpooning from boats. Land game animals existed: deer, elk, bear, and a variety of smaller types such as beaver and mink. In some areas, moose and caribou could be taken. Pitfall and deadfall traps were used for these along with a variety of snares and the bow and arrow for individual stalking. Many wild fowl migrated seasonally through this area and were taken by underwater snares and large nets to entrap them while landing or taking off. Only vegetable foods were not plentiful, although there were many species of wild berries. Such a natural bounty and "harvests" of fish led to a markedly atypical way of life for these societies.

> This made for periods of intense activity, put a premium on the development of techniques for the preservation of foodstuffs, and, once such techniques had been developed, permitted lengthy periods of leisure. In fact . . . not only was there opportunity of leisure, but there was a certain force for seasonal immobility; even a large family group is unlikely to favor a nomadic way of life if they have half a ton of dried salmon to lug around with them. This leisure and temporary immobility was utilized . . . for the development of art and ceremonialism. (Drucker, 1963: 7)

The Quality of Food-Collecting Life

We can now attempt to summarize the general quality of life generated by hunting, gathering, and fishing subsistence technology systems. First of all, with the exception of groups such as those on the Northwest coast, these people live in small groups (259 Netsilik in 1923), and in terms of the territories occupied, population densities are extremely low. "Throughout the world hunter densities rarely exceed one person per square mile; most of the accurate figures reported . . . ranged between one and 25 persons per hundred square miles" (Lee and Devore, 1968: 11). Second, as in the case of the Netsilik and the Washo, most food collectors move around a lot, migrating from place to place in pursuit of game or ripening food supplies. Because of this and because many of their techniques are strenuous, they consume great amounts of energy, although, generally, overall return is greater—perhaps evened out by the use of labor-saving mechanical contrivances such as traps and co-operative collecting techniques. The dependability of hunting, gathering, and fishing techniques is often a matter of concern. This is due both to the rather limited hunting techniques and associated equipment and to the visissitudes of the ecological setting: seals may not come to the breathing hole where the hunter waits, wild fruit may rot before it can be reached. The fact that such a way of life is ultimately successful in procuring food is perhaps more a testimony to the knowledge, skill, and endurance of its practitioners than to the abundance of food. Surplus is likewise often marginal. Here, it is perhaps not so much a case of the people not being able to obtain enough food beyond bare subsistence needs or their inability to control the environment but rather their lack of preservation, storage, and transportation facilities. Because of these, there is often little use in further food-getting activities after a small supply has been obtained. So lack of surplus may be less a matter of acquisition than retention. The mongongo nut is the staple of the Bushman diet and yet may rot on the ground for lack of utilization. All in all, then, we may say that the food-collecting way of life is generally characterized by low population density and low surplus, energy, and dependability. One can also maintain that for most of such groups, survival by such techniques does entail fairly constant work throughout the year, and the price of any consecutive number of failures is apt to be severe. Yet such societies do manage to survive, and their labors are not as unremitting as generally supposed. Speaking again of the African Bushmen, "Even the hardest working individuals in the camp . . . spend a maximum of 32 hours a week in the food quest" (Lee, 1968: 37). On the Northwest coast, the average, if computed on a yearly basis, is prob-

244

ably much less. How does this compare with modern suburban living? We can turn now to the more commonly (if recently) occurring techniques of food production.

FOOD PRODUCTION

We have already suggested that food production was a revolutionary change in human development (chapter nine). It was also pointed out that this was a recent accomplishment. Since that time, however, peoples having domesticated plants and animals have expanded at the expense of food collectors.

> Ten thousand years ago the entire population of the earth subsisted by hunting and gathering, as their ancestors had done since the dawn of culture. By the time of Christ, eight thousand years later, tillers and herders had replaced them over at least half of the earth. At the time of the discovery of the New World, only perhaps 15 percent of the earth's surface was still occupied by hunters and gatherers, and this area has continued to decline at a progressive rate until the present day, when only a few isolated pockets survive. (Murdock, 1968: 13)

One expects, in light of such expansion, to find material (or other) advantages associated with food production. There exists no absolute consensus as to the types of food-producing subsistence technology systems. Generally, however, the following categories are documented: incipient agriculture, horticulture, plow agriculture, and pastoralism. We will discuss and illustrate each of these possibilities in turn.

Incipient Agriculture

Incipient agriculture refers to agriculture that is basically carried on as a part-time pursuit by practitioners who are more dependent upon hunting, gathering, or fishing activities. This suggests that people are aware of the fact that dependability, surplus, and energy returns are not automatically increased because of the presence of domesticated crops. In fact, groups such as the Hadza and Bushmen of Africa appear to recognize that they are better protected from famine than their pastoral and agricultural neighbors since their wild crops are less vulnerable to droughts than herds or cultivated crops. Honigmann (1959) has suggested a number of reasons why the Siriono of Bolivia, who have knowledge of agriculture, do not practice it more heavily. It is difficult for them to clear the land; a mobile game supply takes them away from the crops;

agriculture is considered man's work, but so is hunting (so not enough time exists for agriculture, anyway); and, more importantly, collecting is sufficiently bountiful to produce no real feelings of inadequacy. We will briefly examine one example of an incipiently agricultural society.

Western Apache. Such a society was the Western Apache of Arizona, who were subdivided into a number of smaller groupings.

> Although the Western Apache engaged in subsistence farming, their economy was based primarily on the exploitation of a wide variety of natural resources by hunting and gathering ... agricultural products made up only 25 percent of all the food consumed in a year, the remaining 75 percent being a combination of meat and undomesticated plants. Because they could not rely on crops throughout the year, the Western Apache did not establish permanent residences in any one place...they were almost constantly on the move. (Basso, 1970: 3)

So, as in most collecting societies, the seasonal cycle was predicated mainly on supplies of wild vegetable products. In May, they left their winter camps and journeyed to farm sites in the mountains. Here, they planted corn, beans, and squash in small fields and then set out to gather mescal, the fruit of the sahuaro cactus, and prickly pear. Older people and a few others remained behind for cultivation. In middle and late summer, acorns and mesquite beans became the staple. In the fall, they returned to farm sites to harvest their domesticated crops, but still gathered juniper berries and pinon nuts in late fall to help see them through the winter. Hunting was also intensively pursued at this time (as well as sporadically throughout the winter). They then returned to their winter camp.

Among these people, although the surplus, energy, and dependability of agriculture are seen as somewhat more reliable than among the Siriono, the Western Apache still did not place heavy emphasis upon agriculture, possibly because of the rather arid, limiting conditions of their environment. The idea of agriculture itself spread to them from Pueblo Indian neighbors, who did rely heavily upon agriculture in subsistence. This points up the general notion that agriculture was probably independently developed only a few times; most groups have had the knowledge, if not the specific techniques, spread to them from others.

Horticulture

Horticulture, sometimes called manual agriculture, gardening, extensive agriculture or shifting agriculture, generally involves rather simple tools and a great deal of human energy in some cases. Here, the dependence

The slash-and-burn technique opens new agricultural land by the use of fire. This land will be abandoned when its fertility is depleted.

F. A. O. Photo

upon cultivated plants has become more important in survival, if not the basic contribution to the diet. There is still, however, the necessity for hunting or fishing activities and even some minor collecting of wild-plant foods. Perhaps the most widespread type of horticultural activity is the *slash-and-burn technique.*

> Its general features are as follows. Early in the dry season an area of forested land selected as a garden site is cut, and the trees and under-growth left on the ground to dry. A few months later the dried vege-tation is burned. At the beginning of the rainy season the crops are planted. The wood ashes that remain on the ground restore some minerals to the soil, but otherwise no fertilizer is used. The same plot is replanted until a decrease in the fertility of the soil or . . . invasion of weeds and grass makes it uneconomical to do so any longer. At this point it is abandoned, and a new area of forest is cut down, burned, and planted as before . . . To be able to recultivate a once abandoned plot a . . . farmer must generally wait until a new cover of forest has grown up and shaded out the small vegetation. This usually takes many years. (Carneiro, 1956: 229)

Although cultivation by such horticultural techniques is not absolutely dependable because of the fickleness of nature, it does yield up a greater surplus than that enjoyed by the majority of food-collecting peoples. Moreover, since one knows the yield of his plantings, estimation of the amount of food that will become available in the future is more predict-able. It might also be expected that such farmers are more future oriented in their behaviors as well: being less live-for-today oriented than col-lectors. Sometimes this surplus allows individuals to be freed from ordinary subsistence activities to pursue more specialized crafts or other social activities. It also places a stress on the development of food pres-ervation and storage techniques. Energy is on the plus side, although

247

this is averaged out; sometimes heavier activities are required than at other times. Pospisil (1963) has estimated that among the Kapauku of New Guinea, males worked a little more than two hours a day and females just under this amount. Population densities also increase, and more sedentary, village-oriented life has become possible; one does not generally find the seasonal nomadism of the collecting way of life. Although periodic movements may occur as land loses its fertility, such movements are not always correlated with such needs. Carneiro (1956) has demonstrated that the Kuikuru of Central Brazil, by utilizing only about seven percent of the arable land within an accessible distance, could remain completely sedentary. So, movement for them must involve other considerations.

The Ulithians.   We will examine two different horticultural societies to indicate a little of the variety of such behaviors. Ulithi is an island complex in the Micronesian culture area of the Pacific Ocean. As such it represents some limits (in land) to primitive agricultural potential and also lower population density (421 residents in 1949). Here, subsistence activities are confined mostly to gardening and fishing, supplemented by a small amount of gathering. Garden plots are of two sorts, those in swampy areas and those outside such areas. The staple food stuffs are coconuts (used also for drinks and oil; its leaves and trunks are used for building materials), taro (a root crop) and related aroids, sweet potatoes, breadfruit, and bananas. Taro and sweet potatoes are planted by cuttings and kept in continual cycles of cultivation; other plant foods are of a more seasonal variety. On Ulithi, fishing activities supplement those of agriculture to provide food variety as well as a kind of insurance when bad weather causes food shortages from land-oriented subsistence. Fishing is most productive when schools of fish come onto the outer reef where they can be taken by cooperative effort, drawing a long net in around them. Lagoon fishing inside the reef is more common and involves a number of catching methods: traps, nets, spearing, and angling. In Ulithi, a balance has been struck between production and collection, and all the potentials for surplus at least have perhaps not been obtained. "The adaptation made by the people to their environment is limited by pervasive ecological factors that prevent the economy from rising very far above a subsistence level ... Yet subsistence activities proceed at a sustained and adequate level" (Lessa, 1966: 12).

The Kapauku Papuans.   A more advanced horticultural society are the Kapauku Papuans who inhabit the Central Highlands of Western New Guinea. Here, land is not limited as in Ulithi, and natural resources are more available. Population, consequently, is higher, estimates ranging up to 45,000 individuals. They make their living primarily by cultivating plants and breeding pigs; large game animals are scarce.

> As a result, hunting and trapping of any economic consequence are limited to small birds, bats and rats. Fishing and gathering provide the Papuans with additional proteins and vegetable material. In their fishless rivers and lakes the women net crayfish, dragonfly larvae, tadpoles and water bugs. In addition they collect many species of insects . . . and a large variety of greens and fruits. Since breeding and fattening pigs depends on the harvest of sweet potatoes . . . agriculture assumes an undisputed key role in the native food production. (Pospisil, 1963: 15)

Here there are three types of garden plots. Mountain slopes provide gardens made by slash-and-burn techniques. On the valley floor, the deeper soil permits a greater variety of plants, and only the grass needs to be burned off. Finally, some plots in the valley are used more intensively; rectangular beds are laborously maintained by turning over the soil and fertilizing it so that cultivation can be continued indefinitely. Here, no fallow time is necessary to restore usability.

The Kapauku cultivate a variety of plants: sweet potatoes are the basic crop; sugar cane, taro, bananas, and numerous green vegetables are also grown. Still other root crops such as manioc and yams are of more recent adoption. The pig occupies a place in Kapauku economy not unlike fish on Ulithi, only with greater social implications. It is an important source of protein in the diet and a hedge against any agriculture failure.

Horticultural peoples such as the Kapauku appear to have somewhat greater control over their environments. By being more active than collectors with respect to their environments, they have a greater surplus, energy returns appear to be good, and population numbers appear generally higher. Barring any major environmental problems, dependability also seems better. The degree of knowledge required is also great, although comparison with knowledge among collectors is perhaps unrewarding. Conklin (1954) has pointed out that the Hanunoo of the Philippine Islands (Mindoro) are aware of 430 cultigens and many hundreds of other plants with valuable uses, besides being knowledgeable of varieties of soil and how to match their crops to them for best success. In some respects, we must assume that horticultural techniques are probably as well suited for such areas as more modern methods.

Why do such peoples not progress to more advanced agricultural techniques? Perhaps the primary reason is that they see no real necessity for doing so. The Kapauku, for example, realize that yields of sweet potatoes are better in their perpetually enriched plots of the valley floor than on their mountain plots—in 900 square meters, 640 kilograms versus 380 kilograms of yield. However, the work involved also increases—

450 hours of labor versus 260 hours. Is more food worth more work if one has enough already? One writer on New Guinea has very neatly summed up this situation.

> ... what is the result for human beings of an increase in intensity of land use within a system of shifting cultivation: The total food production of their territory can be increased and the shifting cultivation can begin to merge into a sedentary agriculture with no abrupt change in techniques or crops. But do these changes improve the quality of human life? In several ways, the change seems for the worse. The variety of the food supply is impoverished. The protein-rich leaves of forest trees and ferns become scarce. Game diminishes ... Moreover, because the output of food per hour of labor decreases, the increase in total production within the territory can hardly be said to be economic growth. (Clarke, 1966: 357,358)

In light of the above, why would any society ever take up more intensive techniques? Of many possible answers, two seem most often cited: needs to increase production and pressure on land resources (less land available for cultivation). In both cases, population pressures may ultimately be responsible. Does this have a modern ecological ring? Of course, desires for wealth or status may also be involved; anthropologists have not yet adequately studied all such variables.

Plow Agriculture

We can now briefly turn to another agricultural subsistence system, that of *plow agriculture*. As the name suggests, this is farming with the use of a plow—generally, but not always, drawn by some domesticated animal. It is sometimes called intensive agriculture since the major result is greater productivity from a given amount of land. As a subsistence technology system in primitive societies, it was formerly limited to the Old World, excluding the Americas and the islands of the Pacific. Plow agriculture helps increase productivity in a variety of ways. It permits a single farmer to cultivate a much larger plot of land. It permits the working of heavier soils—how would you like to dig up your backyard with just a sharpened stick? It also reaches deeper to bring up fertile subsoils. In addition, it aids in the planting of various seed-sown crops such as wheat. These can be sown broadcast and then worked into the soil with the plow; hand planting would be too time-consuming. It becomes apparent that plow agriculture can greatly increase surplus and energy in such pursuits. One writer cites two cases in support of this.

> The productivity of plow agriculture may be judged from the following
> figures. A family of 5 Burmese can cultivate from 2 to 3 acres of dry
> rice by manual techniques while a group of the same size easily can
> plow 16 acres of wet riceland ... In a Mexican village cultivation of 2.5
> acres of land by hoe culture occupies from 143 to 180 man-days. The
> same land takes 35 to 78 days to cultivate by the ox-drawn plow ...
> (Honigmann, 1959: 317)

And of course the manure from the draft animals can also be used as
fertilizer. Utilizing these agricultural pursuits, population tends to increase to over 1000 persons per square mile, and fewer people need be
involved in plowing. This creates even more specialists in the society
and greatly multiplies the number of people totally released from the
direct quest for food. As a result, social complexity greatly increases.

Despite the revolutionary aspects of plow agriculture, dependability
is perhaps still less than satisfactory. Not only can insect pests such as
locusts wipe out the crop, but lack of rainfall can severely reduce its
potential. While it remained for more "modern" societies to develop
pesticides, the lack of sufficient rainfall was handled by a number of
primitive agriculturalists by the development of various irrigational techniques. Irrigation is the watering of plants by artificial means. It may
occur not only with plow agriculture but also in horticultural societies.
The simplest variety of irrigation is to employ flood water by diverting
it to the area of crops or catching it in special reservoirs and using it
later on after the flood has receded. Techniques such as these are sometimes called hydroagriculture to distinguish them from more permanent
water works that can pump or divert water directly from its source at
anytime: hydraulic agriculture. In either case, the dependability of the
agricultural process has been given a great push forward, one more
active manipulation of the environment in pursuit of the food supply.
We can turn now to the last major subsistence technology system.

Pastoralism

Pastoralism, or intensive animal husbandry, involves a dependence upon
the herding of various domesticated animals. Of course, agriculturalists
may keep some domestic animals, but here the magnitude of involvement
with such animals is greater.

> The camel is the largest of the domesticated animals of Arabia. Its
> range and scale of uses, its specific adaptations to desert conditions,
> and its limitations are the foundations of Bedouin culture. As a source
> of food it provides both meat and milk ... In the desert and steppe en-
> vironments of north Arabia few other food resources are available.

Pastoralism depends on the herding of various domestic animals and tends to lead to a nomadic way of life. These Masai are guarding their herds in Tanganyika.

British Information Services

... The camel herds provide a more stable food supply. (Sweet, 1969: 159)

Although much of their livelihood may derive from such sources, such groups generally still practice some agriculture, trade for vegetable products, or pursue hunting and gathering activities. One of the greatest misconceptions about such peoples is that they rely absolutely on animals and their products. This is simply not so. Although they may value their animals highly, in some cases derive much subsistence from them and employ them in nonsubsistence areas of life (as items of wealth), they are not characterized by an "animal psychology." As a type of subsistence technology, pastoralism was developed only in the Old World. Here, it was distributed mostly in geographical regions that posed serious difficulties for full-time agricultural pursuits (or agriculture in general) and was excluded from those where agricultural potentials were greater (Forde, 1957). Where it is found, pastoralism is a device for pursuing a viable way of life under conditions of dubious ecological potential.

Because of needs to satisfy the demands of their animals, pastoralists are nomadic. In this respect, they are like food-collecting peoples. Their degree of nomadism, however, is highly variable. To oversimplify, we may distinguish three general types. Among some groups, seasonal movement is held to a minimum since fodder can be collected to maintain the herds at times when local pasturage is in the off-season. This is rare. More commonly, one finds pastoral peoples exhibiting one or another form of transhumance. This involves leaving the home base and taking the herds to seasonal pastures and then returning after that season has ended. Perhaps not all of the group members will actually migrate with the herds. Karimojong women (Dyson-Hudson, 1969) remain in the center of the tribal land and practice agriculture while the men and boys migrate with the cattle. This may involve a great degree of nomadism. These cattle pastoralists move over 500 square miles in a two-year period! Finally, there is what might be called long-range nomadism. This involves seasonal migration over long distances for the

252

entire society, often from summer to winter to summer pastures in an endless cycle. Camel pastoralists in northern Arabia may travel over 600 kilometers a year with their herds. Population numbers vary substantially among various pastoral societies but are generally high, as are the numbers of their domesticated animals. The Karimojong number 40,000 people in an area of about 4,000 square miles; suggesting a high population density. The Pakot, with about the same population, have 112,000 cows, 113,000 goats, and 37,000 sheep. The Rwala Bedouin (in the 1930s) comprised 35,000 persons and 350,000 camels over a huge territory.

Patterns of surplus, energy, and dependability are difficult to calculate for pastoral peoples. Certainly, energy may appear to be equivocal. Although some animal products are there for the taking (just out in the pasture), taking care of the needs of the animals, protecting them from predators, moving with them, and finding them food supplies also require great energy expenditure. It is possible that if they had only domestic animals for subsistence, the energy supply might not be sufficient. Speaking of the Basseri of southwest Asia:

> Wheat is the main staple food of these nomads . . . Other cereals, dates, fruits, etc., are also eaten, implying a heavy reliance on vegetable foods in the diet. Clothing, footwear, craftsman's products and industrial wares are likewise not produced in a pastoral economy . . . Of the totality of objects contained in a nomad's home. . . . only a small fraction have been produced by himself or a fellow nomad; and of the food such a family consumes in a year only a small fraction is pastoral products. (Barth, 1960: 245)

This is perhaps an extreme case, but in general the above equally applies to surplus and dependability. Among the Karimojong, cows give at best only up to two pints of milk per person per day, and there is not a sufficient quantity of livestock products to feed the entire population. Part of this lack of food is to be expected because of use limitations of domesticated animals. A common misconception about pastoralists is that they use their animals for everything. This is, of course, impossible; there are logical necessities involved. If you use a cow for milk you can't use it for meat! In addition, various cultural practices may further restrict the food potential of domesticated animals. For most East African cattle pastoralists, the major food usages are milk and blood (taken from the neck veins). Because of the semisacred nature of cattle, and because of their value as wealth and productive capital and means for creating social relationships (see chapter sixteen), meat is not a very common product. Often the only time they are eaten is in the context of a religious sacrifice or at the time of natural death.

Again, for the Bedouin of North Arabia, camels supply milk but to kill one for meat is a special occasion of hospitality or religion. So, surplus is considerably less than one would suspect, although it is there if you need it for survival. Likewise, dependability may be severely affected by disease or other natural calamities.

Saying that surplus, energy, and dependability are lower in pastoralism than expected and that they require support from other subsistence means should not obscure the fact that the animals of these peoples do supply other necessities besides those of a bare subsistence nature. For the Nuer of East Africa, the cattle have many other uses.

> Their skins are used for beds, trays, for carrying fuel, cord for tethering and other purposes . . . and for the tympana of drums. They are employed in the manufacture of ropes, spears, shields, snuff containers, etc. . . Tail hairs are made into tassels used as dance ornaments . . . Their bones are used for the manufacture of armlets, and as beaters, pounders, and scrapers. Their horns are cut into spoons and are used in the construction of harpoons. Their dung is used for fuel and for plastering walls, floors . . . and to protect wounds. The ashes of burnt dung are rubbed over men's bodies, and are used to dye and straighten the hair, as a mouth wash and tooth powder, in the preparation of sleeping-skins and leather bags, and for various ritual purposes. Their urine is used in churning and cheese-making, in the preparation of gourd-utensils, for tanning leather, and for bathing face and hands. (Evans-Pritchard, 1968: 28, 29)

Elsewhere, domesticated animals have many other valuable nonsubsistence functions, ranging from use of hair as textile material to uses as beasts of burden and for riding. The latter help out the energy factor.

OTHER ASPECTS OF TECHNOLOGY

We have now briefly examined five major types of subsistence technology: hunting, gathering, and fishing; incipient agriculture; horticulture; plow agriculture; and pastoralism. Since how humans extract food from their environments has, as previously stated, profound repercussions on the rest of their behavior, we shall continually refer back to these different livelihoods. There are many other aspects of technology, too numerous to cover in an introductory text. Two may be quickly discussed in concluding this chapter since they generally accompany the topic of food. They are shelter and clothing and ornamentation.

Shelter

Shelter is another aspect of material culture that represents a human-environment interaction. Many animals use or make shelters of one kind or another; in contrast, those of humans show greater intraspecies variability. Certainly, shelter helps us to lessen our need for biological adjustment to the weather. Like clothing (sometimes), shelter is a kind of shield against the environment. It is tempting to believe that one can predict the type of house or shelter a people will have from their environment. In many cases, this is true since primitives face many building limitations. Their raw materials generally must come from their own environmental setting and may be meager or in scant supply. Nevertheless, some societies may make only minimal and unpredictable uses of shelter, perhaps utilizing only a simple windbreak device of brush in an area where temperatures might seemingly dictate otherwise. The Ona of Tierra Del Fuego at the tip of South America, for example, were poorly clothed as well. So, too, we must realize that other cultural used only a hide windbreak in an area of exceedingly cold winters, and behaviors, such as subsistence type and general level of development, have to be taken into account in the understanding of shelter possibilities. A pastoral nomad group will have to have shelter that can be taken apart easily and moved. The classic teepee of the Plains Indians in North America (after the introduction of the horse made buffalo hunting more economical) is a good example: sixteen to twenty-four long poles covered with skins, the perfect camping-trailer development!

Although it is, as suggested, unprofitable to generalize about primitive shelter arrangements, it can be stated that many of these reveal a high level of performance in meeting the demands of the environment. We can also state that very often nearly identical solutions are made in settings with similar environmental problems. We can also suggest that these solutions are often more rational than those of modern societies, which, on occasion, seem more interested in size or appearance.

> An understanding of this primitive experience is of more than academic interest today because ... there is a growing tendency to minimize or ignore the importance and complexity of the natural environment. Not only is the modern architect quite removed from any direct experience with climatic and geographic cause-and-effect; he is also quite persuaded that they don't matter any more. Yet the poor performance of most modern buildings is impressive evidence to the contrary. ... Thus Western man, for all his impressive knowledge and technological apparatus, often builds comparably less well than did his primitive predecessor. (Fitch and Branch, 1960: 134)

255

Following the above authors, we can indicate a few of these environments and the primitive shelter solutions. In the Arctic, we find an area of intense, continuous cold and driving winds. This requires a shelter that retains heat and has high wind resistance. And there are few available building materials! For many Eskimo groups, the result was the igloo or snow hut. This is a dome-shaped dwelling built out of large blocks of snow on a sloping spiral. Heat inside forms a glaze on the inner surface (a lining of skins keeps it from melting) so that heat is retained within the shelter. The dome shape has a stress-deflecting quality so that winds do not subject the dwelling to intolerable stresses. This also means less surface for the chilling effects of the wind. All in all, a beautiful adjustment. Desert regions provide different circumstances: high day-time temperatures and lower temperatures at night. A good response would have a high-heat-capacity wall to absorb heat in the day from the desert sun and then slowly reradiate it at night. A very common response is to utilize materials such as stone, clay, or mud brick, all of which have these qualities. These may be used in block form or the mud or clay may be placed over a framework made of wood. Where seasonal rain might damage such dwellings, there may be an additional layer of leaves or thatch over the outside. A final example of the correlation between shelter and climate occurs repeatedly in tropical forest regions. These pose the difficulties of heavy rainfall and high humidity with intense solar radiation. The solution to these problems should include a building capable of shedding rain and also giving shade and ventilation. In many different tropical areas, from Pacific Islands to the interior of the Amazon River Basin, the resultant shelters look very much the same. They are constructed of leaves and other plant materials to avoid heat buildup, they have high peaked roofs (which often form a major part of the walls) for shedding rain and providing shade, and are often open on the ends to aid in ventilation. So, among primitive peoples, shelter and environment are generally correlated, and despite technological limitations, their constructions are sophisticated and rational. Moreover, although most such structures are living quarters, many are constructed for other purposes: storage, social (club houses), and religious activities. Such buildings may even be better or larger than those used for living concerns.

Clothing and Ornamentation

At first blush, clothing would seem to fit closely into the picture we have drawn for shelter. It would seem to be a basic necessity for a "naked ape" and one would think of its origins and function in terms of protection from the environment. Certainly, the clothing of groups such as the Eskimo, which is tailored with several layers, would appear to bear this out. Yet some groups in very cold environments appear to have been very underdeveloped in clothing and yet managed to survive. The Yahgan (neighbors of the Ona) faced sleet storms with only a loincloth device and a shoulder cape. And, of course, clothing is often worn contrary to the demand of the environment: say, for example, a suit at a dinner party on a sultry August night when a loincloth would be much more apropos. So protection from the environment is a function of clothing but not of universal significance. Modesty is also generally conceded to be related to clothing. Many groups, however, are immodest by our standards since they fail to completely cover genital areas; or it is they who blush if we see them without their nose ring in proper position. And in our society, what about see-through blouses and tight pants, which seem to run counter to modesty? Probably the most universal function of clothing is that it can function as a device for signaling differences in the status and activity of human beings. Clothes may not exactly "make" the man or woman, but they can indicate the social position occupied, sex, and age, or the activity about to be engaged in: for example, the vestments of the priest or the war paint of the warrior about to do battle. Clothes may also reflect the mood of the individual.

In addition to clothing differences, or as a substitute for them in some areas, can be found varieties of decoration or ornamentation. Here there are many possibilities: hairdo, cosmetics, painting of the face and/or body, "hangys" like necklaces and earrings, and various bodily deformations. These last include tatooing, scarification, tooth filing, and the placing of labrets (tubes or plugs) in the lower lip, nasal septum, or ear lobes. Such things can be said (along with clothing) to make up a symbolic language that visually expresses information about a person

Body painting for ritualistic (and other) purposes occurs in our own society as well as in primitive ones. Left, young Aboriginal dancers prepare for a traditional dance; right, body paint as applied by an American.

Australian News and Information Bureau   Courtesy Maybelline Co.

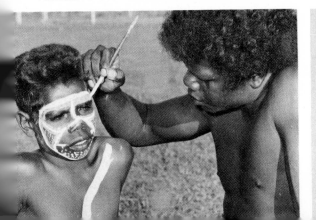

to the others of his or her group. We will close this chapter with a very brief example, the Kayapo of central Brazil (Turner, 1969).

In this society, when a young boy is born his ear lobes and lower lip are pierced. A cigar-shaped labret is placed in the ears and generally a string of beads through the lip. He is painted red—the color of health, energy, and vitality—in complex linear patterns over his entire body. Cotton bands are worn around the wrists, ankles, and knees. At about age four, the infant decorations are discarded and the hair cut short, which is symbolic of suppressing ties to others and is done also by relatives of the dead for mourning. He is losing his infant status. His body is also painted in blocks or bands of red and black, the latter color symbolic of transition. At age eight, the boy is taken to the men's house to live and is painted all black. He is given a penis sheath and can let his hair grow long again. He is also given a small version of the adult male lip labret (the lip is expanded over time). The sheath indicates that control of mature male sex powers is necessary and the long hair that full participation in sex relations is now possible—"you can but you must be careful." He is now a bachelor youth. But he is not too careful, and after the birth of a child he now moves to his wife's house; a saucerlike lip plug (or cylinder) is inserted in the lower lip, and he is now considered a bonafide adult male. Such a visible reference is, of course, handy for self-awareness and self-evaluation as well.

SUMMARY

1. Technology is defined as the tools and associated techniques employed in adapting and adjusting to the physical environment. The core of these efforts revolves around securing food (subsistence technology). Although certain primitive techniques appear simple they are, in reality, often quite sophisticated and successful.

2. Subsistence technology can be divided into two major systems: food collection and food production. These systems may be compared in terms of population numbers supported, energy, dependability, and surplus.

3. Food collection systems include hunting, gathering, and fishing (the most common), and intensive fishing and foraging.

4. Food production systems include incipient agriculture, horticulture, intensive agriculture, and pastoralism.

5. Other aspects of technology include shelter, clothing, and ornamentation. Primitive shelter arrangements often reveal a high level of performance in adapting to the environment. Clothing and ornamentation often function chiefly as devices for signaling the status and/or activity of the wearer.

REFERENCES FOR FURTHER READING

General survey texts of primitive technology are rare. An environmentally oriented text of some value is *The Human Use of the Earth*, by Philip Wagner (1964, Free Press). An excellent reader is *Environment and Cultural Behavior*, edited by Andrew Vayda (1969, Natural History Press). A somewhat different approach to technology is taken by Howard Odum in *Environment, Power and Society* (1971, Wiley). For a consideration of more specific techniques, the student will find *From the Hand of Man*, by Robert Speir (1970, Houghton Mifflin) especially rewarding. For different subsistence usages there is the article by P. W. Porter, "Environmental Potentials and Economic Opportunities," in *American Anthropologist 67* (1965): 409–20. For varieties of subsistence technology briefly illustrated, see Daryll Forde, *Habitat, Economy and Society* (1957, Methuen & Co.). For general treatments of the hunting and gathering way of life, there are a number of excellent sources: Elman Service, *The Hunters* (1966, Prentice-Hall); Carleton Coon, *The Hunting Peoples* (1971, Little, Brown); and *Man the Hunter*, a collection of readings edited by Richard Lee and Irven DeVore (1968, Aldine). The specific examples in this text are drawn from the latter text and from Asen Balikci, *The Netsilik Eskimo* (1970, Natural History Press); James Downs, *The Two Worlds of the Washo* (1966, Holt, Rinehart & Winston); and Phillip Drucker, *Indians of the Northwest Coast* (1963, Natural History Press). The summary statement on hunting by George Murdock is drawn from Lee and DeVore, cited above.

The example of hunters with agriculture is from *The Cibecue Apache* by Keith Basso (1970, Holt, Rinehart & Winston). The quote on horticulture by Robert Carniero is from "Slash and Burn Agriculture: A Closer Look at its Implications for Settlement Patterns," in *Men and Cultures*, edited by Anthony Wallace (1956, University of Pennsylvania Press). Specific agricultural examples are taken from William Lessa, *Ulithi: A Micronesian Design for Living* (1966), and Leopold Pospisil, *The Kapauku Papuans of West New Guinea* (1963), both published by Holt, Rinehart & Winston. The Hanunoo statistics come from Harold Conklin, *Hanunoo Agriculture* (1957, Forestry Development paper no. 12, United Nations). His article "Study of Shifting Cultivation," in *Current Anthropology 2* (1961): 27–61, gives an overview of the range of information available on such peoples. Among the many specific studies of agricultural peoples, an excellent book in keeping with modern anthropological concerns is *Hill Farmers of Nigeria: Cultural Ecology of the Kofyar of the Jos Plateau*, by Robert McNetting (1968, University of Washington Press). A treatment of the relative value of intensive agriculture comes from William Clark, "From Extensive to Intensive Shifting Cultivation," in *Ethnology 5* (1966): 347–59. The comparison of plow and hoe agriculture is from John Honigmann (1959) cited in an earlier bibliography. A classic comparison appears in "Plow Culture and Hoe Culture," by Oscar Lewis, in *Rural Sociology* 14 (1949): 116–27.

A general survey of pastoral nomadism is "Nomadism," by John Myres, in *Journal of the Royal Anthropological Institute* 71 (1941): 19–42. For Africa, from where most examples seem to be drawn, are articles by Alan Jacobs, "African Pastoralists: Some General Remarks," in *Anthropological Quarterly* 38 (1956): 144–54; and Melville Herskovits, "The Cattle Complex of East Africa," in *American Anthropologist* 28 (1926): 230–72, 361–88, 494–528. The specific examples cited in this text are from Louise Sweet, *Camel Pastoralism in North Arabia and the Minimal Camping Unit* (in Vayda, cited above), Harold K. Schneider, "The Subsistence Role of Cattle Among the Pakot and in East Africa," in *American Anthropologist* 59 (1957): 278–300; Fredrik Barth, "Nomadism in the Mountain and Plateau Areas of South West Asia, in *Problems of the Arid Zone*, pp. 341–55 (1960, UNESCO); "Subsistence Herding In Uganda," by Rada and Neville Dyson-Hudson, in *Scientific American* 220 (1969): 76–89; and, finally, *The Nuer*, by E. E. Evans-Pritchard (1968, Oxford University Press). The examples on shelter and clothing are from James Fitch and Daniel Branch, "Primitive Architecture and Climate," in *Scientific American*, December, 1960, pp. 134–44; and from Terence Turner, "Tchikrin: A Central Brazilian Tribe and Its Symbolic Language of Bodily Adornment," in *Natural History* 78 (1969): 50–59, 70. Most standard descriptive anthropological works give data on these topics.

16
economics

We have seen in the last chapter that technology refers to tools and the techniques associated with their use. This is, however, only part of how people relate to their physical environment. Many social activities and relationships are also involved since tools and techniques do not operate themselves. Most of these operations are embedded in what is generally called economic activity. For a majority of anthropologists, economic activities are separated into three spheres of interest. First, the division of labor that exists in a society, the social acts involved in operating the technology: who does what, with what, and with whom. Second, the mechanisms of distribution available to the members of a society becomes a focal point of interest. What happens after a technique yields a result? Who winds up in possession of the final product, and how is this accomplished? How are goods and services allocated? Finally, what are the end results of all such activities? Who owns the tools or the results of their use? This area deals with concepts of ownership, property and inheritance. We can discuss these economic behaviors separately, although in actual behavior they are closely interwoven. One general matter must first be discussed.

ANALYSIS OF PRIMITIVE ECONOMICS

One assumes that many such economic behaviors will be somewhat different in primitive societies from those we ourselves have experienced. There are no local supermarkets, factories for intensive production, or labor-management disputes. Many anthropologists, taking their cue from data that reveals primitive economic activity to be deeply enmeshed in other social relations (rather than such relations being dominated by the economic system itself), have suggested that we cannot use

There are no supermarkets in primitive societies. These Ghanian women are selling feed in the street.

formal economic principles to categorize primitive economic behavior. They suggest that we have to develop fresh methodological approaches to describe a different kind of economic reality, one not based on a "market model" for goods and services, the mainstay of the modern economist. Such anthropologists may be designated as *substantivists*. In disagreement are scholars who might be called *formalists*, who in essence feel that economic theory developed to understand our behaviors are at least partially applicable to primitive forms of economic activity. The present text takes no theoretical side in this controversy, but since the writings of substantivists have supplied much of our data on this topic, much of what follows will necessarily be couched in such terms.

TYPES OF ECONOMY

Perhaps the easiest way for the student to apprehend what causes such interpretative problems for primitive economics is to take note of a basic distinction often drawn by anthropologists in comparing economic behavior in primitive societies with that of modern industrial societies. This is the distinction between a subsistence economy and a prestige economy. In a subsistence economy, production and other behaviors are largely in direct relation to the environment and motivated by immediate survival—production for use and consumption by those producers. A prestige economy, on the other hand, features production for exchange with other producers, a more indirect relation to the environment, a more interdependent mode of survival, and greater emphasis on profit

263

and luxury items as opposed to the basic necessities. Although this fundamental distinction, which categorizes primitives as having subsistence economies, has been attacked by some writers as inexact and misleading, the basic differences may be defended. A recent authority has written:

> The households of primitive communities are not usually self-sufficient, producing all they need and needing all they produce. Certainly there is exchange. Even aside from the presents given and received under inescapable social obligations, the people may work for a frankly utilitarian trade, thus indirectly getting what they need. Still it is "what they need": the exchange and the production for it, are oriented to livelihood, not to profits. . . . Livelihood and gain, "production for use" and "production for exchange" thus pose contrasting finalities of production—and, accordingly, contrasting intensities of production. For one is an economic system of determinate and finite objectives while the other holds out the indefinite goal of "as much as possible." (Sahlins, 1972: 83, 84)

With this overview in mind, we can now examine some of the more specific resulting differences as they relate to division of labor, exchange mechanisms, and concepts of ownership and property.

DIVISIONS OF LABOR

Natural and True Divisions

There are many approaches to characterizing the possible divisions of labor in any society. Perhaps the most traditional anthropological view has been to draw the distinction between the natural and true divisions. In the natural division of labor, the various tasks that must be accomplished are allocated on the basis of the age and sex differences of the

Natural division of labor often allots jobs according to sex.

United Nations

members of the society, with skill requirements distinctly of a secondary consideration. Here, males have certain activities consequent to them and women others; older males different jobs from younger males, etc. It should be immediately pointed out that although these are natural points of differentiation or division, not all peoples agree on the appropriateness of the assigned tasks. It is not "natural" that men should make pottery (and often they do not), but it is natural to employ sex as a dividing criterion for job allocation. It will be remembered that among the Netsilik Eskimos, men do the hunting while women convert the skins into clothing—*all* men and women. It is also of interest to note that youth in most societies, especially males, may have few assigned tasks by any means of labor division.

Most primitive societies appear to rely heavily upon the natural division of labor and have what Sahlins (1972) has called a domestic mode of production, in which the family itself (because of sex-age structure) becomes a miniature economy. It can be so in a subsistence economy since here there are generally simple tools, small labor-force requirements, and limited objectives. Opposed to this is the true division of labor, in which, at least theoretically, all the tasks are allocated on the basis of skill, leading to the great demands for job-training requirements and proper certification found in modern economies. Such an orientation, of course, leads to a loss of family self-sufficiency (never absolute anyway) since the demand for the true labor division correlates with a rise in the complexity of technology, increase in the size of the labor force, and the broadening of productive goals. Of course, this distinction between natural and true divisions of labor is never absolute. Even in a simple hunting society there may be someone outstanding in the manufacture of arrowheads who becomes the major source of supply, and in modern societies the idea that only males perform certain tasks has brought no end of criticism from advocates of woman's liberation.

Individual, Communal, and Organized Divisions

A second way of characterizing labor division is to draw distinctions based upon the numbers of people involved in a task and on exchange factors. Here three major categories have been suggested. Individual labor represents a situation in which people work at various jobs, mostly in isolation from each other and for their own benefit (and that of their family): for example, a Bushman woman going off by herself to gather roots or a solitary hunter stalking deer. This is closely related to the natural division of labor and the family basically relying upon itself for survival. Communal labor is a situation in which groups of people are working together in each other's company but are still basically working toward their own ends or benefit. Here, for example, women may collect cactus fruits together, as among the Washo; males build a stone dam to catch fish, as among the Netsilik; or a Plains Indian group collectively drive buffalo over a cliff to ensure a mass kill. Here again family self-sufficiency is involved, but there are many reasons why communal rather than individual labor is selected. Some tasks may require a greater labor force than a single family can muster (hard to stampede buffalo by yourself). It may also be wise to have women work together in the fields for the protective reasons of group security. Again, some tasks such as house building can be speeded up with group cooperation. There are also less obvious reasons, especially when work is done communally that could as easily be done by more individual labor. "Malinowski has stressed the psychological advantages of simple combinations of labor, the part played by emulation, the feeling of oneness with the group, the spur to concerted effort provided by rhythm of either movement or song" (Beattie, 1964: 188). One might also suggest the opportunity for talk and gossip. The point, however, is that the individual is still participating (along with other family members) in all the tasks necessary for survival. They are still involved in a domestic mode of production.

Basically opposed to the above types, both found mostly in the primitive world, is what has been called organized labor. Whereas communal labor may be organized to some extent in the sense that hunting tasks may be divided up between those who chase the game and those who wait in hiding to shoot it, a real organized division of labor is quite different. Here different tasks are performed by different individuals, singly or in groups, and the results of these specialists are exchanged to ensure survival or other goals. As in the true division of labor, one no longer directly participates in all the tasks necessary for survival. Production is for others (exchange), and skill becomes again an important factor. Some, but not all men, engage in hunting or making pots.

> The social advantages of specialization, which is implied by complex combinations of labor, are sufficiently obvious. The rich and varied life which can be enjoyed ... by at least some members of advanced cultures implies an almost complete dependence on other people, mostly total strangers, for the necessities of life. It is a truism that there is no point in specializing unless there is a possibility of exchange; there must be some means whereby all may be enabled to avail themselves of the special products of each. This calls for some degree of social and economic organization. (Beattie, 1964: 188)

As in the true division of labor, organized labor is mostly a phenomenon of modern industrial societies.

Other Divisions of Labor

There is a final and perhaps more specific way of examining labor differences in modern societies. This approach seems to have been somewhat ignored by anthropologists but represents a fruitful if formalistic view. It has been advanced by a sociologist, Stanley Udy, Jr. In describing differences between industrial and nonindustrial systems he has created a scheme in terms of which these differences as well as any similarities can be noted.

> Any organization manifestly engaged in the production of some material good is a production organization. All such organizations, whether industrial or not, are subject to structural limitations both technological and social in character. The nature of any technological process sets limits on the kinds of organization by which it can be carried out, and the social setting limits the kinds of organization institutionally possible in the society concerned. These limiting mechanisms affect at least four structural variables of any production organization: its permanence or impermanence, specificity or diffuseness, use of achievement or ascription as the basis of rewards for work, and social or territorial recruitment of personnel. (Udy, 1964: 115)

Here, briefly, are the variables of his production organization scheme:

Duration	*permanent*	when its structure outlasts the job spans of members;
	impermanent	if not outlasting the job spans of members.
Objectives	*specific*	if limited to material productive ends;
	diffuse	where additional ends are involved or if objectives are obscure.
Rewards	*achieved*	if they depend upon the amount of work or the energy expended;
	ascribed	if they are allocated independent of work or effort (automatic).
Recruitment	*social*	based upon prior membership in some other social group;
	territorial	based solely on spatial criteria.

Although Udy goes into greater detail on these variables, it can be suggested that, generally speaking, most primitive production organizations tend to be different structurally from those of our own experience. They are somewhat ascribed in rewards because of kinship and sharing responsibilities; even those individuals who do not contribute much to a communal animal hunt may receive the same portion of game as those who make the actual kills. They are social in recruitment. One is a member because the organization is his family or kinship group, not necessarily because he lives in the same village. It is diffuse in objectives since such groups may also utilize their existing organization to accomplish social or even religious ends as well as producing material ends. Duration may sometimes vary, but probably the most potent and reliable organizations in any society have a degree of permanency, although an ad hoc organization may arise to exploit some suddenly appearing resource.

In industrial societies, on the other hand, the production organizations are not only mostly permanent (the Ford Motor Company outlasts the individual worker), but differ markedly from those of primitive societies in the other structural features. They tend to be strongly oriented towards achievement in rewards (the better worker gets the raise, although labor unions seem to attempt to negate this practice); territorial recruitment is necessary to raise the necessary large force; and to maximum profit as well as productive potentials, they are specific in goal orientation.

Although schemes for divisions of labor in human societies could be multiplied, it would appear that from a number of points of view, primitive societies do differ significantly in their manner of organizing labor around their tools and techniques. These differences are perhaps largely contrasts: family-domestic modes of production and general self-sufficiency as opposed to specialized-exchange-oriented modes of production and interdependency. Of course, neither system can be characterized in absolute terms; each incorporates a portion of the other.

MECHANISMS OF EXCHANGE

The next aspect of primitive economics concerns exchange mechanisms. It has been remarked (Bohannan, 1963) that in our society production is complex (with many complicated industrial processes) but the allocation of goods is relatively simple: from factory to store to consumer. In most primitive societies, the reverse appears true. Production as previously demonstrated is simple, but, in the absence of special distributive institutions, allocation of goods is often complex. This is especially the case since usually such distribution is detached from production rather than accompanying it; that is, it is not generally incorporated into a make-sell-profit continuum of activities. Primitive distribution also differs markedly in its bias of a kinship basis for many such operations. When we attempt to understand primitive exchange mechanisms, it is again necessary to go somewhat beyond usual economic theory. One writer, Karl Polanyi, himself an economist, has suggested that in primitive societies there are at least three basic mechanisms of allocation of goods (or services). Every economy will rely upon one of these modes as its primary distributive mechanism and may also utilize the others. These mechanisms are reciprocity, redistribution, and market exchange. We will discuss and illustrate each of these in turn.

Reciprocity

Reciprocity, sometimes called gift giving, as a major mechanism seems to occur in the simpler primitive societies and as a subsidiary mechanism in perhaps all societies. Basically, reciprocity means that people act towards one another in a complementary or reciprocal fashion: "I give to you and you give to me." Diagramatically: A⇌B. It is based on the maxim that even if a gift is unsought and freely given, by accepting it one is placed under a corresponding obligation to return something of equal if not greater value. Such "giving" appears to be highly social, and most, in fact, is, many forms operating under the guise of kinship obligations. Much of it is also based on the fact that having such debts is a kind of social insurance towards some time when one may need more food or some necessary service. Then, too, many items (especially food, which might spoil) cannot exactly be hoarded in primitive societies. By giving some away, one also creates debts in others that may produce notions of prestige in the giver—"my, he's generous"—and prestige *can* be accumulated.

Marshall Sahlins (1965) has postulated the existence of three modes of reciprocity; generalized, balanced, and negative. *Generalized* reciprocity is based on the idea that gifts will perhaps balance out in the long run. It "refers to transactions that are putatively altruistic, transactions on the line of assistance given and, if possible and necessary, assistance returned" (Sahlins, 1965: 147). This form mostly occurs within the circle of close kinsmen, and the matter of a return may not be discussed or even implied. Actual return may never occur, and such a failure usually does not motivate the one-sided giver to terminate the relationship. You give because you feel you ought to do so. One need not dip into the literature on primitive peoples to illustrate this variety of reciprocity. One discovers it in our own (as well as primitive) family behaviors. Gifts and services rendered spouses and children are not expected to be equally reciprocated; if they were, children would be in a lot of trouble! Since such "transactions" are highly social, one gives because of the obligation to do so rather than out of motives of gain. Nonetheless, from an economic viewpoint, when a hunter shares his kill with his family or kin group, goods and services are being allocated although no formal mechanisms are involved.

Balanced reciprocity is a less personal encounter and involves returns asked for or at least strongly implied. Here the material side appears as important as its social dimensions in many cases since there is a more precise reckoning of debts.

> Balanced reciprocity refers to direct exchange. In precise balance, the reciprocation is the customary equivalent of the thing received and is without delay. Perfectly balanced reciprocity, the simultaneous exchange of the same types of goods to the same amounts, is . . . ethographically attested in certain marital transactions . . . friendship compacts . . . and peace agreements. Balanced reciprocity may be more loosely applied to transactions which stipulate returns of commensurate worth or utility within a finite and narrow period. (Sahlins, 1965: 147, 148)

All of this, while still embedded in activities definitely sociable, does strike the observer as economic. Two examples may be given to illustrate balanced reciprocity.

The first comes from the Philippine Islands and is found among speakers of the Tagalog language. It is called by them the Utang Na Loob relation, freely translated as "debt of prime obligation." This relation is established by a person giving an unsolicited gift to someone else or performing a service similarly offered: "Here is a chicken I think you would like to have." By accepting the gift (and one must or risk breeching social relations), the receiver has indicated in a contractual manner that he will in the future meet demands made upon him by the donor. Moreover, the return should actually be a little greater since the act of "free" giving adds an increment to the transaction. The return also must be of a different type of good or service. Generally, the gift has been proffered with a specific return in mind, which is expressed or implied—"that's a mighty fine looking spear you have there." Of course, the counter gift (also "freely" given) now creates a debt in the original giver, who must himself give in the future. This creates a never-ending and constantly alternating state of indebtedness. There are real economic principles involved here. Utang Na Loob helps to regulate the exchange of specialties and resources since the returns must be different. And there are restrictions involved in such transactions. The original and future giver must have a recognized need for whatever is being requested, and the debtor must be in a position to grant it. You cannot strip a man of his last spear! So ideas of supply and demand are involved. "The person with a need has the right to ask from those within his social grouping who have such a surplus. The person with a recognized need will approach someone with a recognized surplus and present him with a gift. ... If it is accepted, he will then have the right to return and ask for the surplus item which to him is a need" (Kaut, 1961: 261).

A second example is found among the Marquesas Islands of the Pacific. Here the reciprocity is in terms of labor service. A man will individually own extensive cultivated fields, the preparation and/or expansion of which is largely male responsibility. This is too much for him alone to accomplish. He does, however, possess many wives. He approaches (at the appropriate season) a number of landless males, who form a sort of floating labor pool, and invites them into his household to help with the agricultural tasks at hand. In return, along with food and lodging, they are granted sexual privileges with respect to his wives for that period of time. Service cancels service; the reckoning is precise and in this case short-term.

The third form of reciprocity is called *negative* reciprocity, and here the intent of one or perhaps both involved parties is "to get the better of one another," to obtain a greater return, or in some way to come out ahead. This is obviously less sociable and more indisputably economic than the other forms of reciprocity. Often transacted with strangers, it is also the furthest removed from a kinship orientation since it runs counter to the idea of kinship obligation and friendship. If gifts make friends and friends make gifts, a gyp situation is apt to make neither. Whereas in balanced reciprocity little of what might be called haggling takes place, here such value discussions are common.

An interesting example comes from the Dobu Islanders of the Western Pacific. These people, like others in their immediate area, engage in trade for largely ceremonial items with trading partners. The items are necklaces and armbands made of different types of shell. They are exchanged for each other and have traditional prestige values. At least for the Dobu Islanders, shrewd dealings with reference to these are also highly valued. Their ideal practice is called wabuwabu.

> To wabuwabu is to get many spondylus shell necklaces from different places to the south on the security of one armshell left at home in the north; or vice versa, many armshells from the north on a security that cannot meet them, promising the one valuable which one possesses to many different persons in return for their gifts that are being solicited. (Benedict, 1959: 144)

Here one promises more than one can give and reaps the benefit of return. Interestingly enough, the defrauded partners seem less angry at the shrewd trader (they do the same thing) than at the man who actually did get an item in equivalent return, and they may employ sorcery against the former person. Moreover, when one comes into possession of more armshells or necklaces (by promising more nonexistent commodities), one can pay off the older debts and so maintain at least minimal trust.

The Trobriand Islanders.   In any society where reciprocity is the basic mechanism, some combination of these three varieties—generalized, balanced, and negative—will occur. Perhaps the best overall account of how they fit together is supplied by Malinowski in his classic work on the Trobriand Islanders, *Argonauts of the Western Pacific.* Among these people, he recognized seven major types of reciprocal transaction. Paraphrasing Malinowski's statements for their comparative value, these are, briefly:

Pure gifts	mostly given in families without expectation of return, although they may eventually have to be returned at the death of the giver (if possible) to his rightful heirs. Also, if an excess of some good occurs (betel nut), the owner may simply give away what cannot be used. (generalized)
Customary payments	which are repaid irregularly without real equivalency—for example, payments received at harvest from a man's wife's brothers—and which are not always equivalently repaid by the husband. (generalized)
Payment for services rendered	are defined by custom each time some service is returned: for example, paying a specialist for his performance of magical rites or for building a canoe. (balanced)
Gifts returned in economically equivalent form	gifts for gifts that must equal out; generally between friends or kinsmen: for example, presents between a man and his wife's father on the occasion of marriage. (balanced)
Exchange of material goods against privileges	here persons exchange what they have for something else, usually of an immaterial nature: knowledge of magic

or the right to perform a dance. In the latter case, one "pays" a set amount to the man or village that invented it. (balanced)

Ceremonial barter with deferred payment

this is based on partnerships and includes Kula Ring transactions—necklaces for armshells—as well as vegetable food for fish to be used in rituals, not for ordinary consumption. The latter occurs between inland and lagoon villages. Here the amounts must be roughly equivalent. (balanced)

Trade pure and simple

here each side attempts to acquire what is needed based on an element of mutual advantage—giving away a less useful article. Much haggling and bargaining occur. The Trobrianders themselves consider this quite different from their other transactions. (negative)

Redistribution

The second mechanism for the distribution of goods is **redistribution**. Karl Polanyi had defined this as a systematic movement of goods to an administrative center and their reallotment by the authorities at that center. Diagramatically: A⇄ Usually such authorities are chiefs or kings or even priests who will reallocate portions of what is received. Some of the goods may be retained at the center to help maintain administrative functions: for example, food for a chief to entertain with and to support immediate henchmen. The redistributed portion may also be used as a reward to individuals or used to aid subsistence or other community services. Some writers call such behavior *pooling*. Structurally, pooling sometimes appears to be a kind of reciprocity, but its overall format is different.

> Their social organizations are very different. True, pooling and reciprocity may occur in the same social contexts ... but the precise social relations ... are not the same. The material transaction that is pooling is socially a within relation, the collective action of a group. Reciprocity is a between relation, the action and reaction of two parties ... Pooling stipulates a social center where goods meet and thence flow outwards, and a social boundary too, within which persons ... are cooperatively

related. But reciprocity stipulates two sides, two distinct social-economic interests. (Sahlins, 1965: 141, 142)

Moreover, although the benefit of redistribution may be of an economic nature, helping to sustain the community or whatever, it is also a reinforcer of that central authority. "The practical benefits may be critical, but . . . chiefly pooling generates the spirit of unity and centricity, codifies the structure, stipulates the centralized organization of social order and social action" (Sahlins, 1965: 143).

It is perhaps reasonable to consider redistribution as having both formal and informal expressions. In *formal* redistribution, the central authority is "political" in the usual sense of that expression and the motives overtly economic. Here an excellent example comes from the Inca of Peru, who at the time of European contact held sway over a vast empire along the west coast of South America. Here the common people had to put in service on state agricultural lands and labor on public works (in addition to efforts on behalf of the religious establishment). Harvest results from such fields were kept in storehouses to support the ruling class, artisans, and the army—the administrative center and its trappings! Such storehouses were also safeguards against famine. In seasons of plenty, a redistribution of such stores would take place to raise the dietary levels of the bulk of the population. Food could also be funneled through the center from one region of the empire to another (where not grown) to vary the diet. One sees here the kind of redistribution that Polanyi had in mind. Such does require some rank system with authority and power to make the system effective. Taxes in the United States on various levels work somewhat the same way, with money going in to run the branches of government and various public benefits such as schools and roads coming back to John Q. Citizen.

Many systems of redistribution, however, are less formal. The movement of goods seems less systematic or economic and the hierarchy of control and aims less "political." Such *informal* redistributive mechanisms may be more common in truly primitive societies. For example, in East Africa among cattle pastoralists, the payment of bride wealth (valuables exchanged for a bride in marriage) may function in such a manner. The father of the groom will put the "bite" for cows or wealth objects on the members of his greater kinship group. They will collect from among themselves the asking price for the girl. This will be forwarded to the appropriate kinship elder in the girl's group, and the bride will be given to the groom. The girl's group will then have the bride wealth redistributed to members who contributed cows in the past (or will in the future) for a male of their group to obtain a bride. If we treat the reciprocators of wealth and girl as constituting an informal center, redistribution has taken place. A is the kin group leader of the groom and B that of the bride.

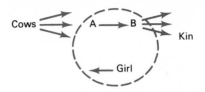

A more classic case of informal redistribution occurs among the intensive fishermen of the North Pacific coast of North America, in our unique collecting societies of chapter fifteen. As we shall see later (in chapter nineteen), these societies were characterized by a rank system, and the various component groups contained a graded series of individuals (based on genealogy), the highest of which held a sort of stewardship over the common property of the group. Much of the prerogative of such individuals and of rank in general was expressed in a curious institution called the *potlatch*. This was an event at which rank was either validated or confirmed and involved extensive giving of food and other presents to members of other groups. So, for example,

> the heir presumptive to a chieftainship would be presented formally to a group of guests at such an affair. His relationship to the incumbent chief would be explained and he would be given a name or the right to use some crest specifically related to the position he would eventually occupy . . . The guests who heard these claims announced and recognized their validity, were regarded as witnesses to the proceedings. As such, they were rewarded and their subsequent good will was insured by giving them feasts and gifts. While at times the demonstration of privileges or the giving away of material goods might appear to overshadow the essential announcement and validation of rights and status, this last-named function was the essence and basic goal of the whole performance. (Drucker, 1963: 132)

The members of the host group cooperated with the "chief" in contributing and assembling the food and other valuables. Here again such a leader is in effect a kind of administrative center to which goods are moving and from which they are dispensed. As such a mechanism, however, informal redistribution appears much more to cater to social than strictly economic needs, as demonstrated by both of the above examples.

Market Exchange

The last mode of distribution to be considered is *market exchange*. In general, this was defined by Polanyi (and economists) as the exchange

Some primitive societies do have market places although money is not used. This is a trading store in Bamenda, Northern Cameroons.

United Nations

of goods based on factors of supply and demand and on prices set by "the market." In a more comparative sense, a producer takes his result to the market and exchanges it for other produce. We differ both quantitatively and qualitatively from primitives in this behavior. We produce for the market, exchanging our product (labor or goods) for money which permits us then to obtain most if not all of our subsistence. In primitive subsistence economies there may well be markets (market places) to which goods are taken, but they do not derive the major proportion of their subsistence by this mechanism; nor is "money" necessarily involved. Put another way, if their markets were to disappear, such people would not perish, although they might well have to cut back on luxury goods consumption. Such unnecessary markets are generally called peripheral markets. So what we really observe is the market "place" rather than the market "principle."

Even in the sense that they occur in primitive societies such markets seem recognizably economic, if only for extra goods. Many writers have pointed out, however, that market places have a great number of social functions as well and that they may, in fact, exist as much for these as for the securing of actual goods. Paul Bohannan has suggested a number of such basically noneconomic motives for West African markets, and the present text follows his discussion. Because the market brings together considerable numbers of people on a regular, periodic basis, a major function is that they can serve as nodes in the network of communication. Either on a formal or informal basis, information can be disseminated. One can exchange news and gossip with friends, and distant kinsmen and chiefs or other officials can make announcements. Then, too, entertainment (other than gossip) finds an audience at the market, not only for dancers and singers but, as Bohannan wryly observes, "the market day usually falls off into a beer drink" (1963: 242). Then there are important political considerations. Control of markets is usually under the direction of political authorities. This is not only

276

advantageous to them but also to those who derive various satisfactions within it since usually the safety of the market place (market peace) is guaranteed to them by such authority. In addition, markets can become focal points for legal behavior. The local chief or his representatives can sit in judgement on dispute cases surrounding past grievances as well as those stemming from the market place itself. Religious activities may also occur. A market is just the place to seek out a seller of magical ingredients, consult a diviner, or witness some more public religious procedure.

> In summary, market places—particularly in areas in which the market is economically peripheral—fulfill many social and cultural needs of the population. Indeed some markets are not regarded as primarily economic institutions by the people. They provide a meeting place where a certain minimum, at least, of security is assured and hence they can be used for political, religious, social and personal purposes. In a society in which collections of people on nonkinship bases may prove difficult, the market place provides the setting for a wide range of social activities. (Bohannan, 1963: 243–44)

MODES OF EXCHANGE

In the discussion of reciprocity, redistribution, and market exchange we have not as yet made clear the *modus operandi* for such transactions. A brief discussion of this will lead us into yet another major difference between primitive and modern economic systems. In many primitive societies, the mode whereby such exchanges occur is *barter*: exchanging one good for another. Such behavior may take two forms. Perhaps the most restricted of these has been called *dumb barter* (silent trade), which involves little in the way of face-to-face contact between exchangers and no haggling. The Pygmies of the Ituri Forest of Africa are generally cited as a case in point. As Putnam (1948) describes it, the Pygmies trade in a regular fashion with their Bantu neighbors, leaving meat, hides, and other forest products in certain agreed-upon locations. These are spots where the Bantu have left piles of agricultural and manufactured products. They leave their own goods and take those in the opposite pile. Neither side, however, can afford to cheat the other, despite the fact that one's partner is absent, since this would be bad for subsequent "business." The Phoenicians, those indefatigable traders of the ancient world, also seem to have traded with peoples of different languages in such a fashion.

Perhaps most of barter is done in the direct sense, with long bar-

Direct barter permits complete freedom of expression and sharper trading. These men are bargaining over a piece of material.

Omikron

gaining sessions or ritual observances often accompanying it. *Direct barter* thus permits a more complete expression of feeling for all concerned and sharper trading since one is better able to secure the quality or quantity of what is desired. Any form of barter, however, has several disadvantages. One may desire some product possessed by another but lack the commodity desired in exchange—you want his chickens, but he doesn't want any more pots. One may also have to accept an undesirable article simply to keep the social aspects of a partnership open in the event of future need. And, of course, there is the overall transportation problem. How to get the goods for barter to the proper location and home again. They may be bulky or perishable. A herd of cattle on the way to market or to a trading partner could lose weight or be stolen along the way (devalued currency?).

Solving these kinds of problems in the modern world, and in some primitive societies, is money. Money not only takes a number of forms— coins, banknotes, etc.—but is really capable of economic application in a number of senses. It may be used as a form of payment, a way of settling debts. It can be used is a standard of value: all goods can be assigned values in terms of it (a chicken equals ten shells, a dozen eggs equals two shells, chickens are worth five dozen eggs). Obviously, this cuts down on the bargaining time necessary in exchange transactions. This leads to a third major function of money, its use as a medium of exchange, which overcomes other drawbacks of barter situations.

In primitive societies, money (lacking the United States mint) takes forms dictated by locally available natural resources.

278

> One of the most exotic kinds of money in the world today is a belt two inches wide and 30 feet long made of glue, fibers and feathers, particularly the downy red feathers plucked from the breast, head and back of a tropical forest bird. The red-feather money of the Santa Cruz Islands of the southwest Pacific nonetheless fits the most rigorous definition of the term "money." It serves as a means of accumulating wealth and as a universal medium of exchange in the highly diversified commerce that flows among these islands. The currency itself is fully interchangeable, each belt having a precisely negotiable value in terms of other belts. (Davenport, 1962: 95)

Supplies of such money depend on the people continually obtaining sufficient red feathers and the going out of circulation of older currency (when the color fades, the belts become worthless). Among its many uses, red-feather money is used (much like cattle in East Africa) in obtaining brides. The minimum payment is ten units or belts, ranging in value from one newly made belt to one that is almost completely faded. From the newest on down, each of these belts is worth twice as much as the next one. For example, say a value of 100 for the top belt, 50 for the next, and so on down to that of hardly any value. Thus, these people can spell out their business deals in terms of dollars and cents. In many primitive societies, however, such forms of money as exist may not be capable of such usages; they may be more limited in their functional applications. Money used simultaneously (or on different occasions) for all functions has been called *general-purpose* money. Money employed in less total senses, for example only payment, has been designated as *special-purpose* money.

In societies that lack money in its general sense we often discover that exchanges for the most part may occur in a number of different spheres marked by different modes of transaction and often displaying different moral values as well. Primitives exhibiting such behaviors are said, as a result, to display *multicentric* economies. With general-purpose money available, a *unicentric* economy emerges with such currency knitting together all areas and aspects of economic behavior. A now-classic example of a multicentric economy has been recognized by Paul Bohannan (1959) among the Tiv of Central Nigeria in Africa. Here, traditionally, there were three economic spheres. The subsistence sphere consisted of exchange of various foodstuffs, raw materials, and utensils. Such goods changed hands either by reciprocity or in the market by bartering activities. The prestige sphere consisted, among other things, of cattle, slaves, medicines, and brass rods. Within this sphere, the latter commodity served as general-purpose money, but not outside this range of activities. In this sphere, "The actual shifts of goods took place at ceremonies, at more or less ritualized wealth displays, and on occasions when 'doctors' performed rites and prescribed medicines" (Bohannan,

1959: 493). The last sphere was one involving rights in people (other than slaves), particularly women. A man would deliver a female ward to an outsider in marriage and receive another woman in exchange who either became his wife or one for a kinsman or a ward to be later exchanged outside again. Although the system is much more complicated than expressed here—conversion exchanges could occur between spheres in certain situations—a general impression can be gained of how lack of a single unitary currency can keep separate major spheres of economic activity.

OWNERSHIP, PROPERTY, AND INHERITANCE

The last major interest area of economics for the anthropologist consists of the concepts of ownership, property, and inheritance. Just as all human societies organize work and distribute its products, so apparently does the effective use of such resources require some sense of their possession and ownership. Ideas relative to ownership and property, however, differ significantly from one society to another, and the forms that property may assume are many. Property may be personal or communal; it may be fixed in position or transportable (land or cattle); and it may be material in substance or immaterial (like a magical spell or a dance). Also, of course, concepts of reciprocity may be involved; one may have to share one's hunting luck—so that what begins as personal property ends up in community hands. Such sharing may include nonconsumable goods. Among the Cuna Indians of Panama, "It is requisite of the ideal character that one be generous and ungrudging in lending his personal possessions" (Stout, 1946: 74).

The concept of property is complex and varies from society to society.

Gabriele Wunderlich

Some degree of confusion surrounds the concept of **property.** Many times we are led into conceiving property in terms of objects. In reality, it is more than the things owned themselves, "For property is a term commonly applied to both objects that are said to be owned as well as the rights exercized over such objects" (Hallowell, 1943: 120). In fact, it is the social aspect that is most important since possessions only become property with the consent of other group members; it consists of patterns of rights, duties, and powers. So, in essence, property represents a complex of social behaviors relative to an object, behaviors involving a number of privileges, responsibilities, and restrictions. So, for example, one "owns" an automobile and has the privilege of driving it, if it is licensed and insured and if one does not exceed the speed limits! Expressed differently, since the group permits the operation of property, it, not the possessor, regulates its effective use. And the privileges granted are never total.

> In all societies, then, property comprises a "bundle of rights," not a single right, nor an absolute right. These rights may be of different kinds. It is necessary to determine, for instance, whether only the right of using is implied or also the right of using up . . . Is there the right to destroy in the case of things which can be used without destroying them, as well as in the case of things destroyed in the using? Is the right of alienation included Does the right likewise include bequest and if there is the right of bequest are there also special limitations imposed? (Hallowell, 1943: 123)

Because of the great diversity of such property rights, no attempt will be made here to describe them, save to give a brief impression of such behaviors. Many things can become objects of property rights. Land is a commonly owned possession, and because it assumes great importance in most societies for agriculture or because of resources located upon it, it often becomes the focus of rights both complex and multiple. An excellent example is given in a general text on economics by Melville Herskovitz (1965). He discusses land tenure among the Ibo of West Africa, an agricultural people.

Ibo Land Tenure

The Ibo have four basic types of land: sacred land, virgin forest, farming land held by groups, and individual holdings. The sacred land consists of groves of trees around religious shrines. This is not normally exploited because of fear of spirits, but if one wishes to clear such land for farming it becomes regarded as his own (if he is not zonked by the resident spirits), and after two years he can do what he wishes with this property.

Virgin forest is also usually not farmed for a variety of reasons. If someone wishes to clear it, however, the act of so doing, again, gives him title to own it and transfer rights for his heirs. In some cases, permission of village elders must first be secured since such land is considered a resource for the entire village. The category of communal holdings by groups is somewhat different. It consists of three divisions. Village land is at some distance from the village and is broken down into individual or small family plots. Ancestral land is closer to the village and is held in common by kinship groups. Here the plot of a specific individual can be alienated by the consent of the entire membership group. Household land consists of the land on which the family dwelling is located and cannot be given away by its owners because of religious reasons; the ancestors would punish the seller! What we observe, then, are a series of different sorts of rights, ranging from "absolute" in the case of land carved from sacred areas, to qualified as in the case of ancestral-kin-group land (if subdivided to accommodate population increase, one may have his amount restricted), to using one's household land but not being able to dispose of it to outsiders. So, much private land is hedged with social pressures. Such have often taken the form of what have been called *usufruct rights.* This is a situation in which one owns something privately but only so long as proper care or use is made of it. In some societies, this terminates at the death of the owning individual—being nontransferable to heirs—or it may even require that the land be kept in constant usage; not farming a parcel of land may permit someone else to come in and do so and come to own it. In primitive societies, usufruct rights often insure that resources are kept productive and represent a recognition that all people have a right to the means to support of life—a kind of active welfare system.

Multiple Rights Among the Tupi Namba

Multiple rights, of course, may be applied to anything that becomes the object of property relationships, even other human beings. For the Tupi Namba of Brazil, such rights involved prisoners captured in warfare. Such unfortunates were the chief cause of warfare since ritual cannibalism was the eventual outcome. A prisoner would belong to the first man touching him. The captor would also be responsible for his care and fattening up. However, the actual honor of killing went to another person, and the feast on the remains was open to all.

> Old women rushed to drink the warm blood, and children were invited to dip their hands in it. Mothers would smear their nipples with blood so that even babies could have a taste of it. The body, cut into

> quarters, was roasted on a barbecue, and the old women, who were the
> most eager for human flesh, licked the grease running along the sticks.
> Some portions, reputed to be delicacies or sacred, such as the fingers or
> the grease around the liver or heart, were allotted to distinguished
> guests. (Metraux, 1963: 124)

The slayer was not permitted to eat the flesh of his victim. Female captives were often taken as secondary wives or concubines and belonged
to their captor. Male captives similarly could temporarily marry. But in
most cases, sooner or later, they were ritually killed, as were perhaps
their offspring! So we observe again privilege bounded by duty.

INHERITANCE

Inheritance, the coming into possession of someone else's property
rights, is also governed by the social privileges granted by society. Most
cases of inheritance follow the demise of the previous owner, and many
primitive customs on such occasions may strike us as less than economically sound. As part of the rituals of death, or out of fear generated by
the situation, much or all of the property of the deceased may be buried
with him or otherwise destroyed for use in the "next life." Here is a
case where you can take it with you! Often, however, compromise with
economic necessity takes place and the destruction of goods becomes a
more symbolic event. It would hardly do for the Nuer to slaughter cows
when their owners die!

Principles of Inheritance

There are many facets to the subject of inheritance in primitive societies.
Out of the welter of detail, however, one can observe the operation of
a number of fairly consistent principles. These are generally different in
nature from comparative features of our own inheritance behaviors. First,
there is generally no ability for a person to will or bequest his property
(testamentary disposition) to whom so ever he chooses—*limitations of
bequest*. I can, generally speaking, leave my earthly goods to whomever I
legally so designate, perhaps even my mistress. In primitive societies
succession to such rights is generally in terms of traditional usage, going
automatically to members of a kinship or other group, to a chief, or
reverting to communal control. Occasionally, one can circumvent such
customs. Among the Boloki of Africa, for example:

> A sick man wished to bequeath some property to a friendly but unrelated medicine man, but there was no possible way of directly doing

so. Accordingly, he resorted to subterfuge. Inviting the doctor to his deathbed, he dealt him a light blow across the ankle. For this "assault and battery" the medicine man sued the heirs, demanding and receiving damages . . . precisely the objects the deceased had wished to give him. (Lowie, 1948: 152, 149)

A second general principal differing from our own practice is what might be called *same-sex* inheritance, in which only males inherit from males and females from females. This means that a spouse is not apt (as they are in our own society) to receive a portion of a partner's estate. Although this strikes one as perhaps unfair, it must be recalled that because of the natural division of labor under which many of these peoples operate a surviving spouse would not be able to use such property anyway: "a woman herd cows—unthinkable!" Moreover, lacking money practice, the spouse could not convert such valuables either. A third interesting feature is what is called *anticipatory* inheritance, in which some of the property must change hands before death even occurs. For example, in some East African cattle-pastoral societies a nephew will inherit part of his uncle's (mother's brother) herd in anticipation of the larger share he will receive after the death of that individual. Not unexpectedly, this may lead to hard feelings in some cases: the one too eager and the other reluctant to give the cows. In some societies, a younger brother will gain a wife by inheriting her from his older brother when he dies. Sometimes he will already be granted sexual, if not economic, privileges with respect to her in acknowledgement of this fact (anticipatory levirate). Can you imagine a young man in our society inheriting the family car in such an anticipatory manner?

Finally, in many primitive societies, is the idea of *unitary* inheritance. Here one person, usually a son or daughter, inherits all the possessions of a parent, with his or her siblings or other possible heirs being disenfranchised. This is often an expedient undertaken to guard against splitting up such possessions: agricultural land, for example, into economically unfeasible portions. How can you divide up a canoe? Again, this is partially due to a lack of money enabling conversion of the property into wealth per se. Generally in such cases the property descends according to some age principle: primogeniture if it goes to the oldest, ultimogeniture if it goes to the youngest. Of these two alternatives, ultimogeniture seems to occur more as an informal mechanism than as a formal rule. "In junior right the youngest inherits the bulk of the property . . . for the simple reason that he stays (home) . . . whereas his seniors have departed" (Lowie, 1948: 152). Such occurs to some extent in our own society. The sibling who stays behind to care for the "old folks" often retains possession of the family home as a reward.

We have seen in this chapter that economics in primitive societies, based generally upon subsistence rather than exchanges for profit, is institutionalized in ways different from those we are familiar with in our own experience. Differences in labor division, distribution of goods, ownership, and inheritance occur. We will turn in the next series of chapters to social behaviors in general, having to do with marriage and kinship, social groupings, and law, government, and welfare.

SUMMARY

1. A people's economic behavior is described by their divisions of labor; mechanisms of distribution of goods and services; and concepts of ownership, property, and inheritance. Generally such arrangements differ in subsistence and prestige economies as does the basic self-sufficiency of social units.

2. The social organization of labor is the natural division of labor based on age and sex; the true division of labor is based more on skill requirements. The two organizations can be differentiated in terms of numbers of people involved and exchange factors (individual, communal, or organized). The production organization approach also offers a perspective on differences between primitive and industrial work efforts.

3. Exchange mechanisms include generalized, balanced, and negative reciprocity (gift giving); formal and informal redistribution; and market exchange. The last is generally of a peripheral nature in primitive societies but accomplishes many important social goals.

4. Property represents a complex of social behaviors granted to individuals or groups by society involving rules of privilege, responsibility, and restriction relative to the use of objects or things. Many different kinds of property rights occur. Inheritance—the transmission of such rights—in primitive societies is often characterized by traditional factors, same-sex considerations, anticipation, and unitary factors.

REFERENCES FOR FURTHER READING

The study of primitive economic systems is in something of a renaissance at the present time, and the total volume of works devoted to this subject is voluminous. Four readers are worth serious perusal: *Economic Anthropology*, edited by Edward LeClair, Jr. and Harold

Schneider (1968, Holt, Rinehart & Winston); *Capital, Savings and Credit in Peasant Societies*, edited by Raymond Firth and B. J. Yamey (1964, Aldine); *Tribal and Peasant Economies* and *Economic Development and Social Change*, both edited by George Dalton and both published by Natural History Press (1967 and 1971). The old standby text, now somewhat out of date, is *Economic Anthropology*, by Melville Herokovitz (1952, Norton). A new text, argued from a special perspective is *Stone Age Economics*, by Marshall Sahlins (1972, Aldine). His article on reciprocity, which I have exerpted from *Relevance of Models for Social Anthropology* (1965, Association of Social Anthropologists Monographs, Praeger), is included in this text. A brief but classic account is by Marcel Mauss, *The Gift* (1967, Norton). A small but useful volume is by Manning Nash, *Primitive and Peasant Economic Systems* (1966, Chandler).

John Beattie has a thoughtful chapter on economic behavior in *Other Cultures* (1964, Free Press), as does Paul Bohannan in *Social Anthropology* (1963, Holt, Rinehart & Winston). His paper on the Tiv is "The Impact of Money on an African Subsistence Economy," in *Journal of Economic History* 19 (1959): 491–503. The article by Stanley Udy, Jr., "The Preindustrial Forms of Organized Work," I have excerpted from *Cultural and Social Anthropology*, edited by Peter Hammond (1964, Macmillan). "Utang NaLoob: A System of Contractual Obligation Among Tagalogs" is by Charles Kaut, in *Southwestern Journal of Anthropology* 17 (1961): 256–72. Much of the work of Karl Polanyi can be found in *Primitive, Archaic and Modern Economies: Essays of Karl Polanyi*, edited by George Dalton (1968, Doubleday). Two volumes of specific studies I have personally enjoyed are *Kapauku Papuan Economy*, by Leopold Pospisil (1963, Yale University Pubs in Anthro no. 67); and *Malay Fishermen: Their Peasant Economy*, by Raymond Firth (1946, Kegan Paul). The classic account of the Kula Ring is by Bronislau Malinowski, *Argonauts of the Western Pacific*, available in paperback (1961, Dutton). The Dobu example is taken from Ruth Benedict, *Patterns of Culture* (1959, New American Library). The potlatch description is taken from Philip Drucker, *Indians of the Northwest Coast* (1963, Natural History Press). A good account of the Inca is available in *The Ancient Civilizations of Peru*, by J. Alden Mason (1968, Penguin Books). The Pygmy example comes from "The Pygmies of the Ituri Forest," by Patrick Putnam, in *A Reader in General Anthropology*, edited by Carleton Coon (1958, Holt, Rinehart & Winston). An excellent book on markets is *Markets in Africa*, a reader edited by Paul Bohannan and George Dalton (1962, Northwestern University Press). The money example is from William Davenport, "Red Feather Money," in *Scientific American* 206, no. 3 (1962): 95–104.

The quotation on the Cuna comes from "Land Tenure and Other Property Concepts Among the San Blas Cuna," by David Stout (my own mentor), in *Primitive Man* 19 (1946): 63–80. A general article on property is by A. Irving Hallowell, "The Nature and Function of Property as a Social Institution," in *Journal of Legal and Political Sociology* 1 (1943): 115–38. The cannibalism example is taken from Alfred Metraux, "The Tupi Namba," in *Handbook of South American Indians*, vol. 3, edited by Julian Steward (1963, Cooper Square Press). An excellent discussion of property rights and inheritance occurs in Robert Lowie, *Social Organization*, (1959, Rinehart).

17

kinship
and marriage

Kinship and marriage are perhaps the basic social facts of life for human organisms. Rather than relating to others of the group by some kind of "herd instinct," primitive peoples especially employ ties of kinship. Also, since the human species is bisexual, we cannot escape from sexual relations and survive. Since problems can arise here, all societies impose limitations on sexual behavior, the most visible of which relate to marriage rules and customs. In the present chapter, we will deal with some general principles of kinship and marriage on an outline level and then see how these translate into the reality of behavior in the next chapter. This chapter is, then, more theoretical than descriptive.

KINSHIP RELATIONSHIPS

As previously mentioned, kinship is a way of creating human groups. Certainly, there are other organizing criteria: sex, age, locality, social status, occupation, and a host of purely voluntary reasons. Kinship however, as we shall see, is not only a natural way to create groups but in many societies kinship-based groups overlap significantly with those brought into existence by the other criteria; for example, the locality group may also be a kinship group. Generally, kinship is thought to refer to ties of biology (in the genetic sense). A person is my kinsman because I am descended from him (my father) or because we share an ancestor in common (my brother). This is a relationship by **consanguinity.** Such a biological connection can easily be the basis for group organization. If we stretch the concept of biology to include sexuality as well, say the relations of husband and wife, still other human beings can be dragged into the net of kinship and the group. Such a relation is called a relation of **affinity,** and the resultant kin are called affinal kin as opposed to consanguineal kin. Out of general relations of affinity and

Kinship is a way of creating human groups. Since relationships need not be strictly biological, large "families" can often result.

consanguinity there are a number of possible ties. Relationships can also exist that are not really kinship-based but are based on a social reality that treats them as if they were. This is fictive or pretend kinship and will be treated in subsequent chapters.

Paul Bohannan (1963) has neatly simplified kinship relations in diagrammatic form. He has suggested that relations by sexuality and descent (affinity and consanguinity) can be either direct or shared (indirect). *Direct* sexuality involves the relation between a man and his wife. Shared sex relations encompass indirect relations created by the direct sex relation: for example, those between the two wives of the same husband or, by extension, an in-law relation (I have a brother-in-law because my wife is his sister). Parents and offspring have a relation of direct descent; they are *lineal* kin. Brothers and sisters have a shared-descent relation since they share an ancestor in common (they are *collateral* kin), as do a person and his father's brother (the grandfather of one is the father of the other). In Bohannan's diagram (1963: 56), these possible relations are given designations:

	Direct	Shared
Sexuality	spouses	co-spouses
Descent	lineals	collaterals

Breaking this diagram down more specifically, we can observe ten basic kinship relationships or positions. These are the primary immediate relatives for any individual. Two of these positions are created by direct sexuality: husband and wife. One is created by shared sexuality, the co-spouse relations, which can be between co-husbands or co-wives. So there are two relations or positions here. Direct descent creates the positions of father, mother, son, and daughter, and the relations of either

290

parent to either child. Shared descent creates the positions of brother and sister and their possible relations. As Bohannan has diagrammed it (1963: 60):

	Direct		*Shared*
Sexuality	Husband–wife		co-wife–co-wife co-husband–co-husband
Descent	father–son father–daughter	mother–son mother–daughter	brother–brother sister–sister brother–sister

Put another way, a male can potentially be a husband, co-husband, father, son, and brother; and a female can be a wife, co-wife, mother, sister, and daughter; and one can have relationships to all the other primary relatives!

KINSHIP ROLES

There are, of course, various ways to examine such relations. We can determine what names (kinship terms) are attached to these positions and to the persons who occupy them. More about this presently. We can observe what kinds of groups actually develop in response to recognition of such ties. This is dealt with in the next chapter. We can also observe the actual behavioral obligations that correspond with these positions. Such an approach is generally discussed with reference to the concepts of status and role, also applied to nonkinship behaviors. Simply put, a **status** is a social position that a person may occupy—such as father, chief or witchdoctor. It is visible and recognizable with reference to other such positions. **Role** is the complex of behaviors associated with that status, defined in terms of privileges, responsibilities, and restrictions. What are the roles of such primary relatives? George P. Murdock, in a very general manner, has discussed some of the more typical as follows:

Husband and wife: economic specialization and cooperation; sexual cohabitation; joint responsibility for support, care, and upbringing of children; well defined reciprocal rights with respect to property, divorce, spheres of authority, etc.

Father and son: economic cooperation in masculine activities under leadership of the father; obligations of material support, vested in father during childhood of son, in son during old age of father; responsibility of father for instruction and discipline of son; duty of obedience and respect on part of son, tempered by some measure of comradeship.

Mother and daughter: relationship parallel to that between father and son but with more emphasis on child care and economic cooperation and less on authority and material support.

Mother and son: dependence of son during infancy; imposition of early disciplines by mother; moderate economic cooperation during childhood of son; early development of a lifelong incest taboo; material support by son during old age of mother.

Father and daughter: responsibility of father for protection and material support prior to marriage of daughter; economic cooperation, instruction, and discipline appreciably less prominent than in father-son relationship; playfulness common in infancy of daughter, but normally yields to a measure of reserve with the development of a strong incest taboo.

Brother and sister: early relationship of playmates, varying with relative age; gradual development of an incest taboo, commonly coupled with some measure of reserve; moderate economic cooperation; partial assumption of parental role, especially by the elder. (Murdock, 1963: 93, 94)

KINSHIP TERMINOLOGY

It can be recognized that the study of kinship is at once both fascinating (different societies have different role expectations for kin) and complex. Different societies also apply linguistic labels (kin terms) in different manners and to different degrees. Before sampling the realm of kinship terminology, it again becomes necessary to present diagrams. It is clumsy to write out (and difficult to visualize) long chains of kinship relationships. To avoid these problems, anthropologists have devised symbols to stand for such relations. A triangle stands for a male, a circle for a female, an equal-sign for a marriage tie, and a line for descent; vertical for direct descent and horizontal for shared descent. So, for example:

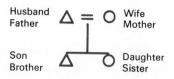

Usually in such a diagram one symbol for a person is designated as *ego,* the position from which the kinship reckoning originates. A little practice in extending this basic diagram out would be a significant exercise for the student at this point. Play the kinship game: give father some brothers and sisters, perhaps an extra wife or two; marry off son and daughter (not to each other); and give everybody children.

Now, the terms that may be applied to such kinsmen are numerous and difficult for the anthropologist to determine. Mostly what we seem to record are terms of *reference*—"he is my father"—terms used to designate a person when speaking about them. These are often really names for the positions (statuses) more than for the occupants. Terms of *address* are used more in speaking to that person—"hey pop"—although the linguistic usage may be the same in both cases. How do such terms originate (apparently, calling everyone by the same term is impractical and confusing)? Different terms originate in a variety of ways.

Numerous anthropologists have suggested criteria that can be employed for differentiation of kinship terms. Among them are the following:

Generation	applying different terms to persons in the generation above and below ego (to differentiate father from son).
Sex	applying different terms to differently sexed individuals (to differentiate brother from sister).
Affinity	applying different terms for relations based on a marriage tie from those based on descent (to differentiate wife from sister).
Lineality	collaterality—applying different terms to those biological kinsmen who are not so close to ego as are lineal kinsmen (to differentiate father from uncle).
Bifurcation	applying different terms to individuals who are linked to ego through male or female links (to differentiate mother's brother from father's brother).
Relative age	applying different terms for relatives in the same category who differ in age (to differentiate older sister from younger sister).
Speaker's sex	applying a different term to a person if the speaker is male or female (two different words for father).

Although there are other criteria, these appear to be the most important in terms of primary kinship term usages and their immediate extensions.

The systems these criteria create differ. Ideally, if they all were simultaneously employed, all individuals would receive separate formal designations (sometimes called a descriptive kinship system). Such a total effort would place greater stresses on the memory of the behaving individuals. Moreover, since many people can be lumped together in the same behavioral categories in terms of role expectations, it is a general occurrence that some overlap occurs in such kinship systems. That is to say, different people are classified together under the same linguistic kin term: for example, the use of the term *uncle* in our own system. Such kinship systems, which have been called **classificatory**, originate when people do not employ all the term criteria simultaneously. Such lumping does not mean, however, that the individuals concerned do not recognize differences between people—they do—only that they consider the behavioral expectations attached to the term roughly equivalent for all the "actors" so designated! So the "inhabitants" of the positions are the same in this sense even though their biology and psychology is different.

Kinship Term Systems

As previously suggested, such relations are complex. Four major kinship terminological systems have been traditionally recognized by anthropologists. These are based upon distinctions drawn by ego with reference to the first ascending generation. We can briefly discuss and illustrate these. The numbers used in the diagrams represent the same kinship term. The first of these systems is our own and is called the *lineal* system.

In this system, the major criteria employed are sex, generation, and lineality-collaterality. There is a separate term for father and mother; they are different terms from those applied to people in ego's own generation, and lineal kinsmen are separated from collateral kin (uncles and aunts), who are lumped together except for sex.

One can be even more descriptive and add the criterion of bifurcation or splitting into two lines and wind up with *bifurcate collateral* kinship terminology.

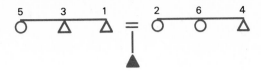

Here the "uncles and aunts" receive separate designations depending on the sex link between them and ego: father's brother from mother's brother and father's sister from mother's sister.

Again, one can do different kinship lumping from that in our own system. In *bifurcate merging* kinship terminology, based on the "equivalence of siblings" one partly overrides the lineality-collaterality distinction.

Here there is a single term for "father" and all his brothers, a single term for "mother" and all her sisters, and separate designations for father's sister and a mother's brother, who are treated as more distant relatives.

Finally, one can more totally lump together people in the generation above oneself. This results in *generational* kinship terminology, which recognizes only the criteria of sex and generation, with merging of lineals and collaterals, not recognizing this last criterion.

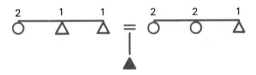

It should be realized that not all people possessing one of these systems employ it in precisely the same manner since one has to take into account people in one's own generation as well as descending generations. And, of course, one must take into account people in the generation above one's parents. Nonetheless, there is a kind of pressure for such criteria to be applied throughout the system. This can quickly be demonstrated with reference to cousin terminology systems. Anthropologists recognize two categories with reference to cousins. Those to which ego is related through members of the parental generation of the same sex (father–brother, mother–sister) are called *parallel* cousins. Those to which one traces through oppositely sexed parental generational links (father–sister, mother–brother) are called *cross* cousins. In a generational system (with Hawaiian cousin terms), the pressure is to extend terms for brother and sister to all cousins because you call their parents by the same terms you apply to your own. Here there are no "cousins" only "brothers and sisters."

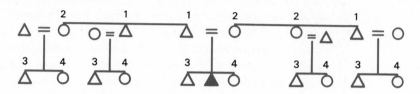

In our own lineal system (Eskimo cousin terms), it will be remembered that we differentiate all cousins from brothers and sisters since they are not the children of "father and mother." We also lump these people together regardless of sex; males and females are both "cousins." Finally, in a bifurcate merging system (Iroquois cousin terms) sibling terms are extended to parallel cousins but there is a separate term for cross cousins (parallel cousins are not different from brother and sister).

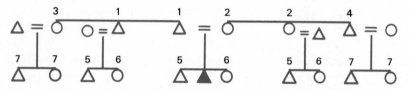

Beyond these simple examples the level of complexity goes past the scope of a general introductory text. It has been seen, however, that such systems do operate by a kind of inherent logic. Understanding how terms are formulated and operate in patterns is necessary because of the kinship orientation of most primitive societies. We can now deal with some general principles of marriage.

MARRIAGE

It was mentioned earlier that sexuality in human societies is regulated in various ways. In so doing, not only is mating limited but marriage institutions are created. Mating itself is simply "sex for the sake of sex" (the pairing off of oppositely sexed individuals under the influence of the sex drive). Although much of mating occurs in marriage, certainly appreciable amounts occur outside of marriage, in premarital and extramarital situations, and exchange (wife lending) forms. Such may or may not be preferred behavior. Marriage itself has been defined as "a complex of customs centering upon the relationship between a sexually associating pair of adults within the family" (Murdock, 1963: 1). This complex of customs defines the relations of the husband and wife to each other, to the various kinsmen of both, to other individuals, and, perhaps most importantly, to any resultant children. As Murdock implies, it is marriage that creates the family, which provides a more or less stable social situation for raising children (among other functions). Put another way, marriage can be defined as a license for procreation. Even where some form of mating is officially encouraged outside of marriage, the procreation of children is not. So marriage is sex with a lot of responsibility and other elements added, as many a young person even in our own society soon discovers.

INCEST

Now, of course, marriage is one way of regulating sex; in some societies you can't indulge (ideally) unless married. There are, however, numerous other controls on sexuality. Since human sexuality is not governed by biological controls, we should expect many learned behaviors in this regard! Probably the most universal and interesting is the incest taboo. This is a rule, often receiving supernatural as well as human sanction, prohibiting mating with a close biological relative and, consequently, prohibiting marriage with such a person. As a rule, this almost always applies to the members of one's immediate family, and because of kinship lumping, it may be extended to other people as well; remember all those "brothers and sisters" in a generational kinship system. It can even be extended to pretend kinsmen.

So, forms of the incest taboo, restricted or extended, occur in all human societies. As in the case of other behavioral universals, a great deal of anthropological "ink" has been spilled over its explanation. At least half a dozen reasons are generally cited. One can be called the inbreeding theory. This holds that incest taboos originated as a guard against the undesirability of inbreeding among individuals too closely related. Generally it has been felt that this would result in bad genetic consequences. Recent studies have shown this to be a possible consequence, but one wonders if early peoples would have been able to correctly assess such results and develop an incest taboo to stop them. Another theory revolves around indifference or revulsion and might be called the psychological theory. In one form, it holds that the taboo results from the normal sexual indifference that people who grow up or live together have for one another, the taboo being an overt recognition of this fact. One wonders if such indifference truly is the case; after all, husbands and wives live together for a long time. Also, if indifferent, why bother formalizing it and why apply the prohibition to people outside the range of common habitation? The other variety of this theory comes from the Freudian concept of the *primal horde*. In the remote past, the young males of a group killed off the old patriarch who ruled the group and monopolized its females in the effort to appropriate the women for themselves. Later (after the orgy), they felt guilt and revulsion over what they had done; he was, after all, also their father and the women their mothers and sisters! So they punished themselves by imposition of the incest taboo. This seems based on a rather dubious reconstruction of the human past.

Another view can be called the demographic theory. It holds that early humans couldn't have had incestuous relations even if they had wanted to. In the case of a male, for example: in your group your mother is past breeding, your elder sister is married, and your younger sister is not old enough. So one has to mate out to mate at all! One again wonders, if so, why the need to formalize the situation? And what happens if you and your sister are of approximate age? Couldn't one engage in sex with a mother even if she is past the breeding age? Still another theory, popularized by Leslie White, can be termed the outside-cooperation theory. In order to maximize cooperation between different human groups the incest taboo was originated to force marriages to occur outside one's own group, thus making friends out of potential enemies.

> If cooperation is advantageous within family groups, why not between families as well? The problem was how to extend the scope of mutual aid . . . Within the definition and prohibition of incest, families became units in the cooperative process as well as individuals. Marriages came to be contracts first between families, later between even larger groups. The individual lost much of his initiative in courtship and choice of mates, for it was now a group affair . . . According to our theory the prohibition of incest has at bottom an economic motivation—not that primitive peoples were aware of this motive, however, for they were not. Rules of exogamy originated as crystallizations of processes of a social system rather than as products of individual psyches. Inbreeding was prohibited and marriage between groups was made compulsory in order to obtain the maximum benefits of cooperation. (White, 1948: 425, 426)

White's view is ingenious, and we can agree that there would have been definite benefits from cooperation. He may have failed to recognize, however, the difference between marrying out (exogamy) and avoiding incestuous relations. Even though we marry out, we could still continue to enjoy sex relations within; and basically this is what incest taboos seem to prohibit (having to marry out would seem to be more a result rather than a cause). Perhaps the best theory is supplied by Robin Fox. In comparing our behaviors along this line with those of wild animals, he suggests that they avoid inbreeding within the group either by instinctive means or by expulsion of the sexually mature young. The human species lacks the first mechanism, instinct, and we can't afford the other because human young are ready sexually before they can support themselves. So we have to proceed culturally with the imposition of the incest taboo. And, in his view, the primary reason we have to do this at all is that otherwise competition within the group would hinder the effectiveness of the stable family groupings. The incest taboo puts the "quietus" on such potentially disruptive behaviors and at the same time, unconsciously, leads to a better gene pool.

> Thus, the human animal had two problems: the problem of the effects of inbreeding, and the problem of competition in the family groups. The latter could be solved ... by some kind of regularized mating in the family—but this would not solve the problem of close inbreeding. The only mechanism by which both these problems could be met and solved was the development of a taboo on intercourse between family members. Natural selection worked, therefore, to promote the survival of those groups that bred out, and failure of those that did not. (Fox, 1967: 65)

One still wonders if somehow we have not missed the main point somewhere along the way. Certainly, the reasons for the origin of the incest taboo are not necessarily those that keep it in force at the present time. Moreover, as Fox himself suggests, incest is not so much prevented as avoided. All this being said, inclusively, we can return to the nature of marriage itself.

CONCEPTS OF MARRIAGE

There are many ways of discussing the concept of marriage. It has been traditional in anthropology to classify marriage according to three sets of criteria. These are the number of spouses permitted a person at any one time, the method of obtaining spouses, and where one lives after marriage has taken place. While the last seems more appropriate to discuss under the heading of family, it must be remembered that any marriage custom may be connected with family behavior. We simply consider residence here as a matter of convenience. We can discuss each of these "types" of marriage in turn.

This Sengalese family illustrates the most common form of polygamy—polygyny (one husband with several wives).

United Nations

Number of Spouses

The first type comprises three varieties of spouse possibilities. Our own rule is **monogamy**, the marriage of single mates. This does not prohibit marriage-divorce-remarriage (serial monogamy) but does mean that at any one time there will be only one husband married to one wife. Not only is monogamy our compulsory rule, but it is an alternate pattern of marriage behavior throughout the primitive world as well—although in some societies it is preferred. A second rule is **polygamy**, the marriage of an individual to multiple spouses. This rule, naturally enough, takes two forms. By far the most common is *polygyny*, in which a man is simultaneously married to several wives. There are many reasons for the occurrence of polygyny. Because of the natural division of labor, males and females may have to be married. So if there is an unbalanced sex ratio between males and females (because of hazardous male occupations or some other factor), then several women may have to share the same husband. The custom may also originate because of economic value of wives. If women work the fields, the greater the number of wives the "wealthier" the individual husband. Again, it may simply be due to considerations of prestige. If ability to support females indicates the worth of a male, polygyny is a tangible way to display such a quality. Finally, among many other possible reasons, it may be brought about because of the desire for children, the opportunities for which, obviously, are multiplied in such situations. Children may be economically useful, if only that female children can be exchanged for wives (remember the Tiv).

It might be thought that polygyny is a great situation for the male, but this is not always so; if one wife can make excessive demands, think how it would be in stereo! Moreover, not only are the opportunities for children increased in such a situation but also opportunities for wives to quarrel. Three expedients occur among primitives to handle this situation. First, a man may marry not just multiple wives but sisters: *sororal polygyny*. This is based upon the somewhat fallacious assumption that sisters have already learned to get along. A second possibility is to give powers to the first female married, making her a kind of foreman over the activities of others. Such a device has other limitations as well.

> In connection with polygyny, it becomes important to draw a distinction between primary and secondary marriages. A primary marriage is typically the first union which an individual contracts; a secondary marriage is any subsequent union. The distinction acquires importance from the fact that many cultures prescribe quite different rules in the two cases. The regulations governing primary marriages ordinarily exclude certain relatives as too closely akin and frequently define other relatives . . . as preferred mates. In secondary marriages, though the choice of a spouse is sometimes wider, it is often much more limited. (Murdock, 1963: 28, 29)

The third expedient is physical separation. In many African societies, each wife and her children will occupy a separate dwelling and the husband will visit each "family" in turn, spending an equal amount of time with each. Friction remains, however, a problem in polygynous situations.

The other variety of polygamy is *polyandry,* the marriage of a woman to a number of husbands. This is a fairly rare phenomenon and most generally comes into existence as a response to an unbalanced sex ratio favoring males. Again, if every male is to have a partner for labor division and procreation, it will necessitate this custom: multiple males sharing the same females. It may also be due to other economic factors: the problem of labor is solved by a number of co-resident males (husbands); and if property cannot be divided up, polyandry is an alternative to unitary inheritance. The classic example is the Toda of India. Among these people, there was the practice of female infanticide. Men only could herd the cattle, and cattle products were exchanged for other foods and commodities. The result was that females had as their main function procreation and few were needed for that, resulting in infanticide and an unbalanced sex ratio.

In polyandry, too, there are opportunities for friction. One response is for brothers to marry the same female: *fraternal polyandry* (sometimes called *Adelphic polyandry*). This is based on the same idea as a man marrying sisters, in sororal polygyny. There is also the new problem of who is dad, not found in polygynous situations, in which there is only one dad and mom is the woman who bore you. Paternity is generally handled by what has been called social fatherhood. In such a case, paternity is institutionalized in some customary way with, perhaps, the oldest male automatically claiming the first born child; the second oldest, the second, and so on. It may also be that the children belong to the fathers collectively. Here it is the social, not the biological, fact that is most important. The concept of social fatherhood can be extended a bit further. From the male point of view, marriage brings with it certain kinds of rights. Domestic rights include those based on labor division and common residence and perhaps even economic claims beyond this (for outside labor of the wife). There are also sexual rights, the right to claim resultant children (rights in genetricem) and perhaps even rights to affiliate those children to a particular kinship group. Here we are reminded of the privileges and obligations that are marriage and how rights can be multiple and complex. For the Toda, only one man at a time had rights in genetricem to offspring, whereas (theoretically) all had sexual rights to the wife.

The last form of marriage in terms of spouse possibilities has been called *group marriage.* This would include plural husbands and wives. Group marriage never seems to exist as a cultural norm and occurs only in a small number of societies anyway, often those which have undergone disruptive experiences. Apparently the problems of friction and the assignment of rights in females pose insurmountable difficulties. Group marriage is frequently mentioned in the older literature of anthropology and by explorers and missionaries today. Here, apparently, true group marriage is confused with the extension of sexual privileges to other people. So, for example, among the Netsilik Eskimo a man will have several wife-exchange partners. These men are reciprocators of hunting success, and the wife exchanges are simply the social lubricants of this more economic relationship. Certainly, a man may be seen with one woman and then with another, and even some economic privileges may be added, but monogamy is their rule of marriage.

Before leaving this kind of marriage classification a couple of notes may be added. First, the choice of who the marriage partner(s) may be is often tightly regulated, and not simply because of the incest taboo. To preserve wealth or privilege within a narrow group one may have to marry within that group (endogamy) or even a specific person, say a cross cousin on one's father's side (patrilateral). Or, a man may have to choose as his first wife an older woman, to learn the ropes, so to speak. As a result, mate-selection potential may range from prescribed (no opportunity for choice) to preferred (little choice) to open (in which a number of possibilities exist). The second note is that some form of trial marriage may take place. In societies emphasizing the procreation of children, a couple may live together long enough to find out if they can bear children, formal marriage only occurring afterwards. Motives, however, may be more general than this. Richard Price (1965) has pointed out how this works in the community of Vicos in the Andes Mountains of Peru. Here the trial marriage relationship is called *watanaki,* the girl coming to live with the boy and his kinsmen. This is the common thing to do and, according to Price, has the following functions: it provides the girl with a period of adjustment to the people she will have to live with; it eases creation of the affinal relations between the different families; it provides time to make the necessary economic preparation for the wedding itself since considerable wealth must be accumulated and a house constructed. Not only can the compatability of the couple themselves be tested, the young couple is also offered a period in which to make the final transition from adolescence to adulthood: this period is their last time free from full adult cares and responsibilities. Of interest is that only one in six of these watanaki relationships terminates without leading to actual marriage—testimony to the effectiveness of this institution.

Methods of Obtaining Spouses

The second major way to classify marriage is in terms of the methods employed in obtaining wives. Here it is traditional to distinguish eight mechanisms, and the account given here follows that of Hoebel (1972). The first of these is *marriage by purchase,* sometimes called *bride price* or *bride wealth.* It is perhaps the most common method and, as previously illustrated, involves the transfer of wealth from the group of the groom to that of the bride. Sometimes it is partly returned. The wealth is not only a tangible symbol of the alliance now formed between the different groups (bride for wealth) but also may serve as a compensation to the group of the girl for raising her as well as for the possible loss of her economic potential. Perhaps most common, however, is the idea that the wealth can be construed as payment for the loss of rights to her subsequent children who may affiliate to her husband's group. This would appear to be a good interpretation since often in such societies the wealth may have to be refunded (or a substitute provided) in the event she proves to be barren. Clearly, it is rights to and desire for children that are involved.

This African wedding party dances on the highway blocking traffic. In order to pass, one must present a gift to the bride.

United Nations

A second method for obtaining a wife is *marriage by service*. Here the groom works for the kin of the bride for a stipulated period of time. This form of compensation may also be accompanied by some wealth exchange. The period of service may be before the marriage, perhaps for a period of a year, or after that event, the termination of the work period usually correlating with the birth of the child.

A third and "cheap" mechanism is *marriage by exchange*. Here a woman from one kin group is exchanged for one of another. Gifts may still be exchanged to symbolize the relationship thus created or continued (if women have been swapped in the past). In their simplest form, exchange marriages involve a man exchanging his sister for the sister of another man, thus becoming double brother-in-laws. The drawback, as in any barter situation, is that required women may not be available. Sometimes this problem is overcome by infant betrothal or deferring returns across generational lines.

A fourth method is *marriage by inheritance*, in which a husband obtains a wife by the expedient of waiting to inherit her from someone else. This may happen upon the death of a father (not your own mother, of course) or a grandfather. In the latter case, he may have married a young girl so that the ages turn out to be roughly equivalent! The most common forms of inheritance marriage are the **levirate** and the **sororate.** In the first, a younger brother inherits the wife of his deceased brother; in the sororate, a sister takes the place of one's deceased wife (or from the female point of view, she gains her sister's husband). Such marriages are often regarded as substitutions to continue the affinal relations established by the original marriages.

The next two mechanisms for obtaining wives are rather restricted in occurrence and appear to be adjustment methods to difficult situations. The first of these is *marriage by adoption*. Here a man obtains a wife by being adopted into her family. It usually occurs as a device for a family to continue its descent line when there are no sons and descent is fixed on the male side. Ancient China is the usually cited case in point. Here, for example, it may be that the Hsu family has both sons and daughters. Wives are obtained for most sons by one or another method but one son is having difficulties. Meanwhile, there is the Chu family: no sons but lots of daughters. What is to become of the Chu line? The two problems are solved by young male Hsu being adopted as a Chu and being given sexual and domestic rights in a Chu daughter. However (and one overlooks the technical incest), young Hsu must give up filiation rights; his offspring are Chu since he is one in the pretend sense. So this is an "expensive" way to obtain a wife. The other adjustment mechanism is of an even more pretend nature and is called *marriage by fiction*. The classic case here is found among the Nuer of Africa and is called *ghost marriage*. It gives offspring to a male who has died without heirs and, hence, continuity to his line. Here the widow takes on a new husband in exchange for that man's loss of in-geneticrem rights. The children of the new marriage affiliate themselves with the deceased husband, their "ghost father." Again a dubious way of obtaining a spouse!

The seventh way to obtain a wife is less a formal procedure than it is a kind of safety-valve device to circumvent tradition. This is called *marriage by elopement*, and we, of course, recognize its existence even in our own society. As a behavior, elopement works in the attempt to get married when no normally acceptable partner exists—you run off with someone of an unsanctioned nature—or as a way to inject personal choice into the mate-selection process. Since many primitive marriages are arranged by kin, elopement gives a boy or girl a chance to avoid an undesirable partner by running off with his or her "true love." As in our own society, over the long run, the marriage comes generally to be accepted. In primitive societies, however, if one is caught at the beginning of elopement, the lovers may be killed for their flaunting of convention.

The last, and perhaps most interesting, is *marriage by capture*. This is going out and abducting a wife, often someone else's. It is doubtful if this is the original "cave-man" method that cartoons would have it. It is never the main way to obtain women, either, although it does occur; it is too counter-productive of alliance relations. As a way to gain a secondary wife, however, it is well documented in the literature of anthropology. And it certainly is adventurous! It is also a way to obtain husbands. The Iroquois of New York State, for example, often made captured warriors take the place of Iroquois husbands who had been killed in battle (also a case of adoptive marriage). More common perhaps than actual capture is what has been termed *mock capture* (our carrying of the bride across the threshold?). This is a pretense at capture that accompanies the more regular procedure. Many theories have been advanced to account for it; it has been seen, for example, as a way of expressing hostility between the different kinship groups who may once have been enemies, or as a way to symbolize the change in status of the newly married pair. My own view is that it is another safety-valve device, a way to "leave them at the church steps" at the last moment. A good example is from the Cuna Indians of Panama. Among these island people, the mock capture seals the marriage bargain already negotiated. The idea is for kinsmen of the bride to capture the groom. Each day for four days they drag him from his house to her house. The first three days he is rescued by his kin and friends. The last day he is not rescued but is taken into her house and tossed into her hammock where she is waiting for him. At this point the marriage contract is sealed. As David Stout relates one such case, on the fourth day the groom was visibly nervous and fought his "captors" more than protocol required. Just prior to being dragged inside her house, he suddenly broke free, ran to the bank where he apparently had hidden a canoe the night before, jumped in and paddled away—breaking off the engagement. Apologies were made, wealth returned, and a new groom sought for the unfortunate girl. Is this not a case of a last minute change of mind? Doesn't mock capture offer a potential bride or groom one last out?

Rules of Residence

The last classification of marriage is in terms of **residence rules**: where the couple reside after marriage. In most societies, such rules are fairly specific; a couple ought to live with a particular kinship group or independent of them. Three behaviors appear to be most common. If the couple establish a residence of their own independently in a new locality, away from either set of in-laws it is said to be *neolocal* residence. This is the ideal pattern for many of us—generally, the more independent and distant the better! If the couple live where the groom resided prior to the marriage, it is *patrilocal* residence (the girl leaves her area), and if they live where the bride lived before marriage, it is *matrilocal* residence (the boy leaves his area). In either of the last two cases, life may be difficult for the in-marrying spouse, perhaps especially so for a girl. Accounts of the position of a young wife in ancient China (moving in patrilocally) are rife with suggestions that her position was little better than that of slave to the demands of her tyrannical mother-in-law. There are tendencies for patrilocal residence to be correlated with the importance of males in the economy, with descent in the male line, and with polygyny. Matrilocal residence is correlated somewhat with female importance in the economy and descent in the female line. There are many exceptions.

There are also some other residence rules of less common distribution. *Bilocal* residence is a situation in which the couple can choose which set of in-laws or areas to affiliate with. In other words, they choose his or her relatives or area. Who lives with whom is often determined by seniority—the oldest or youngest stays at home—or by availability of room or even local resources. It may also be correlated to rank considerations, the spouse of superior status remaining in place. Another rule, *avunculocal* residence, involves a newly married couple going to live with the husband's mother's brother. This seemingly weird situation is often found together with an institution called the *avunculate,* in which that mother's brother becomes more important to a boy than his own father in training, social life, and eventual inheritance of property. In such a situation, the residence rule appears to make sense.

Another restricted rule is *matri-patrilocal* residence. Here there is

To the untrained eye this may look like so many houses on the hillside. It is actually an orderly arrangement which has been planned according to the residence rules of the society.

United Nations

initial residence in the wife's area and then residence in the husband's area. This rule has a degree of correlation to methods of acquiring a bride by service and hence having to live for a period working for his kinsmen. It can also be used to apply to such cases as that of the Dobu Islanders, who move annually between the two areas. And there are still other rules. Many voices have been raised against the more-or-less traditional residence terminology mentioned above. It has been argued, for example, that the term *patrilocal* doesn't tell us if the residence is in the locality of the groom or within the family home itself, obviously a fact of social importance. Such can easily lead to descriptive incompleteness or incorrectness with reference to comparative studies. Moreover, it has been charged that even within the confines of a single society, the above terms may not be sufficiently discrete to correctly illustrate actual practices. Witness the account of Ward Goodenough:

> It was quite a shock, therefore, when I recently found myself differing considerably with John Fischer about the incidence of residence forms in a community on Truk ... where we both collected data within the space of three years ... On the basis of my figures we would not hesitate to classify Trukese society as essentially matrilocal, since nearly three-quarters of the married couples are apparently living in matrilocal residence. On the basis of Fischer's figures, with little more than half the married couples in matrilocal residence and almost a third living patrilocally I would myself be inclined to classify Trukese society as bilocal. (Goodenough, 1956: 22)

The student can imagine that, as a result of such activities, anthropologists have now multiplied both the number of names for residence rules and their approaches towards delineating such practices. Since no consensus has been reached, however, we can still (if partly incorrectly) utilize the terms given here as somewhat approximating the range of residence possibilities in primitive societies.

307

Two Examples: The Nayar and the Tiwi

In order to add a bit of descriptive impact to our account of marriage, we will conclude this chapter with two brief examples of how marriage actually works in a pair of societies. The first example concerns the Nayar of India. This is a case that severely taxes the usual anthropological conception of marriage and that of the family as well. The Nayar were a military caste, and constituent kinship groups in a particular area formed cooperative ties, one of the most important of which was to marry off its pre-pubescent girls (seven to twelve years old) to males in their linked groups. Every so many years, all these girls were ritually married to these males. However, the ritual husbands were not liable to actually consummate the marriage, and, in any event, they had no further obligations to their brides. The brides had only one obligation to their ritual husbands, that of observing a ritual upon the occasion of the husband's death. The girls themselves lived with and were supported by their kin (reckoned through the female side), which included their brothers (who were ritual husbands to girls living elsewhere). The children were also cared for by this group. But whose children were they? It seems that a girl would "receive" a number of males as visiting "husbands." Some of these were high-caste males casually passing through, others were more regular visitors.

> A husband visited his wife after supper at night and left before breakfast next morning. He placed his weapons at the door of his wife's room and if others came later they were free to sleep on the verandah of the woman's house. Either party to a union might terminate it at any time without formality. A passing guest recompensed a woman with a small cash gift at each visit. But a more regular husband from within the neighborhood had certain customary obligations ... Most important, however, when a woman became pregnant it was essential for one or more men of appropriate sub-caste to acknowledge probable paternity ... Although he made regular gifts to her at festivals, in no sense of the term did a man maintain his wife. Her food and regular clothing she obtained from her matrilineal group. The gifts of a woman's husbands were personal luxuries which pertained to her role as a sexual partner. ... (Gough, 1959: 26, 27).

These husbands owed nothing to their children. Is this a real marriage situation? There are really no affinal relations engendered. Gough concludes that marriage is present—group marriage—but her concluding definition has struck many anthropologists as far too broad to be of comparative significance.

The other example, one definitely within the realm of marriage, comes from the Tiwi of northern Australia. These people are of interest because of their insistence that all females must be married all of the time. This was due to their belief that spirits could impregnate a woman at any time. Since a child must have a father, the expedient is taken to provide women with husbands at all times—a bit of logic not without a certain charm. To employ this practice meant that a female baby would be betrothed at birth and widows remarried at the graveside of their deceased husbands. Such a custom led to polygyny since not all males would have to be continually married and not all were as easily able to marry as others. The ability to betroth a potential female infant gave its possible possessor (a man with a pregnant wife) great powers, and he was not apt to use this power just to give a future wife to some non-entity. He would betroth a female infant to a friend or ally or to some-one he wished to be in this position, perhaps some up-and-coming young man to use as "old-age insurance." Or he would employ the power in an exchange-marriage fashion to obtain more wives for himself. Most younger males could offer no such inducement since they themselves were not yet married. This means that the Tiwi comprised older men married to many younger females. Even if one obtained a wife at age twenty-five by betrothal, one would have to wait about fourteen years for her to grow up and be economically and sexually valuable. From this point on, however, success literally breeds success.

> As in our own culture, where the first million is the hardest to make, so in Tiwi the first bestowed wife was the hardest to get. If some shrewd father with a daughter to invest in a twenty-year-old decided to invest her in you, his judgement was likely to attract other fathers to make a similar investment. As a result, for some Tiwi men, the arrival in residence of the first wife . . . was quickly followed by the arrival in residence of a second, third and fourth . . . and from then on he was practically certain to accumulate still more wives as later bestowals grew up and as he was able to invest the daughters borne by his first crop of young wives in transactions which brought in a later crop. (Hart and Pilling, 1964: 16)

So most of the wives were concentrated in the few surviving old men in any one particular group. To avoid permanent bachelorhood, a young man without exceptional promise would have to rely on widow remar-riages since these women were often able to pick their own husbands, generally friends of their own sons.

One gets from these two incomplete examples some idea of the complexity (and excitement) of the actual operation of marriage in primi-tive societies. We can now turn to the results of marriage and kinship practices: the various forms of the family and other kinship groupings.

SUMMARY

1. Kinship is a way of creating human groups. Kinship ties are formed by consanguinity (biological connection and affinity), by sexuality, or by marriage. Biological descent and sexuality may be direct or shared, creating four basic categories of primary kinsmen.

2. Status is the social position that an individual may occupy, and role is the complex of behaviors associated with that position. These concepts are useful in understanding kinship and other social behaviors.

3. Systems of kinship terminology are of four basic types: lineal, bifurcate collateral, bifurcate merging, and generational.

4. A near universal factor in regulating mating and marriage customs is the incest taboo, the existence and real functioning of which is open to interpretation.

5. Marriage systems can be analyzed in terms of number of spouses—monogamy, polygyny, and polyandry; methods of obtaining spouses—purchase, service, exchange, inheritance, adoption, fiction, elopement, and capture; and rules of residence after marriage—neolocal, patrilocal, matrilocal, bilocal, and more restricted customs.

REFERENCES FOR FURTHER READING

There is an almost inexhaustible number and variety of useful books on kinship and marriage. A good starting point for the interested student would be *Social Structure*, by George P. Murdock (1963, Macmillan), although somewhat out of date; *Kinship and Marriage*, by Robin Fox (1967, Penguin Books), and *Social Anthropology*, by Paul Bohannon (1963, Holt, Rinehart & Winston). The best nontechnical account of kinship is *Manual for Kinship Analysis*, by Ernest Schusky (1965, Holt, Rinehart & Winston). General readers abound; four of the most useful are *Kinship and Social Organization*, edited by Paul Bohannon and John Middleton (1968, Natural History Press); *Marriage, Family and Residence* (1968) same editors and publisher; *Kinship and Family Organization*, edited by Bernard Farber (1966, Wiley), for a more sociological approach; and *Readings in Kinship and Social Structure*, edited by Nelson Graburn (1971, Harper & Row). See also *Patterns of Sexual Behavior* by C. S. Ford and F. A. Beach (1972, Harper & Row). A general article of some significance is by Ralph Linton, "Age and Sex Categories," in *American Sociological Review* 7 (1942): 589–603. A good discussion of incest theories is in Fox (cited above), and the specific quote by Leslie

White is from "The Definition and Prohibition of Incest," in *American Anthropologist 50* (1948): 416–34. An excellent general anthropology text with a discussion of marriage mechanisms is E. Adamson Hoebel, *Anthropology: The Study of Man* (1972, McGraw-Hill). The article by Ward Goodenough, "Residence Rules," in *Southwestern Journal of Anthropology* 12 (1956): 22–37, deals with problems relative to the applicability of these in the traditional sense and poses a solution, as does the above-cited text by Paul Bohannon. The two specific cases of marriage discussed in chapter seventeen are the "Nayars and the Definition of Marriage," by E. Kathleen Gough, in *Journal of the Royal Anthropological Institute* 89 (1959): 23–34; and the *Tiwi of North Australia* by Hart and Pilling (1964, Holt, Rinehart & Winston). A pair of excellent texts on plural marriages are *Many Wives, Many Powers,* by Remi Cliqnet (1970, Northwestern University Press); and the monumental *A Study of Polyandry,* by HRM Prince Peter of Greece and Denmark (1963, Mouton). A regional study containing many interesting examples is *Pigs, Pearlshells, and Women,* edited by R. M. Glasse and M. J. Meggitt (1969, Prentice-Hall).

18
social groups: kinship

The number of approaches taken to the study of social groups is enough to overwhelm the hardiest scholar. Such a topic, of course, is not merely the preserve of the anthropologist. Sociologists perhaps have charted its greatest dimensions. The approach of the present chapter (and chapter nineteen) is to present as simple an account as possible of this complex topic. This chapter deals specifically with groups based upon kinship ties since these are among the most important and long-lasting studied by anthropologists. The next chapter deals with those organized along different lines.

THE CONCEPT OF SOCIAL GROUP

Before looking specifically at the various types of kinship groups in primitive societies, some small background on groups in general is useful. It is not easy to define the term *social group* to everyone's satisfaction. The concept is so general and useful (like culture) that different writers express its underlying conception quite differently. One sociologist has defined a *social group* as "a plurality of individuals who are in contact with one another, who take one another into account, and who are aware of some significant communality" (Olmstead, 1966: 21). What he is stressing here is the idea that interaction between members does take place, that they have some kind of principle that brings them together, and they are aware of this and have a sense of their own identity as a group. In this sense, a social group is different from what some writers call a *social category* or a *statistical aggregate*. This is simply a collection of people assigned to one another without possessing the attributes of a true group: for example, all college students in the United States or a crowd of people at a bus stop who are together (as the college students are not) but who have little feeling of identity and hardly take one another into account, especially with today's lack of manners! Although it is the feeling of having something in common that is perhaps most important in social groups, one might add a last often-mentioned criterion —that they usually have some degree of persistence over time.

Primary and Secondary Groups

Another basic consideration relative to social groups is a distinction made years ago by Charles H. Cooley (an early sociologist), a distinction between those social groups that are *primary* and those that are *secondary*.

> By primary groups I mean those characterized by intimate face-to-face association and cooperation. . . . The result of intimate association . . . is a certain fusion of individualities in a common whole, so that one's very self, for many purposes at least, is the common life and purpose of the group. Perhaps the simplest way of describing this wholeness is by saying that it is a "we"; it involves the sort of sympathy and mutual identification for which "we" is the natural expression. (Cooley, 1920: 23)

In such primary groups, the quality of interaction between members gives them great satisfaction because that interaction is usually face-to-face, the numbers of people involved are usually small, and duration is usually long, perhaps for the lifetime of the individual. It is a group, as the sociologists are fond of saying, in which one can be oneself, one in which the person is an end in himself rather than a means to some end. The family is the usually cited illustration, and its warm, intimate, and personal ties are indicative of relations within primary groups.

The secondary group is considered as the opposite of the primary group in many of these behaviors. Although it does share in the general aspects of "groupness," the face-to-face interaction is of less duration or may be indirect. The groups are usually larger, and the social relationships that exist are less warm and intimate and generally impersonal; the other persons become primarily a means towards realizing some end.

> The nature of secondary contacts is obvious. They may be face-to-face, but if so they are of the touch-and-go variety. The contact with . . . the bank cashier is a perfect illustration. Many contacts are entirely indirect, being handled through long-distance communication . . . Actually a great part of the essential business of the modern world is handled through impersonal contacts. . . . Such contacts do not necessarily imply any identity of ends as between the parties concerned, any interest in the other party as an end in himself . . . or any sentiment whatever attaching to the contact. They do not require that the parties know each other.

... One party may be substituted for another without affecting the relationship The contract is viewed purely as a means to an end and is dropped as soon as the end changes. (Davis, 1966: 302)

Just as primary interaction characterizes primary groups, so such secondary interaction (contacts) characterizes secondary groups. Because of the kinship nature of many primitive groups, and for other reasons we shall pursue later, it can be assumed that many primitive societies are composed of groups that fall on the primary end of the above distinction. In modern society, on the other hand, most would appear to be of secondary nature.

Varieties Of Kinship Social Groups.   Most anthropologists divide up the social groups based on kinship into two major and overlapping varieties. In the first, the members form residential units. They live in a common house and area and they are composed of kinsmen based both on affinal and consanguineal ties (marriage and descent). These have been designated *familial* or *residential* kinship groups. The other variety, called *descent* or *consanguineal* kinship groups, is comprised of members united by real or assumed biological ties. Such members (at least some of them) may also reside together. We will consider the many types of each of these varieties.

Familial kinship groups are brought into existence by some of the rules of marriage—numbers of mates and residence—and are forms of the family. "The family is a social group characterized by common residence, economic cooperation, and reproduction. It includes adults of both sexes, at least two of whom maintain a socially approved sexual relationship, and one or more children, own or adopted, of the sexually cohabiting adults" (Murdock, 1963: 1). This definition fits most such groups encountered by anthropologists. It would be hard to belong to a group more primary than this one! There are two basic formats of the family. The first is called the **nuclear family** and is our own familial kinship group. Typically it consists of a nucleus of a man, his wife, and their offspring. It occurs in conjunction with monogamy in marriage and since, at least ideally, offspring will move away after marriage, with neo-local residence. The nuclear family, however, may include other people, perhaps a child who never marries or a spinster aunt. This form of the family has also been called the elementary family because it is basic to all societies and is a building block of larger familial groups. Sociologists often designate it as the conjugal family (joined by marriage), although this is somewhat inappropriate terminology.

As a reproductive and economic unit, the nuclear family is highly functional. Within it "We thus see assembled four functions funda-

It is possible to belong to a family of orientation and a family of procreation at the same time. There is considerable overlapping among the three generations shown here.

Suzanne Szasz

mental to human social life—the sexual, the economic, the reproductive, and the educational" (Murdock, 1963: 10). The spouses can gratify each other sexually (although this is not necessarily exclusive to this unit), reproduction licensed by the marriage can occur, and the parents can serve to help educate the offspring so procreated, teaching appropriate behaviors. Finally, based upon age and sex, such a family can be an efficient technological unit in terms of the natural division of labor. Perhaps this helps account for its almost universal distribution in both primitive and modern societies.

There are a number of other points of interest relative to the nuclear family. First of all, any one individual can belong to more than one such unit at the same time. That of a child can be called a nuclear family of *orientation*, into which he was born and where his role is generally rather passive in terms of authority and responsibility. After one marries and has children, one assumes the parent-spouse roles and has founded a nuclear family of *procreation*, with appropriate authority and responsibility. Diagramatically:

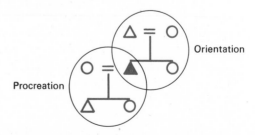

Such dual membership carries a certain degree of behavioral confusion along with it, especially in our own society where such groups are usually residentially separate. After lecturing one's own children on the way "home" for some holiday one then has to "take" a similar lecture from one's own parents. Although one's own children often see

316

the humor in the situation, you seldom do! Also, of course, there may arise the problem of to which family one owes one's primary allegiance. Divorce courts are full of cases in which a spouse and parent could not keep such ties separate from those involving their own parents.

A second point involves the functioning of the nuclear family in our own society. Due to the modern division of labor and the phenomenal number of specialized institutions—schools, clubs, and nonfamily associations, it has been claimed that the nuclear family is becoming obsolete, that other forms of organization perform its functions better. In some senses they probably do. Few families can produce directly for all of their economic needs; few parents can transmit all the needed skills and knowledge to offspring; and the sexual revolution threatens to rob the family of even this sort of gratification: sex perhaps being more available before marriage than in the past. Yet we can expect the nuclear family to endure because of the satisfactions it can provide due to its intrinsic nature as a primary group. Few other groups in modern society can cater so beautifully to the emotional needs of the individual—a function increasing in importance in a society that is perhaps becoming ever more impersonal. At least in the family a person remains a person rather than a number!

The last point has to do with another intrinsic aspect of the nuclear family. By its very nature there are inherent limitations of various sorts. If associated with neolocal residence (as is the independent type discussed above) and with monogamy, it is discontinuous over time; when children marry and move away or parents die, it is terminated. There may also be other factors such as the presence of competing groups of greater importance to the individual that can weaken its functional integrity. Finally, when many of the major technological and economic activities are pinned to it, the simple nuclear family can be severely impaired by the death of a single member. For example if the husband-father dies, who will perform adult male activities? To escape from such problems, the nuclear family in some primitive societies becomes a dependent kind of unit; it is submerged as part of some larger family grouping or is overlapped with nonfamilial types of kinship groupings. Speaking of the people of Ulithi in Micronesia in the Pacific, William Lessa observes:

> The nuclear family is strongly dependent in character, for it must compete with three other kin groups—the extended family, the commensal group and the lineage. These other groups assume some of the roles of the nuclear family, which may be, and often is, scattered among other units for purposes of eating and sleeping. Adding to these impinging influences are the extremely common practices of adoption and remarriage. . . . The result of all this is that the feeding, sheltering, training,

and other services which the family provides the individual are so dissipated that his nuclear family loses much of its importance in his life. ... The nuclear family does not usually exist in its ideal form. Attached to it for purposes of residence may be any of various kinds of kinsmen. At the other extreme are residential units consisting merely of husband and wife ... A canvass of households in the village of Mogmog reveals that only one fourth consist of a husband and wife and their offspring. (Lessa, 1966: 21)

The other variety of family in primitive societies may be called the *Composite family*. This represents a combining of nuclear family units into larger family groupings because of a rule of plural marriage or because of the operation of some of the rules of residence after marriage. We will consider each of these possibilities in turn.

The **polygamous composite family** involves nuclear families linked together by plural marriages. As a unit, this is generally larger than any single nuclear family, but if residence is neolocal, it may still not be permanent over time. There are two types of polygamous composite family, based on whether the plural spouses are male or female. Diagramatically these are:

Polygynous family   Polyandrous family

Put another way, in each situation, one person, either husband or wife, plays duplicate roles in two or more different nuclear units: husband-father or wife-mother in each. And, of course, a greater number of statuses and roles exist, not only co-wife and co-husband but half brothers and sisters as well. As we mentioned for plural marriages in general, friction may also be expanded, if only because there are more people to cooperate and take each other into account. However, the technoeconomic advantages increase proportionately. Here there are more people to pursue labor-division tasks. And at least the death of one of the multiple spouses does not threaten this unit as much as in a nuclear-family situation. Authority patterns are along the lines of the nuclear family: the husband in the polygynous case, and usually the eldest male in the case of polyandry, assume control.

Based upon actual situations, some anthropologists have suggested that the real building block in the polygynous case is the *matricentric* family, consisting of a woman and her children, and that the closest familial ties are joined here. In some cases, it is probably valuable to analyze behavior from this perspective. Comparable behavioral data from polyandrous situations is meager, but most descriptions affirm the primacy of the female-children bond at least for early upbringing; later on, the husbands take greater or even exclusive interest in "their" sons. So this concept may be generally valuable. In any case, we observe the polygamous family to be a more effective unit for technoeconomic operations, education, and sex and reproduction, at least in primitive societies.

The other possibility of composite familial kinship group is called the **extended family**. It is created by the operation of residence rules other than that of the neolocal type. Some offspring, usually only males or only females, remain at home in their nuclear family of orientation and add an additional family of procreation by bringing in a wife or husband from the outside. Such groups are not only larger than the single nuclear family but have greater persistence over time than any family type previously discussed. Here the additional social complexity can be thought of as both horizontal—more males/females at any one time—and vertical—grandparents and grandchildren added as well. Ideally, the extended family can go on forever, the newest generation replacing the eldest as it dies off. There are four types of extended families generally cited by anthropologists: patrilocal, matrilocal, bilocal, and avunculocal. All tend to increase technoeconomic potential of labor division, and in all of them on the death of a spouse there is usually another adult male or female to take his or her place. Domestic authority, with exceptions, is generally in the hands of the oldest adult male. We will very briefly diagram and discuss each type.

The *patrilocal* extended family consists of a man and his wife, their sons and unmarried daughters, and the wives and children of the married sons.

This type of extended family is ideally suited to technoeconomic operations requiring a labor force of cooperating males. Not that the other situations lack the necessary males for such mobilization, but there they are all fathers and sons rather than being otherwise related. In patrilocal situations, however, the females (as observed in chapter seventeen) may be considered as having less value, existing only to be exported in exchange for wives for their brothers.

The *matrilocal* extended family consists of a woman and her husband, their daughters and unmarried sons, and the husbands and children of the married daughters.

This type of extended family has a greater problem in authority allocation. Since the males who marry in are often strangers, they may find cooperation difficult, and are often resentful of orders issued by their father-in-law. Moreover, the outmarrying brothers may still retain (for reasons we are about to examine) some degree of authority over their sisters—conflicting with that of the husbands, who may also have obligations outside the family. Much depends upon the distance away the brothers are. In some American Indian Pueblo societies, the brothers live just across the street and can be extremely effective in organizing their sisters' behavior (interfering with it). If brothers are many miles away, their influence may have to remain symbolic.

The *bilocal* extended family "unites the nuclear family of a married couple with some but not all of the sons, with some but not all of the daughters, and some but not all of the grandchildren of either sex" (Murdock, 1963: 35). This includes, of course, the inmarrying husbands or wives. This sounds like a "shifty" family unit and is, often being correlated with food collectors. Here the possibility exists for a man and his wife to join that family unit in which resources are most plentiful and to change membership if necessary. Of course, if all sons and daughters in one generation choose to live in the areas of their spouses, their own unit could terminate. Some offspring must remain at home!

Finally, there is the *avunculocal* extended family. Here, remember, a boy takes up residence with his maternal uncle at marriage, in some cases, actually even prior to this event. Here he rears his own children and eventually is joined by his own nephew and his wife.

> Avunculocal residence mitigates somewhat the conflicts inherent in the avunculate. Instead of working with his father to develop resources that will be transmitted to the older man's nephew, under avunculocal residence a youth at an early age begins to cooperate with his mother's brother. This means permanent leave-taking of his own home. In the new residence he marries and rears his own children. . . . Meanwhile he receives his sister's son. If in any generation a man lacks a sister to produce a son, the avunculocal family may cease, just as matrilocal or patrilocal may cease without female or male births. (Honigmann, 1959: 381)

Sometimes one sees even more "binding" marriage customs to knit together such residential units. Among the Haida of British Columbia, for example, not only does a nephew move in with his uncle, but he may marry that man's daughter as well—his cross cousin on his mother's side.

> Consequently, a typical Haida household consists of the householder, his wife or wives, his young sons and unmarried daughters, several of his sisters' adolescent but unmarried sons, a sister's son who is married to his daughter, the young children of the latter couple, possibly other married nephews or daughters with their families, and occasionally even a grandnephew or two. In this instance, the associated nuclear families are linked through two relationships, that between parent and daughter and that between maternal uncle and nephew. (Murdock, 1963: 35)

Outside of these illustrated extended families there are, of course, atypical situations. Remember the Nayar solution to family living in which brothers and sisters and the children of the latter all reside together. This has been called by some authorities the natolocal extended family. The above cases, however, are most commonly found in primitive societies and generally illustrate the potential of these kinds of residential units. The following simple chart summarizes these major family types.

Familial (residential) kinship groups

Nuclear family
Composite family:
    Polygamous family (polygynous, polyandrous)
    Extended family (patrilocal, matrilocal, bilocal, and avunculocal)

VARIETIES OF KINSHIP SOCIAL GROUPS: DESCENT

We can now consider the other main variety of kinship social groups, descent (consanguineal) kinship groups. These groups exclude kinsmen based on ties of sexuality and often many possible biological kinsmen as well. On the other hand, they may choose to include numbers of pretend kin. As in the case of the familial kinship groups, there are organizational criteria. Here, instead of mates or residence, the criteria are the rules by which descent connections can be reckoned. There is substantial agreement among anthropologists as to the variety of these rules, although sometimes differing terminology may be employed.

There are two major ways by which one can trace descent. A majority of primitive societies trace descent in a **unilineal** fashion. This is to say that they trace exclusively through either male or female lines back to some ancestor(s). In this one-line fashion, there are various potentials. In *patrilineal* descent, one goes through only male links. This is sometimes referred to as agnatic descent. In so doing, an ego ignores his or her mother's side of the family, at least for purposes of reckoning descent. However, one still recognizes her existence! In *matrilineal* descent, the reverse situation occurs. One traces exclusively through female links. This is sometimes referred to as uterine descent. Here, of course, one ignores the father's side. The rules of patrilineal and matrilineal kin reckoning are exclusive in the sense that they systematically exclude numbers of potential kinsmen.

> The unilineal principle has some obvious advantages. For a start, it assigns an individual to one group only, thus avoiding the problems of overlapping groups. If the society is divided into groups based on unilineal recruitment, these will be discrete groups. From the point of view of neatness of organization this is a great convenience. Also, the unilineal principle restricts the numbers of a man's heirs; it prevents the indefinite proliferation of inheritors that . . . (some other principle) . . . demands. (Fox, 1967: 49)

There is a third type of unilineal descent, one often beset by confusion in the writings of anthropologists (for reasons shortly to be considered). This is called *bilineal* descent and should be defined as a situation in which ego traces descent to both patrilineal and matrilineal kinsmen but for different purposes. This is to say that each set of kinsmen thus defined will stand to ego in a different sense. This has sometimes been called double descent or double unilineal and quite possibly has been reported as more common than in fact it actually is.

The second major form of kinship reckoning is called **cognatic descent**. In ancient Roman law, *cognates* were kinsmen traceable through any sex links. This way of descent reckoning thus includes all the descendants of a particular ancestor. Put another way, it is different from bilineal descent (which also goes on both sides) in treating all the involved kinsmen as members of the same group. Ego traces back through both father's and mother's side for the same thing. Such a principle of descent might well be called inclusive, as opposed to those of an exclusive nature. This principle of descent has also been referred to as nonunilineal. Cognatic descent is our own particular device of genealogy but is, apparently, not as common as unilineal descent in the primitive world. The reason may well be its nonexclusivity. The cognatic groups have a tendency to overlap, causing individuals holding dual (or greater) memberships problems in keeping obligations and responsibilities separate. We will discuss this difficulty presently.

The different methods of reckoning descent lead to the various types of descent groups encountered by anthropologists. The terminology applied to such social groupings is in the process of becoming almost unmanageable so the present text will present the more traditional usages. Since unilineal principles appear to be most common in primitive societies we can first examine social groups based upon them. These may be called *unilineal descent groups*. Of these, by far the most common, and structurally the smallest, is the **lineage.** This is a group of kinsmen who trace themselves back through a one-sided series of genealogical links (male or female) to a common ancestor. It is important to add that these genealogical links actually exist. Members of a lineage can actually trace their kinship connections to that ancestor and to each other.

What are the functions of such a group for the individual? The lineage will probably not form a residential group comprising all of its members, so membership usually does not comprise the basic work group. However, a considerable number of other functions may characterize the relations of the individuals that comprise them. They are often exogamous groups; that is to say that, because of feelings of incest, members must seek spouses and mates outside the lineage. So they help regulate marriage. Such groups also generally have religious functions; they, rather than the family group per se, may be the worship group (the lineage that prays together stays together). Often such groups will own objects of "magical" potency in common. Obviously, the religious activities of this group are intensified if the religious system itself is based on ancestor worship. Another common lineage function is revenge activity in grievance and warfare situations. The obligation usually exists to help a lineage mate press his claim in some legal action or to revenge his death in the event of his demise in hostilities. Male members of one's matrilocal extended family could hardly be expected to feel the same genuine concern! Such kinship groups as the lineage (if extended over many generations) also provide a greater potential for general aid to a member than can his or her immediate family members; they can mobilize a greater number of people. In many cases, lineages also become corporate in their common ownership of property and privileges of inheritance, which is another reason why spouses may traditionally be debarred from inheritance—they are not members of this group. Because of the authority patterns generated to supervise lineage functions and control property, such groups may also become political units, especially if more formal political leadership is lacking. For reasons such as these, the lineage often assumes greater social importance for the individual than the family itself.

Based on patrilineal and matrilineal descent rules, the lineage assumes two formats. These are not, however, mirror images of each other. *Patrilineages* represent the most clear cut of these situations. Diagrammatically (members are shaded in):

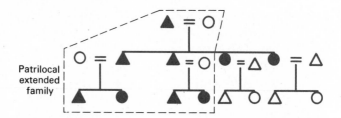

This diagram shows how an exclusive descent rule restricts the number of potential kinsmen. It also points up a common student misapprehension about such groups. Patrilineal descent goes only through male links but does include both males and females as group members; it's not just a group of male kinsmen. Patrilineages usually are correlated with patrilocal residence, so, at least for the males (who hold the authority), they neatly combine both familial and descent groups. The related males actually live together, and their authority and control is not diffused. Such groups can develop corporate status very easily. This helps explain the feeling that daughters and sisters in the group exist mostly as wife-exchange objects. Because of patrilineal descent, they will not be a factor in the reproduction of the lineage; only the offspring of males count. This means that sexual, domestic, and reproductive rights in them are enjoyed by members of other patrilineages. This can be seen in the preceding diagram.

Matrilineages are more difficult to organize functionally. Here daughters and sisters are more important because they reproduce the group. Diagramatically (members are shaded in):

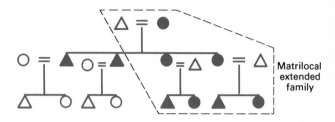

Matrilocal
extended
family

Expressed another way, a husband will enjoy sexual and domestic rights to his wife, but the reproductive rights are fixed in her matrilineages! There exists a definite correlation between the matrilineage and matrilocality in residence. Here it is a core of women who are the organizing principle; lineage women remain at home in the extended family. But since authority and control are vested in males, if the male lineage members live very far away there are major difficulties in coordinating corporate or political activities or even in fulfilling religious or other obligations to the group. In such situations, women often assume a greater role. The Iroquois Indians of New York State are a good illustration of this: the women owned most of the property, and although they did not themselves occupy positions of political power (formal positions existed), nonetheless they played a prominant role in the selection of such officials. Of course, if the males live in close proximity, their supervision of matrilineage affairs becomes more important and continual.

There exist situations in which males can "sneak back" to power (by being able to operate as a group) in matrilineal situations. When the matrilineage exists in conjunction with avunculocal residence, for example, at least some males of the lineage are residing together, and uncles and nephews can play an essentially patrilocal role. Diagrammatically:

Avunculocal
extended
family

In light of the desires of such male matrilineage members to exert on-the-spot influence and control, the Nayar seem not so weird in behavior after all. Here the male and female members of the matrilineage are all living together—perhaps an ideal solution, but one gained at the expense of the usual family group.

There are some other aspects of lineages worthy of mention. Over time, there exists a strong tendency for the numbers of people making up the lineage to expand; patrilineal sons, for example, have sons and daughters, and the sons have offspring. This causes problems such as pressure on territorial space and difficulties in coordination.

> If a man has two sons, and they each have two sons who will have two sons and so on, then at the tenth generation there will be 512 male descendents of the original ancestor. If we asume that generations eight, nine and ten are all alive together there will be 896. The more sons there are who live and themselves have sons, the larger the lineage will be, and if we include the female members, even at the two-and-two rate of progress there will be over a thousand descendants. (Fox, 1967: 123)

As a response to such pressures, and sometimes even in their absence, what is known as *segmentation* takes place. This is the splitting up of the original lineage into a number of segments or sublineages. Sometimes this is an automatic process—every so often males leave and found their own lineage segment (the drift method). It is much easier to accomplish segmentation in a patrilineal system. Here all a son has to do is obtain a wife and procreate children. In a matrilineal system, he must talk a sister into leaving with him and also find her a husband for procreation. In the former case, he not only has control but is the descent link as well. Here he only has control. Then again, the splitting of a lineage into segments may be perpetual; every so many generations a split occurs, the eldest male in each unit becoming or remaining the lineage heads. Such regularity places even greater stresses on matrilineal systems.

By either method of segmentation, two systems of relations may come to exist between the resultant segments. One of these might be called the hierarchial system (also called the principle of the spinal cord). In it, one lineage remains senior to all the others, which become, in effect, side branches. Often this system occurs when kingship or chieftainship passes in a line from father to eldest son to eldest son. Younger brothers "split off" the "royal" line and found segments of decidedly lesser rank. Diagramatically (and leaving out females):

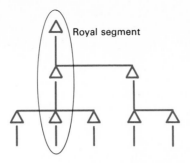

The other possible system of segmentation might be called the separate-but-equal system. Here each of the split off lineage segments are approximately equal in rank, although seniority still plays a role on generational levels. Diagramatically (again leaving out females):

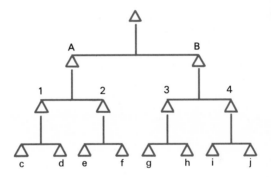

Here *A* is equal to *B*, *1* equal to *3*, and *e* equal to *h* at their own level; there is no super segment line. It has been remarked in a classic paper by Marshall Sahlins that such a lineage system may have a built in advantage for territorial expansion over dissimilarly organized surrounding groups. He discusses the Tiv lineage system (previously discussed in chapter sixteen of this book for their economic behavior). This system bands together a number of small segments (200 to 1,000 people) who live in a small territory. Adjacent to them is another comparably sized and organized group (*c* and *d*, with reference to the above diagram). These, in turn, comprise a larger segment with a larger territory of the total lineage (*1* in the diagram). These more inclusive segments again combine until one has reached back to the original founder and has reached the boundary of the total land claimed by the Tiv, comprising approximately 800,000 people!

The segmentary lineage system consists of this: the focal lines of primary segments can be placed on a single agnatic genealogy that accounts for much (all in the Tiv case) of the tribe. The closer the genealogical relation between focal lines, the closer their respective segments are on the ground. Primary segments whose focal line ancestors are siblings, comprise a territorial entity of higher order, a minor segment, usually named after their common ancestor, the father of the siblings. They comprise an entity, however, only with reference and in opposition to an equivalent lineage segment, one descended from the brother of their common ancestor. In turn, minor segments comprise a higher level entity, a major lineage, in opposition to the descendants of the brother of their common ancestor. The buildup of inclusive segments can proceed to the level of the tribe itself. Always the level of consolidation has a spatial counterpart; all segments of the same inclusive one form a geographical bloc. (Sahlins, 1961: 328, 329)

Now the advantage here is this. Most of the time Tiv minimal segments operate in terms of themselves. But as new segment lands are cleared for agricultural purposes, internal groups (segments in the middle of Tiv territory) must secure land beyond that they presently occupy. To gain it, they have to move against land gained by some other nearby minimal segment, hopefully the most distantly related one in the area. As the struggle escalates, dragging bigger segments into the issue, it sets up pressures on the whole system (d against e can become 1 against 2). As bigger and bigger segments are mobilized, "those who are being pushed from the inside are induced to expand outward, which movement automatically allies both pushers and pushed, as companion segments, against still higher-order Tiv lineages, and ultimately a large sector of Tiv are pressing foreigners" (Sahlins, 1961: 337). When the foreigners defend themselves they unite the entire Tiv, for whom they are not a match. There even appears to be a kind of pecking order among Tiv segments as to who pushes whom to initiate the expansion.

We have examined a little of the variety and structure of the lineage and we can now pass on to larger types of unilineal descent groups. Lest the student despair, let it be mentioned that most of these are built in the "image" of the lineage. That is to say they are functionally and structurally organized in a complementary fashion. There are three of these larger groupings and each will be very briefly discussed. The clan (often called sib in the literature) is a group of kinsmen tracing descent back to a common ancestor through male or female links: patriclans and matriclans. However, the common focus (ancestor), or the links by which all members trace to it, is dubious; all members cannot actually trace such a relation; there may not even be a real ancestor. Ideally, what we observe here are a number of lineages that have for some reason banded together and that have affirmed clanship in the effort to develop solidarity. For all intents and purposes, they behave as if they were kin. Among the Western Apache of North America, for example:

> Members of the same clan were scattered throughout Apache country, thus creating an extensive and intricate network of relationships that cut across bands and local groups but at the same time served to join them together. The members of a clan considered themselves related through the maternal line, but they were rarely able to trace the genealogical links involved. This is not surprising when it is understood that the Apache thought of a clan as being composed of the descendants not of a common ancestor, but of the group that established the first agricultural site with which the clan was associated. Each clan had a name which referred to this legendary place of origin ... The clan's main functions were to regulate marriage, extend obligatory relationships beyond the extended family, and facilitate concerted action in projects requiring more manpower than was available in the family cluster or local group. (Basso, 1970: 9)

In still other cases, the clans may well comprise actual lineage segments who have forgotten the precise nature of their kinship links. Moreover, clans often postulate the common ancestor in mythical terms, or represent them as species of animals or plants (bear clan, hawk clan, etc.); this latter is sometimes called (incorrectly in most cases) the clan totem.

The next-sized group in terms of structure is the *phratry*. Again, ideally, this descent kinship group consists of a number of clans that have affirmed a unilineal connection between themselves. Here the pretense at kinship is even more pronounced and fictional, and the solidarity of the group and the occasions of common functions less marked.

Rules of exogamy, however, usually remain well developed. Often the size of the society is not sufficient for more than two clan clusters, at which point, confusingly, they are called **moieties.** "Briefly, the phratry could be defined as any grouping of two or more sibs provided there are three or more such groups within a society. Where two or more sibs are linked forming only two major groupings, they are called moieties ... " (Schusky, 1965: 67).

So the term *phratry* is useful to designate unilineal kinship group ties between the clan and the division of the society into halves based upon imagined male or female links, if such intermediate groupings exist. Moieties would exist in the United States if there were only two political parties and one was a member of one or the other by patrilineal descent from a donkey or elephant ancestor! Moiety bonds are also generally weaker (except for marriage) than those of the clan; functions, however, may be well defined. Among many groups of American Indians, for example, each moiety engaged in games and other contests with its opposite; they often divided up religious activities; and they buried each other's dead. In terms of unilineal descent groups, then, in the ideal sense, the building blocks of a society would appear structurally as follows:

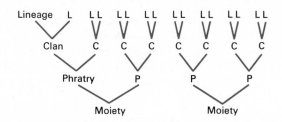

There is a final type of unilineal-descent-group situation, that based upon bilineal descent. Here there must actually be two kinds of descent groups in which an individual holds simultaneous membership. Such a possibility has often been reported in the literature of anthropology but sometimes reflects a misapprehension of actual conditions. In many societies, an individual will affiliate himself to his father's group and trace descent to them but also have some relations with his mother's group. However, since he does not trace descent through them, he is still a member of only one unilineal group. You are aware of the other side but not as ancestors or kinsmen. We must also be careful that double-descent situations are not simply cases in which people affiliate to groups by kinship links for purposes other than descent.

> This is a method of affiliating people to groups or organizations through kinship links. But it does not carry any implications of descent. All the members of such a group do not necessarily regard themselves as descended from a common ancestor or even from subgroups descended unilineally from a common ancestor. Thus they are not unilineal descent groups, even though they recruit unilineally . . . A society in which a man gained descent-group membership through his father, but was affiliated to a religious group through his mother, would not, then, in our definition, be a double descent society. (Fox, 1967: 134)

Nevertheless, there *are* societies in which true double descent creates dual kinship groups for individuals. Fox cites the classic case of the Yako of Nigeria in Africa. They number approximately 11,000 people and live in one big town divided up into areas, each inhabited by a patrilineal clan called a *kepun*. Each patriclan is subdivided into small lineages, the males of which reside together in compounds housing patrilocal extended families. From these patrilineal kinsmen—to whom one traces descent—come the rights to houses and land. To some degree, they are also a group for the protection of members. An individual Yako also holds membership in a matrilineal clan, the *lejima,* and also traces descent to these relatives. The functions of the matriclan for the individual are as a peace keeping device (because it crosscuts the other groupings); in the conducting of religious activities (there is a shrine to its spirit); and as a group within which movable property and wealth (money and livestock) pass. So an individual inherits different things from each group and traces descent from different kinsmen for different purposes. Because of kinship and descent ties, both patriclan and matriclan are exogamous units. In such cases of true double descent, it is often suggested that the society in question was originally exclusive on one side or the other in descent and that the present duality represents an intrusion of the opposite rule of descent, say a matrilineal intrusion into a formerly wholly patrilineal society. In such bilineal situations, the emphasis may still be greater on one side, or to one group, anyway.

There are also some "strange" systems in some ways resembling bilineal descents. This reminds us that the abstracted categories of the social scientist are only ideal types. Among the Mudugamor of New Guinea, for example, a situation called "ropes" exists, in which land is passed on patrilineally from a father to his son, but all other goods are passed by cross-sex ties, father to daughter and mother to son. These ropes of "descent" have been explained in terms of a male-hostility situation. This is a society having sister-exchange marriage, but often a father will use daughter to obtain extra wives for himself rather than for his son, hurting the latter's chances for marriage. The hostility is said not to interfere with land inheritance since land is plentiful, but, in the case of other goods, males simply do not trust other males. It is hard to determine, however, if actual descent groups result from all of this.

Finally, there are situations in which the operation of double descent not only recognizes the existence of dual descent groups but also creates (recognizes) groups out of the overlap of membership between them. Here the classic cases are taken from various groups of Australian aborigines. Such groups, which have been called *sections* or marriage classes, often postulate totemic ancestors and may engage in corresponding religious activities as a unit. In the simple four-section system, the community is divided into two sets of groups in terms of both patrilineal or matrilineal descent. An individual will belong to one of the

patrilineal groups—that which his father is in—and one of the matrilineal groups—that of his mother. Diagrammatically:

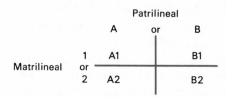

In this overlapping situation an individual will belong to section *A1*
(patrigroup *A*, matrigroup *1*) or any of the other three sections. A major
function of these sections becomes that of regulating marriage. Because
of exogamous considerations, an individual must marry someone from
both the opposite father's group and the opposite mother's group. Knowledge of section membership simplifies this search considerably. If I
am an *A1* person, I know I will have to marry a *B2* woman. When one
begins to work out the ramifications of this system, one begins to realize
who the "section mates" of a person will turn out to be. If a male *A1*
marries a female *B2*, their children will be *A2* (*A* from the father and
2 from the mother). If an *A2* son marries, it must be to a *B1* female,
and their children are *A1* (*A* from father, *1* from mother). So I am in
the same section as my grandchildren (by my son), and my wife is in
the same section with her grandchildren (by our daughter). The sections
skip generations. Diagrammatically:

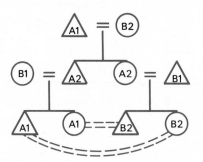

As might be expected, this system can work very effectively with marriage systems emphasizing sister exchange.

The other variety of descent kinship group is based upon cognatic
descent and may be called a *cognatic descent group*. These have been
less studied by anthropologists, although in the last few years this situation has been partially rectified. Work on this topic is extremely impor-

tant because "at least a third of the societies of the world are not unilineal, in the sense that they do not employ either patrilineal or matrilineal descent as a major organizing principle in the grouping of kinsmen" (Murdock, 1960: 2). In light of the lack of general terminology for these groups, the following remarks will necessarily be brief and simplistic. Ideally, an *unrestricted type* of cognatic descent group consists of all the descendants of a person, traced through both the male and female sides. This is to say that both males and females can reproduce the group; you get back to that ancestor through any possible link! Diagramatically:

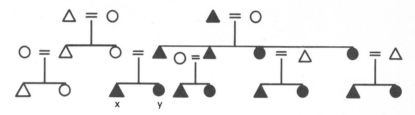

In such an inclusive system, however, there is bound to be an overlap. An individual will belong to as many cognatic descent groups as he can trace biological ancestors on either side. So, for example, x and y in the above diagram also belong to a cognatic descent group through their mother, a group containing people not related to members of their shaded-in group. Such can become a disadvantage. Without unified groups, problems of support and obligation may become a problem. If those two different groups get involved in a hostile situation, which group do x and y support? And how do you remember all those kin links, anyway? Perhaps because of problems such as these, such groups are less commonly found in primitive societies. On the other hand, there are some advantages. As Robin Fox (1967) has pointed out, cognates can take up residence in areas of other kinsmen where home-base lands cannot be further expanded. It may be of no little coincidence that many cognatic descent groups are found in island situations. Moreover, if there are problems of whom one supports, such overlap (as in bilineal situations) may also serve the cause of peace. People who belong to different groups can serve as intermediaries and peacemakers.

In cognatic situations, the actual recognition of cognates for any one individual may well be restricted: "situationally selected." Instead of using the founding ancestor(s) and all the intervening links as points of reference as to who group members are, one can use oneself, forming an *ego-focused* group. Strictly speaking, this is not a group based upon descent: it employs laterality more than lineality and is a more purely personal group. Such a group can even come to include some affinal kin; the term *kindred* has often been employed to designate such a group. So, for example, among the Kalinga of Northern Luzon in the Philippines:

> The bilateral (cognatic) descent group is quite a different kind of organization from the personal kindred. While in bilateral descent groups the whole group receives emphasis, in personal kindreds the individual is the focus of attention. In the personal kindred every individual is a hub in an enormous wheel of relatives spiraling outward and bounded in the outer perimeters by great-grandparents, third cousins, and great-grandchildren. ... the personal kindred among the Kalinga is important primarily with respect to the blood-feud system. (Dozier, 1967: 20, 21)

So there may well be nondescent groups based on kin ties as well as those of a strict descent nature (based on relating back to some ancestor). As in the case of familial kinship groups, we may conclude by summing this up in chart fashion.

Descent Kinship Groups

Unilineal:
    lineage
    clan
    phratry, plus bilineal situations
    moiety
Cognatic:
    unrestricted
    ego-centered-like kindred

It is evident that anthropology has a long way to go in establishing the character, dimensions, functions, and appropriate terminological distinctions for such kinship groupings. The individual, of course, has membership not only in familial and descent groups but also in a number of other social groupings that are not (primarily at least) based upon kinship principles. It is to these that we now turn in the next chapter.

SUMMARY

1. Many different types of kinship and nonkinship social groups occur, some primary or secondary, some instrumental, others expressive.
2. Kinship social groups are divided into two main types: familial or residential, and descent or consanguineal.

3. Familial kinship groups include the nuclear family and the composite family, the later being based upon rules of plural marriage or on rules of residence. The composite family has two basic expressions: the polygamous family and the extended family. In primitive societies, the composite family has certain advantages over the nuclear family in that it supplies a greater number of people to carry out the demand of the natural division of labor, and in that it has greater permanence.

4. Descent kinship groups are based upon unilineal and cognatic ways of reckoning biological affiliation. Unilineal descent groups consist of the lineage, clan, phratry, and moiety as well as some bilineal types such as the section. Groups that are reckoned patrilineally have fewer structural problems than those based on descent through females. Cognatic descent groups have been less studied. They may be unrestricted or ego-centered like the kindred.

REFERENCES FOR FURTHER READING

A good quick introduction to social groups is provided by M. S. Olmstead in *The Small Group* (1966, Random House); and in two sociological classics: *Social Organization,* by Charles H. Cooley (1920, Scribners); and *Human Society,* by Kingsley Davis (1966, Macmillan). Murdock, *Social Structure* (1963, Macmillan) also discusses kinship groups themselves. Three general texts on the family contain excellent illustrations of this variety of kinship group. They are *The Family in Various Cultures,* by Stuart Queen and Robert Haberstein (1967, Lippencott); *The Family in Cross-Cultural Perspective,* by William N. Stephens (1963, Holt, Rinehart & Winston); and *Comparative Family Systems,* edited by M. F. Nimkoff (1965, Houghton Mifflin). Two general works taking special approaches to kinship groups are *Kinship and Social Organization,* by Ira R. Buchler and Henry A. Selby (1968, Macmillan) and *Primitive Social Organization,* by Elman R. Service (1962, Random House). A good introduction to cognatic forms of social organization is *Social Structure in Southeast Asia,* edited by G. P. Murdock (1960, Quadrangle Books), whose own essay is especially helpful. Text examples in chapter eighteen are drawn from *The Cibacue Apache,* by Keith Basso (1970); *The Kalinga of Northern Luzon, Philippines,* by Edward Dozier (1967); and *Ulithi, A Micronesian Design for Living,* by William A. Lessa (1966), all published by Holt, Rinehart & Winston.

19

social groups:
nonkinship

*A*ll human societies probably have groups of people organized on the basis of principles other than kinship. These groups may well contain kinsmen, but the causes that bring such groups into existence are not of a kinship nature. Such nonkinship groups not only may cut across kinship lines but can help provide solidarity, integration, and social control for the entire society itself. Moreover, they can supplement or replace the function of the kinship groups for the individual—technologically, socially, and religiously. Because of the visibility and "glamour" of kinship groups, anthropologists have not made nonkinship groups the primary objects of their studies. Hence, we have not advanced very far in our analysis of nonkinship groupings. We have especially not come to any terminological agreements relative to their varieties. For purposes of illustration, the present chapter divides nonkinship groups into three major varieties. The first variety brings people together on the basis of pursuit of some purpose or goal or the inherent satisfaction from membership itself. The second variety is based upon considerations of status and rank. People in different social strata, especially in small primitive societies, may actually comprise an interacting group with feelings of identity and solidarity. Finally, nonkinship groups derive from the fact of territoriality; people living in the same area can develop a feeling of self-recognition. We will consider each of these in turn.

ASSOCIATIONS

The first form of nonkinship groups (based on purpose and satisfactions) perhaps offers the greatest difficulties in classification. Associations occur in a bewildering variety, their overlapping natures make their exposition even more difficult. Generally speaking, they answer the needs of human beings to pursue activities that kinsmen either cannot or will not help the individual accomplish. This may be merely the playing out of desires for companionship of the nonkinship sort.

337

Certainly, no single psychological motive is involved. Often, however, they are formed because kinship groups are rather small and cannot possibly cater to all the needs of their members. Also, as Paul Bohannon has remarked (1963), relations between kinship groups may be difficult to regulate by kinship means, intermarriage often being the only kinship links available. We will presently examine more specific motivations and functions. Generally, however, the great proliferation of such groups in modern society (check a sociology text) reflects the lack of availability of kinship groups and the need to extend social relations.

What do we call such groups? To be perfectly honest, almost anything we want to! There are almost as many names as there are writers on this topic. Many authors distinguish between voluntary and involuntary associations on the basis of freedom of membership. Can the individual choose the group he or she wishes and can they choose not to join at all? Is one's choice potential restricted by membership in some other group or by having to join, like it or not? Another membership possibility has led some writers to distinguish those groups that are exclusive from those of an inclusive nature. In the first case, only a few individuals in the society hold membership in the group; in the inclusive situation, everybody belongs. It is doubtful that this latter case ever truly occurs in this type of nonkinship group. Again, such groups can be distinguished on the basis of their autonomy. Do they exist independent from centralized political controls or are they in one way or another subservient to, or incorporated within, the government of the society? Finally, among many possible variables, such groups may be divided in terms of the goals or purposes themselves. They may be *instrumental*, in which case people organize themselves into groups to work for the achievement of rather restricted goals, say a headhunting expedition. They may also be *expressive*. Here members are organized more for the intrinsic satisfactions that the group membership itself has to offer, perhaps the good times shared by habitual drinking companions. However, seldom will even the most "self-satisfied" group not also pursue goals in common or a specific-purpose group not derive mutual satisfactions. All of these possibilities overlap. For purposes of convenient designation, we will call all forms of these groups by the commonly employed term *associations* (sometimes called sodalities). We can examine some of the varieties of these on the basis of what the most obvious organizing principle of each appears to be, realizing that other principles may also be involved.

Associations Based Upon Sex Distinctions

The first variety of association is based primarily upon *sex* distinctions. Basically, this means that anthropologists discover groups of males and groups of females in a society that cut across kinship lines. Associations of males, sometimes called tribal fraternities, appear much more commonly than do those for women. This may be partly due to the fact that the males assume positions of social control, whereas females generally do not. Hence, organization of such groups may reflect this. "I do not claim that females have no organization . . . but female organizations affect political activity far less than male ones do . . . females generally exert less political influence than do males" (Tiger, 1970: 179). Perhaps male associations also aid males in the playing out of their more public roles. However, more must be involved than this. Tiger sees the cooperation in hunting procedures by males as bonding them together in such groups, and we could add the demands of warfare as well. Although we can dismiss the existence of a greater "social instinct" in males, it can be suggested that availability of time may be a factor of considerable importance in explaining the greater number of male groups.

> Male and female are not comparable in terms of "superiority." They are, however, comparable in another regard: females as a category have to spend more hours, calories, and reveries on childbearing and nurturing than males have to spend on child begetting and provisioning . . . The fact remains that men have more time on their hands and uncommitted energy in their bodies than are usually vouchsafed to women. They use their time and energy not merely to provide for their women and children, as most men in most cultures do in some degree, but also to create situations that are as satisfying to themselves as the domestic positions of women . . . can be made for most women in most societies. (Bohannon, 1963: 145)

Certainly, more than one reason must be involved but, just as certainly, the enhancement of sex solidarity among the males at least is a covert,

Social clubs and organizations based on sex distinctions occur in both primitive and modern societies. Left, a men's club in Woleai; right, American boy scouts.

United Nations   Wayne Miller/Magnum Photos

if not an overt, function of male groups, even in groups in which other purposes are discernible.

That solidarity is involved is borne out when one considers that a common activity of the male associations is the initiating of young boys into manhood and into the group at the same time. Among the Yahgan of South America, for example, both males and females in the past went through a general initiation rite (the *ciexaus*). This was accompanied by endurance tests and restrictions on behavior, vocational and moral instruction, songs and dances, and was concluded by a feast and a mock battle between men and women. All this gave the youth of both sexes their membership in the tribe. Later, however, a special rite only for males was held (the *Kina*) in which women were kept strictly away. As a part of it, males secretly painted themselves to impersonate various spirits and danced publicly, threatening the women with severe penalties if they did not yield to the will of the men (Cooper, 1963). Such proceedings gave the boys membership in the male association. Again,

> In ... New Guinea the Bukaua men mystify and terrorize the female population throughout a boy's long initiation festival . . . A demon, the women learn, craves their sons' flesh, but by bringing plenty of food they can appease the monster, who will regurgitate the youths he has swallowed. The hoax is bolstered up in various ways ... The tyros themselves undergo a severe test. Their seniors lead them blindfolded, to their several months' retreat, where concealed guards frighten them with sounds and weapons. Just before the operation (circumcision) the men produce an awe-inspiring din by shouting, swinging bull-roarers, and rattling shells. When the novices finally discover the truth, they are forbidden—on pain of horrible punishment—to breathe a word to the uninitiated. (Lowie, 1959: 297)

Of course, all cases of initiation are not correlated with associations of adult males and many male associations exist without specifically being involved with initiation procedures. A classic example comes from various Plains Indian societies in North America. Among the Cheyenne, for example, when a boy was old enough to engage in warfare activities, he joined a military society, a number of which were organized on a tribal basis. The boy could join any society of his choice and might be able later to shift his affiliation. Each military society was equal in status to all the others, although at any one time one might be more popular. They differed only in their dances and songs and in dress and ornamentation. Each was controlled in its activities by four leaders who were also the main war chiefs of the tribe. Unlike some other tribes in this area, the Cheyenne military societies did not grade their memberships into subgroupings based on age. They functioned to glorify war (a focus of Plains Indian behavior) and also performed other activities on behalf of the community at large. As one writer has so neatly summed up such functions (for these groups in general):

> As regards the functions of the military societies . . . we may distinguish private and public functions. For the individual his society was a club, and at its lodge he would lounge, sleep, eat, dance, sing, and generally have a good time with his fellows. But there were also serious public duties that devolved on either a special society in the series, or on all of the societies, or on one after another. Foremost among such obligations was the policing of the people at crucial times, such as the collective hunt, the march, or the Sun Dance . . . the majority of these organizations fostered the warlike spirit so typical of the area. (Lowie, 1963: 111)

In contrast to tribal fraternities composed of all the males, military societies—at least individually—are exclusive and voluntary since choice and limited membership exist; a truly inclusive men's group is involuntary. Frequently, men's associations will have a special house or common residence. This can help symbolize (and strengthen) the bonds of male solidarity, and many activities can become associated with it. It may be a dormitory for unmarried males (and hence often a place for sexual activity); even married males may sleep there. In any case, it becomes a social center where technological activities, education, and just plain "chewing the fat" may take place. In a few societies, it becomes a kind of arsenal and military rallying place as well.

Associations Based Upon Age Distinctions

Although very few associations are based primarily on age differences, *age* usually plays a decisive role in creating nonkinship groups. And, of course, like sex, age is a good "marker" for group membership. In all societies, people are divided into categories according to age. These categories may not always become socially recognized groups. If they do, they are generally called age sets by anthropologists. An *age set*, then, is a group of people who belong to the same age category; for example, elders as a group of old men. An interesting example comes from the Swazi of South Africa, who recognize about eight periods of individual growth. For three months after birth, a person is simply a "thing" and is not named. After this time, one becomes a "person" and is given a name and receives greater attention. This baby stage lasts until weaning, about three years. Then one becomes a "toddler" and expands the social horizon to include peers of one's own age. At about the age of six, a small slit is made in the ear lobes, and now a person has to engage in more adult types of activities. Training in activities appropriate for later life also commences. The attainment of puberty is not a public event but still is a high point in individual development. After this time, sexual experiences can take place. Girls may marry soon after (to older males), but boys join a "regimental" age class (set). These are formed by the king, based upon a nucleus of similarly aged males who are attached to his own household. A set is brought into existence every five to seven years, when the previous group is considered ready for marriage, when they are "ready to spill their strength in children." These age sets of males are called *emabutfo,* and in the past they were primarily warfare groups, although they also performed as labor groups, primarily with regard to agricultural activities.

> Age groups cut across the boundaries of local chiefs and across the bonds of kinship, incorporating individuals into the state, the widest political unit. Between the members of the same regiment, and particularly those in permanent residence, there is a loyalty and camaraderie. They treat each other as equals, eat together, smoke hemp from the long hemp pipe that is part of their joint equipment, work together, and have a central meeting place or clubhouse in the barracks. ... Towards other age sets there is often openly expressed rivalry and occasional fights, usually provoked by disputes over beer or women, do occur. Young regiments resent the marital privileges of the older men who, in turn, attempt to keep the young from monopolizing as lovers, girls old enough to become wives. To prevent feuds between the regiments national policy dictated periodic action against an external enemy. (Kuper, 1963: 53, 54)

Unlike in some other African societies, all the members of Swazi age sets did not live permanently in the vicinity of the king. Those who did held special rank. Formerly, among the Zulu, the warriors did reside with the king. After initiation into the appropriate age set, the youths went to the king's village and became part of the standing army. They conquered neighboring tribes, collected tribute, as well as acted as a police force within the tribe itself. After about ten years, a man would return to his own village and marry. He became a member of the elder set and engaged in subsistence activities (twenty-five to sixty years of age). Beyond this set was a group of "ancestors" who engaged in ritual activities.

Dorothy Hammond (1972) cites an example of the Tiriki age sets (in Kenya). Here there are seven sets whose members move as a unit about every fifteen years. Each set has strict rules of etiquette for public behavior and strong feelings of solidarity within the set; in fact, set members even practice exogamy. The sets included the uninitiated, initiates, warriors, elder warriors (for general leadership and administration), judicial elders (for legal activities), ritual elders (who run the initiation cult itself), and the most senior set (whose members are either senile or deceased).

In thinking of the above examples, we can observe the functions of age-set types of associations. Obviously, they form an ideal organizing principle for warfare activities, creating a draft system automatically including all the eligible males of the tribe. They can also form the basis for cooperative work groups, especially (but not always) for public projects. They can give a communal organization to education and training, forming "open door" colleges, so to speak. Political functions are almost always found. Elders have political power and social-control potential in their hands, often buttressed by a monopoly on major ritual activities as well. And, of course, age sets are a neat and useful device for marking off the progression of individuals through the various stages of their lives: who am I? I am an elder warrior, that's who! Finally, there is the overall function of supplying solidarity, not only for the various different sets of people themselves but, on a higher level, for the society itself (since such ties cut across group loyalties of a kinship nature). As Hammond has put the matter:

> What unites the Tiriki, transcending clan loyalties to create an integrated society, is their system of age-graded associations . . . This pattern of age grading so prevalent in East Africa has its primary purpose in warfare and adds support to the concept of warfare as a major dynamic factor in the formation of masculine associations. The societies of this area share not only a predilection for cattle raiding, they also tend to lack formal political organizations. The age groups cut across family, lineage and clan affiliations and by uniting the men with one another provide the society with whatever integration it has and its base for cooperative action. The age-grade system serves then as a partial functional alternative to government. (Hammond, 1972: 10, 11)

Such sets can be cyclical, in which case their names are repeated at regular intervals, or progressive, in which case each set receives a unique designation. There are also exceptional cases in which special residential features are added to the system, besides that of a temporary unity of the warriors. The Nyakyusa of Africa (Wilson, 1949) are perhaps the best example of this. Here, because a wife must avoid her in-laws, a male set will set up a peripheral age-set village before marriage and will later live there with their wives. Among these people, then, male identity and solidarity are geographical as well as social.

Associations Based Upon Special Interest

So associations are brought into existence on the basis of both sex and age. What other major types of nonkinship groups occur? Another type,

Special interest groups in America often take the form of ethnic organizations. Shown here is a Greek-American parade.

Suzanne Szasz

which might be called a *special interest* or *agreement* group, is composed of individuals who have particular goals or interests in common. This type of association develops especially where kinsmen cannot meet the needs of the individual. It forms the basis for much of the writings of sociologists on associations. Such groups are often founded on what has been called a contract. A *contract* "is an initially voluntary agreement between two or more people to carry out certain obligations and gain certain rights, when these obligations are not part of any other relationship in which the contracting parties stand to one another" (Bohannon, 1963: 156). The contract may not always be formal, and the result of such "contracting" is generally to the benefit of the group itself. Perhaps the simplest variety of this group is based upon one or another form of friendship, constructed perhaps more on trust and affection than on obligation. Hammond (1972) cites the case of the Plains Cree Indians of North America, in which a male would develop three types of friends. One was gained in boyhood. In the second, a boy would act as a "squire" to an older warrior. The third, developed in later life, involved married men who exchanged wives and who gave each other gifts. All such friendships provided support in warfare and related activities. Among the Netsilik Eskimo, sharing partners were chosen by a boy's parents at the time of early childhood. These were lifetime friendships. Only most distant relatives or nonrelated individuals are eligible for such "contracts." Although such people had food-sharing obligations, the real motive was social, as we have observed for associations in general.

> . . . in the winter it was absolutely essential that several extended families live and work together in the interest of common survival. The system of formal partnerships, of which food sharing was a part, worked to overcome these latent hostilities toward non-relatives and

344

> gave the camp social cohesion. It constituted a permanent set of alliances independent of kinship connections, renewable at each generation, decisively contributing to camp peace. (Balikci, 1970: 138)

Such associations, of course, can be considerably expanded both in scope and membership. Kenneth Little has written of how migrants to urban areas in West Africa have formed a multiplicity of such organizations. Such individuals have come to urban areas to live and work, but most of their real social attachments remain in the tribal areas of their origin. To combat rejection by "city slickers," and to ease their sense of disorganization, they join an association. These serve as functional substitutes for older patterns of stability, taking the place of family and lineage. Such groups provide protection, mutual aid, and ease of transition of the urban migrant to city life. Here men and women often belong to the same organization. Group meetings are held at regular intervals, and fraternity and sociability of members are also values derived from such relations. In such groups, the concept of contract and obligation are more formal than those usually found in friendship situations.

> Membership of an association means submission to its discipline and a person is not admitted unless he agrees to abide by its rules. These are generally laid down in, and form an important part of, the constitution which is usually written or typed in a book. They prescribe a specific code of personal and moral conduct which is designed to regulate the public behavior of members as well as their relations with each other. (Little, 1969: 9A)

Another example of the functioning of interest associations is supplied by George Foster for the Mexican peasant community of Tzintzuntzan. Here he points out that people organize social contacts outside the family by means of permanent contract relationships between two individuals. These dyadic contracts, as he calls them, are in essence relations of reciprocity; balanced between people of similar socioeconomic status, more generalized if they are of different socioeconomic status (with more given by the higher-status person). The nature of such exchanges concerns services and goods in both ritual and nonritual contexts. In the first case are such things as help at life crises such as aid or gifts at marriage and death; in the latter situation (nonritual), help on some building project and borrowing of food. These associations are established by an individual selecting a number of people of different sorts to enhance his personal, economic, and emotional security. Such associations are necessary in Tzintzuntzan because the basic kin group is only the nuclear family. Law and religion are in the hands of outsiders, and, because of plow agriculture, basic technological activities are handled by the individual himself. Hence, if one wants to broaden his social relationships, he must (as in modern society) create new social ties; these dyadic contract situations result from such an endeavor. As Foster has summarized:

> This model rests on the assumption of a structure in which critical social relationships inherent in all institutions beyond the nuclear family are contractual . . . rather than ascribed. . . . In the absence of corporate units, contracts can occur only between pairs of individuals; they must be dyadic. In the absence of legal or ritual validation, contracts must be considered informal or implicit. Informal or implicit contracts can be validated and maintained only by means of recognized reciprocal obligations, manifest by the continuing exchange of goods and services. . . . The contractual principle enables an individual to disentangle himself from the weight of ideal role behavior implicit in the totality of ascribed and achieved statuses he occupies in a society and to make functional such relationships as he deems necessary in everyday life. (Foster, 1969: 18A)

One type of person that is chosen as a candidate for this special dyadic relation is a spiritual parent (ceremonial kinsman). In many areas of Latin America, this institution is called *compadrazgo* and functions to extend the social horizons of the individual. It is the acquiring of ritual god-parents and co-parents for one's own children. Such people (*compadres* and *comadres*) can be acquired on many occasions throughout life, and, if exploited for the ritual obligations owed, they form a kind of ego-centered association. In Tzintzuntzan, however, only a few are selected for the development of any effective working relationship.

    A final example of special-interest associations can be given. Often such groups are formed around some cultlike religious motivation. Such a case is the peyote cult found in many American Indian societies. Among the Taos (a southwest Pueblo group), such membership can be demonstrated to have functions of general social integration beyond, perhaps, the scope of the membership group itself. Peyote is a small, spineless cactus with a general propensity for production of visual color hallucinations when eaten in either the dried or green state. It is used in the peyote cult as the major sacred element, much like the Host in a Catholic church. Among the Taos, the peyote cult is one of three religious groupings. The traditional religious system still survives (Kiva religion), but it is mostly the older and more conservative who hold active membership, and as they die off its secrets disappear with them. Younger people, who are not initiated into the traditional religion, are more involved in the local Catholic church, which they see as modern and up-to-date. Older people also attend, but it is more a *pro forma* activity for most of them. Both young and old people (especially males) attend the peyote activities, perhaps mostly because of the individual-istic religious experiences derived from the visionary nature of this cult. However, peyotism seems to be becoming an increasingly common ground for religious participation for many Pueblo members. This is in a real rather than a nominal sense since membership and participation are entirely voluntary. For the older participants, such activities are a way of remaining at least partially Indian without being rooted in an obsolete religious past or being ultratraditional. These older members can participate with younger adults in an activity that is Indian and not introduced from the outside in the same manner as Catholicism. For the younger participants, who are disillusioned with traditional practices and want to be a part of the larger society, it is the only real mechanism for meaningful religious contact with the older people in a context out-side traditional religious activities. It is a way to be nontraditional while at the same time confirming a degree of Indian identity. So the peyote cult association is a mechanism for maintaining a common and vital religious and social identity for the Taos as well as being valuable for its own individualistic benefits. Both young and old, with different in-terests and points of reference, can unite through this interest group in meaningful social and religious interaction.

Secret Associations

The fourth and last major variety of association is the secret society. This is a group whose members have secret knowledge that non-members do not possess. The nature of their secret may be supernatural powers, ob-jects, or the actual identity of the members themselves. Now, of course, the men's association previously discussed had secrets from the females. As considered here, however, a true secret society has a more limited membership, and the function of the group is not specifically that of group solidarity. In the general sense of the word, probably all groups have some "secrets." Perhaps the most clear-cut example of true secret societies are various groupings of "medicine men" found among Pueblo Indians in the American Southwest. Speaking of Sia Pueblo, Leslie White defines such groups as:

> . . . an organization of men, or of men and women, established according to Sia belief, in the mythological past, by a supernatural being who thus became the society's "father," or patron. The societies were en-dowed with supernatural power and were provided with songs, para-phernalia, rituals, and in some instances dances, through which this power was expressed or used for certain purposes such as curing sickness, hunting or warfare. The societies of the modern era are simply continuations of these original organizations. (White, 1962: 136)

Each of these secret societies has a special headquarters. One joins voluntarily, as a consequence of sickness, or for less common reasons, such as coming too close to an area tabooed to nonmembers and hence being "forced" to join. Each society has different sets of functions to perform. The Flint society, for example, treats patients suffering from any serious illness and specializes in wounds caused in warfare and lightning shock. They also perform weather-control ceremonies.

Camilla Wedgewood (1930), in a general article on secret societies, distinguishes between associations that are social and antisocial. Social secret societies (like the Sia) are those whose functions are supportive of the established social order and recognized by everyone as beneficial. Antisocial secret societies, on the other hand, may exist to gain power for themselves. " . . . they are in opposition to the government which, theoretically at least, symbolizes the will of the community" (Wedgewood, 1930: 136). This is not always a distinction easily drawn. Moreover, any secret societies, in addition to their avowed purposes, can also serve the specific needs of their members. Along with everything else, they bestow a sense of exclusiveness; one is different from one's fellows by virtue of membership, and possession of the secret gives a sense of social prestige.

We have briefly discussed four overlapping types of associations, those based upon age, sex, special interests, and possession of secrets. Almost all have in common the fostering of wider social integration for society because they cut across kinship bonds. In this way, even those of a private nature may come to cater to real public needs. Then, too, they supplement groups of a kinship sort by providing other organizational opportunities to assist the individual.

> Simpler societies have fewer associations, and they are more limited in type. Cultural homogeneity, and the relatively few multifunctioned roles do not provide the prerequisites for the formation of a wide variety of associations. Most societies, however, that have some minimal economic surplus and population density develop associations for the achievement of goals that could not be attained by the individual or by the family. Transitory informal groups could develop spontaneously in response to any perceived need and could readily become perpetuated in a more formal organization. (Hammond, 1972: 19)

Most writers characterize such associations as "way stations" between the family and the development of centralized political organization. However, great debate has occurred over how associations actually fit into this situation. In terms of wider social integration, they aid in its development, but they can also work against such purposes and support more private goals and interests. And often where a high degree of political organization is achieved, associations are either agencies of that control or are restricted in number. We will consider this in greater detail in chapter twenty-one. We can now turn to a consideration of the second major variety of nonkinship groups, those based upon social stratification.

STATUS AND RANK GROUPS

Social stratification in human societies may be said to exist when individuals or groups of individuals are conceived of as occupying higher or lower social levels or strata. These levels and their occupants have more or less "worth" or value in terms of certain characteristics. Generally speaking, these are differences in power, occupational prestige, wealth, material possessions, and often educational or religious knowledge. There are also differences in moral and personal attributes. The positive aspects of these characteristics are most developed on the higher strata and tend to decrease as one descends to the lower levels in the society. Such systems of ranking have been called hierarchies of differential privilege since higher levels reflect possession of more of the "goodies" available in the society. Although the occupants of these strata are basically representatives of social categories of people, such may lead to the formation of actual social groups, and (as we shall see) although kinsmen tend to hang on the same level, collective status and rank are the groups' organizing factors here. One also retains family- and kin-group identity. Put another way, each stratum in the society will be composed of a group (or groups) of people occupying a collective position as "better or worse" than those of other groups. As a result, not only do they share certain behaviors in common that are part of the strata culture, but, in light of membership and similarity, they have the potentiality for common interaction, especially in a small primitive society. So, ideally, a system of social stratification will include a series of groups that are hierarchically arranged on various levels in terms of power, prestige, and other defining characteristics.

There is certainly a conceptual muddle when it comes to describing such groups. Thomas Lasswell (1965) has pointed out that at least seven somewhat different approaches have been taken in the attempt to understand the ranked groups that make up systems of social stratification Some scholars take a single-structure approach, assuming that the ranked groups comprise a single hierarchy; others assume a plural structure, with no single group (at the top) having all the power and prestige. Some writers look at the whole system in terms of the labor division in the society, seeing the groups as the attempt to articulate this; others look at the situation in terms of the characteristic attributes of the populations, which, they believe, define the group boundaries. Still others emphasize the aspects of interaction between the groups as the key to their understanding. Certainly, some combination of approaches is most fruitful.

Caste and Class

Despite such different theoretical approaches taken with respect to the study of social stratification, there is agreement among scholars that such systems take two major forms: caste and class. Simply put, **castes** are hereditary membership groups: placement within them is ascribed by birth. They have a fixed nature. **Classes** are groups of a more open nature. One may be born the child of a "middle-class" family, but subsequent achievements can place one higher or lower in the society. Caste systems are rigid systems of groups because mobility (upward or downward movement) in the hierarchy cannot take place. "Caste systems rank people by birth ascribed group membership rather than by individual attributes. Class systems . . . define the rank of their members according to their individual attributes and behaviors. In a caste system, one displays the attributes of his caste because he is a member of it. In the class system, one is a member . . . because he displays its attributes . . . " (Berreman, 1968: 334). Caste members are ranked in terms of ascribed rather than acquired worth. Because of the "frozen" nature of caste systems, the constituent groups assume a more distinctive nature. Not only are individuals easy to place because of birthright, but the groups themselves have recognized names and a tighter set of common cultural behaviors, including (usually) a common occupation. Moreover, caste systems assume that "superiority and inferiority" are inherited and unchangeable and worry about "contamination" resulting from unguarded contacts between members of different castes.

Class systems are characteristic of western societies. The Duke of Windsor gave up his position in the aristocratic class of England when he married an American commoner.

United Press International

True caste systems are much more rigid than class systems. This untouchable woman is assigned the task of cleaning bathrooms in a Bombay apartment building.

Marilyn Silverstone/Magnum Photos

True caste situations are not easy to discover in the simpler primitive societies, but special forms of caste are often discernible in more complex types. In many Pacific Island cultures, a caste situation existed in which the majority of people were basically undifferentiated but there was a caste of priestly families that were insulated from everyone else by an elaborate system of taboos (supernatural prohibitions). Members of this special group possessed a concentration of religious/magical power (*mana*), and as a result were ritually superior to other people. They were "isolated" from ordinary people so that they could perform supernatural tasks relative to the benefit of the entire population. Through such powers, they gained political power and other rewards. Another special form of caste occurs in which there is a separate caste on the bottom of the social order that exists in isolation to perform certain tasks considered as impure or contaminating for everyone else. Such a group is sometimes called an *outcaste* or *pariah group*. The Eta of Japan are an excellent example. Until recently, they traditionally worked as leather workers, butchering and handling dead animals. Religious concepts relative to spiritual pollution set them off as a people apart, requiring of them endogamy and special behaviors.

> The Shinto concept of uncleanness as the greatest tsumi [things displeasing to the gods] contributed to the development of the Eta. Disease, wounds, death, and the necessary activities relating to death were regarded as causes of uncleanness . . . [after the introduction of Buddhism] . . . uncleanness was now attached to meat eating and a minority who continue to practice this ancient custom began to be despised . . . Since the Eta were held to be defiled not only were they prohibited from participating in the worship of the gods, but individuals coming in contact with these defiled people were treated with disfavor, for defilement was thought to be contagious. (Prince, 1966: 17, 18)

The classic case of an extensive caste system is from India. In fact, some scholars would limit the use of this term to its developments there. This caste system appears to have begun when "Hinduism matured into an institutionalized religion and began transforming the social organization of Indian state systems to accord with its metaphysical, philosophical, theological, and ritual presuppositions" (Gould, 1971:10). Very briefly, the priests developed the power to blend religion and the occupational order into one system of ranked groups, with themselves on the top! Four occupational strata (*varnas*) came into existence, with, perhaps, an untouchable group outside the system.

Brahman:	priestly duties
Kshatriya:	governmental duties (probably split from *Brahmans*)
Vaisyas:	merchant and commercial duties
Sudras:	agricultural duties

Out of these levels, many castes and subcastes and specific ranked occupations historically developed.

In the Hindu belief system, attachment to and involvement with the ordinary things of life meant entrapment in the dreary and necessary cycle of birth and rebirth associated with life; they believed in individual reincarnation. To stop the cycle, one had to cut one's ties to this (unreal) world, and this meant rising through the caste system until enlightenment at the top allowed one to gain eternal rest. Of course, each *varna* represented a stage in this process better than the one beneath it since less earthly attachment was demanded in the duties of its occupants. And, one is reborn into a higher stratum only by conforming to the expected conduct of the stratum one currently occupies. So the religious conceptions and occupational realities were blended together into a system of ranked and distinct levels for caste formation.

> The conclusion was drawn that in both the occupational and religious domains of experience the degree of immersion in life could be gauged by the extent to which a person's activities put him in proximity to blood, death, and dirt. Contact with the offal and decay of life was impure and defiling and unequivocally opposed to those attributes of being that survived after mortal existence has been transcended. In mortal existence, therefore, status was determined by the degree of immersion in life process ... In the context of occupational conduct, this meant that the rank of any given profession was determined by the relationship that was obtained between its practitioners and defiling things. (Gould, 1971: 11)

Thus, differences in innate purity, coupled with occupations, were at the heart of the caste system in India.

A caste system of extremely parallel dimensions (although with a special twist) occurred among the Natchez Indians of the southeastern United States. Here there were two basic divisions, the aristocracy and the commoners (called *Stinkards*). The aristocracy (high caste) was subdivided into three groups or ranks called *Suns, Nobles,* and *Honoureds,* each worth a lesser amount in the scheme of social worth. The Suns on the top were mythically believed to have descended from the gods themselves and had ritual purity similar to that of the *Brahmans* of India. The political ruler (the Great Sun) came from this group.

> The principal offices in the Natchez state were prerogatives of members of a matrilineal royal family, all the members of which were denominated Suns. The king was known as The Great Sun; his mother, or, in the case of her death, his sister,—was The White Woman, or, merely, the Sun Woman. Aside from the king all Sun males were known as Little Suns; and apart from the White Woman, all other royal women were denominated merely Sun Women. As concerns rank within the family, primogeniture seems to have been the rule. The king would seem to have ruled directly over the Grand Village, or capital; the outlying villages, at least those of the Natchez population, being ruled by other members of the royal family in order of rank. (MacLeod, 1924: 202)

The lower aristocratic groups performed merchant and military types of activity and the Stinkards (*sudras?*) kept the system going. Such groups displayed different behaviors and practices in dress, diet, and housing, as well as distinctive forms of address. It is even claimed that the Stinkards spoke a separate language. The highest people of all were carried on litters. Unlike the endogamy of most caste systems, however, all these aristocratic subcastes were obliged to marry down and take Stinkards as spouses. Their offspring, in true caste fashion, were assigned to the appropriate level. If an aristocratic male married a female Stinkard their male children fell one level. If a female aristocrat married a Stinkard male, they took the social position of their mother (via matrilineal descent). In addition, apparently, daughters of Stinkard females remained Stinkards! Diagrammatically:

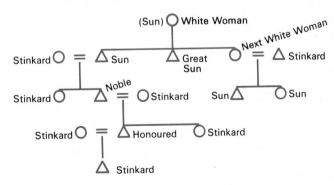

So, in a regular fashion, a genetic line could have at least male representatives in all four categories, although women apparently were either Suns or Stinkards only. Still, in most cases, wherever you were born, there you stayed; the regulation of behavioral differences and worth were absolute. The lot of a Stinkard husband of a female Sun was not pleasant. He acted in her presence like a servant, and at her death (since she was ritually special), he was killed to accompany her into the next life. So, in all, the system of social stratification among the Natchez seems more caste than classlike in its operation.

Class systems of one degree of development or another may also be discovered in primitive societies. Once again, groups of North American Indians provide interesting examples. In these class systems, the individual belongs to the class because he has achieved the attributes of that class. Among the Kiowa (of the Great Plains area), there was a system of stratification into four classes: "distinguished," "second best," "propertyless," and "useless."

> There are five prerequisites of [the distinguished] grade. Every [distinguished] should possess good looks. "He should be handsome on a horse." He should have property enough to validate his rank by distributing it when necessary. He should be generous. He must be aristocratic in his bearing and courteous. Above all else, he must have distinguished himself in war. The last overweighs the other four taken together and suggests the fundamental difference between the first and second grade. (Mishkin, 1940: 36)

Much of the wealth possessed by such upper-class people was counted in horses, often obtained on raiding expeditions. The second-bests consisted of persons who had wealth, were generous and noble but lacked the formal war exploits (see chapter twenty-two) of their betters. The propertyless individuals had neither wealth nor war honors and for the most part were dependent upon more fortunate relatives. They borrowed horses and performed tasks for their benefactors. But, "they persistently tried to raise their rank . . ." (Mishkin, 1940: 36). The lowest class consisted of shiftless, lazy, and less-than-honest individuals who were disowned for all intents and purposes by their kinsmen. They had no more status than captives and survived mostly as retainers to upper-class households by performing menial tasks. In effect, they formed an outcaste type of group. The upper three classes were less sharply demarcated.

A second class system comes from the Taos Indians (whom we discussed with regard to the peyote cult). Here the chief variables of the ranks are education and community-mindedness instead of war and wealth. This is a system of stratification that emerged only in recent times. There are three classes of people. In the first (upper) are found the most highly respected members of the community. Such people are highly educated in traditional Indian ways. This amounts to having been educated by initiation and membership in religious practices and groupings. "They are aware of how to act according to the Indian way of thinking." But they mostly lack the ability to read and write English. Most of the important official governmental positions at the pueblo are occupied by individuals of this class. They are considered to be working for unselfish goals and the good of the community. Members of the second rank (middle class) are usually well-educated from a non-Indian point of view. Many such people have spent much of their youth away from the pueblo and may be highly acculturated to white behavior. However, they usually lack a knowledge of "real" Indian behavior, not having undergone initiation into religious secrets. They are interested in their community, however, and use their knowledge for public affairs, often serving as secretaries and interpreters for the upper-class leaders. The members of the bottom rank (lower class) are felt to be careless, useless, and are little respected. They are often heavy drinkers and troublemakers for the pueblo. They appear to be fallen members of the other classes. This means that they may be well-educated from either an Indian or white perspective but they are not community-minded and waste their education and potential. As I have summarized this elsewhere:

> There appears to be at least three ranking categories at Taos Pueblo. Rather than all members of the Pueblo being considered equal some, because of their education in traditional Indian ways and in community application, are ranked as the best members of the community. Other community members are not as qualified, lacking sufficient "cultural Indian behavior." Yet their White education is useful to the Pueblo and, if they make the attempt to integrate themselves into community affairs, they are respected. These are considered "good Indians" although slightly suspect. A last category of individuals may have either kind of education but these persons make no attempt to apply themselves in community life. They occupy a distinctly inferior rank though they are capable of upward mobility. . . . (Collins, 1972: 49)

So caste and classlike systems of social stratification exist in primitive societies. Such an avenue for the creation of groups offers still another social dimension for human membership and anthropological study.

TERRITORIAL GROUPS

The last possibility for nonkinship grouping derives from the fact of territoriality and geographical proximity. Exactly how these groups are organized and how they differ from other types in behavioral terms seems not yet to be clearly understood by anthropologists, and few texts deal with the topic. Yet people who live in the same area may develop some or all of the characteristics of social groups. Such groups may even draw boundaries between themselves and others in such terms. In a negative sense, isolation may provide group solidarity and collectiveness, but usually these are groups bounded by a common degree of functional interdependence in terms of self-protection, economy, and, in many cases, overriding political considerations (see chapter twenty-one).

The Local Group

It is probably a truism that the smaller these kinds of groups are, the easier they are to recognize and define. A typically small territorial nonkinship group has been called a *local group*. In ideal terms, this is composed of a number of unrelated families who occupy, or are in some way identified with, a given geographical area or region. They reside in it or exploit it technoeconomically. Although many of these people may in fact be related by kinship, the essential character the group presents to the outside world is not primarily of a kinship nature. It has been somewhat traditional among anthropologists to divide the local group into two varieties, the *band* and the *village*. The *band* is a mobile type of local group and is correlated with food collecting and pastoralism as subsistence techniques. Among the Washo Indians of Nevada, for example, the band was called a "bunch."

> ... various families tended to move together in an informal but recognized social unit called the "bunch." This unit seems to have been what we have come to call a band ... Most frequently a bunch was identified with its leader and would be referred to as "so and so's bunch." The assumption of leadership of a bunch was an informal matter ... Usually men of the same bunch formed together to form hunting parties. The bunch might as a unit move to the west side of the Sierra to pick acorns or go to the ocean to gather shells for trading. In time of emergency the men of the bunch usually stood together in defense of attacks ... In general, we might say that the bunch consisted of a minimal number of families that could cooperate to do those things which an individual family could not do for itself. ... Should a family decide to move to some area where they had heard that a good gathering crop was available, they were in no way compelled to remain with their erstwhile companions. (Downs, 1966: 44, 45)

This description points up the essentially nonkinship nature of the band, its interdependence, its small size, and its lack of stability in terms of membership.

The other variety of local group has been called (rather inelegantly) the *village* and refers to a more sedentary unit. Such groups tend to correlate more with situations in which subsistence patterns either allow or require people to stay clustered together for relatively long periods of time: for example, in agricultural societies. Anthropologists are not in any agreement as to the actual permanancy or size requirements for this group, although sociologists have constructed elaborate typologies ranging from tiny hamlets to large metropolitan areas. More often, anthropologists have concerned themselves with the nature of this sort of group. Eric Wolf (1955), for example, has dealt with such units as being closed or open communities. This is in terms of whether there is a sharp distinction made between members and nonmembers, whether economic behavior is geared to serve and supply members or outsiders, whether interaction with the world beyond occurs, and other related matters. All this is the basic distinction between being self-contained or being articulated to a larger social field of behavior. Such discussions are beyond the scope of the present book. We can say, however, that village membership is apt to shift less often than that of the band (at least in primitive societies), and the sense of identification and solidarity may also be greater. Speaking of the Mexican village of Tepoztlan, Lewis points out that:

> The village is a corporate body which enjoys legal status . . . It is an administrative unit and most of the social, economic, and religious activities of the villagers take place within it. The stability of residence and the predominance of endogamous marriages . . . encourage village identification, a trend which is further enhanced by the absence of well-developed class distinctions. Because each family, rich or poor, owns a house and house site and has recognized status as a villager, each villager can proudly say "this is my village and the village of my ancestors." (Lewis, 1960: 48)

This sense of identification is buttressed by a form of collective labor that requires every able-bodied male between the ages of twenty-one and fifty-one to work twelve days a year on public works projects such as improving roads and constructing public buildings.

The Maximal Group

If anthropological analysis has been less than adequate on small territorial groups, we are, in essence, just beginning our study of those of a more comprehensive nature. Such groups—tribes and nations—are sometimes called *maximal groups*. In such groups, of course, there is less direct social contact—especially of the primary group sort—and the size varies greatly. Ideally, a maximal group would be composed of all the local groups that felt a higher common unity among themselves. In the absence of political integration, however, such recognition is often lacking and the creation of maximal groups is more of an abstraction made by the anthropologist. We lump local groups into larger units based upon consideration of linguistic and other cultural similarities. Recent research employs the term *ethnic group* to designate such a unit and generally defines it along the following lines:

1. is largely biologically self-perpetuating
2. shares fundamental cultural values, realized in overt unity in cultural forms
3. makes up a field of communication and interaction
4. has a membership which identifies itself, and is identified by others, as constituting a category distinguishable from other categories of the same order. (Barth, 1969: 10, 11)

As already observed, however, unless there is political unity, such larger identification is certainly less real for many primitives than it is for ourselves.

> While the Washo clearly differentiated between themselves and all other peoples, using various cultural criteria, it is clear that they felt no overall obligations simply because of this relationship. War was one of the mechanisms for dealing with non-Washo people, but it was generally a local matter resorted to to resolve local problems and not considered a "nation-wide" affair. (Downs, 1966: 53, 54)

All this suggests that although there are territorial group identifications, the anthropological study of such groups, and of more complex societies in general, is just beginning. We can now turn to a quite different dimension of the interpersonal dimension of cultural behavior, the realm of social control: law, government, and warfare.

SUMMARY

1. Nonkinship groups fall into three major classes: those based upon the common satisfactions of members, those based upon considerations of status and rank, and those based upon territoriality. These groups often overlap with each other as well as with kinship groups.
2. Satisfaction groups, or associations, can be based on sex or age distinctions and may be voluntarily or involuntarily joined; they may be exclusive or inclusive, and may or may not pursue limited

interests. Such groups may be formally or informally conceived. Many such groups are formed around political or religious activities in primitive societies. Finally, such groups may or may not be secret societies.

3. Social stratification exists when individuals or groups are conceived of as occupying higher or lower social levels or strata, representing differences in power, wealth, occupational prestige, etc. Many theoretical approaches have been taken in the study of these systems. Castes and classes, and closed and open groups are two common forms of social stratification. Caste systems often exhibit connection to religious beliefs and behaviors.

4. Territorial nonkinship groups are derived from geographical proximity. They consist of people bounded not only by territory but by a common degree of functional interdependence in terms of economy and self-protection. Small groups are called local groups and may be bands or villages depending upon their degree of mobility. Larger groups, tribes, or nations may be called maximal groups and often coincide with ethnic boundaries although political unity may be poorly developed.

REFERENCES FOR FURTHER READING

A thoughtful discussion of associations is provided by Robert Lowie in *Social Organization* (1959, Rinehart). General articles include "Associations," by Dorothy Hammond (Addison-Wesley Module 14, 1972), "The Nature and Functions of Secret Societies," by Camilla Wedgewood, in *Oceania* 1 (1930): 129–45; "The Organization of Voluntary Associations in West Africa," by Kenneth Little, both quoted in John Collins, *Readings in Social and Cultural Anthropology* (1969, Selected academic readings); and George M. Foster, *The Dyadic Contract* in the same volume. An interesting discussion of male groups is found in Lionel Tiger, *Men in Groups* (1970, Random House). Some general volumes dealing with class and caste systems are: Gerhard Lenski, *Power and Privilege* (1966, McGraw-Hill); *Class and Stratum*, by Thomas E. Lasswell (1965, Houghton Mifflin); *Class and Caste: A Comparative View*, by Harold A. Gould (Addison-Wesley Module 11, 1971) and Gerald D. Berreman, "The Concept of Caste," in *Encyclopedia of the Social Sciences* 2 (1968): 333–38. The case of the Eta is taken from *Japan's Invisible Race*, edited by George DeVos and Hiroshi Wagatsuma (1966, University of California Press). A consideration of territorial groups is found in *Ethnic Groups and Boundaries*, edited by Fredrik Barth (1969; Little, Brown); as well as in John Honigmann, *The World of Man* (1959, Harper & Row). The examples used in chapter nineteen were drawn from *The Pueblo of Sia, New Mexico,* by Leslie White (1962, U.S. Government Printing Office); *The Netsilik Eskimo,* by Asen Balikci (1970, Doubleday); "Reputational Rank at Taos Pueblo, New Mexico," by John Collins, in *Agora* 2 (1972): 47–49; *Rank and Warfare Among the Plains Indians,* by Bernard Mishkin (1940, University of Washington Press), *The Swazi,* by Hilda Kuper (1963); *The Two Worlds of the Washo,* by James Downs (1966); and *Tepoztlan,* by Oscar Lewis (1960), all published by Holt, Rinehart & Winston. The Natchez example came from "Natchez Political Evolution," by W. C. MacLeod, in *American Anthropologist* 26 (1924): 201–29. For ritual kinship see S. M. Mintz and Eric Wolf, "An Analysis of Ritual Co-Parenthood (Compadrazgo," in *Southwestern Journal of Anthropology* 6 (1950): 341–68.

20 law

Probably all human societies make attempts to regulate and control the behaviors of the individuals and groups that constitute them. They also attempt to order relationships with other societies. Although much of ongoing behavior needs no formal or special institutions to guarantee its "correctness" (by employing guilt or fear of shame), there are special directive or inhibitory attempts at social control. These are generally labeled as law, government, and warfare, and may or may not be effective. This chapter deals with those mechanisms commonly called law or legal behavior.

THE CONCEPT OF LAW

Mechanisms of law generally attempt to punish and redress deviations from the rules of a society, and ultimately, ideally, prevent such misconduct from occurring. As we observed in previous chapters, such behaviors often become organized in primitive societies in ways somewhat outside the scope of our own experiences. As a result, the legal anthropologist faces a number of conceptual difficulties in defining the term *law* and in clearly apprehending its applications and interconnections with other cultural behaviors. In essence, we wish to determine whether law is universal and, if so, to ascertain its characters. In such a pursuit, however, we have often taken extreme positions. One view treats law so narrowly so as to make it coincide with the politically organized state. With a bias toward Western legal behavior, it defines law as being composed of "codes and courts." This definition has little comparative value since law, so defined, is not a universal human behavior: not all primitive societies have codes and courts. E. A. Hoebel, in a survey volume on primitive law, has illustrated an older variety

362

of this concept of law. He quotes the work of Cardozo, who defines law as "a principle or rule of conduct so established as to justify a prediction with reasonable certainty that it will be enforced by the courts if its authority is challenged" (Hoebel, 1954: 22). In practice, this boils down to the elements of rules, regularity, enforcement, and courts. It is not always easy to discover all of these elements in all societies. If we see an enforcement mechanism in operation, we can perhaps ascertain its regularity and discover the rule that was broken. The idea of a court, however, at least in the Western sense is often difficult to recognize. Not all groups employ courts in our specialized sense. Hoebel gives various examples of such "courts," among which is the following:

> Consider the Eskimo way of handling recidivist homicide. Killing on a single occasion merely leads to feud . . . but, among the Eskimos, to kill someone on a second occasion makes the culprit a dangerous public enemy.
>
> Now arises the opportunity for some public spirited man of initiative to perform a community service. He may undertake to interview, one after the other, all the adult males of the community to see if they agree that the killer had best be executed. If unanimous consent is given, he personally dispatches the murderer at the first opportunity, and no revenge may be taken on him by the murderer's relatives. (Hoebel, 1954: 25, 26)

He goes on to opt for a wider definition than this in an effort to avoid such definitional problems, and stresses legal behavior as involving legitimate use of physical coercion by socially authorized agents. This represents the second definitional approach, one that wishes the term *law* to be broader in its range of application. This view seeks for some manner in which legal behavior can be legitimately studied in cross-cultural perspective. As Laura Nader has suggested, some broader definition is required since:

> How people resolve conflicting interests and how they remedy strife situations is a problem with which all societies have to deal, and usually they find not one but many ways to handle grievances. In any society also there are remedy agents which may be referred to when a grievance reaches a boiling point, and an understanding of all such agencies is necessary for a comprehensive analysis of social control and for a sophisticated contextual analysis of the court system, should one exist. (Nader, 1965: 23)

There is perhaps an unfortunate tendency in this approach to equate any process of social control with law, removing any real definitional significance from this term.

The notion of law in western society, typified by a courtroom, judge, and jury is not universal. Many primitive societies react as a whole to modes of behavior which are thereby approved or disapproved. Left, an American courtroom; right, an African village meeting.

LAW AND SOCIAL SANCTIONS

This chapter treats law as a definable "something" that not all primitive societies exhibit, although most, certainly, have regularized mechanisms of social control. We consider law as part of this wider context. All social-control mechanisms can perhaps be most usefully considered as resulting from the application of social-sanction behaviors. Social sanctions have been defined by one anthropologist as "a reaction on the part of a society or of a considerable number of its members to a mode of behavior which is thereby approved . . . or disapproved" (Radcliffe-Brown, 1952: 205). These reactions help to regulate the conduct of the individual to conform to expected behavior. Those social sanctions that are negative, in disapproval of certain behaviors, result in the social-control mechanisms that are most easily perceived and examined by anthropologists. This is because one seems to be more often punished for deviation than rewarded for conformity. It's not what you do right but what you do wrong or don't do that seems to attract attention—poor psychology, perhaps, but a fact of social life! Radcliffe-Brown discussed, among others, four major types of such sanctions, which we can consider in this negative sense and somewhat redefine. An *organized* negative sanction is a response in disapproval of some action carried out according to some definite recognized procedure ("I would like to report my car has been stolen."). The outcome is predictable. One knows what people involved will do in a given situation and what the result is likely to be. A *diffuse* negative sanction is a response of disapproval to some act that is a more spontaneous expression. It is often simply a sense of moral approbation ("He shouldn't do that, it really isn't right."). The procedure itself in terms of choice and outcome is not definite or predictable. There are numerous possibilities for action, and a selected technique may or may not be effective; the "guilty" party may or may not suffer any consequences. A *primary* negative sanction is a disapproving response to some behavior that emanates from the whole community or its authorized representative(s) when direct communal reaction is not feasible (The police and courts represent my interests.). Everyone feels concern and involvement either directly or indirectly. A *secondary* negative sanction is a response to some disapproved behavior that involves only a person or some small group acting in terms of its own concerns ("The color of that house is going to spoil this neighborhood.").

These four negative sanctions are easy to recognize in ongoing behavior and present no problems of definition. Everyone is concerned or they are not; they have definite procedures or merely possibilities. Moreover, in actual behavior, we can recognize a kind of overlap between them. They tend to operate in combination and actually result in four basic sanction clusters that may function in the social control of disapproved behaviors. These are represented below.

	Primary	*Secondary*
Organized	Definite recognized procedures with predictable outcome on the part of community or representative.	Definite recognized procedures with predictable outcome on the part of a person or group for themselves.
Diffuse	Spontaneous expression with no predictable outcome on the part of a community or representative.	Spontaneous expression with no predictable outcome on the part of a person or group for themselves.

These four areas of social-control possibilities may be observed in operation in any society. Possibly all four may occur, but generally one area will predominate over the others as the major mechanism of social control. Perhaps in a small number of groups one mechanism will be the only device for regulating conduct, the only way to express disapproval. We will examine each of these areas in turn and illustrate typical behaviors from representative primitive societies.

Organized-Primary Sanctions

The first of these negative areas represents the sanction combination **organized-primary**. It is recognizable as the kind of disapproval response that most frequently occurs in Western societies. Here there are authorities and courts acting on behalf of society. Regularized procedures exist and they have predictable outcomes. Such are responses that meet the narrower definition of law since such sanctions require higher levels of political organization. They display what we have earlier referred to as codes and courts. As one anthropologist has observed, such sanctions require a unicentric (single) system of power and authority so that "... some of the customs of some of the institutions of society are restated in such a way that they can be applied by an institution designed ... for that purpose" (Bohannan, 1965: 36). So such a sanction combination represents legal behavior.

Although the majority of effective disapproval expressions in Western behavior may assume this form, other possibilities certainly exist. Neighbors can exert spontaneous disapproval over the color a house is painted or businessmen censure a colleague for unethical but not necessarily illegal practices. The point, however, is that the outcome of such behaviors is not predictable, and they are not engaged in on behalf of the whole community. Primitive societies exist that institutionalize at least some of their negative sanctions in this organized-primary manner. Such are usually politically organized on a chiefdom or state level (see chapter twenty-one). Even in these societies, it has been observed that such practices often lack the formality and completeness of Western legal practices. They also appear to display more concern with human relations and the total context of the dispute situation.

An interesting example occurs in the Pueblo Indian society of the Taos in New Mexico. As among other Rio Grande Pueblos, here there exist a series of official governmental positions, most of which are of annual election. They are divided into two main groupings. The first comprises the governor, lieutenant governor, and their staff members; the second, the war captain, his chief assistant, and their staff. The former are concerned with internal pueblo affairs, the latter with those of an external nature. The governor and his group are of great importance in organized-primary sanction expression. He himself is first and foremost an arbiter of trouble cases and theoretically acts as a deterrent in this area. We can represent a typical expression of such activity in the following outline.

1. If some difficulty, say a dispute, is felt by one or more of the contending parties to be serious enough to warrant the governor's attention, he is informed of it.
2. During the report to the governor, the disputants give an account of their difficulty, the circumstances surrounding it, and other evidence they feel is pertinent.

3. The governor then schedules a trial, after first conferring with his staff members to make sure there is enough evidence to permit such a trial.

4. The governor then brings together the contending parties once again, in private, in the attempt to resolve the difficulty "out of court." Failing this, the trial is held as scheduled.

5. The governor opens the trial with advice to the jurors and his staff members, and urges all concerned to follow acceptable procedures and tell the truth.

6. In order of their rank, the staff members question the contending parties and openly discuss the merit of the positions of each.

7. The governor then calls a halt to the proceedings and sums up the evidence on both sides. He next summarizes the discussions of his staff members and gives his opinion. (Throughout the trial he has also acted as a kind of umpire.)

8. Finally the lieutenant governor, who has sat on the sidelines, so to speak, renders the official decision. Almost always, this is in accordance with the opinion of the governor. The lieutenant governor then decides a fine or other punishment for the guilty party.

As previously indicated, although such behavior may seem less complete than legal behavior among ourselves—judge, attorneys, and jury being combined among the Taos—nonetheless, there are definite procedures for an aggrieved individual to follow; there are officials acting on behalf of the society; and the outcome is generally predictable, so much so that disputants will often settle out of court. Such is a clear example of law in a non-industrially organized society. Similar examples are found in other world areas; for example, in Africa, where numerous tribal groupings are organized on centralized levels represented by paramount chiefs. Many primitive peoples, however, lack such political sophistication. In most such societies, one or both of two other negative-sanction combinations predominate.

Organized-Secondary Sanctions

One of these disapproval areas is **organized-secondary**. This is recognizable as the kind of "self-help" activity that is often cited in works dealing with social-control behaviors among primitives. In the absence of properly constituted authority or the involvement of the whole community, it is up to the aggrieved individual or his kinsmen to express disapproval on their own behalf. There do exist regularized procedures they can follow, and, up to reasonable limits, a predictable outcome exists within the frame of custom. As one anthropologist has stated, such societies have numerous centers of power, and dispute situations occur between people who often represent equally powerful units. "In such a situation, all trouble cases are settled by some form of compromise, more or less in accordance with a set of overt rules. Instead of decisions there are compromises" (Bohannan, 1965: 39). Instead of some binding decision by an official *adjudicating* body with enforcing powers, as in organized-primary situations, here each party to the dispute tries to *negotiate* the best decision according to acknowledged standards of dispute settlement. Although not "legal" as in our first area, since the whole community does not express disapproval, there are, nevertheless, recognized avenues of approach to the problem of resolving disputes and generally predictable outcomes. It is not enforcement, however, but compromise. The negotiations may be direct—between the conflicting parties—or indirect—by employing the services of go-betweens or high-status mediators.

A good example of organized-secondary settlement occurs among the Daflas of the Indo-Tibetan borderlands. Here it may happen that individual A will arrange to buy a valuable item from individual B for two cows. He pays one cow, promises the other, and receives his goods, but for some reason delays full payment. B, the aggrieved individual, if his kin group is equal to that of A, will try to take by force what is due him. If weak, he will pass the debt on to his son for later possible restitution. He will seize a cow (often of greater value than compensation calls for) to cancel out the debt. This act follows customary procedure of self-help and the kin, and friends of B can be counted on for support. But A has lost face and is likely to seek revenge, usually taking the form of kidnapping a B kinsman (who is treated well). Now a further customary course of action is pursued: B sends a mediator from his group to A to determine the amount of ransom. If neither side wishes to continue the quarrel, the ransom is set to restore normal relations and secure the release of the captive—not justice, perhaps, but settlement. If the ransom is set too high for B's satisfaction, he will have to pay it to secure release but will himself plot revenge. "He will now have an added grievance, for the quarrel began with A's refusal to pay a freely contracted debt, and the extraction of an exorbitant ransom adds to the injury . . . yet there exists no tribal authority to which he can appeal. Everyone may agree that he has been wronged but nobody makes any move to redress the wrong . . ."(Von Furer-Haimendorf, 1967: 61). B generally raids A to secure his own captives for ransom, an extreme form of self-help supported by force, although killing generally does not occur. Now a more formal go-between is selected to arrange a meeting to bring the chief opponents together so they can discuss their differences. He has, however, no authority to impose any solution, being solely the medium for negotiating a settlement. After arguing to a mutually acceptable conclusion, the appropriate ritual will reestablish their normal relations.

> Although there is no administration of justice in any sense of the word, questions of right and wrong are continuously discussed in the course of a dispute. In the mind of the Dafla there is a great difference between justified retaliation and unprovoked robbery, and when hostile parties meet to discuss the settlement of a feud both harp on the details of custom, each trying to prove that their own actions were justified and those of their opponents were a breach of custom. (Von Furer-Haimendorf, 1967: 67)

Much the same kind of procedure occurs among the Nuer of Africa, more formally negotiated by the Leopard-Skin Chief—a sacred personage whose own dwelling can become a place of sanctuary for murderers and other wrongdoers. As with all formal negotiators, such persons may even become a rationale for settlement. Even though they lack any real authority, their prestige serves as an excuse for the contending parties in a dispute to settle without any loss of face: "We will compromise but only to honor him, not because we were wrong or don't seek vengeance." So self-help is often effective in dispute settlement. Even in a few societies in which formal courts exist, it may still be left up to the "winning" party to employ the actual enforcement by applying the appropriate retaliative sanction. Then, too, in some groups such as the Yurok of California each side in a dispute may select mediators who, as a collective body, will cross back and forth between the contenders and arrange a collective settlement. Such behaviors certainly contain the germs for development of more legal authority since the mediators themselves make the decision. In all organized-secondary situations, however, such expressions of disapproval may degenerate to the level of continuing hostility and result in feud situations. So although settlement is likely to occur, its security is less assured than in the legal organized-primary practices.

Diffuse-Primary Sanctions

The third negative-sanction combination is **diffuse-primary.** This, too, is common in many primitive societies as a device for disapproval. In this case, the whole community or its representatives are involved, but there is no definitely recognized procedural mode, and the outcome is not predictable, save that some disposition is made of the problem that aroused disapproval. In such cases, the actual guilt or innocence may be secondary, and a given instance of trouble may or may not lead to such sanctions.

Published accounts of some Eskimo procedures seem to reflect this kind of disapproval. The much-publicized *song duels* are an example. An injured party will nurse his grievance (often adultery) until such time as he and his opponent and other community members are gathered together. At this point, he will actually sing his indictment and hope in such a manner to crystallize the force of public opinion in his favor. His opponent is given rebuttal time. E. A. Hoebel has characterized these activities as follows:

> Song duels are used to work off grudges and disputes of all orders, save murder. . . . The singing style is highly conventionalized. The successful singer uses the traditional patterns of composition which he attempts to deliver with such finesse as to delight the audience to enthusiastic applause. He who is most heartily applauded is winner. (1954:93)

Further:

> The song duels are juridical instruments insofar as they serve to settle disputes and restore normal relations between estranged members of the community. One of the contestants receives a judgement in his favor. There is, however, no attempt to mete justice according to rights and privileges defined by substantative law. It is sufficient that the litigants (contestants) feel relieved—the complaint is laid to rest—a psychological satisfaction attained and balance restored. (1954: 98, 99)

In such a case, the entire community expresses disapproval, and the loser in the "contest" may even be shamed into leaving that particular community.

The drawbacks to systems of unorganized collective disapproval in which a guilty party may win by virtue of verbal skill (or physical strength in some cases) are obvious. Yet, in the absence of more organized procedures, such systems aid in social control by at least restoring normal social relations. Certainly, the moral force of public contempt, criticism, or actual ridicule can be as effective as prolonged negotiation or actual adjudication in resolution of at least overt friction in a society. We might designate such a solution *consensual resolution*.

Diffuse-Secondary Sanctions

The last negative sanction combination is **diffuse-secondary**. This represents the weakest of the four modes of disapproval. Not only are there only a few individuals who feel the need to express sanctions towards some disapproved behavior, but the procedure undertaken is unorganized and, consequently, will entail no predictable outcome. Sometimes a difficulty will be resolved, perhaps more often not. This is an area of dubious social control; as a type it may be called *indecision*. It is undoubtedly represented in all societies, but it appears to be the most common (if it is ever common) in the simplest of primitive societies. Such groups on occasion seem to lack many sanctions, even those of the organized-secondary and diffuse-primary types. Among the Andaman islanders (near India), for example:

> There does not appear to have been . . . any such thing as the punishment of crime. . . . The murderer would as a rule leave the camp and hide himself in the jungle, where he might be joined by such of his friends as were ready to take his part. It was left to the relatives and friends of the dead man to exact vengeance if they wished and if they could. If the murderer was a man who was much feared it was probable that he would escape. In any case, the anger of the Andamanese is short lived and, if for a few months he could keep out of the way of those who might seek revenge, it is probable that at the end of that time he would find their anger cooled. . . . Quarrels were more likely to occur at the meetings of different local groups. . . . and might occasionally end in the murder of someone. In such a case the quarrel would be taken up by the group to which the murdered man belonged. Such was one of the common causes of or the origin of the petty warfare that formerly existed in the Andamans. (Radcliffe-Brown, 1964: 48–50)

What we encounter here is the absence of any negative social-control mechanism of a definable kind; either nothing is done or, if revenge is taken, it degenerates to continual feud. Perhaps the main lubricants of good relations in such societies are positive social sanctions. Little deviation from custom occurs in such societies because one gains the good will of one's fellows by keeping to those customs. This provides tangible benefits based on reciprocity in terms of food sharing and other economic considerations (see chapter sixteen). This situation in simple societies is analogous to the dubious state of international law between modern nations. Its alternative in any society is a feud/warfare situation.

In summary, there are four negative-sanction combinations, each an attempt at social control. The first, *organized-primary* (adjudication) is definitely within the realm of legal behavior as law is narrowly defined. *Organized-secondary* (negotiation) and *diffuse-primary* (consensus) types are also useful social-control mechanisms but are not themselves law. As anthropologists have pointed out in different contexts, it is not law that utilizes reciprocity and publicity to keep itself in force but rather custom. Some have called such devices rudimentary law. It may be that such behaviors form a basis for such development, but in practice they are not legal sanction combinations. Hence they must be differently designated. Finally there are *diffuse-secondary* (indecision) sanctions that are not in themselves an adequate base for negative control of behavior. A formalization of either moral concern or definite procedure presumably leads to developments in their effectiveness. Every human society, potentially, has areas of social control that fall into these categories. Western politically centrally organized societies rely primarily on adjudicative sanctions and have law. Primitive societies more often rely on the intermediate sanction areas of negotiation and consensus, at least in the majority of cases. A few of the simpler groups may have had to make do with sanctions of an indecisive nature. Seen from such a perspective, law becomes one of a number of potential social-control mechanisms that are defined in terms of a specific negative-sanction category—one in which there exist definite regularized procedures, with predictable outcomes, undertaken by a society or its representatives to regulate behavior by expressing disapproval. Thus, many primitives, in contrast to ourselves, lack law but do exhibit other behavior-regulating devices.

Social Control and the Supernatural

There are a number of related social-control topics that, in various dimensions, crosscut or relate to the preceding discussion. Perhaps the most often cited is the variable connection between social control and supernatural concepts and behaviors, often called the **ritual sanction**. There is no doubt that fear of punishments by supernatural agencies plays a role in suppressing disapproved behaviors. This can range from fear of breaking a prohibition (taboo) attributed to some deity to the fear that an aggrieved person will use witchcraft or sorcery in retaliation for injury. But if no official human representatives are involved, the sanction behavior is outside the realm we have categorized as law, and if the effects of supernatural intervention are solely restricted to such an agency, it is probably outside the realm of social control as we have previously discussed it. It may still be extremely effective, however, and, certainly, in any connection, human and supernatural sanctions can reinforce each other. Perhaps the easiest way to see some of these relations is to suggest two poles of sanction behavior:

Breaking human norms (rules) = crime,	Breaking supernatural norms (taboos) = sin,
punished by human agencies	punished by supernatural agencies

A woman does a ritualistic dance over a dead chicken that has been sacrificed by a medicine man in an attempt to protect herself from punishment by supernatural powers.

Peter Buckley

In any society, we may expect certain behaviors to be part of one or the other pole exclusively and subject to independent enforcement. Issues of greater public or personal concern may be covered by sanctions from both areas, crime becoming sin and vice versa. As many writers have pointed out, this may especially become the case when the effects of sin are felt capable of spreading by "contamination" to other members of the offender's group. Such, then, becomes a double coercive situation: to prevent the behavior in question that both humans and gods prohibit. Both the Ten Commandments and the New York State Penal Code treat theft as a NO NO! Probably even simple societies exhibit some such behaviors. Some Eskimo groups, for example, have spirits who punish an offender for breaking a hunting or food-handling taboo by withholding game from him (and from others of his group). A *shaman* (medicine man) will "finger the culprit," force a confession and then exact penalties in human terms. Here the two types of sanctions work as a team in rapport.

There are other ways by which supernatural beliefs may help retard deviant behavior. Often they become a sort of substitute control when human sanctions are ineffective or when moral indignation is slow to develop. Such a case has been well documented by Beatrice Whiting in her study of the function of sorcery among the Paiute Indians of North America. Here, if one was accused and convicted of sorcery activities, he was formerly certain to be killed or excluded from the group. On this, public concern was genuine. The steps leading to this greatly-to-be-avoided situation ran about as follows. First an individual got a reputation for being mean and uncooperative by deviating from normal social conventions and expectations. This led to the second step, which

373

involved discussions by other people as to the cause of such irregular behavior; guesses often involved suspicions of sorcery, although no formal accusations were made. The third stage consisted of circumstantial evidence: the suspect happened to be near the scene of some sorcery-interpreted catastrophe and, with the background already in existence, was given the blame. "Joe walked by her house just before she died." Joe got (with his dubious reputation) the job of fall guy! Since most people were aware of such steps to personal disaster, most attempted to avoid such involvements. They were careful to be correct in their behavioral relations with others, avoiding that dubious initial reputation. Thus, conformity to the norms was maintained in the absence of more formal repressive measures. Broader studies indicate sorcery as important in most such societies lacking formal controls on behavior, but perhaps in many of these it acts more in the sense of a personal retaliatory measure.

We may conclude the discussion of the intertwinings of supernaturalism and social-control behavior by mentioning a last connection. Supernaturalism may be a distinct aid when the usual human techniques are not up to eliciting adequate evidence on which to "judge" some difficulty. When actual guilt is in question, for example, some form of divination may be used to reveal the hidden knowledge by supernatural means. This may be accomplished *in absentia* or with the participation (often unwilling) of a suspect. A classic case of the former variety occurs among the Azande of Africa. Here, if a person seeks to ascertain guilt in a case of adultery, he will engage the services of a diviner to test and possibly confirm his suspicions. This special person will give a poison to a chicken in the divining ritual and the oracle will be addressed. "If person A is guilty of adultery, let the poison kill this chicken." If the chicken dies, A is guilty. A second chicken is then prepared and given the poison. If this chicken lives, the verdict is felt to be correct. Often many trials are required before proof of guilt is positively established. Then the appropriate sanction can be applied by the aggrieved party. One comes away from this, and related practices elsewhere, with the feeling that perhaps the "verdict" is manipulated to affix guilt on a party acceptable to most people in the community! When the suspect participates in divination, it usually takes the form of the ordeal. An excellent example comes from another African society, the Bushong. The event is occasioned by repeated deaths, unusual happenings, or failure in hunting and fishing and is the attempt to discover the identity of the witch believed responsible. It is . . . the most powerful rite they know. It has as its ambitious aim to eliminate evil and death. Much more than a judicial procedure it is also a meeting of the supernatural with the human" (Vansina, 1969: 245). In the rite, the suspect (always a woman) must submit herself to the ordeal of swallowing poison (after much preliminary ritual). If she finally sickens and begins to die, she is judged guilty and, in the past, was then suffocated to death. If she vomits the poison, this is taken as a sign of her innocence. Refusal to take the poison, of course, is taken as an expression of guilt. In either event, supernatural beliefs and practices have aided (if unfairly) the usual social-control procedures.

FUNCTIONS OF LAW AND SOCIAL CONTROL

We will conclude this chapter on law and social control with a discussion of the general functions of such behaviors in human societies. Hoebel (1954) has postulated four such basic functions for law, and, since he treats this term as broadly coincident to social control, we can apply them with respect to the previously discussed sanction categories.

Function one: The definition of human relationships for the members of a society.

Law and social control make people aware of those activities that are permitted and those that are not. They set the rules. Law, as defined narrowly, by formalizing such rules in codes for conduct, performs this task more rigorously and perhaps more efficiently than do the other negative-sanction categories, which rely more on custom. Yet, in any sense, it is a basic function both for behavior and the evaluation of it. Even minimal guidelines appear necessary. Many writers have suggested that in some primitive societies there is little deviation from such norms for conduct inasmuch as such rules merge with kinship obligations anyway—"you naturally want to do what you have to do." This situation is contrasted to the laws of politically well-organized societies in which rules regulate conduct more in terms of nonkinship relations. It is assumed that, as a result, the codes are broken easier and more frequently in the higher developed societies. This appears to make some logical sense but how much "noble savage" philosophy and how much actual statistics can be adduced as proof for such an assertion is open to question. As Robert Lowie pointed out many years ago,

> If the native errs less frequently against group standards, it is presumably because they are actually those of his group, not those imposed from outside. . . . However, individuals differ enormously in their capacity to risk temptation; accordingly, ethnographic literature records many transgressions of the social standard. . . . There can thus be no question of an automatic submission to (rules). (Lowie, 1948: 172–73)

Function two: The allocation of the authority (privilege) to employ means of enforcement.

Someone or some group has to be given the right to step in and rectify difficulties. In Western societies and in some primitive groups, this allocation often occurs in a full-time, specialized manner—where police, judges, and courts exist. In many primitive societies, however, such authority may last just for the amount of time necessary to restore the situation, and, as we have already noticed, it may be in the hands of the aggrieved individual or his kinsmen. It has also been pointed out that the authority in developed societies tends to be more transpersonalized, residing in a social status or office rather than in individuals themselves.

Function three: The handling of trouble cases as they arise.

This is, perhaps, the most visible of primitive control behaviors. Deviation has occurred and to correct or resolve and restore the situation something must be done; things must be brought back to normal. Here the differences in practice between ourselves and primitives appear to loom large.

> Most of the trouble cases do not, in a civilized society, of themselves loom large on the social scene, although in a small community even one can lead directly to a social explosion if not successfully cleaned up. Indeed, in a primitive society, the individual case always holds the threat of a little civil war if procedure breaks down, for from its inception it sets kin group against kin group—and, if it comes to fighting, the number of kinsmen who will be involved is almost always immediately enlarged. . . . Relatively speaking, each run-of-the-mill trouble case in primitive law imposes a more pressing demand for settlement. . . . than is the case with us. (Hoebel, 1954: 280)

It is, perhaps, in line with this situation that primitive cases are resolved in ways that strike us as being less than fair: someone paying the witchcraft price for bad hunting in Africa, or a guilty but better singer among Eskimos being judged the winner in a song contest over adultery.

Two other customs common in primitive societies may also be explained in light of the above. One is the wide-spread practice of collective responsibility, which means that members of kinship groups may become functional substitutes for each other. Revenge against a guilty party may be gained at the expense of a wife or son. Members of a murdered man's group may be able to kill any member of the murderer's group to resolve their difficulty in an acceptable fashion. The validity of such a custom has occasionally led to kin "policing their own ranks." Here the case of an elderly Eskimo woman strangling her young son while he slept because he had become a public nuisance strikes us as exceedingly different from our own practices. Nonetheless, such was motivated by the desire to avoid involvement by kinsmen in unpleasant situations! Allied to such devices to keep or restore conditions to normal social relations is the idea that many times primitive social difficulties are settled by the substitution of "blood wealth" for actual revenge, the wrongdoer and his group receiving no actual physical punishment at all. Certainly, settlement of trouble cases in such societies departs in many ways from behaviors with which we are familiar.

Function four: The redefinition of social relations as the conditions of life change.

As such changes occur and call for new or altered human relationships, the rules that govern such behaviors must change or be flexible enough to cover this situation. Otherwise, the rules and their enforcement devices frustrate behavior rather than aid it. Among the Taos, whose court mechanisms were previously described, this judicial process, while serving to dispose of trouble cases as they arise, seem also an able mechanism for rendering a decision in the best interests of all concerned. It is a decision in keeping with the surrounding circumstances. During the period of intensive questioning (step 6) ample opportunity exists for all facets of a difficulty between contending parties to be brought out into the open and given full discussion. By so doing, each case is carefully weighed on the basis of its own merits, and a decision not necessarily based upon old precedent is given. Each case is treated as a separate kind of difficulty to be handled in terms of what the majority feels to be the best disposition of the matter. Thus, the function of maintaining adaptability of rules and their adjustment to the conditions of life at any given time is secured. We can turn now, in the next chapter, to another aspect of social control in human societies—that of government or political organization.

SUMMARY

1. Every society has mechanisms of social control that attempt to punish or redress deviations from its rules and, ideally, prevent such misconduct from occurring.
2. The concept of law has presented definitional problems for anthropologists since many of the features usually associated with it—codes and courts—were not always present in primitive societies.

Some scholars solve this difficulty by expanding the scope of application of the term law, rendering it meaningless in the process.

3. Social sanctions are reactions to behavior, in approval or disapproval. They help regulate behavior, and negative sanctions (in disapproval) become overt social control mechanisms.

4. Four negative sanction combinations exist, each of which may be the major mode of social control in a given society. They are organized-primary, organized-secondary, diffuse-primary, and diffuse-secondary. The first is the realm of legal behavior (adjudication), and the last an area of limited effectiveness (indecision). The middle two are very common in primitive societies and involve negotiation and consensus.

5. Ritual sanctions involve the use or threat of use of supernatural devices to constrain behavior. These range from instilling fear that the offender is breaking a taboo to the use of witchcraft. Such sanctions may reinforce ordinary sanctions or may be substituted for them.

6. Basic functions of law include defining or redefining human relationships, allocating authority, and settling trouble when it occurs.

REFERENCES FOR FURTHER READING

There are a number of good introductory and survey volumes on primitive law. The now classic text is the *Law of Primitive Man*, by E. A. Hoebel (1964, Harvard University Press). More recent discussions are *Politics, Law and Ritual in Tribal Society*, by Max Gluckman (1965, Aldine); and "The Ethnography of Law," edited by Laura Nadar, in *American Anthropologist 67*, no. 6 (1965): part 2. This last work contains a number of very provocative articles of both a theoretical and descriptive nature. An excellent reader along similar lines is *Law and Warfare*, edited by Paul Bohannan (1967, Natural History Press). The most recent statement is *Anthropology of Law*, by Leopold Pospisil (1971, Harper & Row). Helpful chapters on legal behavior occur in *Social Organization*, by Robert Lowie (1948, Rinehart); and in *Social Anthropology*, by Paul Bohannan (1963, Holt, Rinehart & Winston). See also his article in Nadar (cited above). The basis for my scheme of social-control categories comes from chapters eleven and twelve in *Structure and Function in Primitive Society*, by A. R. Radcliffe-Brown (1952, Cohen & West). Specific examples on primitive law are taken from *Morals and Merit*, by Christopher von Furer-Haimendorf (1967, Weidenfield & Nicolson); *The Andaman Islanders*, by A. R. Radcliffe-Brown (1964, Free Press); "The Bushong Poison Ordeal," by Jan Vansina, in Mary Douglas and Phyllis Kaberry, editors, *Man in Africa*, (1969, Tavistock); and *Paiute Sorcery*, by B. B. Whiting in *Viking Fund Publications in Anthropology* no. 15. (1950). The example of the Taos is from "Law Function and Judicial Process at a New Mexican Pueblo," by John Collins in *International Journal of Comparative Sociology* 9 (1969): 129–31.

21 government

It is not always easy to differentiate adequately between government and law and the other social-control categories that were discussed in the last chapter. Law can be seen as comprising the rules and sanctions of a society. Government relates more to the functionaries and institutions that organize such rules and employ the sanctions. Many writers would seem to lump both law and government together as part of the larger concept of political organization. "In studying political organization, we have to deal with the maintenance or establishment of social order, within a territorial framework, by the organized exercise of coercive authority through the use, or possibility of use, of physical force" (Radcliffe-Brown, 1963: xiv). Or, as a more recent writer has stated it, political organization is a "system of regulation or relations between groups or members of different groups within a society at large and between one society and another" (Hoebel, 1972: 522). Seen from this perspective, political organization is more than just government, it includes legal and other social-control behavior as well. The present chapter deals only with this governmental side of political behavior.

ASPECTS OF GOVERNMENT

How do we describe the functioning of government in primitive societies? One can imagine discovering the same problems that plague us in comparisons of legal behavior. Many typologies do, in fact, exist, and terms such as monarchy, democracy, theocracy, and the like are often used, but these are not always applicable in primitive societies in the same senses as they are used in the modern world. Nor do they really give a good indication of the quality of governmental behavior. Perhaps the best approach is first to examine some of the concepts that may be

381

involved in this aspect of political organization. John Beattie (1964) has listed three aspects involved in such behaviors, and we can add to these and expand them slightly. The first is the idea of **centralization.** If this is developed to a high degree, then there exists a central authority that is acknowledged by the various component groups within the society, within Radcliffe-Brown's "territorial framework." This central authority may be a single leader (a king or chief) or it could be a group of individuals, for example, a council. At the opposite extreme, where the degree of centralization is low, the society would comprise a number of various groups that are distinct in acknowledgement of authority, say a number of lineages, each with its own leader.

A second aspect is the degree of **specialization.**

> Is there a person, or are there persons, vested with specifically political authority, that is, with the right to issue orders and administer sanctions in a certain territory, such activity being generally directed, and seen to be directed, towards the maintenance of the existing social order. ... Or are there no such roles in the society? This criterion is not the same as the first one. For it is possible to have specifically political authorities in a society which is non-centralized ... and there are some societies in which ritual or religious authority is acknowledged on a tribe-wide basis, but little or no political authority is attributed to the central figure. (Beattie, 1964: 144)

One could perhaps add here that it should be noted whether the specialized governmental official has the right to issue orders or apply sanctions all the time or whether he is limited in such exercise to particular times or occasions. Often such powers may have restrictions: for example, applying to peace but not warfare situations.

The aspects of centralization and specialization lead to a third consideration not specifically discussed by Beattie. This is the degree of **absolutism.** How absolute is the right of the leaders to issue orders and apply sanctions? Can the activities of the leader be questioned and disregarded and if so, is compliance to them backed up in any way? The possibilities here may be seen as running from a high to an almost non-existent degree. The editors of a recent text on political organization (Schwartz et al., 1966) have pointed out that there are three ways to secure such compliance. One way is by the use of force and physical coercion: to make people do what you want them to do. This can be called *coercive power.* If a leader or leaders have henchmen or armies at their command, this becomes a possibility but is a tenuous one over the long run. The more often it is used, the greater the staff needed to apply it since its only sanction is its own effectiveness. A second possibility is to employ what is called *consensual power.* Here the effectiveness is based on the idea of legitimacy. This is:

> ... a type of support that derives not from force or its threat but from the values held by the individuals formulating, influencing, and being affected by political ends ... The derivation of legitimacy from values comes through the establishment of a positive connection between the entity or process having legitimacy and those values. This connection can be established in a number of different ways ... but in all cases it involves a set of expectations in the minds of those who accept the legitimacy. These expectations are to the effect that the legitimate entity or process will, under certain circumstances, meet certain obligations that are held by those who view it as legitimate. (Schwartz et al, 1966: 10, 11)

Here, in essence, one goes along with decisions because one feels that one will eventually benefit or is benefiting in a generalized way. Finally, compliance may be brought about by *persuasion*. This works by motivating people to accept a decision or by changing their previous beliefs or attitudes. This is accomplished in many ways: for example, by the giving of inducements (political reciprocity), as well as by simply making people feel it will be in their own best interest to act in a particular way. With high absolutism one may find some combination of all three, with consensual power perhaps most important in maintaining the system. The government of the United States certainly depends upon this but has coercive power as a backup, and, of course, a strong president also has great powers of persuasion. At the opposite end, the leaders in many primitive societies probably rely upon persuasion with some degree of consensus power. They often lack the ability to apply force and coercion.

The last aspect discussed by Beattie is **allocation**. How does one gain a governmental position? As he sees it, this may be either ascribed or achieved (hereditary or elective). One becomes the leader because of some automatic consideration—the eldest son of the king becomes the next king—or it may require some effort and accomplishment. One may have to run for the office or be the most outstanding and admired member of his group. Of course, some combination of these possibilities may be involved. The senior man of a lineage may be its leader only if he is capable of retaining the confidence of its membership, and even kings may be deposed if found incompetent.

So there are four aspects that government may reflect: centralization, specialization, absolutism, and allocation. We can examine such behaviors in any society in terms of these criteria and employ them for comparative purposes. Because of the overlap in all but the first one, however, Beattie concludes that the criterion of centralization is the best for purposes of classification. He draws a contrast between centralized and uncentralized societies. Those of the primitive world are generally of the latter variety, and he suggests four types of politically uncentralized societies. Very briefly, these are:

1. ... very simply organized communities, whose members usually live by collecting or hunting, in which the largest social units are cooperating groups of families or close kin, and in which there is no formal grouping of any kind above this level.
2. ... societies which are made up of separate village communities, related to one another by various economic and kinship ties, but administered internally by more or less formally appointed councils.
3. ... societies in which political control is largely conceived in terms of an age set system.
4. ... those in which political functions are effected through groups organized in terms of unilineal descent. (Beattie, 1964: 147, 148)

The above varieties offer some interesting comparative government contrasts. However, a simpler approach is one that offers a developmental perspective on such behaviors. Some recent attempts in this direction are basically in agreement. Before briefly considering them we can tighten our focus and look just at the positions of leadership themselves in light of the above criteria. We can then place them into the larger systems of which they are a part.

POSITIONS OF LEADERSHIP

Perhaps the simplest and most commonly found position of leadership in primitive societies is that of **headman**. This is also probably the earliest type in development. A headman is a person who has earned the respect, support, and confidence of a following of people. He does this primarily in an achieved fashion. He may be the best hunter, orator, or craftsman. In a sense, the "man makes the office." As it has been put for the Siuai of the Solomon Islands (Bougainville), "Widening influence accompanies increasing renown, but renown itself is acquired mostly directly by competitive giving ... one man gives material goods to another with the hope and expectation that the receiver will be unable to return material goods of equivalent value. Instead the giver acquires renown theoretically equivalent in value to the unrequited gift" (Douglas, 1967: 388, 389). Such a person attracts followers because of his behaviors and the strength of his personality. His actual powers are informal. As many anthropologists characterize the position of headman, he is a kind of advisor to a group of people—an advisor whose force of character and observed knowledge and skills make his advice well worth following.

An excellent description of the position of headman (unfortunately,

The position of headman is earned rather than inherited. It is the simplest and most common form of leadership found in primitive societies.

Marc and Evelyne Bernheim
Woodfin Camp

he uses the term *chief*) is supplied by Levi-Strauss (1967) for the Nambikuara of Brazil. We can briefly paraphrase his account. This is one of the least developed of South American societies. The total group consists of a number of small nomadic bands (local groups), each under a leader. During the rainy season they often come together for horticultural activities but spend most of their time pursuing separate existences. When the bands split up, the members do so on a "free-choice" basis, choosing to follow men who have acknowledged reputations as good leaders. So the man is making the office: the band more or less develops around the leader rather than the leaders existing because of permanent band needs. In fact, the term for this leader is "he who unites or joins together." For much of the year the headman is solely responsible for the welfare of his particular band. He directs all food-collecting operations, selects routes of migration, and keeps a lookout for hostile groups.

> These rather versatile duties ... are not facilitated by any fixed power or recognized authority. Consent is at the origin of leadership, and consent, too, furnishes the only legitimacy. Disorderly conduct ... and unwillingness to work on the part of one or two discontented individuals may seriously jeopardize the chief's program and the welfare of his small group. In this eventuality, however, the chief has no coercive power at his disposal. ... Thus he must continuously display a skill belonging more to the politician trying to keep hold of his fluctuating majority than to an over-powering ruler. (Levi-Strauss, 1967: 53)

So the method of compliance is built upon persuasion and also upon consensual power. The band come to rely upon him for their safety and survival. His very effectiveness is a basis for his legitimacy. And, if he does not solve the food problem, his group will drift away. Individuals

385

and families will leave and join up with a better managed band. If his own band membership drops below a certain number, he may have to do so as well. So headmanship is not a permanent position. Yet, although temporary, it does suggest a degree of centralization, but only in terms of the local band since the Nambikuara as a whole do not relate to the same individuals. How does he maintain consent for his "orders"? By generosity and ingenuity. He must somehow acquire a surplus of food, tools, and other necessary items, and be willing to part with them to those in need within his band. And he must display great skill and initiative.

> He must have a perfect knowledge of the territories haunted by his and other groups, be familiar with the hunting grounds, the location of fruit-bearing trees and the time of their ripening, have some idea of the itineraries followed by other bands, whether hostile or friendly. Therefore, he must travel more and more quickly, than his people, have a good memory, and sometimes gamble his prestige on hazardous contacts with foreign and dangerous people. He is constantly engaged in some task of reconnoitering and exploring and seems to flutter around his band rather than lead it. (Levi-Strauss, 1967: 55)

Such qualities in a headman are repeated from society to society. Speaking again of the Siuai, the leaders must possess ambition, industriousness, skill, and goodness. Certainly, headmanship may be an onerous and burdensome activity!

A second position of leadership in primitive societies has been rather loosely called chief. Generally speaking, this position is represented as a permanent office and reflects a situation in which the "office makes the man." As a result, centralization and specialization have increased. And the ability to secure compliance includes not only persuasion and consensus but may also include coercive power. Although some degree of achievement is involved in attaining chieftainship—possession of knowledge, oratorical skill, and the like—the position may be limited to certain descent lines or families; heredity can play a role. Chieftainship often emerges where there is the necessity to coordinate different activities for different groups; where a headman-oriented kind of leader might not be sufficiently powerful to accomplish such a task. So leaders of the chiefly type are more recognizable as a formal governmental structure.

A classic comparative statement on headman versus chiefs is that of Sahlins (1963), in which he contrasts leadership in the islands of Melanesia and Polynesia. He discusses the Melanesian position of the Big Man (headman) as a "free-enterprise" type of leader. The Big Man behaves in such a way as to draw a circle of kin and lesser people around him. The ability to give feasts and sound advice and to persuade

The presence of a chief implies a more formally structured government. Shown here is the chief of the Zulu Indians.

South African Information Service

others to do his bidding give him "personal power." "Big Men do not come to office, they do not succeed to ... existing positions of leadership over political groups" (Sahlins, 1963: 289). Outside of their own groups of followers, such leaders may acquire a reputation for renown but lack any real directive functions. In Polynesia, on the other hand, groups are larger and require greater coordination, and true chiefs exist. They had a greater "fund of power" than in Melanesia and backed their authority with a corps of warriors and claims to a sacred nature. They could be called *sacredotes*, sacred chiefs, combining as they did secular and supernatural power and functions. This political move is found elsewhere and really centralizes and specializes the exercise of securing compliance to decisions. As Sahlins beautifully summarizes the headman-chief differences:

> And these Polynesian chiefs did not make their positions in society—they were installed in societal positions ... Power resided in the office; it was not made by the demonstration of personal superiority. In other islands, Tahiti was famous for it, succession to chieftainship was tightly controlled by inherent rank. The chiefly lineage ruled by virtue of its genealogical connections with divinity, and chiefs were succeeded by first sons, who carried "in the blood" the attributes of leadership.

Further:

> The productive ability the big-man laboriously had to demonstrate was effortlessly given Polynesian chiefs as religious control over agricultural fertility and upon the ceremonial implementation of it the rest of the people were conceived dependent. Where a Melanesian leader had to master the compelling oratorical style, Polynesian paramounts often had trained "talking chiefs" whose voice was the chiefly command. (Sahlins, 1963: 295)

Here we are dealing with really well-developed concepts of leadership and government.

387

On a somewhat lesser developed level of chieftainship are the Cheyenne (Plains Indians), whose description by Hoebel (1960) we can briefly summarize. The Cheyenne spent part of the year in separate bands consisting of cognatic groups and families. The band leaders were the headmen of these groups. Forty-four of these headmen were also members of a tribal council that functioned when the entire tribe came together during the summer months in one large encampment. These peace chiefs held positions sanctified by myth; each chief was chosen for a ten year period in office, and each could choose his own successor from his own particular band. This ensured that band representation on the council remained constant. Each band had about the same number of representatives. Frequently, a man chose his own son to follow him into office, but certain chiefly qualities had to be in evidence. "The personal requirements for a tribal chief ... are an even-tempered good nature, energy, wisdom, kindliness, concern for the well-being of others, courage, generosity, and altruism" (Hoebel, 1960: 37). So chieftainship was not an entirely ascribed position. Among these chiefs are five sacred chiefs who were chosen from among those individuals who had already served as regular chiefs. They represented supernatural beings and had priestly functions relative to the spiritual well-being of the entire tribe. Their leader, and presiding council officer, sweet-medicine chief, held a special medicine bundle (object of supernatural power).

During the summer months, the council deliberated on questions of tribal interest: movement, alliance to other tribes, and war. They also acted as a judicial unit in legal situations. "In governmental affairs, it further serves as executive and legislative authority over the military societies, which act as the administrative police branch" (Hoebel, 1960: 47). However, the military societies, which acted to enforce the decisions of the council, did have a more direct say in matters of a warfare nature. This, coupled with the fact that the council operated as a body only part of the year, suggests that the Cheyenne were in a state of political evolution.

The last kind of governmental official or leader commonly found in primitive societies has been called a king. This is in some ways perhaps the loosest designation since kings, while not exactly coming in all shapes and sizes, nevertheless do vary in function and composition. The position itself is generally correlated with societal types more complex than those we have used as examples so far. The idea, apparently, is that leadership becomes hereditary and powerful to introduce stability into governmental processes. Africa is the case in point usually cited for such leaders, and one writer, Jan Vansina (1964) has adequately summarized most of the constituent features of African Kingship. "We should define African Kingdoms as sovereign political groups,

King of the Ibo tribe, Nigeria.

Peter Buckley

headed by a single leader who delegates authority to representatives in charge of territorial units into which the country is divided" (Vansina, 1964: 250). Involved here are the following features. The king is "the" leader. There is only one king in these societies, and such centralization and specialization is buttressed by the notion that the king has special supernatural powers. These are either inherent in his person or are acquired by special ritual activities. As such, his well-being and that of his people coincide. This also means, of course, that assumption of office is basically ascribed rather than achieved. Second is the allied notion that the king "owns" the land and the people; he has ultimate control over them. He has at his disposal all the mechanisms for achieving compliance to his decisions, including the ability to marshall a standing army (at least seasonally) for coercive activities as well as expansion of his political prerogatives.

Another idea concerned with African Kingship (and elsewhere) is the delegation of such authority and power to lesser representatives: chiefs and other more localized officials. They become the instrument of kingship on the village level and not only have governmental decision-making capabilities but apply their legitimacy to the rendering of legal judgements as well. Thus, they often operate local courts and treat minor offenses. This delegation also operates in a reverse direction in connection with levies for taxes and labor.

> Once tribute is collected by a local chief he hands it over to a higher-ranking chief and so on up the pyramid until it reaches the capital and the king. But each of the intermediary chiefs has a right to retain some proportion of it. Compulsory labor is called for as needed by any official

in his territory . . . Taxes are paid by market-users for the use of the facilities of the market or even for any commercial transaction in a market. Tolls exist in some areas on roads or bridges. Dues have to be paid when bringing a case to court, and fines are often imposed in courts. Another source of revenue is the king's or chief's claim to intestate property. The produce of all of these sources of income goes to the king but part of it is retained by the collectors, the officials in charge . . . and so on. (Vansina, 1964: 252)

In all these behaviors, we have come a long way from the generosity and persuasive abilities of the headman! Finally, among other attributes of kingship, is the idea of the council. Where government is highly developed, with real power and authority (and often where is is not), some balance of interests is necessary. In Africa, councils of various types exist, and quite often they assume considerable powers, their decisions being binding upon the king himself. And, of course, they can serve purely advisory functions as well since no ruler of this sort can possess a headmanlike knowledge of what it takes to govern wisely. So kings are more highly formalized in terms of the attributes of leadership behavior.

We can examine one concrete example of African Kingship to convey the flavor and complexity of such behavior. Hilda Kuper (1963) has given a neat account of political structure among the Swazi of South Africa. Here the centralized leadership is divided between the king and a queen mother. All powers are concentrated in their hands—legislative, executive, administrative, and religious—and they are surrounded by attendants and set apart by unique costume and ornamentation. In the case of the king especially, "The well-being of the nation is associated with the king's strength and virility, and he must neither see nor touch a corpse, nor approach a grave or a mourner. The major episodes in his life . . . are heavily ritualized" (Kuper, 1963: 29). The king and the queen mother strike a balance in activity. He presides over the highest court, she over the second highest. And a special place (shrine) in her homestead becomes a place of sanctuary for those seeking protection. Again, he has the power to allocate land, but they must work together (with rain magic) to make it fruitful. She has control over sacred national objects, but their use requires his cooperation. Moreover, while she resides in the capital he remains in a village some distance away.

A further check on kingly "malpractice" is evidenced by his circle of advisors. His main counselor is a prime minister who resides at the capital and who both advises the king on the mood of his people and acts as their representative to him. This person can also hear legal cases. Beyond this functionary there are two formal councils. The first, or inner council, consists of senior princes (from the lineage of the king) and the prime minister. Although they do not meet regularly as a body, their compliance is necessary in the case of important decisions. A second and larger group consists of leading members of the inner group plus all chiefs and headmen of the kingdom. Here, too, the aim is to reach agreement. A king is also "aided" in his functioning by a number of specialists in the supernatural who aid his powers by means of ritual manipulations. They are drawn from selected nonroyal clans. Also from such groups come sets of "blood brothers." These ritual kinsmen help him carry out his ritual duties as well as routine tasks. The first two of these are of his own age and have grown up with him, undergoing puberty initiation, marriage, and other activities with him. "Swazi believe that any attack by evil doers against the king will be deflected by . . . (them) . . . whose bodies serve as his shield" (Kuper, 1963: 32).

The Swazi king delegates his authority and power to local chiefs. These officials are princes of the royal lineage or local clan heads who have been so appointed. Each chief rules over a district, and if his mother is alive, she shares in his authority. The local leader also has a council composed of local headmen and has a prime minister. So the national government is duplicated on the local level. The quality of leadership, however, is less well marked.

> Swazi political authorities are criticized by their subjects if they are aggressive and domineering. Qualities such as ability in debate, efficiency in organizing work, and knowledge of law are admired, but they are not considered essential for a chief because it is expected that his counselors will provide them. He is constantly reminded that his prestige depends largely on the number of his followers, and he is aware that they have the right to migrate from his district if he does not fulfill demands that they consider legitimate. (Kruper, 1963: 35)

We can now turn to considerations of a developmental nature on political behavior.

PRIMITIVE GOVERNMENT IN DEVELOPMENTAL PERSPECTIVE

Some years ago, Elman Service (1962, 1963) presented the notion of describing primitive societies on the basis of levels of structural complexity. "Simply stated, greater complexity implies more parts to the whole, more differentiation or specialization of these parts, and firmer integration of the parts within the whole" (Service, 1963: xix). The implication is that the history of human culture has been involved with the development of higher levels of such complexity. He suggested the existence of four general levels of development: bands, tribes, chiefdoms, and states. By briefly summarizing the major character of these, we can place the leadership positions previously discussed into a developmental perspective. This will also provide the student with a review of some other materials.

Bands

The band level is integrated primarily by personal and familial ties. The family, with its domestic mode of production, is the central group, although seldom does it exist as the only social unit. Generally, the band consists of a number of cooperating families. Leadership here is in the hands of the heads of families, and decisions are either collective or suggestions made by a headman type of individual, based on mechanisms already described. Band societies are generally egalitarian (Fried, 1960, 1967), all the individuals in any given social category (such as adult males) having equal access to prestige and resources. Bands are usually associated with food-collecting technological systems, and the main mode of distribution is reciprocity.

> ... kinship ties, structured in their nature by marriage rules, are the integrating mechanism in band societies. The social bodies, the parts of the society, the differentiation of persons into statuses, and so on are all familial. ... Social differentiation makes parts and statuses in the society that exist irrespective of the particular personnel who fill them. In band society all of these are familistic differentiations: every person is one or another kind of consanguinal or affinal, relative. (Service, 1963: xxi)

Tribes

The tribal level of development evolves from the band level. It is suggested that this is in response to increases in population, which, in turn, may be due to occupation of an area rich in natural resources or developments of food-producing technology. Tribal society "... consists of a much larger number of kinship and residential segments [groups], each segment being composed of individual nuclear families" (Service, 1963: xxi). These segments look like a collection of bands sharing the same language and culture, but they are united by somewhat different means of integration. This new form of cohesion Service calls a *pantribal sodality*—an organization of people not built upon a residential basis but on the mere fact of membership. These groups crosscut the various family-oriented bands and may include larger kin groups such as clans

as well as associations of nonkinsmen such as men's clubs, military societies, or religious groups. Such broader integration, however, need
not be permanent; it may exist only for special occasions, when some
need beyond the band level arises. The tribe remains egalitarian, and
a domestic mode of production and reciprocity are the major technoeconomic mechanisms. For such activities, each segment (band) is still
largely independent and self-sufficient, and leadership still remains at
the headman level. As previously observed, the Cheyenne seem to have
been evolving away from this general level.

Chiefdoms

A chiefdom is different from a tribe in a number of ways. It is larger,
more complex, and has a new system for the integration of its parts.
This new device of organization is the position of chief, with its more
formal powers and authority. Its occupant has become sufficiently strong
to impose his leadership over not only his own group but other groups
in his society. Chiefdoms are developed food-production societies, and
a central function of the chief is to serve as the agent for redistribution
in economic behavior. A more organized division of labor, with specialization, has developed.

> There are two distinct and separable kinds of specialization which
> could lead to redistribution . . . One . . . is the regional, or ecological,
> specialization of different local residential units; the other is the pooling
> of individual skills in large scale cooperative productive endeavors. A
> great many . . . chiefdoms exist in habitats that consist of several eco-
> logical zones . . . [which] . . . promote a local differentiation in the kinds
> of crops grown as well as in the distribution of natural products . . .
> Without agriculture, people would take advantage of that variation by
> moving themselves around with respect to the products. With agriculture
> and permanent settlements, the local specialization is most advantageous
> to the inhabitants when the *products* are moved. (Service, 1962: 145)

In essence, the idea appears to be that such potential for productivity
will promote the development of chiefs as coordinators, which then
facilitates greater productivity and specialization. Such controls are
easily transferred to the other areas of social life and the power and
authority of the leadership position becomes solidified. So a new solidarity exists on this level of complexity, and a new kind of society as well,
since the beginnings of social inequality are in evidence. These are rank
societies (Fried, 1960, 1967) since the chief, his kinship group, and retainers come to possess greater wealth and power than other individuals
in the society. The egalitarian notion of band and tribe may still char-

acterize the mass of people. In addition, not only are there some persons who are different from others, but labor specialization has also led to unlike parts.

States

The last type to be discussed is the state. States are generally societies with large populations and with intensive agricultural techniques supplemented by numbers of domesticated animals. To redistribution, market exchange is added as an economic mechanism for distribution, and even greater labor specialization has occurred.

> The means of integration characteristic of states as distinguished from chiefdoms particularly, and from all the lower levels generally, is of course that special control, the use of force and constant threat of force from an institutionalized body of persons who wield the force. A state constitutes itself *legally*: it makes explicit the manner and circumstances of its use of force, and it outlaws all other use of force as it intervenes in the disputes between individuals and groups. (Service, 1963: xxvi)

The governmental leaders in such primitive societies tend to be of the kingly type as previously defined. An important basis for compliance to decisions is obviously coercive power backed by the use of military force, although some degree of consensual legitimacy is also necessary. Centralization is highly developed and many specialized political officials exist. In many cases (as was previously observed), political and religious leadership are combined in the same office; they are theocratic states.

There are some other features associated with the state. The society is crosscut by classes or castes. The rank nature of the chiefdom has been supplanted by a full-scale system of social stratification, not only politically but socially and economically as well (see chapter nineteen). In addition, states are coordinated in terms of territorial organization. The kinship basis of life has now almost completely given way to integration in geographic terms. Individuals in the state exist as part of divisions of territory and derive their various rights and responsibilities by reference to this membership. The territorial nonkinship group has gained the center of the social stage.

Just exactly how states evolve from the chiefdom level is not a matter of scholarly agreement. Many writers have suggested that although military conquest (and the setting up of a ruling class), or the spread of the idea of the state itself, are often responsible, in the beginning the first states may have arisen as part of the development of advanced irrigation techniques.

> The implication of the "hydraulic theory" ... is that the development of
> the state as an internal phenomenon is associated with major tasks of
> drainage and irrigation. The emergence of a control system to ensure the
> operation of the economy is closely tied to the appearance of a distinctive
> class system and certain constellations of power in the hands of a mana-
> gerial bureaucracy which frequently operates below a ruler who com-
> mands theoretically unlimited power. (Fried, 1960: 730)

So the leadership positions of headman, chief, and king are generally
correlated with the levels of structural complexity of the band, tribe,
chiefdom, and state. We have also noted that the progressive development of these positions is also accompanied by other changes in technoeconomic activities, in the size of the governed group, and in terms of
social differentiation. Culture is indeed an integrated phenomenon.

OTHER ASPECTS OF GOVERNMENT

There are many other aspects to the topic of government. One final
idea that can be presented here is the concept that basically nonpolitical
associations may help or hinder the exercise of governmental power and
authority. Paul Radin (1957) has given the intriguing example of the
antiwitch society among the Nupe of Africa. This group of males has received supernatural power from spirits so that they have the ability to
control witches. The head of this society is confirmed in his position by
the king of the Nupe kingdom. Usually about harvest time each year this
leader appears at the court of the king to report that witches, who are
always believed to be women, are getting out of control throughout the
country. The king agrees and suggests that the society mobilize its
local branches to combat this threat. These local members begin a
series of dances that will harm any women who are witches. The local
women are terrified—what if they really are witches?—and they often
collect wealth to bribe the society members into performing only a harm-
less dance. The bribe is accepted! Meanwhile, the local chiefs are having
their own problems.

> ... the activity of the society has plunged the community into wild un-
> rest. Households are dissolved, women neglect their duties, and money
> becomes scarce. As a result, a number of the village chiefs band together,
> collect a large sum of money, and bring it to the king, beseeching him
> to recall the members of the society ... the society members at last leave.
> The head of the society himself appears at the king's court, this time,
> however, to divide the spoils. The king receives one-third while the head
> of the society keeps two-thirds. There are always spoils to be divided

because ... the date of the ceremony is set for the harvest time, when money is plentiful everywhere in the country. (Radin, 1957: 48)

What a neat device for balancing or adding to one's budget!

In other cases, the association can function to ensure that the behavior of the king or chief remains within his traditional prerogatives. In West Africa, the Poro Society·often acts in this manner. This is also a men's society which controls spirits and possesses supernatural "medicines" of great strength. Although chiefs can call upon the Poro leaders and membership for aid, and although they are expected to act as a check on Poro activities, "In ordinary circumstances it was the prerogative of the society in any given political unit ... to watch the chief; to ensure that his actions as ruler conformed with customary practice" (Little, 1965:69). So the process of government is not limited to those leaders or institutions that are overtly political. Having now briefly discussed law and government as aspects of social control in primitive societies, we can now examine this area of human behavior in which pure coercive power is the central facet of activity: the area of warfare.

SUMMARY

1. Government is related to law and other functionaries, mechanisms, and institutions of social control that organize rules and employ sanctions.

2. Systems of government differ in terms of centralization, specialization, and absolutism. Absolutism—the power to apply sanctions—also takes a variety of forms: coercive power, consensual power, and persuasion. Positions of government may be allocated by ascription or achievement.

3. Positions of "governmental" leadership commonly found in primitive societies are headman, chief, sacredote, and king. These positions may or may not be associated with a council.

4. Political organizaton may be examined on levels other than the type of leader it has. A general scale of development exists as one goes from band, to tribe, to chiefdom, to state. These vary not only in size and type of political leadership but in type of subsistence, economic mechanisms, and degree of social stratification.

5. Many distinctly nonpolitical groups and associations may help or hinder the exercise of governmental power and authority.

REFERENCES FOR FURTHER READING

There are no really satisfactory general texts on government in primitive societies. Three books dealing with African situations are *Primitive Government*, by Lucy Mair (1962, Penguin Books); *Government and Politics in Tribal Societies*, by I. Schapera (1967, Schocken Books); and the classic *African Political Systems*, edited by M. Fortes and E. E. Evans-Pritchard (1963, Oxford University Press). The quote in this chapter by Radcliffe-Brown is from the introduction to this work. A recent reader containing some excellent samples of anthropological writing on various aspects of government is *Comparative Political Systems*, edited by R. Cohen and J. Middleton (1967, Natural History Press). The quote from Levi-Strauss on the Nambikurara is from this text. Two other readers of some value are: *Political Anthropology*, edited by M. Swartz, V. Turner, and A. Tuden (1966, Aldine)—the introduction is especially significant; and *Political Systems and the Distribution of Power*, (1965, Association of Social Anthropologists Monographs, Praeger). Important chapters on government are found in *Other Cultures*, by John Beattie (1964, Free Press) and *Anthropology: The Study of Man*, by E. A. Hoebel, 4th ed. (1972, McGraw-Hill).

The concept of levels of development comes from two works by Elman Service: *Profiles in Ethnology* (1963, Harper & Row); and *Primitive Social Organization* (1962, Random House). Somewhat parallel to these are two works by Morton Fried: "On the Evolution of Social Stratification and the State," in S. Diamond, ed., *Culture and History* (1960, Columbia University Press), pp. 713–31; and *The Evolution of Political Society* (1967, Random House). Two specific works on some of these levels are *Tribesmen*, by Marshall Sahlins; and *Formation of the State*, by Lawrence Krader, both published by Prentice-Hall in 1968. Specific examples cited in chapter twenty-one are "Poor Man, Rich Man, Big Man, Chief: Political Types in Melanesia and Polynesia," by Marshall Sahlins in *Comparative Studies in Society and History* 5 (1963): 285–303; *A Solomon Island Society* by Douglas Oliver (1967, Beacon Press); *The Cheyennes*, by E. A. Hoebel (1960, Holt, Rinehart & Winston); and *The Swazi*, by Hilda Kuper (1963, Holt, Rinehart & Winston). The general discussion of African kingdoms is from Jan Vansina, "A Comparison of African Kingdoms," in *Cultural and Social Anthropology*, edited by Philip Hammond (1964, Macmillan). The two examples of associations interacting in government are from "The Political Function of the Poro," by Kenneth Little, in *Africa* 35 (1965–66): 349–65 and 36: 62–71 and *Primitive Religion*, by Paul Radin (1957, Dover).

22 warfare

Every human society regulates the behaviors of its members by employing legal, political, and other means. It must also interact with other societies or groups, if only for such purposes as trading. Settled people especially may have to be concerned with the integrity of their borders. Failure in any sense to regulate relations with other societies may result in warfare. Warfare and hostile relations both within and between human societies are, unfortunately, common, although some societies engage in them more often and value them more highly than others. We can document such activities all the way back to the dawn of the human species. As many a historian has put it, much of our history has been that of war and of weapons development. Although some peoples do appear to lack war, its common occurrence has led many writers to suggest that aggressiveness is in our genes, that it is innate. We will consider this issue at the conclusion of the present chapter. We will first place warfare in its proper context.

DEFINING WARFARE

Warfare is somewhat difficult to define in ways that are meaningful for crosscultural comparisons. Certainly, it involves the members of one group or society attacking those of another group or society. Certainly, they are attempting in some way to further their own interests at the expense of the other group, and there will be at least some destruction of life and property. It is mostly, however, a question of the scale involved.

> Warfare is defined as armed combat between political communities. Armed combat, which is fighting with weapons, is performed by military organizations. When political communities within the same cultural unit

engage in warfare, this is considered to be internal war. When warfare occurs between political communities which are not culturally similar, this is referred to as external war. (Otterbein, 1970: 3)

Many writers would amend such a definition to say that "true" war must include a number of qualifying features. One scholar (Turney-High, 1971) has suggested that at least five characteristics must be present in true warfare activities. First, they must involve tactical operations with some sense of organization. Second, leadership must be developed. Command and control are necessary for tactical operations to be organized! Third is the idea that the ability must exist to sustain the military operations until the aim is reached (or cannot be reached). Fourth, the motive must have some clarity in the minds of the combatants. It is generally conceded that it must be a motive shared by the group: for example, in the modern world, a political reason. Finally, there is the suggestion that there must be either an adequate supply system or a short war.

WAR IN PRIMITIVE SOCIETIES

Many primitive societies fail to meet all of these considerations in the conduct of their hostilities. Their generally small-scale operations are usually of short duration, relying upon hit-and-run, surprise-attack tactics. They often terminate hostilities short of winning any clear-cut goal; and leadership, command, and military discipline may be very poorly developed. More than one writer has commented on the "every-man-his-own-general" nature of such activities. And the motives seem generally different from our own. As we examine the dimensions of warfare, tactics, motives, and the like, we can enlarge upon these distinctions.

One scholar, in an attempt to quantify such differences, has emphasized some basic elements of war. He has suggested that political organization and warfare are interrelated. The greater the degree of political centralization, the more organized and professionalized warfare becomes. The military organizations themselves are important, and, in politically centralized communities, they are apt to become more professional.

Professionals, in contrast to nonprofessionals, devote a substantial part of their time during their early adulthood to intensive training, which may include not only practice in the use of weapons, but also practice in performing maneuvers. They may belong to age grades, military societies, or standing armies, or they may serve as mercenaries. Societies with age grades, military societies and standing armies are considered to have military organizations composed solely of professionals; socie-

Many primitive societies practice ritualistic activities to insure victory before engaging in war. Pictured here, a ceremonial war dance in New Guinea.

Omikron

ties which employ mercenaries to lead, train, or assist untrained warriors are classified as having both professionals and nonprofessionals in their military organizations. (Otterbein, 1970: 20)

A few societies lack military organizations in any sense. In the present chapter, we will be loose in our definition of war, treating it simply as armed combat that differs from that of a "legal" nature. Although this facilitates data presentation, there are still problems in terms of where legalistic regulation leaves off and warfare begins. The Yanomamo of Venezuela offer an interesting example of this problem. Here all the villages are hostile towards each other, especially those in the center of the Yanomamo territory, where the villages are closer together, since here there is less opportunity to escape hostility by migration. Villages also form alliances with each other by creating shortages in certain goods to increase interdependence. This is reflected in feasting alliances in which women are exchanged and refuge is given, as well as actual aid in raiding common enemies. Most warfare is confined within the tribe itself and is part of a series of forms of patterned violence. At the lowest level is the chest pounding duel. This occurs between villages that are in alliance and occurs in response to accusations of cowardice or excessive demands for food or women. Here a man represents his village at feasts and offers his chest to be beaten upon. Someone from the "insulting" village takes up the challenge. "Fierce fighters will take as many as four blows before demanding to hit the opponent. The recipient of the blows has a chance to hit the first man as many times as he was hit, unless he knocks him unconscious before delivering all the blows" (Chagnon, 1968: 133). Serious injury or unconsciousness terminates the matter, and the disputants usually patch up the quarrel. This, then, is legal violence. There are also club fights that occur between and within villages over adultery and theft of food. Here the offended party takes a long pole (club) and insults his opponent who then comes with his own pole, and they alternately strike each other in the head. At the first sight of blood these often turn into a free-for-all with other men

401

joining both sides. Theoretically, the village headman, armed with bow and arrows, will shoot anyone deliberately trying to kill his opponent or escalating the violence level. Often, however, a village may split into permanent factions over this, or the different villages will terminate their alliance. The club fight is regulated combat. The next violence level, that of the raid, is actual warfare. It takes place between unrelated villages and those who have broken their alliances. Here a war party practices throwing spears into a grass dummy representing the enemy, and before leaving they "psyche" themselves up by singing their war song ("I am a meat-hungry buzzard"). They attack early in the morning, trying to pick off and kill some one individual and then retreat back to their home territory without being detected.

> The ultimate form of violence is the nomohoni, or "Trick." It involves the collaboration of two or more allied villages, one of which invites a different group to a feast. The unsuspecting guests are treacherously murdered and their women abducted and distributed among the confederates in the incident. For example, if village A and B are at war, one of the groups may persuade the members of a third village to hold a feast and invite the other to it. The third village must be on visiting terms with the victims. The feast is conducted, the guests fallen upon at some point during the festivities and brutally killed with clubs and staves. Those who manage to escape the slaughter inside the village are shot from ambush by the other principal in the treachery. (Chagnon, 1968: 138, 139)

This last form of violence is true warfare indeed. Having dealt with some definitional problems, we can now look at the various dimensions of warfare, beginning with techniques.

TECHNIQUES OF WARFARE

Turney-High (1971) lists about fourteen different aspects of techniques, a few of which we will examine in brief detail. Weapons are perhaps the most overt cultural aspect of warfare, increasing tremendously the ability of humans to harm their fellows. We began with stones and we progressed to better things! Basically, weapons fall into four basic categories. *Projectile* or fire weapons are designed for getting at an enemy from a distance while the user remains (theoretically) somewhat safe. Such weapons include arrows, spears, throwing clubs, sling stones, and similar objects. Among primitive peoples, such weapons are usually used as a preliminary to the "main event," perhaps to soften up or disorganize the enemy. For modern peoples, one suspects that we rely upon our projectile weapons—missiles and bombs—as the weapons of ultimate victory. A second class of weapons are *shock* weapons. Held in the hands and used for close-in fighting, these include the "crushers and piercers," such as swords, axes, knives, and similar objects. For primitives, these are usually the ultimate weapons of victory. For us, however, "if they are close enough to hit with a rifle butt, they are too close."

Then there are other weapons. *Mobility* weapons like horses and boats (war canoes) allow one to get to and away from the enemy. Like the modern tank, some of these can combine mobility with projectile and shock potential: shooting arrows from horseback or ramming other boats. For many primitives, such devices are underdeveloped, leg power supplying all the mobility required. Finally, there are the weapons of *protection*. These defensive weapons exist not only to protect the individual fighter (body armor), protect groups (palisades and trenches), but also may function to warn of the coming of the enemy (traps and modern radar). The Jivaro of Ecuador exhibit an instructive example of such protective devices. Here the local group inhabits a single house on a hill or at an angle in a river. These dwellings are made of thick chonta palm poles and are double-walled with a lookout tower on one end. They also employ a number of traps. One involves a round hole in the ground with pointed stakes projecting up from the bottom. Anyone falling in (in the dark as they approach the house) has these enter his body, and his screams serve to awaken the inhabitants. Observing the maxim that a good offense is the best defense, a second trap type occurs. Here a flexible tree limb is bent back and up to eight sharp stakes attached to it at right angles. It is tied back like a bow, and when an invader comes down the trail and trips a "trigger" vine laid across it, the limb is released to whip around and impale him in the chest. Nowadays they tie the vine to the trigger of a rifle, with the same results. Of course, in all cases, one of the most important aspects of weapons is their use.

A warring primitive tribe. Note the use of projectile weapons (spears) and protective weapons (shields).

American Museum of Natural History

Skill is necessary and often the crucial factor. " . . . a clever man with a club can kill an ignorant man armed with a rifle" (Turney-High, 1971: 18). Otterbein (1970) has pointed out that some weapon varieties (cavalry, shock, and body armor) are significantly correlated with professional military organizations. Also, more permanent field fortifications such as walls and trenches require a developed subsistence technology and high political centralization.

Tactics are another aspect of warfare techniques and, like weapons, reflect the culture and technology of the societies that use them. Many writers dealing with tactical operations differentiate between line fighting and ambush techniques. In the former, one faces the enemy in a modern kind of military engagement, in the latter, one surprises one's enemy on a more hit-and-run basis. As previously mentioned, this latter technique indicates the manner in which many primitives fight and perhaps derives from hunting activities. As the degree of political centralization (and motives) for war increase, so does the tendency to employ both line and ambush procedures. The Jivaro also provide a good example of the use of surprise, and some of their behavior will be described in detail to suggest other elements of promitive war as well.

In the case of internal warfare within a tribe, the course of action runs about as follows. Someone dies, and the medicine man cites witchcraft as the cause and names a guilty party. The relatives of the deceased decide to take revenge. They consult the spirit world by divination to assess the success of their attack (by drinking a narcotic liquid and dreaming the answer). They may, in this case, inform the enemy of their eventual coming. They do this by making a small head in his likeness and placing it near his house. They then actually prepare themselves by performing a war dance with their lances every night for a week prior to the attack. The last night, they paint themselves black. Early the next day, they attack.

> The attack is carried out in different ways . . . Sometimes the victim is attacked in his house at night, sometimes while he is working outside or traveling. In the former case the assault is made a little before dawn . . . Since it is difficult or impossible to force the entrance, the enemies generally avail themselves of the opportunity when he opens the door to perform his necessary duties. At this moment, they rush upon him and kill him with their lances. . . . It is, however, easier to kill the enemy while he is outside the house . . . The conspirators beforehand carefully inquire about the movements of the intended victim, and ambush at a place along the path where he has to pass. . . . [when he does] . . . the enemies rush forward and pierce him with their lances or shoot him to death. The dead body is left lying on the path or is thrown into the forest. (Karsten, 1923: 18)

On returning home, the avengers, because of their supernatural beliefs, have to observe certain precautions, including sexual abstinence for two or three months.

Feuds between Jivaro tribes are on a larger scale and are true wars in any sense of that term. Either a whole tribe or allegiances between local groups are involved; and a common leader is elected, and all concerned swear obedience to him. During the preparations, dream divination again is very important. In a more practical sense, they also employ spies to observe the number and condition of the enemy. They hope to catch them unprepared, and no warning is given in the case of external war. War dances are held: to heighten courage and confidence, as well as to generate the magical effect of being able to escape from the lances of the enemy. They paint themselves for mutual identification and to appear as terrifying as possible. They usually attack the enemy house at dawn, killing the person who first opens the door and then massacring its inhabitants. Often they set fire to it and kill everyone on the way out. They then go to the next house in the attempt to exterminate all of the enemy if possible. The victims' only defense is to break out and run or, if forewarned, to stay inside and signal for help.

> The victorious enemy without mercy wreaks his savage vengeance not only upon the fighting men, but also on old people, women, and small children, nay, sometimes even on the domesticated animals. The younger women are, however, often spared and carried off as prisoners of war, their fate being later to add to the number of their victors', and especially the chief's, wives. ... For the rest, the Indian does not content himself with merely killing his enemy. He wants to shed as much blood as possible and delights in mutilating the body of the slain enemy, being especially anxious to secure his head. The scene of a battle between Jivaro Indians, therefore, generally appears a dreadful spectacle of savage lust of destruction and thirst for blood. (Karsten, 1923: 28)

Many writers have commented upon the "joy of killing" evidenced by some tribes of primitive peoples. The Jivaro also, like so many groups, display the mixture of religious and warfare activities: divining the outcome; preparations including magic to insure victory; and purifications afterwards.

Another aspect of warfare techniques revolves around the size of the engagements and their actual organization. Plains Indians in North America, generally speaking, divided their hostile activities into two basic types: raiding and revenge expeditions. In the raiding variety, the size was generally restricted to about six to ten individuals; such small groups could stay out a long period of time. An aspiring leader simply interested a few friends who got a few of theirs to join. The usual motive was to steal horses or women. The revenge variety was larger, usually involving over 100 individuals, and was tribal in character. Because so many men (hunters) were involved, it had to be of short duration. Recruitment also differed. A prominent warrior might send a tobacco pipe to each military society leader who, if approving the venture, would present it to his men. Those who smoked signified they would join in the proposed activity. The motive here was generally revenge of some sort, which, interestingly enough, was often taken on the first enemy encountered, not necessarily those prompting the expedition in the first place! Line as well as ambush techniques could be employed in such situations. Although there are many other aspects of tactics, the above ideas and descriptions perhaps give a bit of the flavor of such activities.

MOTIVATIONS FOR WARFARE

A second dimension of warfare is found in its *motivations*. Why do people engage in such activities? One immediately thinks of political and/or economic motives for war since these have occupied so much of Western history. In such cases, subjugation of an opposing political unit often results in obtaining territory, tribute, economic advantages, captives for slavery, and plunder. The expansion of the Roman Empire documents such motives—matched very closely in the primitive world by the expansion of the Inca in South America. In many cases, hostages are taken to ensure the future cooperation of the losers. These kinds of motives, however, require a high degree of political centralization, and even purely economic advantages are less common motives than those to be mentioned next. Plunder, of course, can accompany any war activity as a subsidiary motive; and for pastoral peoples, gaining the stock of their neighbors (camels, cattle) may often be the prime motive. Would the use of the slain or captives for cannibalistic purposes be considered economic?

A second motive is that warfare can offer its participants a route to earning *honor and status*. Perhaps few males could deny wishes for glory and advancement, and war exploits and success in many primitive societies can offer a good means for obtaining them. Of course, not all societies emphasize war in such a fashion. In fact, some groups, such as the Pueblo Indians, consider war a defiling activity. Perhaps the acts of purification even in war-oriented groups suggest that war does create at least mildly uncomfortable states of being. Nevertheless, some societies positively fix war as the mode of social advancement. The

Plains Indians are generally cited as the classic example. Among the Kiowa, for example, one proved one's worth by accumulating credit-bearing deeds in war, many of which included the phenomenon of counting coup—being the first to touch a living or dead enemy. The outstanding person was a warrior who had at least four heroic deeds in his past plus all varieties of warfare experience. Such deeds were ranked in classes or groups.

Group I
1. Counting first coup.
2. Charging the enemy while party is in retreat, thereby covering retreat.
3. Rescuing a comrade while party is retreating before a charging enemy.
4. Charging the leading man of the enemy before the parties have met (which is tantamount to suicide).

Group II
5. Killing enemy.
6. Counting second coup.
7. Receiving wound in an honorable action (hand to hand combat).

Group III
8. Dismounting, turning pony loose and fighting on foot.
9. Counting third and fourth coup.
10. Serving as (leader) often.
11. Success in stealing horses.
12. Efficiency in war camp life (obeying orders, good scouting, etc.). (Mishkin, 1940:39)

Each group takes precedence over the one below it. After a major battle (and with supernatural oath-taking to preclude the claiming of false deeds), the action was reconstructed and appropriate deeds properly assigned to the combatants. This was followed by an extensive publicity campaign; deeds being recited in the military societies and by relatives as they feasted or simply rode about the camp singing the praises of their "famous" kinsmen. Even in societies where war is not the major avenue to status, the war hero may be the object of at least temporary honor and attention.

A third motive for war stems out of *grudges and desires for revenge.* Related here too is the idea of defense. Once a hostile situation has come into existence, real or fancied grudges and desires for revenge may keep the affair alive almost indefinitely. It could be initiated by wife stealing, suspected sorcery or witchcraft, killing, or some other "insulting" activity. Recall the way the Yanomamo club fight can escalate into a breech of alliance and lead to raiding activity. In most such cases, the attacked group can fight first to protect their home base and then go over to the offensive themselves in retribution to even the score. It is certainly true, however, that such "accounts to settle" can provide the rationale for the expression of some other type of motive.

A fourth reason for war, perhaps the most common and variable in primitive societies, is the motive associated with *supernaturalism*. We have already observed war and supernaturalism to be closely related in practice, and the supernatural beliefs can facilitate war as well. There are many such religious or magical motives, and we can examine a few as being representative. The Aztec of Mexico, for example, offered thousands of victims each year to pay off their debt to the gods who had created them. Since these gods had shed their own blood (in myth) to bring the bones of people of past creations to life as the Aztec, the Aztec had to pay them back (with interest, it would seem) in human blood. Such sacrifices included cutting open the chest cavity of the victim and pulling out the still beating heart! The Skidi Pawnee of North America

> . . . strove to capture a beautiful enemy maiden on each of their raids. This girl was then adopted into some very honorable Pawnee family where, to her surprise, she was treated with more consideration than the real daughters of the lodge. She became the pampered darling. Yet late one night she was rudely seized, stripped of her clothing, and her body half painted down its length from head, through groin, to foot with charcoal. She thus symbolized the junction of night and day. She was then strung up between two upright poles with cross pieces. Her adopted father was compelled to shoot an arrow through her heart just as the sacred Morning Star was rising. The arrows of the priests soon followed, and her body was horribly mangled before it had served its purpose. This rite of appeasement to the Morning Star was considered essential to Pawnee welfare, to success in all things and agriculture in particular. (Turney-High, 1971: 189, 190)

The Jivaro give still another dimension to supernatural motivation. These people severed the head of a slain enemy from the body and, by a series of techniques (including removal of bones), shrunk it down in size. Such shrunken heads (*tsantsas*) were not merely trophies of war and prowess, but after a lengthy series of ceremonies the soul of the enemy was incarcerated in the head and became the helpless and obedient slave of the slayer. To gain such supernatural aid is a worthy reason for involving oneself in war activity. Somewhat related are the practices of the Creek Indians of the southeastern United States. Here scalps were taken from the slain enemy and by harming these one could also work evil on the survivors.

Finally, although there are many other motives for war, there is

a class of reasons we might label as *recreation and excitement*. Although these motives may seldom occupy the center of the stage in warfare, they may lurk not too far away in the wings. War can become for males, at least, a kind of leisure-time activity, and a successful raid (especially one that brings back captives) may provide recreation and excitement for all concerned. A perhaps excessive example is found in various Iroquoian tribes of Northeastern North America. Among the Huron, prisoners were tortured, often for as long as five to six days. The entire village, and often guests, assembled to enjoy the spectacle as well as to participate in it.

> The prisoner was forced to make his way back and forth from one end of the longhouse to the other, while all those who were present armed themselves with a brand or a burning piece of bark, which they thrust at him as he passed. To increase his torment, the Huron also tried to force him to run through the hearths that were lighted down the center of the longhouse. At the ends of the cabin he was frequently stopped and made to rest on hot ashes taken from the fire. Here the bones of his hands were broken, his ears pierced with burning sticks, and his wrists burned or cut through by wrapping cords around them and pulling them back and forth as hard as possible. Later fire was applied to his genitals. . . . Now, when the prisoner was no longer able to run about, torture was applied to the rest of his body, mainly by the youths of the village. They made cuts in his arms, legs, thighs and the other fleshy parts of his body, quenching the flow of blood by thrusting glowing brands into the wounds. (Trigger, 1969: 50, 51)

And it got worse! In a less dramatic fashion, the training and practice for war, its preparations, victory celebrations, and recitation of war stories provide excitement and recreation. As Otterbein (1970) points out, there are many reasons for the waging of war in primitive societies, and, in general, the higher the level of political centralization, the greater the number of such motives. It can be assumed, however, that revenge motives (even if only as a rationale for others) and defense are the most common causes. This suggests that political conquest, warfare in the modern sense, which can be correlated with the politically centralized state, is not an inevitable feature of human existence since it is absent in many primitive societies. We can now examine a different dimension or aspect of war.

FUNCTIONS OF WARFARE

War is often said to have functions, to perform necessary things for its practitioners, beyond those gratifications of motivations.

> That war should have functions at all is of course in itself a hypothesis, and alternative hypothesis, e.g., to the effect that war is a nonfunctional pathological condition of society, may be and indeed often have been presented. . . . The examination of . . . functions may also have practical implications for the prevention of war. If we should indeed find that war constitutes a counteracting response made by a system when a variable or activity within the system has been disturbed in some way, we can then proceed to try to prevent war either by seeking to eliminate the disturbances whereby the variables or activities in question are moved from their proper, desired, or acceptable state or else by looking for alternatives to war as a counteracting response to the disturbances. (Vayda, 1968: 85, 86)

Anthropologists have suggested a number of possible functions. One is psychological. All societies have to handle the anxiety, tensions, and hostilities of their members. If these exceed certain limits, social disharmony could develop. It is not socially useful to expend hostility on the local people who may have helped contribute to its development. War or hostile relations with members of other social groups are ways of bringing such feelings out into the open and working them out without overly socially disrupting the local group (unless you lose). A second possible function is a sociological one. In most cases, the waging of warfare, either in offense or defense, creates and/or reinforces feelings of solidarity among the various groups involved. Hence, it can serve as an integrating function in the absence of overreaching kinship or formal political ties. This is especially significant for the local group among primitives, but may also operate (remember Yanomamo alliances) to at least temporarily knit together larger groups of people. There is nothing like a good revenge expedition to remind a Plains Indian society of its common identity! Then there are a number of less commonly advocated possible functions of war. Some writers see the taking of war captives for adoption as counteracting social imbalances between groups and the plunder as serving to counteract economic differences, say in camels among Bedouin. War is sometimes seen as providing males with something "valuable" to do in societies where females are important in subsistence technology or where descent and residence are biased in their favor. Many objections can perhaps be made to such theories, but, as was previously pointed out, the search for functions is not an anthropological apology for war; it is motivated by a desire to see if less harmful substitute activities for war are available.

CONSEQUENCES OF WARFARE

Finally, we can discuss the consequences of war. Because of the face-to-face, close-quarters nature of much primitive warfare, the most immediate result is the killing of many physically fit and important individuals of the involved groups. Although women and children may also be killed by the victorious side, generally women are excluded from the use of weapons, at least offensively. This is perhaps due to the fact that the weapons for primitive war are mostly adapted from hunting, a male domain. At any rate, estimates of battlefield casualties run higher than one might think possible without the use of bombs and modern paraphernalia. In one Zulu (of Africa) battle, the combined casualty rate was eighty percent. Generally speaking, however, "the higher the degree of military sophistication the higher the casualty rates" (Otterbein, 1970: 82). Longer-term consequences can include loss of property, livelihood, and freedom, as well as the dispersal of people. With the sophistication of modern military technology and political interests, the consequences of even a localized conflict, of course, may have world-wide repercussions.

> Warfare depends upon the establishment of unequivocal and mutually exclusive identities and loyalties, today represented by national boundaries. As long as there exists a permanent definition of their own group, within which to kill is murder, and others, whom it may be or is virtuous to risk one's own life to kill, warfare or the threat of warfare with its accompaniments of uncontrolled violence among smaller nations or subnational groups, can be easily invoked. (Mead, 1968: 222)

How frequent is war in primitive societies? One gets the general impression that at least feuding operations are rather continual, and peace (as one wag put it) is merely a period of cheating between active hostilities. And yet more permanent and actual periods of peace often occur, along with formal mechanisms for implementing and preserving it. The Kalinga of Northern Luzon in the Philippine Islands provide a good example of this. Here, formerly, headhunting between regional areas was common—surrounded by rituals—and occupied an important place in their culture. It was a prime mechanism whereby a man could gain status and renown and become a *Mangngol* or "brave warrior." Warfare included feuding and, in the extreme, included all the manpower of one region pitted against that of another. It was usually terminated by the combatants instituting peace after the death of a few individuals. Peace pacts between rival groups intensified in recent times as the former isolation of groups was lessened and the introduction of rifles upped the casualty rate.

Peace pacts, in essence, extend "law" to interregional situations, they are initiated by two individuals from different regions who hold the pact as binding on their whole area. They meet on neutral ground, review past grievances, and exchange spears. A period of truce begins. The next step is the *Simsim* or "tasting," in which there is the actual meeting of leaders from the two regions and the holding of a small feast. At it, all past difficulties are brought into the open and discussed. If a basis seems to exist for settlement, a date is set for the next stage, the *Lonok*. This is a big feast where the issues that were discussed previously are reviewed and extensive sets of provisions for the peace are set up. Many people from both sides are in attendance. Of considerable interest are the speech-making activities, which speakers begin in a complimentary manner and conclude by castigating the other side. By doing this, they appear to work off hostility that might endanger the peace. Such a pact is renewed if either of the holders dies or wishes it transferred and in the event of trouble between the two regions. If serious hostility breaks out, all the steps must be repeated.

ULTIMATE CAUSES OF WAR

Certainly, there are sufficient cultural motives for war, and we have previously suggested some of these, such as desires for status and the like. Given the long record of human hostility, however, some writers have suggested that although we fight for basically cultural reasons, we have, underlying these, an instinct for hostile aggression. Many such writers (Ardry, 1966; Lorenz, 1966) tie such aggression to territoriality and innate responses to its defense. From some such accounts, one gets the impression that we cannot help being nasty and brutal creatures and, except for rats, perhaps the worst of nature's forms since we are a species that kills its own kind! If all this is true, and war is in our genes as an instinctive compulsion, then it is only the *forms* of war that are culturally patterned. Some writers, while still holding to a view of the innateness of aggressive behavior, do not feel its expression to be an absolute necessity. Anthony Storr discusses the physiological mechanisms of aggression. "If . . . the cerebral cortex receives the impulse of an external threat . . . it will send down messages to the hypothalamus, releasing it from inhibitory control and stimulating it into action" (Storr, 1970: 14). This triggers a number of physiological changes and aggressive emotions and behavior. The view is held, however, that although such is an inborn propensity, it need not necessarily be initiated. If no threat occurs, aggressive behavior is not manifested. In this case, aggression does not so much seek discharge as it is discharged by external stimuli, which presumably could be controlled.

The other main view, held perhaps by most social scientists (a bit too naively?) is that not only the forms of aggression but aggression itself is a learned behavior. Such writers point not only to the basic lack of aggressiveness (at least of a killing nature) in our closest primate relatives, but also to pervasiveness of cultural conditioning.

> As Lorenz points out, aggressiveness can be taught. It is also intensified when it is exercised . . . When men began to settle in communities, they learned the irritations of being crowded. By then they had probably learned the use of weapons, originally for the purpose of killing game. And since they had already acquired at least a rudimentary speech, they could absorb from one another, and preach, animosity . . . Perhaps that is the way—culturally rather than genetically—that human aggressiveness arose. (Carrighar, 1968: 49)

There is little doubt that aggressive behavior can be systematically taught. Speaking again of the Yanomamo, our first example of this chapter:

> Yanomamo boys . . . fear pain and personal danger. They must be forced to tolerate it and learn to accept ferocity as a way of life . . . [adults] . . . forced all the young boys from eight to fifteen years old to duck-waddle around the village periphery and fight each other. The boys were reluctant and tried to run away, afraid they would be hurt. Their parents

Is the tendency toward aggression innate or learned? War is as prevalent today as it has been since the beginning of recorded history; only the methods have changed.

United Press International

> dragged them back by force and insisted they hit each other. The first
> few blows brought tears to their eyes, but as the fight progressed, fears
> turned to anger and rage, and they ended up enthusiastically pounding
> each other as hard as they could, bawling, screaming, and rolling in the
> dirt while their fathers cheered them on and admired their ferocity.
> (Chagnon, 1968: 130, 131)

Such activities certainly reinforce the cultural importance of aggressiveness in this society. Do they supply its raw materials as well? One
suspects that neither view of aggression (innate versus learned) is
exclusively a sufficient explanation. Aggressiveness may well have a
biological base. Certainly, basic psychology is involved, but such behavior is also definitely affected by learning and cultural traditions.

> Nothing could more effectively prolong man's fighting behavior than a
> belief that aggression is in our genes. An unwelcome cultural inherit-
> ance can be eradicated fairly quickly and easily, but the incentive to do
> it is lacking while people believe that aggression is innate and instinctive
> with us . . . (Carrighar, 1968: 50)

Just as effective in prolonging war as a human institution is the idea
that in becoming the cultural animal we no longer have to take biology
into account in our search for explanations of behavior!

SUMMARY

1. Warfare and hostile relations occur both within and among societies.
   War, in a sense, is the use of pure coercive power.

2. True warfare involves tactical operations with a sense of organization, developed leadership, and, generally, adequate means of provisioning combatants.

3. The greater the degree of political centralization, the more organized
   and professionalized warfare becomes.

4. Weapon types include projectile, shock, and mobility weapons. Some
   exist solely as protective devices. The use of these weapons in
   primitive societies is often different than our own use of the same
   weapons.

5. Motivations for war in primitive societies include economic gain,
   notions of honor and status, grudges and desires for revenge, and
   various motives of a supernatural nature. Recreation and excitement needs may also be involved. One can also discern unconscious
   motivations.

6. The ultimate causes of war and hostility have not been determined.
   Although cultural motives and their reinforcement are certainly

involved, some scholars suggest that the initial stimulus may be biological. Great controversy surrounds this view that war may be innate in the human species.

REFERENCES FOR FURTHER READING

There is a distinct lack of general texts on the subject of primitive war. Perhaps the most succinct is *The Evolution of War*, by Keith Otterbein (1970, HRAF Press), a study based on comparisons of twenty-six variables of war for fifty societies. An older and descriptively useful book is *Primitive War*, by H. H. Turner-High, republished in paperback (1971, University of South Carolina Press). A provocative reader is *War, the Anthropology of Armed Conflict and Aggression*, edited by Morton Fried, Marvin Harris, and Robert Murphy (1968, The Natural History Press). Part Three of *Law and Warfare*, edited by Paul Bohannan (1967, Natural History Press), also contains some useful articles. There is also the classic attempt by Quincy Wright, *A Study of War*, available in an abridged paperback edition (1970, University of Chicago Press). Specific examples quoted in chapter twenty-two are taken from the following: *The Huron*, by B. Trigger (1969, Holt, Rinehart & Winston); *Blood, Revenge, War and Victory Feasts among the Jibaro Indians of Eastern Ecuador*, by Rafael Karston (1923, Bureau of American Ethnology Bulletin no. 79); *Rank and Warfare Among Plains Indians*, by Bernard Mishkin (1940, University of Washington Press); and *Mountain Arbiters*, by Edward Dozier (1966, University of Arizona Press).

The quotes from Andrew Vayda, *Hypotheses about the Functions of War* and Margaret Mead, *Alternatives to War* are found in the Fried, Harris, and Murphy text cited above, pp. 85–91, and 215–28, respectively. The Yanomamo material by Napolean Chagnon, *Yanomamo Social Organization and Warfare* is cited from the same text, pp. 109–59. The literature on the aggression problem is enormous. Three paperback texts serve as a useful introduction: *Human Aggression*, by Anthony Storr (1970, Bantam Books); *Aggression in Man and Animals*, by R. Johnson (1972, W. B. Saunders, Co.); and *Man and Aggression*, edited by M. F. Ashley Montagu (1968, Oxford University Press). The quotes from Sally Carrighar, *War Is Not In Our Genes*, is taken from the Montagu text, pp. 37–50. For an intriguing discussion of the greater aggressiveness of males and the role of learning, see *Biology and Social Behavior*, by A. Mazur and L. Robertson (1972, The Free Press). Two books that have sparked great controversy on the topic of human aggression are Robert Ardry, *The Territorial Imperative* (1966, Atheneum); and Konrad Lorenz, *On Aggression* (1966, Harcourt, Brace & World).

23 supernaturalism

Human beings have to adapt to their physical environment and to their fellow human beings—to the natural and social worlds about them. So far as anthropologists have been able to determine, humans have created and then adapted as well to the world of the supernatural— to the world of postulated mysterious beings, powers, and events. The result is human religious and magical behavior. This chapter cannot survey all the high points of such behaviors, but it does attempt to provide the student with an appreciation of the structure and variety of supernaturalism.

THE CHARACTER OF PRIMITIVE RELIGION

We have already discussed some differences between primitive and modern societies in terms of such things as economic, legal, and political behavior. We can expect comparable differences to exist with respect to the supernatural realm of experience and behavior. One writer, William Howells (1948), has suggested that primitive religions differ from those of modern societies in the following ways. First, modern systems of belief have a sense of history, going back as they do to historical figures of an outstanding nature (Buddha, Christ). Primitive religions, certainly, have founders, but they are usually lost to memory. Second, there is the fact that most modern religions are world religions. Either because of the migrations of their adherents or active missionizing, they have spread beyond the original borders of their development. Most primitive faiths are indigenous; they have developed among those people who believe in and practice them. They are "native cults," as Howells calls them. There are Buddhist temples in Los Angeles and Christian churches in Africa, but no Pygmy church in India or the United States. Third, there is the idea that most modern religions are characterized by the notion of exclusivism or intolerance. They feel

Most modern religions are world religions. The Muslim population is estimated at 400,000,000.

United Nations

they are the one true creed ("there is no god but Allah . . ."), or, among competing creeds, they consider themselves the best or truest. This also generally leads to modern religions being associated with a well-worked-out system of beliefs to export out to "pagans." Inconsistencies in belief have been worked out into what we might call a consistent theology. Most primitive systems, in contrast, lack the sense of having an exclusive handle on truth and are basically tolerant of the creeds and practices of other peoples. They " . . . are open to any suggestion and will accept any idea that seems appealing or useful, sometimes even if it opposes a prevailing one. And although they may look on the gods of other people as enemies, they are quite willing to recognize their existence and do not try to grind them out by denying them belief" (Howells, 1948: 5, 6). As a result, primitive religions often become what Howells calls "a regular junkyard of the supernatural." There are, however, similarities in all human societies in the supernatural dimension of existence, and some of these will be discussed presently.

A DEFINITION OF RELIGION

What exactly is *religion*? There are almost as many definitions of religion as there are scholars interested in its study. Remember the problems in defining culture? In the interests of simplicity, we can define *religion* as beliefs in the existence of supernatural beings and the practices associated with relating to them. Such a definition suggests that religion will have a number of elements of thought and behavior associated with it. Its basic assumption is that there exist gods or spirits who have powers greater than those of human beings. If humans wish to gain something beyond their ordinary capabilities, they must turn to supernatural beings to accomplish these things. The supernaturals have the special powers that humans lack. Although such gods and

418

spirits may or may not help humans in these matters, religion basically presupposes a dependency relationship.

William J. Goode (1951) has suggested a number of characteristics of religion that follow from what has been said above. Some of these are as follows. Religion has an attitude of supplication. Humans ask or beg the gods for help. This is often done "on bended knee" to show our powerless and dependent state. Such requests are often accompanied by offerings or sacrifices to show our devotion and/or earnest desire. This is often accompanied by some degree of emotionalism. Because supernatural beings are so much more powerful than humans, we often display fear and awe in our dealings with them. Religion is also generally a public and group-oriented phenomenon. Its practices are meant to benefit a wide circle of people—the congregation or perhaps everyone in a small society. Its ends are basically group ends. Religion is democratic; the gods exist for everyone. Goode characterizes the relationship of leaders and followers in religion as the shepherd-flock relationship. Although we depend upon the gods to accomplish special things for us, we ourselves can do very little. Nonetheless, there are some people who by special training are able to know the "will" of these gods better than others, and such people can shepherd the rest of us in ways pleasing to these beings. Finally, among other things, the goals of religion tend to be of a general or other-worldly variety. This is perhaps more true in modern societies, but religious behavior need not always have some specific goal in mind. In fact, religious behavior is often thought to become an end in itself rather than being a means to an end. We attend religious services because of what we get out of the service itself.

THE CONCEPT OF MAGIC

In addition to religion, there is also the concept of magic. This area of supernaturalism is generally conceived in somewhat different terms. It, too, has been the subject of many definitions. We can define it simply here as a set of supernatural techniques by means of which humans can accomplish things beyond their ordinary capabilities. This presupposes that humans can themselves play a godlike role, if on a lesser level. The magician often accomplishes this by imitation, by symbolically pretending to do what he wants to happen: for example, the classic idea of sticking pins in the image of a person to cause his injury. This is generally accompanied by some kind of verbal element: a spell or incantation. Because humans gain or utilize power in magic,

magic has a number of basic characters that contrast with those of religious practice.

Goode (1951) has indicated some of the characteristics of magic as follows. Magic has an attitude of manipulation. The procedure is an ordering rather than an asking. This means that if you can deal in the supernatural, if you can put X and Y together to accomplish Z; there is no need for much emotionalism. Hence, most magical behavior is detached and impersonal; no real fear or awe is involved, only respect. After all, if you don't handle electricity right, you could get hurt; magic appears to work in much the same manner. Then again, magical practices are for the most part private activities; they are oriented around individuals and individual needs and desires. Magic, as such, really doesn't have a "church." The leader-follower interaction Goode characterizes as the professional-client relationship. The magical practitioner has the knowledge and techniques to secure certain things, and other people engage his services for such ends, just as we go as clients to specialists. A big difference often said to exist between magic and religion is that, at least potentially, magic can be evil. It can be directed against other people in one's own group. There is black magic. Is there black religion? Perhaps not in the strict sense. Finally, among other things, is the notion that magic is directed more to specific goals than is religion. Magical practice is always supposed to result in something; it does not become an end in itself. So magic and religion can be seen to function as somewhat different approaches to the world of the supernatural.

NATURALISM AND SUPERNATURALISM

How do magic and religion fit in with other human behaviors? Many writers have designated magical and religious behavior as being sacred or holy and have used terms such as *profane* or *unholy* to describe areas of behavior not connected with supernatural beings and powers. Such terms, however, carry unfortunate connotations. Edward Norbeck (1961) suggests the use of the term supernaturalism for the kinds of behavior we have been describing. By this term he means " . . . to include all that is not natural, that which is regarded as extraordinary, not of the ordinary world, mysterious, and unexplained or unexplainable in ordinary terms" (Norbeck, 1961: 11). Supernatural means more than natural, and this is not the same thing as superstitious! Naturalism, on the other hand, is the view that things happen because of the operation of perfectly ordinary, nonmysterious causes and circumstances. This is the world of science rather than of magic and religion. Further is the idea in supernaturalism (probably more developed in its religious manifestations) that its special world transcends the purely natural one; it is more real than that which is normally perceived by and dealt with in purely scientific terms. The view is often held that human existence can only realize its potential in proportion to our acceptance of and reliance upon the world of the supernatural. We are only real in other words as *Homo religiosus*, not as *Homo scientificus*. Man, in this view, cannot be self-made. "It is he who has made us and not we ourselves. . . . " In any event, human beings usually merge these two views in some way.

> . . . man interprets his universe in two principal and different ways and on the basis of these interpretations he is afforded patterns of behavior with relation to that universe so that he may know how to act. One of the kinds of interpretation we may call naturalistic, the other supernaturalistic. Naturalism and supernaturalism are both ways of adjusting to the universe. Man's behavior has been based upon both of the principal lines of interpretation, separately, alternately, and in combination; and they have affected his life in ways of which he has not always been aware. (Norbeck, 1961: 12)

REASONS FOR SUPERNATURALISM

More than one writer has asked why human beings continue to believe in and practice supernaturalism in the face of scientific advances. After all, an "ignorant savage" thinks that magic causes the rain or he prays to a rain god, but "rational" modern people know better. Why has science not dislodged supernaturalism? Most attempts to answer this question revolve around the nature of human beings as thinking and self-questioning animals who are concerned with the meaning of their experiences.

Unpredictability

As Talcott Parsons (1952) has expressed it, we are interested in the fit between what we expect to happen to us and what actually happens. In such a situation, we often meet with frustrations. These frustrations, Parsons feels, fall into two main categories. Sometimes things happen to us (a surprise quiz or a car accident) that we could neither predict nor prepare for. At other times, our behavior may be surrounded with more general uncertainty. Here we may have the skills to meet a situation (the final exam) but there may be unknown factors involved. In either of these cases, supernaturalism can be a useful mechanism of adjustment. Science hardly provides the living with ways to adjust to the death of a close friend or relative, even if it can explain that death; and even the most skilled hunter has some doubts as to the complete probability of his success.

Cognitive, Substantive, and Expressive Needs

Melford Spiro (1966), in a somewhat more elegant fashion, has summed up the human needs that supernaturalism, in the absence of naturalistic means or explanations, can function to meet. These can be represented as follows:

Need	Function	
Cognitive	"...to know, to understand, to find meaning..."	Adjustive
Substantive	"...desires for rain...crops...victory . . . recovery from illness..."	Adaptive
Expressive	" . . . powerful drives which seek reduction and powerful motives which seek satisfaction."	Integrative

(Spiro, 1966: 109–15)

So human beings want to have knowledge of things, they want to accomplish things, and they have the need to handle their own fears and anxieties. If science, the view of naturalism, cannot cater to these, says Spiro, then supernatural beliefs and practices will step in to perform adjustive, adaptive, and integrative functions. It can satisfy such needs and desires. We can now examine some of the aspects of supernaturalism in primitive societies.

SUPERNATURAL LEADERSHIP

One of the most interesting area of supernaturalism deals with the areas of the leaders (professionals or shepherds) of such behaviors. Traditionally, anthropologists have concentrated most of their attention on these types of individuals rather than on the laymen as such. In an ideal sort of way we recognize two basic and contrasting types of leaders, and these can briefly be discussed.

Shaman

The shaman is the type of practitioner found predominantly on the magical side of supernaturalism. Although leaders designated as shamans vary considerably in the details of their practice, their general behavioral

A modern shepherd with a substantial flock is the young guru, Maharaj Ji. His followers claim he has given them "perfect knowledge."

United Press International

characteristics can be stated as follows. First, the powers of the shaman come from direct contact with the supernatural. They not only have magical techniques but are usually aided by spirit powers as well. Generally, one is recognized early in childhood as a likely candidate for such a position, evidenced by nervousness and unnatural behavior—signs of spirit contact. One must, however, usually undergo special experiences to gain control of the power requisite for office. According to some groups of Australian Aborigines, for example, the potential shaman must visit a cave occupied by spirits. After a time, these emerge and "kill" the novice, and take him inside to receive new internal organs and magical substances. He is then brought back to life. In this, as in most cases, the shaman must then apprentice himself to others already in the practice to learn how to use his powers effectively.

A second characteristic of the shaman, obviously, is that he can actually accomplish extraordinary things. If others can use magic, his is doubly effective. Perhaps the most common shamanistic activities are curing the sick (from variously supernaturally caused illnesses) and divination of the future and discovery of hidden knowledge. In such tasks, shamans perform as part-time practitioners; they are not fully supported in their role by the other members of their society. They do, usually, receive some compensation for their services. Although shamans exist in most societies, they tend to hold the center of the supernatural stage in the technologically simpler societies. It should be added that where they are the only type of supernatural leader they often occur as "lone-wolf" practitioners working in competition and often in conflict with each other. As societal complexity increases they often go into cooperative group practice, and phenomena such as curing societies emerge (as briefly noted in chapter nineteen).

Finally, and most visibly, shamans are characterized by unusual psychological and physiological behaviors. Perhaps the most striking of these is the trance state associated with much of their activity. This condition of withdrawal during which they may perform is usually interpreted by primitive peoples as cases in which the shaman's soul has left his body or as his being possessed by a spirit. In both of these

423

cases, however, the shaman is considered to be the master of the situation; it is part of their behavioral repertoire. Since such practitioners appear to be able to slip into such states pretty much at will, it is assumed by scholars of comparative religion that there are means for inducing such conditions. These range from auditory (by drumming) and other external stimuli, to alcohol and various drug stimulants. Much speculation concerns the apparent deviant nature of the shaman and the types of individuals who become such leaders. It is generally assumed by anthropologists that the shaman is the earliest developed type of supernatural practitioner.

Priest

Anthropologists have generally employed the term **priest** to cover the type of leader usually associated with religious types of practices. If there are different types of shamans, there are literally scores of varieties of priests. Nonetheless, a general sampling of their characteristics would include the following traits. First, although they may receive a "call" to their office, they undergo no experiences with spirit beings; they receive no supernatural gifts. They *learn* all the prerequisites of their positions. As a result, secondly, they cannot "traffic" directly in the realm of the supernatural. They have no extraordinary powers and they accomplish no marvelous things. Their behavior, for the most part, is confined to leading communal rituals, giving advice, and to administration types of activities (around cult or church affairs). Based upon greater religious knowledge, they often can also interpret the will of the gods. Third, priests generally are full-time practitioners; they are supported by other members of their society. Their societies, incidentally, are usually the more complex food-producing types that have surpluses necessary for the rise of such specialists. Fourth, priests are usually found in cooperative groupings, often arranged in some hierarchical fashion. Apparently, if one lacks powers oneself, one requires as much help as one can get! Finally, almost always the priestly type of supernatural leader is "normal" (and supposedly exemplary) in his behaviors. Generally speaking, the priest ought to be a well-integrated person; what sheep want to follow a freaked-out shepherd?

The notions of shaman and priest are, of course, like magic and religion, ideal concepts. Speaking of the Nyima of the Nuba Mountains of Africa, S. F. Nadel describes three types of supernatural leaders.

> ... the shaman, who is full a servant of spirits; the medoeran or Hill Priest, whose office illustrates the encroachment of shamanistic concepts; and the shirra or Rain Maker, whose office is non-shamanistic ... The

Hill Priest is conceived of as the guardian of the hill on which the community lives—the Hill being understood in a mystical, sacred sense. He officiates in the most important community rites, which are concerned with the land, the seasons, and circumcision, that is, with the continuity . . . of life on the Hill. The Hill Priests' office is hereditary, being transmitted from father to son. But, since the mythical founders of the hill community and its rituals have become spirits, their reincarnation equally enters into the qualifications for this priesthood. (Nadel, 1946: 33)

The shaman himself functions mostly in divination situations: to discover the nature of disease, auspicious times for work, war, and other, activities, and counsels how to avoid misfortune. The Rain Maker is primarily concerned with rain, health, and fertility and is free from spirit possession in his practice. The Hill Priest seems to be between these two types; he functions in religious situations but with shamanistic behaviors and powers. Thus, anthropological concepts are only useful guides; reality does not divide itself up into neat categories. We can now examine some supernatural practices of various kinds.

SUPERNATURAL PRACTICES

Supernatural practices, sometimes called rituals or ceremonies are of many different types. Although there is some debate among anthropologists as to the most useful classification to employ with respect to them, for the illustrative purposes of this book we can assume the existence of three major types. The first we can call **critical supernatural practices.** These rituals occur in response to some crisis or need, and hence they occur intermittently—whenever such a situation arises. These include activities surrounding such things as war, sickness, and wanting to know what the future holds, and their occurrence usually cannot be predicted. A second major type of supernatural practice may be called **cyclical.** These rituals occur in a fairly predictable sequence but are not tied down to any specific dates throughout the year. They may be held perhaps every so many years. Initiation of young people into adulthood is perhaps the best example of these. A group will wait until enough young people exist to make such a performance worthwhile, but one knows that the ritual will occur. Finally, there are supernatural practices of a **calendrical** nature. Since these are activities tied in with the yearly calendar, their prediction is absolute. For example, every fall the harvest festival occurs to give thanks to the gods for crops; we go to church each week at a given time. There is a strong tendency for practices we have termed magical to be of the critical sort and calendrical rites to be more religious in nature. Cyclical types often display a combination of both. We can now illustrate each of these areas of supernaturalism.

Critical Rituals

One of the most commonly occurring critical rituals is one or another form of *divination:* the attempt to discover hidden knowledge and/or predict the future. Such attempts take many forms in primitive societies. Basically, the supernatural techniques of divination fall into two broad categories. Internal divination involves some kind of alleged change in condition in an individual, and the answers sought come from within that person. Internal types range from a shaman being possessed by a spirit, and that spirit giving the desired information, to an ordinary person having a dream and then interpreting its significance. The other main type of divination may be called external divination. Here the answers come from outside the individual. This ranges from deliberately manipulating objects designed to provide the answer (casting dice) to merely taking note of some natural phenomenon (a flight of birds) as an omen.

Divination certainly caters to Spiro's human need for explanation and helps us deal with our "should-I-or-shouldn't-I" situations. It gives the person immobilized by a difficult decision not only an answer, but provides the assurance on which one can then proceed with confidence. Thus, divination is a useful behavior and goal-oriented. Some writers have even suggested that divination gives answers even more functional than this. George Park (1963), speaking of the Yoruba of West Africa, points out that the selection of a house site by a young man is often surrounded by difficulties beyond the choice decision itself since the selection also aligns him to a social group and, importantly, to a rejection of others. To avoid bitterness over the result, he can consult a diviner, thus removing the blame from himself and transferring it to the world of the supernatural, where the decision is obviously beyond reproach.

We can briefly survey some of the divination practices in one society to capture a bit of the flavor of such activities. Divination among the Barotse of South Africa has been described most adequately by Barrie Reynolds (1963). Among these people, there are seven major divination varieties. One is *pattern divination*. By this " . . . is meant the use of a number of material symbols which, being shaken together and cast on the ground, provide answers by the positions they take up relative not only to each other but to some outside factor or factors" (Reynolds, 1963: 100). There are many forms of this, perhaps the most interesting being the "divining-basket" technique used by a professional diviner. This consists of the use of a shallow, flat basket containing about 100 symbols representing life, death, good fortune, etc. The basket is tossed up and down several times until the top objects form a pattern relative to one another that can be interpreted by the diviner for the answer.

Another variety is *pointing divination*. In this case, the answer comes in simple yes-no fashion by pointing at one of two symbols or at a person accused of some crime. One type of many here involves the use of a turtle shell that has been filled with "medicine" and that has a feather sticking from one orifice, on which rests the hand of the diviner. By its direction of movement taken on the ground, towards symbols or suspect, the answer is given. Needless to say, this method (with its obvious capacity for manipulation) is most effective at night under poor lighting conditions.

A third variety is *revolving divination*. This technique works by revolving an object on an axis. The direction and speed of movement supply the sought-for answer. Here, for example, an antelope horn is filled with "medicine." A string is attached to its open end, and it is suspended from a stick held by the diviner. The point of the horn touches the ground, and the top revolves on it. The direction of the swinging (clockwise-counterclockwise) and the speed indicate the answer.

A fourth variety of divination among the Barotse is *magnetic*, operating on the idea of objects sticking together. One type uses an axe:

> This is one of the commonest methods . . . and is to be found among many . . . African peoples . . . The axe, which is an ordinary working axe, consists of a wedge-shaped piece of iron tang-hafted in the bulbous head of a normal wooden handle. The axe is laid on its side, on the ground or on the back of a grindstone, is held by the diviner at the head of the shaft, and is slid gently forwards and backwards while he poses the question. The answer is indicated by its refusal to move in response to the pressure of his hand. The diviner taps it with his knuckles thereby releasing it, and a second question is then posed. (Reynolds, 1963: 114–15)

A fifth variety is based on *reflecting*. Here one peers into some substance to "see" the answer. Water, "medicine"-filled containers, and actual mirrors are employed in this technique. The sixth variety consists of a number of internal types, *mental* varieties, as Reynolds calls them. These include spirit possession, communication with spirits through carved figurines that act as intermediaries, and dreams. The last major variety consists of various forms of the *ordeal*. These work on the same principle as previously discussed for the Bushong in the chapter on primitive law.

Cyclical Rituals

One of the most common cyclical supernatural practices, as already indicated, is that of initiation rituals. These kinds of activities have as their overt function the conferral of adult status on young males and females, although the rites for males are usually more common and more elaborate than those for females. The rites operate by removing young people symbolically from their youthful status in their society, providing them a period of transition during which discipline can be applied and knowledge imparted, and reintegrating them back into society as adult members. Covertly, the rites can also express the importance of such individuals to their group as well as reinforce the social unity of the entire group. " . . . they create and renew feelings and experiences of social unity and cohesion; they ensure respect for the tribe's moral and social sanctions" (Elkins, 1964: 189). The author just cited has presented a kind of composite account of male initiation rites among the Australian aborigines in terms of eight ritual stages, which we can paraphrase here.

The first stage is the *taking of the novice.* When the appropriate leaders decide that there are enough pubescent boys to initiate, the youths are taken from the camp in an elaborate manner. The women usually make a symbolic resistance since their sons will now be "dead" to their youthful status. Sometimes the boys are painted with human blood. They may also be subjected to other rites at this time, being tossed into the air, or having the septums of their noses pierced. Then comes what Elkin calls the *ceremonial welcome and combat.* All the local groups involved come to the designated sacred area, and various rituals take place to integrate these various groups together. Past difficulties are settled by a mock battle followed by a feast, although formerly, in some areas, some people were killed and eaten. Then comes the *preliminary ceremonial,* which carries out the symbolism of the death of these novices. Sometimes the boys will be placed on a platform made by two lines of men crossing their spears. The women weep as the "dead"

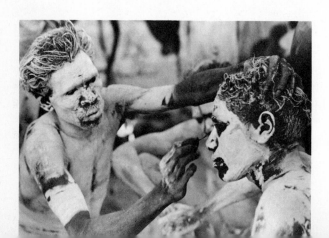

Aborigines painting up in pipe-clay in preparation for an initiation ritual.

American Museum of Natural History

young boys are carried about. The next stage consists of the *ritual body operations* applied to the boys. These include knocking out incisor teeth, scarification, circumcision, and subincision (slitting underneath the penis). One is now certainly entering the sacred and secret world of adulthood. Generally, one of these operations is emphasized over the others, and usually the adult males form a "living" table on which such activities take place. Then comes the *period of seclusion.* This continues the death symbolism, and the novices are isolated. Usually it is during this recovery period that the secret lore that enables males to function as protectors of their group is taught to the novices. In many areas too " . . . the youths seem to spend a good deal of their period of seclusion in pairs, thus assisting one another to get food . . . Each novice has a special guide and instructor . . . who sees him from time to time and supports him through the ceremonies and ordeals. They frequently have a special language code for their own use" (Elkin, 1964: 182).

The next portion is called the *blood ceremony* and consists of smearing blood over the bodies of the initiates and giving them some to drink. The blood may be taken from the arm veins of the adult males, or they may reopen their old subincision wounds to provide it. The older males may also smear themselves and drink blood and dance.

> This blood is sacred; there is a secret name for it, and it is usually associated with some mythical hero's act. It gives life, strength and courage and so fits the candidates for the revelations which are to be made. At the same time it unites them with the elders of whose blood they have partaken; indeed, it does more; it unites them to the initiation heroes, for the blood taken under such conditions is the hero's or ancestor's life, and so to drink it, brings the initiated into the mythical world. (Elkin, 1964: 183)

The *fire ceremony* occurs next as a kind of purification before the young men return as adults to their respective groups. It varies from gazing at a fire, being "smoked" over it, and collectively stomping it out with their feet. Now they can all safely return to the world of ordinary things. The initiation is then concluded by the *washing and return.* Blood and other decorations are washed off, and the young men finally return as reborn individuals.

Calendrical Rituals

We may now briefly describe one calendrical supernatural practice. An excellent example of this variety of ritual is the Bear Festival among the Ainu of Northern Japan. The performance of this activity, as described by Joseph Kitagawa (1960), is connected to the Ainu belief in *Kamui* or gods (this term may be used for supernatural power in general). These gods regularly visit this world in animal disguises,

The decoration of Christmas trees is the subconscious continuation of a pre-Christian calendrical ritual commemorating the Winter Solstice.

especially the bear. They cannot return to the spirit world, however, unless humans rob them of their disguise by ritually killing them. Humans benefit from this "chore" since some "soul or spirit" remains behind to protect human potency. The following is a perhaps oversimplified description of the Bear Festival, which involves such beliefs.

A bear cub is caught towards the end of the winter and is cared for until about October. It is said to have been nursed as a human baby by an Ainu woman since it is an honored visitor. If treated correctly, its spirit will return again and again. During all this time, the bear is kept in a cage surrounded by magical objects, and preparations are made for the feast itself. After all the guests arrive, the main portion of the rite takes place, presided over by three elders (priests) and their assistants. The Kamui are asked for their assistance, and the person who originally caught the bear prays to it, requesting it to return to the spirit world. Then, dancing occurs around the cage to encourage the bear to behave appropriately. Then, the bear is roped and taken from the cage and paraded around a sacred area. The people shoot it with blunt arrows to obtain good luck. Finally, a real arrow is fired into its heart, and the blood is collected and drunk by the elders. About the same time, the bear is strangled to death by two poles clamped about its neck. The bear is then skinned, prayers are offered to the kamui, and dancing takes place. An offering is placed before the bear. The skull is then prepared and taken to a sacred "fence" and placed on a pole in the center. An arrow is shot towards the eastern sky—symbolic of safe departure—and the skull is turned to face west. The main rite is concluded.

Such calendrical supernatural practices as the Ainu Bear Festival not only function to meet substantive needs and desires—in this case, to gain potency and honor the gods—but may indirectly cater to a host of other needs as well. These would include the enhancement of solidarity and the repetition of the beliefs central to the group, just as in the case of cyclical rituals. Not all supernatural beliefs and practices, however, function in such overtly positive ways. As previously mentioned, at least magical practices can be directed against other members of one's group. We can now turn to this darker side of supernaturalism, to the area of sorcery and witchcraft.

Witchcraft

Witchcraft involves the use of supernatural power in such a manner as to cause harm to one's fellow human beings. The witch is perhaps closest to the shaman in practice, although the two are seldom thought to be identical.

> . . . I would suggest that the essence of the witchcraft idea is simply this: People believe that the blame for some of their sufferings rests upon a peculiar evil power, embodied in certain individuals in their midst; although no material connection can be empirically demonstrated between those individuals and the ills they are supposed to have caused. The witch then is held to be a person in whom dwells a distinctive evilness, whereby he harms his own fellows in mysteriously secret ways. To this central mystical idea each society adds its own embellishments. (Meyer, 1970: 46–47)

An Aborigine witch-doctor shows how a magic bone is pointed at a victim intended for death. The ceremony is performed in secret but the victim always learns of it and usually dies.

Australian News and Information Bureau

The elements involved in witchcraft can generally be stated as follows. First, the witch derives his or her powers from within; the skills are not learned, although it is often thought that they can be increased by use. Because of such an internal nature, witchcraft powers are often inherited in a family line. Second, the powers of the witch may be used consciously or unconsciously. One can harm others without realizing it before one recognizes one's witch potential. This is partly the reason, one suspects, that people may readily confess to witchcraft if accused—"if they say I harmed someone, then maybe I am a witch." In any case, third, witches are usually thought never to use their powers for good causes; they are absolutely evil. They are also incapable of redemption. Whereas a shaman guilty of malpractice can repent and return to his generally helpful role in society, the witch is addicted to his or her deviant behavior. The evil witches do is generally with respect to their own kinsmen and neighbors; witchcraft is localized and the types of misfortunes they are said to cause are generally definitely categorized. They usually include things out of the ordinary. Fourth, witches are so evil that they are seen to reverse normal human standards in their behavior. "They particularly delight in unnatural practices such as incest or bestiality; they eat their own children, they dig up corpses" (Meyer, 1970: 48). Finally, among other characters, witches often have animal familiars, creatures (owls, bats, etc.) with whom they can converse, as well as forms into which they can transform themselves if they wish to go somewhere to do their evil unobserved.

Sorcery

Sorcery is also the use of supernatural power in an unacceptable way, but it has a somewhat different character from witchcraft. A sorcerer if often thought of as having to learn his or her techniques. Instead of being inborn and automatic, it is more a case of black magic. Because of this acquired nature, sorcery powers may only be used consciously; hence, the practitioner is generally not considered innately evil. They are "regular" types of people who for one reason or another have chosen to act in a disapproved fashion. As a result, the sorcerer may not only be capable of redemption, but the powers may be used for beneficial purposes. Finally, and this is a point of some debate among anthropologists, sorcery practices do seem to be attempted; it is a belief *and* a practice. Although witchcraft is certainly a well-defined belief, many scholars have suggested that witchcraft is not really attempted—that, like unicorns, there really are no witches, only the belief in them. Such types of people really don't exist even in the societies holding such beliefs! At any rate, both witchcraft and sorcery relate to the idea of the misapplication of supernaturalism.

How do such things work? Clyde Kluckhohn (1944) has described the variety of evil activities among the Navaho of Arizona, and we can briefly indicate these to demonstrate the flavor of such beliefs. There are four major applications of such powers in this society. The first involves the preparation of a potion made from the flesh of corpses. This preparation is ground into a powder and used to contaminate people or the objects they may come into contact with. Such practitioners form groups and meet together to initiate new members, plan activities, and do immoral things such as have intercourse with corpses. One achieves initiation by killing a close relative. A second type may well be a branch of the first variety. Again, one must kill a close relative to participate. The main practice is to take some possession of one's intended victim, bury it along with material taken from a grave, and then (most importantly) recite an evil spell over it. In the third variety, the main technique is to project a disease-causing object (bone, stone, etc.) into the victim. This is accomplished by placing the object in a special basket or buckskin pouch and then causing it to fly into the victim by spell recitation. Although one has to kill a close relative to confirm one's powers here too, there appears to be no group activities. A last type is employed to gain extraordinary success (which makes it bad apparently) in trading, gambling, and especially lovemaking (maybe not all bad). In this last case, there are special plants one uses that are ground up and put in food that will be eaten by the "victim." The potion can even be transferred from the "seductor to the seductee" by kissing!

FUNCTIONS OF WITCHCRAFT AND SORCERY BELIEFS

What is the function of such misdirected supernaturalism?

The theories that have been advanced in the discussion of witchcraft beliefs as they can be observed today are of different kinds. Some ask why such beliefs are so tenacious and so widely held. Some, considering beliefs and accusations together, ask what is their "function"—that is to say, what do they do for the societies in which they are found? Do they contribute something indispensable to the maintenance of ordered social relations? Others seek to make correlations between different ways of directing accusation or between the total number of accusations, or the proportion of misfortunes ascribed to witchcraft, and the structure of different societies. (Mair, 1969: 199)

We can give two examples of such speculations. S. F. Nadel (1952) has neatly demonstrated how witchcraft beliefs may arise from and cater to areas of social tension in human societies. One of his examples is the Nupe of Africa, part of whose beliefs in witchcraft were discussed in the chapter on government. It will be recalled that among the Nupe, only women are witches. Why is this so? Nadel suggests that the witch beliefs provide a way for men to "get even" with them. In this society, many wives engage in trading activities that give them a superior economic position with respect to their husbands, who lack such opportunities. Further, because wives have wealth, they often assume male activities such as furnishing the bride wealth for a son when he obtains a wife by purchase. Men resent this situation but can do little about it. Finally, these trader wives become morally lax during trading activities and are not only unfaithful to their husbands because of this but dad has to stay home and watch the kids while all this is going on, adding insult to injury!

> In practice, then, the men must submit to the domineering and independent leanings of the women; they resent their own helplessness, and definitely blame the "immorality" of the womenfolk. The wish to see the situation reversed is expressed in nostalgic talk about "the good old days" when all this was unheard of ... Equally, it can be argued, the hostility between men and women plus this wish-fulfillment are projected into the witchcraft beliefs ... in which men are the "real" victims but the "utopian" masters of the evil women. A final item of evidence ... lies in the identification of the head of the witches with the official head of the women traders. It relates the "projection" in a direct and overt manner to the conscious hostility and the concrete situation evoking it. (Nadel, 1952: 21, 22)

So, by using witch beliefs in such a manner, the men not only give themselves a sense of worth—they are too good to be witches—but their annual witchhunt makes them the "master" their male egos demand that they be.

The study by Kluckhohn already cited also deals with the functional aspects of witchcraft beliefs. He lists some eight possible uses of such beliefs for the Navaho. We can mention a few of these possibilities. One function, generally cited for many other societies as well, is the notion that such beliefs are an important device for explanation. They provide answers for why things happen: why a curing ceremony fails, why people get sick and die in the first place, why some unusual event occurs. Then too, the stories that describe witches and tell of their evil activities have a certain value as entertainment; they are the Navaho equivalent of the late-night mystery movie. And, importantly, these stories may have moral or educational overtones; they present and highlight the behaviors that are forbidden to normal people. They become a "morality play."

Another function suggested by Kluckhohn is the idea that individuals may utilize such beliefs to gain attention, to gain the center of the "social stage." If one is struck down by a witch (exhibiting the typical symptoms in public), one immediately secures the attention and compassion of other people as they attempt to rectify the situation. Kluckhohn suggests that most such victims are low-status individuals who are perhaps receiving less than their required share of attention from others and are utilizing the beliefs as a device with which to secure it. Finally, among other possibilities, the Navaho can employ such beliefs to allow for the expression of hostility and antagonism. During daily living, a person will build up hostility and aggressive impulses—people bug you—but because of kinship obligations and the necessity for co-operation, one cannot always strike out at those who cause such feelings. However, one can, indirectly, express the hostility by venting it onto some unnamed witch and by participating in antiwitchcraft activities. Here the expression of hostility is permitted. This is generally called the scapegoating function of witchcraft beliefs. Moreover, it is also suggested that the aggression might even be of a direct nature. One can subtly suggest that one's real target of hate might just be a witch! This is the use of innuendo. So, in terms of the needs suggested by Spiro discussed earlier, although bad supernaturalism appears to be an unreasonable way to cater to substantive desires, it may also (if out of the level of conscious awareness) function to secure cognitive and expressive needs.

MYTHOLOGY

Supernaturalism results not only in ritual practices but also in beliefs, and one form taken by these is mythology. In fact, many early students of myth felt that these beliefs and ideas were prior to ritual and that supernatural practices were simply enactments of such myths. Later on this notion was reversed—the supernatural practice serving as the stimulus for myth, to justify it. As Clyde Kluckhohn (1942) has pointed out, this controversy as to the priority of myth or ritual is not completely amenable to solution. Rather, the important thing is their interdependence; they often go together, reinforcing each other and catering to the needs of humans that are generally expressed in supernaturalism.

Myths

What is the nature of mythology and what are its varieties? William Bascom has discussed myth in terms of a larger context of prose narratives—a " . . . category of verbal art which includes myths, legends, and folktales. These three forms are related to each other in that they are narratives in prose, and this fact distinguishes them from . . . other forms of verbal art on the basis of strictly formal characteristics" (Bascom, 1965: 3). There are also other forms of prose narratives. As Bascom defines the three major types, they differ from each other in certain ways. "Myths are prose narratives which, in the society in which they are told, are considered to be truthful accounts of what happened in the remote past" (1965: 4). The protagonists and actors in myths are usually gods or animals, although humans may play supporting roles. The world in which the actions are set is a world different from the present, or perhaps a different world altogether: for example, the spirit world. As Bascom points out, these myths are accepted as true and because they deal with the doings of the gods they are usually considered sacred and unquestionable as well. They may justify or be connected with ritual and they may be part of the theological system of the believing society.

Legends

"Legends are prose narratives which, like myths, are regarded as true by the narrator and his audience, but they are set in a period considered less remote, when the world was much as it is today" (1965: 4). Generally speaking, humans are the principal actors in legends, although their activities may take on a superhuman element. By this reasoning, the *Odyssey* and *Paul Bunyon* should be discussed as legends. Although considered true, legends seldom develop sacred overtones; they are more secular in nature and often comprise the folk history of some past event. They can, however, refer to less substantial subject matter.

Folktales

Finally, Bascom defines folktales as "prose narratives which are regarded as fiction" (1965: 4). Even to the people who tell and listen to them they are not considered as true but rather held in the sense of amusing stories (once upon a time, etc.). Because of this, their format is much less rigidly defined than either myth or legend. The heroes can be god or animal or human (although most often of the latter types), their setting can occur in any time or place, and, of course, they do not have sacred identifications. Aesop's fables are a good example of folktales.

Of these three types of prose narratives, myths—with their sacred and ritual connections—are of most interest to anthropologists. Social scientists in general have taken more than just a "story-line" approach to such stories. They have been perhaps even more interested in social and cultural connections. Who tells the myth, who listens, what is the occasion, how does the content reflect social and cultural behaviors, and what are the functions of myth? Students of myth with a humanities orientation are often only interested in myth as a variety of comparative literature to study. We will reproduce a single myth here (an origin myth) to indicate the flavor of such stories, and then briefly indicate a few of the functions that myth and, to a lesser degree, legends and folktales have been said to demonstrate. This myth is found among some of the intensive-fishing societies of the North Pacific coast of North America mentioned in the chapter on technology.

Before people were on the earth, the Chief of the Sky Spirits grew tired of his home in the Above World, because it was always cold up there. So he made a hole in the sky by turning a stone round and round. Through this hole he pushed snow and ice until he made a great mound that reached from the earth almost to the sky. Later, people named it Mount Shasta.

Then the Sky Spirit stepped from a cloud to the peak and walked down the mountain. When he was about halfway down to the valley below, he thought, "On this mountain there should be trees." He put his finger to the ground here and there, here and there. Wherever his finger touched the ground, a tree began to grow. In his footsteps the snow melted and the water ran down in rivers.

The Sky Spirit broke off the small end of the giant stick he had carried from the sky and threw the pieces into the rivers. The longer pieces became beaver and otter; the smaller pieces became fish. From the big end of the stick he made the animals.

Biggest of them all were the grizzly bears. They were covered with hair and they had sharp claws, just as they have today, but they walked on two feet and could talk. They looked so fierce that the Sky Spirit sent them away from him, to live in the forest at the base of the mountain.

When the leaves dropped from the trees, he picked them up, blew upon them, and so made the birds.

Then the Chief of the Sky Spirits decided to stay on the earth, and to bring his family down from the sky. The mountain became their lodge. He made a big fire in the center of the mountain and a hole in the top so that the smoke and sparks could fly out. When he put a big log on the fire, sparks would fly up and the earth would tremble.

Late one spring, while the Sky Spirit and his family were sitting around the fire, the Wind Spirit sent a big storm that shook the top of the mountain. It blew and blew, and roared and roared. Smoke blown back into the lodge hurt their eyes. At last the Sky Spirit said to his youngest daughter, "Go up to the smoke hole and ask the Wind Spirit to blow more gently. Tell him I am afraid he will blow the mountain over."

His little daughter was glad to go. As she started, her father spoke again, "Be careful when you get to the top. Don't put your head out. If you do put it out, the wind may catch you by your hair and blow you away. Just thrust out your arm, make a sign and then speak to the Wind Spirit."

The little girl hurried to the top of the mountain and spoke to the Wind Spirit. As she was about to start back, she remembered that her father had said the ocean could be seen from the top of their lodge. He had made the ocean since the family moved from the sky, and his daughter had never seen it.

She put her head out of the hole and looked toward the west. The Wind Spirit caught her long hair, pulled her out of the mountain and blew her down over the snow and ice. She landed among the scrubby fir trees at the edge of the timber and snow line, her long red hair trailing over the snow.

There Grizzly Bear found her when he was out hunting food for his family. He carried the little girl home with him, wondering who and what she was. Mother Bear took good care of her and brought her up with their family of cubs. The little red-haired girl and the cubs ate together, played together and grew up together.

When she became a young woman, she and the eldest son of the grizzly bears were married. In the years that followed they had many children. The children did not look like their father or like their mother. They were not so hairy as the grizzlies and yet they did not look like spirits either.

All the grizzly bears throughout the forest were proud of these new creatures. They were so pleased and were so kindhearted that they made a lodge for the red-haired mother and her strange looking children. They built the lodge near Mount Shasta—Little Mount Shasta it is called today.

After many years had passed, Mother Grizzly Bear knew that she would soon die. Fearing that she had done wrong in keeping the daughter of the Chief of the Sky Spirits away from her father, she felt that she should send him word and ask his forgiveness. So she asked all the grizzlies to join her at the new lodge they had built. Then she sent her oldest grandson to the top of Mount Shasta, in a cloud, to tell the Spirit Chief where he could find his long-lost daughter.

The father was so glad that he came down the mountainside in giant strides. He hurried so fast that the snow melted off in places under his feet. Even today his tracks can be seen in the rocky path on the south side of Mount Shasta.

As he neared the lodge, he called out, "Is this where my little daughter lives?"

He expected to see a little girl exactly as she had looked when he saw her last. When he saw the strange creatures his daughter was taking care of and learned that they were his grandchildren, he was very angry. A new race had been created, and he had not known about it. He frowned on the old grandmother so sternly that she died at once. Then he cursed all the grizzlies.

"Get down on your hands and knees. From this moment all of you grizzlies shall walk on four feet. And you shall never talk again. You have wronged me."

He drove his grandchildren out of the lodge, put his daughter over his shoulder and climbed back up the mountain. Never again did he come to the forest. Some say that he put out the fire in the center of his lodge and took his daughter back up to the sky to live.

Those strange creatures, his grandchildren, scattered and wandered all over the earth. They were the first Indians, the ancestors of all the Indian tribes.

That is why the Indians living around Mount Shasta would never kill a grizzly bear. Whenever one of them was killed by a grizzly, his body was burned on the spot. And for many years all who passed that way cast a stone there until a great pile of stones marked the place of his death (*Indian Legends of the Pacific Northwest*, edited by Ella E. Clark, University of California Press, 1958: 9)

FUNCTIONS OF MYTHOLOGY

Using the above myth, we can illustrate two of the most common functions of mythology. One is that myths can serve as devices for *explanation*. Why are things the way they are? Where did we come from? Why are humans better than animals but less than the gods? In the above myth, humans were born of animal and goddess, so they have a mixed—"in between"—nature. Why are the gods no longer on earth? Because they were wronged when they were here and went back to their own world. This certainly fits well with the concept of cognitive needs as defined by Spiro. Another function is *entertainment*, although this would seldom be the main value of myths. Lacking the many diversions of modern society, primitive people can recite these stories, like those of witchcraft indicated earlier, to pass the time away in a pleasant manner. They are not just stories, they are artistic stories filled with adventure and marvelous happenings.

Myths not only explain why things are the way they are, but also become kind of a charter for traditional behavior. Thus, mythology may also have a function in *validation*.

Myth, as a statement of primeval reality, which still lives in a present-day life and as a justification by precedent, supplies a retrospective pattern of moral values, sociological order and magical belief. It is, therefore, neither a mere narrative, nor a form of science, nor a branch of art or history, not an explanatory tale ... The function of myth, briefly, is to strengthen tradition and endow it with a greater value and prestige by tracing it back to a higher, better, more supernatural reality of initial events. (Malinowski, 1954: 146)

In this sense, myths can also play a role in *education*; since they convey values and information, they can be utilized as pedagogic devices for transmitting such knowledge from generation to generation, as well as reinforcing the behaviors of adults. Finally, among many other possibilities, myths and other prose narratives can serve certain psychological functions, the most obvious perhaps being that of *escapism*. These stories reveal humans' frustrations and their attempts to retreat in fantasy from the rules and regulations imposed by society, as well as from their own personal failures. This might be called the Cinderella function and is perhaps the equivalent of our own James Bond escape-reading tactics. At least in such stories we can escape from our own reality in vicarious fashion.

We have briefly and incompletely surveyed a few of the forms of supernaturalism and dealt with magical and religious practice and belief from a functional point of view. It has been suggested that humans live "not by bread alone," but have needs and desires that science alone cannot completely gratify or not meet at all. Our own current revival of supernaturalism in young people in the Jesus Movement, and in people of all ages with reference to interest in the occult, is testimony for this idea. Supernaturalism is alive and well in rational, technological America just as it was and is in the primitive societies of the world.

SUMMARY

1. Primitive religions differ from those of the modern world in a number of respects: there is no sense of historical development, they are localized and tolerant, and they are often inconsistent theologically.

2. Religion is the belief in the existence of supernatural beings and the practices associated with relating to those beings. Its characteristics (ideally) are supplication, emotionalism, public- and group-oriented behaviors, and often other-worldly motivations. Magic—supernatural techniques through which humans can accomplish things beyond ordinary capability—is manipulative, impersonal, private, and individualistic—behaviors that are specifically goal-oriented and often antisocial.

3. Both religion and magic are manifestations of the supernatural view. Both supernaturalism and naturalism are found in all societies in various combinations.

4. Supernaturalism in either manifestation helps to alleviate human frustration in areas of unpredictability or dubious control. They meet cognitive, substantive, and expressive needs and serve adjustive, adaptive, and integrative functions.

5. The two major practitioners of the supernatural are the Shaman (associated with magic) and the priest (associated with religious practices). They differ in the derivation and scope of powers, and in the forms of their behaviors.

6. Ritual practices fall into three major categories based upon the scheduling and causes of such activities. These are critical, cyclical, and calendrical rites; each has many specific forms of expression.

7. Supernatural beliefs and practices may also be antisocial and take the forms of witchcraft and sorcery, depending upon the innateness or learned quality of the behaviors involved. The mere belief in witches may perform powerful functions for the members of a society.

8. Mythology—myths, legends, and folktales—serve functions of explanation, entertainment, education, escapism, and the validation of behavior.

REFERENCES FOR FURTHER READING

There are a great many excellent books on supernaturalism. Some of the best general texts include the following. An engagingly written text is *The Heathens*, by William Howells (1948, Doubleday). A somewhat more structured account is that of Edward Norbeck, *Religion in Primitive Society* (1961, Harper). The most speculative introduction is *Religion: An Anthropological View*, by Anthony F. C. Wallace (1966, Random House). *Religion Among the Primitives*, by W. J. Goode (1951, Free Press), is the source of many differences between magic and religion. Two other texts written basically from nonanthropological points of view and of great value are *The Sacred and the Profane*, by Mircea Eliade (1961, Harper), and *Understanding Religious Man*, by F. J. Streng, (1969, Dickenson).

Collections of readings abound on this topic. Perhaps the standard is *Reader in Comparative Religion*, edited by W. Lessa and E. Vogt (1965, Harper & Row), now available in a revised paperback edition. Three readers, all published by Natural History Press and all edited by John Middleton, are: *God and Rituals; Magic, Witchcraft and Curing;* and *Myth and Cosmos*, all published in 1967. Talcott Parsons' idea of the religious functions is suggested in his article "Sociology and Social Psychology," in *Religious Perspectives in College Teaching*, edited by H. Fairchild, pp. 286–305, (1952, Ronald Press). A more comprehensive article by Melford Spiro, is "Religion: Problems of Definition and Explanation" in Association of Social Anthropologists monograph no. 3, *Anthropological Approaches to the Study of Religion*, pp. 85–126 (1966, Praeger). In the same volume, pp. 1–41, is an excellent article by Clifford

Geertz, "Religion as a Cultural System", which deals with problems of the content and definition of religion.

The quotation on shamans and priests is from S. F. Nadel, "A Study of Shamanism in the Nuba Mountains," in *Journal of the Royal Anthropological Institute* 76 (1946): 25–37. The most comprehensive study of shamanism is Mircea Eliade, *Shamanism* (1964, Princeton University Press) and a comparable study of priests is presented in E. O. James, *The Nature and Function of Priesthood* (1955, Vanguard Press). An intriguing approach to supernatural practices is taken by Victor Turner in *The Ritual Process* (1969, Aldine). The specific material on divination cited in the text is from Barrie Reynolds, *Magic, Divination, and Witchcraft Among the Barotse of Northern Rhodesia* (1963, University of California Press). The description and quotes on initiation rites is from *The Australian Aborigines*, by A. P. Elkin (1964, Doubleday). The Ainu calendrical ritual is from Joseph Kitagawa, "Ainu Bear Festival" (Iyomante), in *History of Religions* 1 (1960): 95–151. The material on witchcraft and sorcery is enormous. The best introduction is that of Lucy Mair, *Witchcraft* (1969, McGraw-Hill), and the best specific-readings book is *Witchcraft and Sorcery*, edited by Max Marwick (1970, Penguin Books); the quotation from Philip Meyer, "Witches," is from this text, pp. 45–64. The data on witch beliefs and functions among the Navaho is from Clyde Kluckhohn, "Navaho Witchcraft," in *Peabody Museum Papers*, no. 22 (1944 Cambridge). The Nupe example and quotation comes from S. F. Nadel, "Witchcraft in Four African Societies: An Essay in Comparison," in *American Anthropologist* (1952): 18–29.

There are many texts dealing with myth from various perspectives. Three of these are useful paperbacks: *The Making of Myth*, edited by Richard Ohman (1962, G. P. Putnam's), *Myth, A Symposium*, edited by Thomas Scheok (1970, Indiana University Press), and *Studies on Mythology*, edited by Robert Georges (1968, Dorsey Press). The quotations in the text are from "The Forms of Folklore: Prose Narratives," by William Bascom, in *Journal of American Folklore*, 78, no. 307 (1965): 3–20; and *Magic, Science and Religion*, by Bronislaw Malinowski (1954, Doubleday). A most excellent collection of prose narratives is by Stith Thompson, ed., *Tales of the North American Indians* (1968, Indiana University Press).

24 language

We have already briefly described a number of systems of cultural behavior. We can turn now to yet another system, that of human language. **Language** is so common a behavior that we who use it seldom reflect upon it. And yet, from a number of points of view, language is our most important cultural possession. It is and has been our most important way of communicating information. As such, it is the most important way in which human culture itself is learned and transmitted from generation to generation. This being so, and the acquisition of culture supplying the major arena for human behavior—that which makes us different from other animals—then it is the possession of language that has "made" the human species.

If we tend to take language for granted, there is also the notion that a particular language is somehow innate, that we are born speaking English or Eskimo. This feeling is perhaps due to the fact that the young child is already adept at speaking his language by age four and that we seem to be able to use language quickly and effortlessly without having to put much conscious thought into the process—"but how hard it is to learn a foreign language." Nonetheless, specific language behaviors, as well as linguistic communication itself (like the rest of culture), must be learned, and if we do not recall our own first clumsy attempts, we can find them amusing in our own children. Our own speech patterns are no more "natural" than eating with chopsticks, or tracing descent matrilineally! Another common misconception is the notion that some languages—those of industrialized peoples—are "better" or more developed than those found in the primitive world. After all, is not French the language of love? Such a view is incorrect. Primitive people do not speak by grunts and gestures. Every human language known appears to be capable of expressing much the same things, if in a somewhat different manner. They have equal potentialities. This does not imply that they have an equal number of sounds and vocabulary items or that their structures operate the same. Some have demonstrably fewer words and expressions. And different languages certainly reflect the concerns of the speakers in terms of what *they* feel is important to communicate. Yet, for reasons that will shortly be observed, they can quickly increase their potential for communication if necessary and can effectively adapt what they already possess. Although language may indeed have been "less developed" at some time in the past, this is surely not the case for any human group at present. Linguistic ethnocentrism is clearly inappropriate.

How long has language been in the possession of the human species? This is a matter of some debate. The issue generally hinges on the question of how much culture must exist to reflect the facilitating influence of language. Some writers suggest that developed languages (like those existing today) can only be ascertained by looking at technological advances as these are revealed in the record of archaeology. The late Paleolithic period is often given as a likely point in time. This would correlate with the arrival of modern humans on the scene. Languages of undeveloped types are conceded as being earlier. Other scholars have suggested that since much of human culture cannot be directly fossilized—social and other behaviors—developed human language probably goes back still earlier in time. Could the Neanderthals have conceived of a necessity to bury their dead without its use? A few writers even hold that humans became distinctive in their reliance upon tools only because of the presence of a developed form of communication. This suggests that the earliest tool traditions reflect language of a modern type. The most certain fact here is that we will probably never be able to pinpoint either the precise time of the development of language or the stages of that development. All we can say is that the languages presently amenable to study are "mature" and are equally valuable systems.

TYPES OF LANGUAGE STUDY

Language itself is the object of attention in the field of study known as linguistics. Such a study, of course, is not limited to anthropology. Many linguists are not anthropologists, and the pursuit of language study is prior to the development of the field of anthropology. Anthropologists became interested in language as part of their fieldwork experiences and the necessity to learn and understand the unwritten languages of primitive peoples. As opposed to the linguist who studies language per se, the anthropological linguist is equally interested in relating language analysis to the rest of culture. The study of language has become more a means to other ends than an end in itself. Linguistic study basically falls into two branches: *structural* linguistics deals primarily with language at a given point in time and inspects the nature or construction of language; *historical* linguistics deals with the changes in language over time and the relations among languages. Since such studies have been pursued and refined for some time, the number of technical terms is enormous. The present chapter, then, will necessarily take a very simplistic approach.

UNIQUENESS OF LANGUAGE COMMUNICATION

As the basic mode of human communication, language is a unique phenomenon. This is not to suggest that other animals lack communication, only that their systems are not like human language in terms of sophistication, flexibility, and complexity.

> Language is a purely human and noninstinctive method of communicating ideas, emotions, and desires by means of a system of voluntarily produced symbols. These symbols are in the first instance, auditory and they are produced by the so-called "organs of speech." There is no discernible instinctive basis in human speech as such . . . Such human or animal communication, if "communication" it may be called, as is brought about by involuntary, instinctive cries is no, in our sense, language at all. (Sapir, 1949: 8)

How can this fundamental difference be conveyed? There are two somewhat different approaches towards indicating the gap between human and other animal comunication systems. The first is to make the assertion that the content of human language is *symbolic* communication. This is an approach taken by Leslie White. As he states the situation, "A symbol may be defined as a thing the value or meaning of which is bestowed upon it by those who use it. . . . The meaning or value . . . is in no instance derived from or determined by properties intrinsic in its physical form . . . [although] . . . All symbols must have a physical form otherwise they could not enter our experience" (White, 1949: 25). For example, mere inspection of the peace symbol recently worn by many college students could not reveal its meaning—it could as well be a neat "one-hamburger-at-a-time" barbecue grill! There is nothing inherent in the red traffic light that means stop; or in the sound "tree" or the American flag, to indicate what they stand for. The value and meaning in these cases have been determined by the humans who employ these things. White then discusses the concept of a *sign*, which he also defines as a physical thing that functions to indicate something. But in this case, the meaning or value is either inherent in, or identified with, its physical form. This at first appears confusing since we do respond to the sound "tree" and the traffic light in sign fashion. And for humans there does exist this overlap between symbol and sign.

> But a thing which in one context is a symbol is, in another context, not a symbol but a sign. Thus, a word is a symbol only when one is concerned with the distinction between its meaning and its physical form. This distinction must be made when one bestows value upon a sound-combination or when a previously bestowed value is discovered for the first time; it may be made at other times for certain purposes. But after value has been bestowed upon, or discovered in, a word its meaning becomes identified, in use, with its physical form. The word then functions as a sign, rather than a symbol. Its meaning is then grasped with the senses. (White, 1949: 26, 27)

Thus, things like words in language are both symbols and signs to human beings. We bestow value and meaning and then respond to them as signs because the meanings have become identified with the sounds. And, of course, with this symbolic faculty, we can alter meanings or invent new ones all the time; we can symbolize whenever it becomes necessary for communication.

White seems to suggest that no other animals can duplicate this process. Other animals can respond to signs or react to new ones (I call my dog home by saying, "Rover, come home"), but they cannot "create and bestow" the value and meaning. They are, so to speak, passive in their processes of communication. Baboons have calls for food, danger, etc., but baboons did not assign the meanings for these —"ooga-ooga will stand for danger." Apparently, their biology has assigned these meanings, just as when we place our hand on a hot stove we cry out—every one else recognizes our pain even though we didn't say, "a scream will indicate pain." Humans are active in communication, giving symbolic substance to their signs, and therein is contained the difference in communication.

A second way to access human and nonhuman communication is supplied by Charles Hockett in an article dealing with the origins of speech. He pursues what can be called a design-feature approach. This is " . . . the basic features of design that can be present or absent in any communicative system, whether it be a communicative system of humans, of animals or of machines" (Hockett, 1960: 3). Although he employs this approach in the attempt to see how human language may have developed from earlier forms, we can cite a few of these features to indicate communication system differences. Hockett considers human language to have thirteen design features. Some other animals (primates) may have as many as ten of these, but most creatures have to make do with far fewer. The possession of all thirteen in human language makes it unique. One of these features is called *displacement*. This means that the message being communicated can refer to things remote in space and/or time in reference to where/when the communication takes place. I can talk about the final exam well in advance of giving it ("there will be" as opposed to "here it is"), and I can talk about something not physically in sight, like the library. Displacement gives the communication process great advantages. One can "program" the young of the species for events or situations they have yet to encounter, greatly aiding their adaptation. We can acquire information and then retain it for later communication. Most primates appear to lack this trait. If a baboon, for example, sees a stalking leopard, he emits the danger call immediately—in the ear of the leopard; he doesn't creep back and whisper the information and may pay the obvious price. Bees, on the other hand, do appear to exhibit this feature since in their "dancing" both the direction and distance of flower pollen are roughly communicated to other bees.

Another design feature is *productivity:* " . . . the capacity to say things that have never been said or heard before and yet be understood by other speakers of the language" (Hockett, 1960: 4). Humans, because of their symbolizing faculty, are constantly saying new things by rearranging old things in new ways. Instead of being a closed system of calls—either danger or sex—our system of communication enables us to talk about dangerous sex or sexy danger. Again, if productivity characterizes the communication system, then its users have no limitations on what can be communicated and dealt with. A third design feature is *specialization*. In essence this means that the " . . . bodily effort and spreading sound waves of speech serve no function except as signals" (Hockett, 1960: 4). As Hockett puts it, a panting dog may communicate that it is hot, but the energy expenditure and sound are biological activities. Moreover, in human language, although body effort is expended primarily for communication purposes, it is also rather slight: we can talk all day long without burning up too many calories. Bee dancing, on the other hand, is pure energy, and (after the first few minutes) they would not make lively guests on a television talk show! Perhaps the less energy expended the better the communication system.

Finally, among other features is the idea of *interchangeability*. This means that the species member can both send and receive messages. I can communicate to you, and you (if you understand) can communicate back to me. Most animals have this rather basic feature, but some species of crickets appear to lack it, only males being capable of generating messages. The main idea, then, is that, by possession of all thirteen features, human linguistic communication becomes demonstrably superior to that of other creatures, even though some communication overlap occurs. Although a skateboard and a car both possess wheels and a "floorboard," the car's possession of additional features, such as an engine, makes all the difference in the world when it comes to transportation. So also with human language. We may now examine the structural nature of language itself.

THE NATURE OF HUMAN LANGUAGE

What exactly is the nature of human language? It often appears, on hearing a foreign language, to be just noise, and so it is, although it might be better to say it is meaningful sound. And, indeed, almost any kind of sound that the human vocal apparatus can make is probably used in some way in some human language. Many discrete and recognizable sounds can be produced by utilizing the so-called organs of speech: the lips, tongue, palate, nose, etc. After sound is produced, these organs "chop it up" into the distinctive and repeated sounds utilized by each particular language. They do this by modifying " . . . the shape of the air passages and cavities open to it. Thus, if voice is produced by the vocal cords, the sound will be quite different according as the oral passages, the nasal passage, or both are open to it, and according to the shape of the oral passage" (Gleason, 1955: 193). Although all discussion of mechanics for producing this rich variety of sounds is beyond the scope of this chapter, it can be noted that no language employs more than perhaps thirty to fifty such sound possibilities. Those utilized become distinctive and repeated by the speakers of a language and are called phonemes. For example, in English: /k/, /t/, /s/. There are sound variations for each phoneme.

Sounds by themselves, however, are only a place to begin. As such, phonemes usually do not occur singly but appear in combinations or sequences, and, just as there are limits as to which phoneme possibilities a language employs, so also are there traditions for establishing these sequences. Speakers of English recognize *gone* but not *ngoe*, even though they can produce this sequence. So there exist certain conventions with regard to phoneme order. Since our alphabet does not perfectly equate with the phonemes of English (forty-six in all), linguists have utilized the International Phonetic Alphabet (IPA) to aid them in recording the sounds of language. So, for example, to see the different "pronounciations" of *just*, the linguist may write / jɘst/ or /jɨst/. Think of the different sounds at the ends of *dogs* and *cats*. The initial *th* sound between *thy* and *thigh* is represented by the symbols ᴆ and ⊖ . Such symbols permit recording of all sound possibilities.

Why is it that a language can make do with only a relatively few phonemes? It is because of their countless possibilities for combination despite some limitations. So, for example, the word *pin*, by substituting the initial phoneme, can become *bin, kin, sin, din*, etc. Or, often, the phoneme order can be reversed with *pin* becoming *nip*. So, although there are relatively few phonemes, their combinations yield numerous possibilities. When arranged together in their distinctive "shapes," the phonemes form what linguists call morphemes, repeated and distinctive sequences of phonemes that have a meaning. We are now dealing with what has traditionally been called the grammar of language. Upon reflection it becomes apparent that these morphemes are not always words; they are merely what is significant grammatically and may even consist of a single phoneme: for example *a* as in *a* dog, or the *s* that comes after *cat* in *cats*. This leads to the linguistic distinction between what are called free and bound morphemes. A *free* morpheme is one that can stand by itself; it can occur independently. Examples would be *a* or *dog*. A *bound* morpheme occurs only in combination with other morphemes: for example, the *s* in cats. Bound morphemes have, so to speak, grammatical but not independent meaning by themselves; in the example, *s* indicates the plural. A more complicated morpheme series would be found in *unlovingly*, in which only *love* is a free morpheme.

Just as there are conventions for placing phonemes into sequences, so also are there rules for arranging morphemes into words and sentences and longer linguistic utterances. These, of course, like the sounds themselves, vary from language to language in the details of their construction. So, for example, German verbs are often placed at the end of the sentence. Within any given language the rules governing the pattern of morphemes (*syntax*) exercise a kind of subtle tyranny over its speakers; to deviate very much is to destroy the communicational meaning. If I say "the jumped dog over the table" by reversing the normal order of *dog* and *jumped*, I seem to be referring to a particular dog rather than any action. Although what I meant to say might be figured out by my listeners, if I said "the dog table over the jumped," I make no sense at all. Meaning can also be altered in terms of how the units themselves are put together, even if in the correct order. These "junctural" phenomena are also considered by linguists to be phonemic and make the difference between *I scream* and *ice cream*. There is a more open transition in the first case. Such juncture can also occur at the end of sentences, and fading or raising of the sound can alter the meaning significantly. *What are we having for dinner, mother?* is different from *what are we having for dinner?, mother*. This, too, is classified as phonemic phenomena and aids the linguist in the analysis of language. In terms of what has been said, the structure of language can be over-simply defined as sounds arranged into shapes that make

The English language has changed so much since its origination that it is nearly impossible to "translate" an Old English piece of writing.

The Granger Collection

sense; phonemes arranged into morphemes that are combined to convey meanings.

LANGUAGE CHANGE

It is the student of historical linguistics who is interested in language change and comparisons. Although we may think of our language at present as being a static phenomenon, it is, nonetheless, undergoing continual changes—out of the awareness of its speakers, for the most part—in sound, shape, and sense. Except for things such as an obviously borrowed word or the invention of a new one, change is only discernible when we use hindsight, when we inspect a language at widely separated points in time. We can also use the comparative method to discover similar words (*cognates*) having phonemic and meaning correspondences in different languages: for example, English *brother*, *father*, and *man* versus German *Bruder*, *Vater*, and *Mann*. Because of these and other correspondences, these languages are seen as being related and must both be derived from some earlier common language. It should be mentioned that the degree of correspondence must include more than just a few similarities that might otherwise be due to chance.

The comparative method is valuable inasmuch as it permits comparison of languages not represented by writing systems. Comparison of a language to its earlier manifestation does require written documentation, and, given the recent development of writing systems and their lack of universality with respect to languages, this severely limits the field of possibilities. English is the usually cited example. Its initial records go back to about 900 A.D. and, with only a few gaps, run up to the present—modern English beginning about 1550. In less

451

than one thousand years the changes have been so great as to render the reading of an Old English document almost an impossibility for most of us today. For example, one wore *shoon* instead of shoes and lived in a *hus* rather than a house, and man was still *mann*. Indeed, as Sapir has so neatly characterized it:

> Language moves down time in a current of its own making. It has a drift. If there were no breaking up of a language into dialects ... it would still be constantly moving away from any assignable norm, developing new features unceasingly and gradually transforming itself into a language so different from its starting point as to be in effect a new language. ... The drift of a language is constituted by the unconscious selection on the part of its speakers of those individual variations that are cumulative in some special direction. ... In the long run any new feature of the drift becomes part and parcel of the common, accepted speech, but for a long time it may exist as a mere tendency in the speech of a few ... (Sapir, 1949: 150, 155)

This brings up the question of how language change comes about. Sapir suggests that the process is both individual and unconscious. Certainly, the "board of language control" is not responsible for such changes. In the process of learning and using language, many changes occur, and these may happen basically in two ways. External change involves receiving elements from outside the language (or dialect). For example, the word garage coming into Old English from French. Changes may also be internal, worked out from within by the members of that speech community. One source for these changes is what might be called mistakes, which linguists call *analogical replacement*. By analogy with other "correct" forms, a speaker is apt to transfer this use inappropriately. For example, dog–dogs, cat–cats, and octopus–octopuses, instead of octopi or octopodes. At some juncture in time, one of these forms is seen as better than the others and the new form becomes part of the language behavior. Will oxes replace oxen?

Since language has meaning, the morphemes can be conservative or their significance can be altered. The meaning, for example, can become more restricted. *Garage* in Old English meant any kind of storage place; today (what with old newspapers and all) it is more specifically a place for the family car. This is called *narrowing*. Another type of change in meaning is *degeneration*. Here the meaning of a particular word becomes unfavorable (*madam* as the keeper of a brothel) and is not used in its former contexts. Such linguistic preferences may involve more acceptable substitutions, although to someone learning the language such usage is not always well communicated. So at a recent party my son bursts into the room and announces to all, "Dad I have to piss"—"You mean you have to use the bathroom", say I.

"Yeah, that's what I said." Then, too, among many other possibilities, is the change called *widening*. Here the meaning becomes expanded in scope, the oft-cited example being barn–coming from an Old English word (*bern*) meaning a place to specifically store barley. Here again, however, the changes are by use and are validated by use, not by official decree.

LEXICOSTATISTICS

Deriving from the use of the comparative method in linguistics has been the grouping of languages into various related groupings or "family trees." A recent application, one of great potential value despite shortcomings attributed to it, is what has been called lexicostatistics (or glottochronology). It attempts to date the times of divergence or separation of different related languages based upon the ratio of retention of words in them. The words selected for analysis and comparison are said to be those forming a basic vocabulary relating to fundamental aspects of human existence—words for body parts, sun, rain, women, etc. These so-called "culture free" words will occur in all languages, and the technique employs a list that numbers from 100 to 200 items. Words in this basic vocabulary appear to be retained in the language at a constant rate; about eighty-one percent of the terms remain per thousand years of time. It is suggested that this rate is approximately the same in all languages. The statistics are based upon languages for which the history is fairly well known. By comparison of the cognate words for these basic items between two languages we can calculate the number of years of separation. This technique is a "carbon-14" method for language, and if the concept can withstand criticism, promises to be a great aid to the linguist. We can now turn to another aspect of language.

THE RELATION OF LANGUAGE AND CULTURE

It has already been pointed out that all languages are adequate for the needs of the people who speak them, that languages reflect what these speakers feel is necessary to communicate. Language and culture are related. Some writers have suggested that language does more than just communicate—that it defines the means by which human beings apprehend the nature of the world. Benjamin Lee Whorf has pointed out that people have always thought that thinking and interpretation of reality were somehow independent of language rather than a special-ized extension of language. He disputes this notion. The grammar

> ... of each language is not merely a reproducing instrument for voicing ideas but rather is itself the shaper of ideas, the program and guide for the individual's mental activity, for his analysis of impressions, for his synthesis of his mental stock in trade. Formulation of ideas is not an independent process ... but is part of a particular grammar, and differs, from slightly to greatly, between different grammars. We dissect nature along lines laid down by our native languages. The categories and types that we isolate from the world of phenomena we do not find there be-cause they stare every observer in the face ... We cut nature up, organize it into concepts, and ascribe significances as we do, largely because we are parties to an agreement to organize it in this way—an agreement that holds throughout our speech community and is codified in the patterns of our language. (Whorf, 1957: 212, 213)

In other words, he is suggesting that humans do not see the same reality, merely placing different labels on it, but that they apprehend a somewhat different reality altogether. Put simply, if I speak a language with a triangular structure, do I perceive the nature of reality as triangu-lar, and if a square structure, that same reality as square? We are con-strained, says Whorf, in the dissection of nature by the particular mechanics supplied to us by our language.

The proof of this idea, called the **Sapir-Whorf hypothesis** (also after Edward Sapir who aided in its formulation) is difficult to come by. Do speakers of different languages really perceive a different reality? Possibilities are numerous, but their true significance is a matter of contention. The Eskimo, for example, have a number of separate words for snow (falling snow, crusty snow, etc.) whereas speakers of English have but one. This enables the Eskimo to speak of environmental con-ditions with great precision, but does this also indicate a different opera-tional reality for them? Again, the Hopi Indians class together all flying objects (except birds) under a single term; airplane, pilot, and insect together! Do they see flying differently from ourselves? Hopi is also traditionally cited as an example of a "timeless" language. As opposed to the verbs of such languages as English that treat time as a divisible entity having a past, present, and future, Hopi verbs have to get along without such tenses. Their verbs do, however, indicate the suggestion of the validity intended by the speaker of some statement: it is a factual report of an event or the expectation of it (instead of present and future). Do time and validity say the same things? Once an anthropologist studying a society that spoke a "timeless" language was sitting with his informant for an extended period. As they sat he kept probing for reactions to time. "Is time passing slowly?" "Is time dragging for you too?" And, finally, in desperation: "Time is like a river, isn't it?" After

Anthropology

人类觉学

outline

As an extralinguistic form of communication, writing is dependent on the spoken word. Compare these different ways of translating speaking to writing. (Left to right: English, Chinese, shorthand.)

much reflection the informant replied, "No, I am the river." Does this mean that he perceived reality differently from the English-speaking anthropologist? Does he move while all about him is static? This hypothesis is very suggestive but cannot be accepted as clearly proven at the present time. The notion has, however, stimulated much research in the area of language and culture interrelations.

OTHER FORMS OF HUMAN COMMUNICATION

Extralinguistic

All human societies communicate by the use of language. In addition to language, many societies possess what might be called extralinguistic forms of communication. These forms are not themselves language, but they do depend upon language for their existence. We might think of them as secondary symbol systems; they represent language that is in itself symbolic. In such systems, language is represented graphically or by some other means. Writing is the oldest of these means. Since almost everyone in our society learns to read and write, we often confuse language and writing, thinking of them as the "spoken," as opposed to the "written," language. From what has been said above, this is clearly inappropriate since language is sounds arranged into shapes that make sense and writing merely a graphic representation (and an imperfect one) of language.

We have noted, in the first part of this text, that writing systems are recent in development and, in the present chapter, that not all peoples possess them. Most primitive peoples known to anthropologists are nonliterate. We have also noted that attempts at graphic representation began as picture-writing. True writing develops when the written symbols come to represent sound features in language. Such symbols may represent morphemes (7) or they may have phonemic reference (b). When a writing system predominantly represents individual phonemes, it is alphabetic writing. Chinese is usually cited as a case in which the majority of the written symbols represent morphemes. This necessitates a large inventory of symbols but can yield certain advantages.

> China is today ... a country in which a number of languages ... are spoken. Many of them do, however, have certain basic similarities, which are produced in part by common origin and in part by common civilization. The result is that the morpheme inventories can be more or less matched up. On this basis ... any morpheme in any Chinese language can be written by using a character which a neighboring language would use of a morpheme of the same meaning. Thus the grapheme 人 is used in each language for some specific morpheme having the meaning "man." (Gleason, 1955: 308, 309)

He goes on to suggest that Europeans do the same thing with $2 + 3 = 5$, each being read in a specific language differently.

Writing is certainly a valuable supplement to language. Especially when coupled with the means of duplicating written records, it greatly aids the diffusion of information without necessitating intermediaries (such as teachers) or face-to-face contact. We can read the newspaper, a book on beekeeping, or write a letter to our love. Writing also aids us in supplementing memory. Whereas nonliterate peoples must rely upon the resources of their own memories, aided perhaps by mnemonic (memory) devices, we can store up information for retrieval at some point in the future, say the night before the final exam. Seen this way, a library is a kind of artificial "group memory." So there is great value in possessing a writing system. It may not be an unmitigated blessing, however. It has become, say some critics, one of the contributing factors in the development of impersonality in the modern world. This is perhaps made less so by the recent development of visual media, (movies and television), which bring us back to the primacy of language itself.

Nonlinguistic

There also exist what might be called nonlinguistic forms of communication. These are often "packaged" with language but are not dependent upon it. If we are aware of these forms, they increase the content of linguistic communication. They are most often represented by gestures and body movements and comprise what is popularly (and incorrectly) called body language. The study of communication through body motion is technically called *kinesics*. Some gestures or movements are easily recognized: for example, the thumbing of a hitchhiker, or an obscene

Body movements and gestures can effectively communicate without speaking. Left, a conductor uses non-linguistic communication in conducting a symphony. Right, a religious group communicates elemental concepts in nonverbal forms.

"giving them the finger." Others are less obvious—the closing of books and putting away of pencils five minutes before the end of class. Still other movements, like a moderately furrowed brow or a shoulder twitch may only reveal meaning after one has made a special study of the context and situation. Is it possible to know if a person is "on the make" just by observing their body motion? Some students of this area of communication believe so. Some scholars (Birdwhistell, 1970) have developed an approach for studying kinesics similar to that of language itself, breaking down the flow of action into distinctive repeated units (*kines*). This promises to be an exciting area of inquiry since it will have great practical value for fields such as psychiatry and for the general understanding of human behavior.

Proxemics

Stimulated by developing fields such as kinesics, other scholars have attempted to see if communication value exists in other neglected areas of research. One writer, Edward T. Hall (1969), has begun to examine the use of space by human beings. He calls this **proxemics**. Based on an appreciation of theories on territoriality in other animals, he has developed the idea that in our encounters with other human beings we maintain certain spacing arrangements. These are reflected in *intimate distance* (close contact, up to eighteen inches), *personal distance* (normal spacing, eighteen inches to four feet), *social distance* (beyond touch, four feet to twelve feet), and *public distance* (outside the circle of involvement, twelve feet plus). How we utilize this space is part of our general process of communication.

> ... how people are feeling toward each other at the time is a decisive factor in the distance used. Thus people who are very angry or emphatic

about the point they are making will move in close, they "turn up the volume," as it were, by shouting. Similarly—as any woman knows—one of the first signs that a man is beginning to feel amorous is his move closer to her. If the woman does not feel similarly disposed she signals this by moving back. (Hall, 1969: 114)

Like body movements, the use of space varies crossculturally from one society to another. So the process of human communication is not limited to language alone, nor to writing, but involves a number of other behavioral arenas, some of which are just beginning to come under careful scrutiny—as is the area of the relation of language to the rest of culture in general.

SUMMARY

1. All languages are on the same level of development and can be used to communicate generally about the same kinds of things if necessary. Language in a developed sense possibly began as a correlate of, and necessity for, the first tool traditions of prehistory.

2. Language study falls basically into two branches: the nature of language at a given point in time—structural linguistics; and changes in language over time and language relationships—historical linguistics.

3. Language is phenomenon unique to human beings. As a form of communication it is both symbolic as well as sign-functioning, and it incorporates a series of design features that does not occur together in any other animal communication system.

4. Language consists of distinctive repeated sounds—phonemes—arranged into distinctive repeated shapes—morphemes—which, when placed into larger utterances, make sense in a given society.

5. The Sapir-Whorf hypothesis suggests that different languages may present their speakers with differing views of reality.

6. Besides linguistic communication (language), human communicators may employ other communications devices of extralinguistic and nonlinguistic natures such as writing and bodily gestures. The use of space may also have communicative potential.

REFERENCES FOR FURTHER READING

Without formal training it is difficult for the beginning student to make a great deal of sense out of linguistic theory and data. Some fairly clear introductory texts include the following. *An Introduction to Descriptive Linguistics*, by H. A. Gleason (1955, Holt); *A Course in Modern Linguistics*, by C. F. Hockett (1958, Macmillan); *Aspects of Language*, by D. Balinger (1968; Harcourt Brace Jovanovich); the classic *Language*, by Edward Sapir (1949, Harcourt, Brace & World); and especially useful is *Anthropological Linguistics*, by Joseph Greenberg (1968, Random House). *The Story of Language*, by Mario Pei (1966, Mentor Books), has been condemned by some linguistics but should certainly whet the appetite of the reader for more substantial linguistic fare. Perhaps the best nontechnical account is *Linguistics and Your Language*, by Robert A. Hall, Jr. (1950, Doubleday). A more specific collection of readings in language is *Universals of Language*, edited by Joseph Greenberg (1966, MIT Press), which contains some very useful articles.

The quotations on human versus nonhuman communication are from Leslie White, *The Symbol: The Origin and Basis of Human Behavior*, from his book the *Science of Culture*, pp. 22–39 (1949, Farrar, Straus); and Charles D. Hockett," The Origin of Speech," in *Scientific American*, September, 1960. Two excellent texts on historical linguistics are W. P. Lehmann, *Historical Linguistics: An Introduction* (1962, Holt, Rinehart & Winston); and *Linguistic Change*, by E. H. Sturtevant (1965 edition, University of Chicago Press). Although the latter is out of date, it is still useful. There are now many texts and articles on the relation between language and culture. The chapter quote is from Benjamin Lee Whorf, *Language, Thought and Reality* (1957, MIT Press). See also Edward Sapir, *Culture, Language and Personality* (1962, University of California Press). For a specific reaction to this hypothesis see Joshua A. Fishman, "A Systematization of the Whorfian Hypothesis," in *Behavioral Science*, 5 (1960): 323–39. An excellent modern text is Robbins Burling, *Man's Many Voices: Language in its Cultural Context* (1970, Holt, Rinehart & Winston). Excellent readers include *Language in Culture and Society*, edited by Dell Hymes (1964, Harper & Row); *Language, Thought and Culture*, edited by Paul Henle (1965, University of Michigan Press); and *Language and Culture: A Reader*, edited by Gleason and Wakefield (1968, Merrill). Two specific publications on recent work in this area are "Transcultural Studies in Cognition," edited by A. Kimball Romney and Roy D'Andrade, in *American Anthropologist* 66, no. 3, part 2 (1964); and "The Ethnography of Communication," edited by John Gumperz and Dell Hymes, in *American Anthropologist* 66, no. 6, part 2 (1964).

For the history and variety of writing systems, there is the excellent work by I. J. Gelb, *A Study of Writing* (1963, University of Chicago Press); and P. E. Cleator, *Lost Languages* (1962, Mentor Books), a more popularized approach. For body "language," see Roy Birdwhistell, *Kinesics and Context* (1972, Ballantine); and for the communicational possibilities of space and other matters, see two books by Edward T. Hall, *The Silent Language* (1959) and *The Hidden Dimension* (1969), both published by Doubleday.

25 culture change

In the previous chapter it was mentioned that languages undergo constant change. This is also true with respect to all the other systems of culture behavior. The "genes" of culture are constantly being shifted about and added to, and new traits, patterns and complexes of behavior are arising. Certainly, in some societies—those of the industrialized world—these changes are rapid and highly visible to the people concerned: "progress is our most important product." It can move so fast that it divides generations. Even in the most traditional and most conservative societies, although slower and perhaps outside of the awareness of the people involved, culture change does occur. And, of course, as a result of recent contacts many primitive societies have undergone devastating alterations. This being so, even the anthropologist interested in ascertaining the functioning of a cultural system at a given point in time must still be alert to change. His explanations may have to take the dynamics of change phenomena into account.

THE STUDY OF CULTURAL CHANGE

Generally speaking, one can study the topic of change from two perspectives. The dynamics of such situations can be analyzed. Why has a particular change taken place or a new culture trait—say the hula hoop—come into existence? Who originates the new trait, who accepts it, and why? The other approach is to look at the stability of the situation and investigate the factors underlying conservatism in culture. Why have some traits or whole areas of culture behavior not changed or demonstrated great resistance to it? Why are some less innovative than others? We appear to have spent most of our time on the investigation of the former topic.

461

Culture change occurs in all societies, although differently. These three societies have solved the same problem in different ways.

Students of culture have devoted far more attention to studying change than to analyzing stability. There are two principal reasons for this. One derives from the historical development of ideas about the extreme conservatism of nonliterate folk held by scholars in the earlier period of anthropological science. The second reason, however, is inherent in the problem. For it is much easier, methodologically, to study change than to study stability. (Herskovits, 1964: 145)

FACTORS IN CHANGE

The above author has also pointed out that change and stability in any given human society can be encouraged by some very general factors. We can briefly examine these before pursuing some more specific factors. Certainly, the physical *environment* itself offers possibilities for, and sets limits to, change. Not only can one explain the past lack of agriculture among the Eskimos as a result of an unfavorable environment rather than to a lack of inventiveness, but "Certainly a very difficult habitat, to which a people have made an adjustment, does not encourage experimentation . . ." (Herskovits, 1964: 150). This is a case of "don't rock the boat." Then, too, there is the notion of the operation of *historical factors*. There may occur what is called historical *accident*, a development unforeseen or unpredictable from the way a cultural system is organized that orients it in a new behavioral direction. The acquisition of the horse by groups of Plains Indians is a classic example of the operation of this factor. Originally such groups were fairly small, sedentary, agricultural societies—little developed. After acquiring the horse, many gave up agriculture, became heavily dependent upon hunting buffalo, highly mobile, and more complexly developed socially and

462

politically. The horse became an object of wealth, status, and warfare, transforming these societies in a truly revolutionary fashion.

An opposite factor to accident is historical *drift*. Here the "inner logic" of the cultural system and its value and goals seem to push for a given direction or sequence of development. One might point to our own society as an example of this factor. Once we got onto the idea of substitution of machines for human labor (automation) on industrial assembly lines, this idea became a kind of "trend" which spread to other areas of behavior—from processing checks in banks to teaching-machines in schools. And such changes are still spreading in our culture. Such sequences of change are predictable in a way that accidents are not and appear to occur whether the human beings involved with them really desire such behaviors or not, often to their disadvantage. Ever try to argue about your registration with a machine punchcard?

Finally, as a general factor serving as a background for change, there are aspects of human *psychology*. Of course, some elements here are very specific—needs and desires. Herskovits deals, however, with the more general phenomena involved in the learning of culture. It will be remembered that culture is a learned and socially transmitted system of behavior. In the process of learning one's distinctive way of being human, the stability or dynamism of that system can be affected. In early life, individuals play a rather passive role in the acquisition of culture. They are generally not in a position to accept, reject, or change the basic patterns transmitted to them. They are conditioned and "seduced" by their culture. Not only does their dependent position more or less preclude rejection, but they may be unaware of any alternatives to these behaviors: "what are chopsticks?" The early process of learning culture—often called *enculturation*—is certainly a prime factor in cultural stability and conservatism. Later on in life, the factor of choice, knowledge, and the power to make changes begin to operate, and the mature individual has more active options for acceptance and rejection or substitution.

> Thus the mechanism of enculturation leads us to the heart of this problem of conservatism and change in culture. Its earlier conditioning level is the instrument that gives to every culture its stability; that prevents its running wild even in periods of most rapid change. In its later aspects, where enculturation operates on the conscious level, it opens the gate to change, making for the examination of alternate possibilities, and permitting reconditioning to new modes of thought and conduct. (Herskovits, 1964: 151, 152)

It should be mentioned, however, that such mature changes are seldom of a wholesale nature. Once a person has invested so much time and effort in learning culture and acquiring an ease of behavioral facility with one way of being human, he is usually reluctant to change much of this except in very selected ways.

PROCESSES OF INNOVATION

Perhaps the master idea in the study of social and cultural change is the concept of innovation. We generally use this term to refer to something new, but, as many social scientists employ it in a wider context, it refers to all the processes involved in the creation of some new idea, activity, or artifact, as well as how it spreads within and between societies. As such, innovation covers a great variety of behaviors. We can divide these into two main areas. The first of these is the process of origination. This refers to the first part of innovation—the bringing of some new culture trait into existence. It has been somewhat traditional among students of change to make a basic distinction between those originations that are discoveries and those that are inventions. Unfortunately, not only is this a rather semantic distinction, but also not all writers make it the same way. Honigmann (1959) sees the process of discovery as an addition to knowledge, and invention as using this knowledge in some novel form. Others see the former term as an accidental occurrence and invention as a deliberate attempt at origination. In this text, discovery will be defined as becoming aware of something new that is totally new; that is to say, it was not previously known or perceived. Probably the first person who realized that wild grapes that had fermented gave a greater "kick" than those picked fresh from the vine should be credited with a discovery—as would whoever ascertained that fire could be used to cook food. Invention may be considered as the creation of something not absolutely new or unrealized previously. It represents a synthesis or alteration of previously existing elements into some new form or shape. It is putting together *A* and *B* to make *AB*. A usually cited example is the steamboat, both the steam engine and the boat having been previously known and in existence. Another example would be the animal-drawn plow, plows pulled by humans or pushed by hand and domestic animals also existing previously. It is probably a truism that such originations that arise as new combinations and alterations from what had prior existence is more common than the process of discovery, although in the early days of the human species discovery certainly must have played a larger role.

To what has been said above concerning invention we can add two other notions. First is the idea that invention may not simply represent a single, one-time placement of elements in a new form. Often it works by what might be called the accretion of parts, parts evolving together. A speculative possibility for the invention of the bow and arrow is given by one writer as follows.

> A bow must have passed beyond a certain threshold of effectiveness before it can have any utility as a weapon. It seems dubious whether any primitive, starting from nothing and thinking up a bow and arrow by insight, could give it the several points of efficiency needed ... On the other hand, a string on a bent stick is under tension and will twang. Just such a "musical bow" is used by many primitive peoples ... set against the teeth. The same strung stick could also be bounced in a game, or have sticks bounced off its string. From that it would be a short step to sliding or shooting light sticks at a nearby mark. Now, with something to build on, both in the way of a working instrument and manipulative skill, a little more strengthening of both bow and arrow would much more easily result in a workable weapon. (Kroeber, 1963: 164).

From this consideration comes the second notion. When we talk about the creation of some new trait—idea, activity, or artifact—we should really consider it from a number of perspectives or aspects. H. G. Barnett (1942) considers traits to comprise form, function, principle, and meaning. Besides the recognized form (shape or structure), it has a function (what it does) and a meaning to those who use or value it. The principle "is the scheme or theme about which the form is organized..." (Barnett, 1942: 14). It manifests itself when the form is in action. As he puts it, "... the genus of invention lies in disencumbering form of its traditional associations, of seeing it objectively with respect to its active principle and its possibilities for other meanings and functons" (Barnett, 1942: 17). Diagramatically, for example:

Here, conceivably, principle 2 in the same or different form can be used to meet function *1*, substituting a new trait for the old trait *1-1-1* (poisoning the mouse rather than breaking its neck). This is a new way of doing something old or (if trait *2-2-2* already exists) possibly an old way of doing something new!

If there have been disputes over the nature of the difference between discovery and invention, there does exist some agreement on the notion that there are some standard varieties of origination in general. At least two sets of such distinctions can be mentioned here. One set is determined by the degree of purpose involved in the process of creat-

The automobile revolutionized not only transportation, but many other behavioral patterns as well.

United Press International

ing something new. A *deliberate* origination represents the result of a conscious attempt at invention or discovery, say a better mousetrap or a cure for cancer. An *accidental* origination is one that arises either as a byproduct of a deliberate attempt (look for one thing and come across something else) or as a pure change situation. Given the simplicity of the "strike-a-lights" method for making fire (by striking flint and iron pyrites together), the discovery of how to make fire may have been an accidental byproduct of early tool-making. "Penicillin was 'invented' as a result of Fleming's working with staphyloccus cultures and noting that where these became infected with mold the adjacent colonies of bacteria were dissolved away" (Kroeber, 1963: 162).

EFFECTS OF ORIGINATION

Another set of terms for varieties of origination is based on the ultimate effects of the new trait. As used in this text (it has different usages elsewhere), a *basic* origination is one that creates a potential for change in other aspects of cultural behavior. The automobile is the oft-cited case. Not only did it revolutionize the transportation potential of American society but also the distribution of goods and many other economic patterns. It also changed our dating habits. Now we go to the drive-in teller at the bank to get some money to take our date to a drive-in restaurant before going to the drive-in movie. A *nonbasic* origination is one that may change behavior in its own limited sphere of culture but does not have other repercussions. It is doubtful if a new-shaped glass for wine or a smoking pipe for tobacco will have very profound effects. Also, many inventions or discoveries of the basic variety may cause changes in other areas of behavior not only because they have the potential to open up new possibilities, but also because they may render many other aspects of life obsolete or incompatible with the new origination. This forces change elsewhere to recreate the integrated nature of

466

the culture. This phenomenon is often called *accommodation*. We can now turn to a brief consideration of the many factors that facilitate or inhibit the process of origination.

FACTORS IN ORIGINATION

Traditionalism

One factor of great aid or hindrance to change is the degree of what might be called traditionalism in a society. Some peoples are more traditionally oriented or conservative than others with respect to how they tolerate change. If societies welcome change and desire new ideas, activities, and artifacts ("progress is our most important product"), then the process of origination is facilitated. Here the would-be originator seeks a socially approved goal and is encouraged to do so and rewarded. Where custom is more difficult to break, where change or departure from past behavior is perceived as a threat (perhaps as an affront to the gods who initiated human behavior), the task of the originator is made immeasurably more difficult. Such traditionalism may place definite limits on the freedom of inquiry and the means or facilities necessary to pursue innovation. Even in progress-oriented societies, some areas of cultural behavior may permit less freedom than others, religion and politics being cases in point. Although we reward the inventor of the better mousetrap, we are suspicious of the nonconformist theologian and the political radical arguing for an update of a 200-year-old system of government.

Needs

Another factor is that of *need*. The old quote that "necessity is the mother of invention" certainly has the ring of truth. If a people have some need, or feel a given trait or complex of behavior to be in some way inadequate, they may set about deliberately to resolve that situation by origination; to invent or discover a way to curb pollution, make a faster racing car, or a burpless cucumber. Such needs may, of course, be actively encouraged by competition among individuals within a society for a greater share of the rewards (via artificially induced needs); or by competition between societies, often in warfare situations. Certainly, the so called "space race" between the Soviet Union and the United States, with international prestige as its competitive motive, has fostered more than its share of originations. On the other hand, if no real needs or inadequacies are felt by the members of a society, origination will correspondingly be discouraged. In fact, even when some needs are perceived, if the individuals feel that nothing will improve their lot anyway, if they adopt an attitude of fatalism about their condition, then invention and discovery will still be retarded.

Accumulation of Culture Traits

A final factor, among others (and to some scholars the single most important factor), is the idea of the *accumulation of cultural traits*. "The size and complexity of the cultural inventory that is available to an innovator establishes limits within which he must function . . . Some societies are much richer than others in cultural possessions; hence their members have an initial advantage that is denied individuals in less well endowed societies" (Barnett, 1953: 40). In essence, this means that the more you have the more you get. If I exist in a society with few material traits—a stone axe, a spear, a basket, etc.—my opportunity for combining these to invent some new item is minimal. In our society, on the other hand, with more material items than even Sears and Roebuck can keep up with, my task is immeasurably simpler. I can combine a hammer and a screwdriver (the scrammer). Now when I can't turn a screw through the wood I can bash it in! It must also be remembered that many traits are combinations of many different kinds of things. Think of something as technically "simple" as a bicycle—dependent upon wheels, gears, rubber, ball bearings, iron, etc. In most cases, out of very little comes very little!

Some writers would go even further. As Leslie White has stated it, not only does an originator require the necessary cultural elements, but "When the requisite materials have been made available by the process of cultural growth or diffusion, [spread of ideas and things] . . . the invention or discovery is bound to take place" (White 1949: 205). This view makes culture "the mother of invention" and denies the validity of the "great-man theory," that outstanding humans are the cause of changes. This has been put most elegantly by A. L. Kroeber:

> To a certain extent we may even speak legitimately of the inevitability of inventions . . . Given knowledge of electric current and electromagnetic induction and of sound vibration—especially with telegraphs in successful operation for thirty years—and the idea of the telephone is bound to occur to a number of technicians. It is only a question of who will first work the idea out feasibly . . . To his society, and to the world at large, the "Who" is really a matter of indifference . . . because the invention was going to be made anyway about when and where it was made. We cannot always see this fact at the moment . . . But after the

event . . . we can recognize the piling-up of the antecedants until the invention or innovation follows as their consequence. (Kroeber, 1963: 172, 173)

This is regarded by some scholars as an overstatement of the situation; nonetheless, it points out the crucial nature of the inventory of cultural traits available to the would-be originator. Although there are other important factors involved in the creation of new cultural items, traditionalism, need, and the accumulation of necessary materials certainly occupy the center of the stage of origination. We can turn now to the second main aspect of the nature of innovation, the process of **diffusion.**

DIFFUSION

Types of Diffusion

Diffusion refers to the process by which originations spread within and between societies. When diffusion occurs within the originating society it is often called *primary* or *internal* diffusion. If it refers to new ideas, activities, or artifacts spreading to other societies, it is often referred to as *secondary* or *external* diffusion. Anthropologists, because of their great concern with ways of being human other than their own, and because of their emphasis on the fieldwork situation, have tended to be more concerned with the latter type of diffusion—examining how things come in from the outside. They have attempted to define the specific conditions of acceptance and rejection. This has been a fortuitous circumstance since only a relatively small number of culture traits are the results of the discovery and invention originating within that society. Hence, in the explanation of culture change, diffusion is seen as the more important innovative process.

There does exist a special form of diffusion that is somewhat exceptional with reference to the above distinction made between origination and diffusion. This has been called *stimulus diffusion.* "It occurs in situations where a system or pattern as such encounters no resistance to its spread, but there are difficulties in regard to the transmission of the concrete content of the system. In this case, it is the idea of the complex or system which is accepted, but it remains for the receiving culture to develop a new content" (Kroeber, 1940: 1). An excellent example this author gives is the invention of porcelain in Europe in the eighteenth century. Porcelain had been imported from China for a considerable time, but the nature of the manufacturing process had been kept a secret. Due to the expense of importation, deliberate experimentation was undertaken to duplicate this product. After a time, this result was successfully achieved. As a process, stimulus diffusion appears to be between pure origination and diffusion. It is only partial diffusion since the entire nature of the trait has not spread. It is origination, but with an assist. "If it were not for the pre-existence of Chinese porcelain, and the fact of its having reached Europe, there is no reason to believe that Europeans would have invented porcelain in the eighteenth century . . . if at all" (Kroeber, 1940: 2).

FACTORS IN DIFFUSION

In cases of true diffusion there are some very general conditioning circumstances. Diffusion may be a *planned* activity. Traits may be deliberately taken from one society to another with a view towards their introduction. Missionaries, the Peace Corps, military occupation, and other situations are the frameworks in which this usually occurs. Individuals from within the receiving society may also play such a role.

Second is the idea of *geographical marginality*. Here contact must usually take place for cultural traits to spread among different societies. If a society is geographically isolated, say in inaccessible mountain areas or inpenetrable swamps, then originations added to the mainstream of human culture are less likely to reach them, as are traits of a more limited nature.

Finally, among other general circumstances, is the condition of the *contact situation*. Over-simply, the circumstances of contact may be friendly or hostile. If the former condition prevails, traits are more often apt to be acccepted with the active participation of the "borrowing" society. If hostile contacts occur, not only are the conditions for acceptance made more difficult or hazardous, but such traits may become unfavorably identified with the situation itself. And, of course, even after military defeat, great resistance may be demonstrated in a situation

These evidences of western culture were probably deliberately introduced to these primitive societies.
United Nations   United Nations

of forced diffusion. We will discuss an issue closely related to this at the close of the chapter.

As was the case with origination, there are a great number of more specific reasons for the acceptance or rejection of diffused culture traits. We can briefly examine a few of the more common of these reasons. Many things favor the process of diffusion. *Needs* and their recognition certainly favor the acceptance of a newly introduced trait if it meets them, as it does origination in general. If people feel that some part of their system of behavior is inadequate they may be quick to change it when alternatives present themselves. As ingenious as Eskimo hunting techniques were, most groups quickly realized the potential of rifles when these were introduced to them and utilized these for the hunting of many game animals.

A second specific factor is the notion of *compatibility*. If a newly introduced trait fits into previously existing behaviors in the recipient society (in terms of social forms, cultural values, resources, motor habits, etc.), it obviously has a better chance of being accepted. For example, in one region of Mexico, a UNESCO education program

> . . . has been successful in introducing chicken farming in a number of villages. The local people have kept chickens for centuries, and the White Leghorns have generally been recognized as superior birds. Here the fit between values, social forms, and economic possibilities has been good and the program has been gratifying in its results. Contrast this with a similar case in China several years ago: White Leghorns . . . were introduced . . . But the innovator was unaware of a tabu against raising and eating white birds, and consequently little progress was made. (Foster, 1962: 163)

Of course, much of this "fit," or cultural compatibility, ultimately depends upon the perceptions of the individuals involved themselves. Barnett (1942) has pointed out that the form of the item (more than its principle, function, or meaning) is more likely to determine acceptance/rejection of traits undergoing diffusion. If the form of that trait—designed to provide for a previously existing function—is misperceived, the trait is likely to be rejected. The example given is of white settlers not picking up the idea of the potlatch even though their customs of Christmas giving and parties (in principle and function) were much the same. Of course, the process may also work in reverse. If a different trait is misperceived because of its form, it may be accepted anyway. Witness, for example, the tying of sewing thimbles to the fringes of dance costumes for decoration among the Tsimshian of North America. Thus, form "analysis" may lead to rejection in cases of actual compatibility. In this connection, material traits and items of technology appear more acceptable in cases of diffusion than do items in other behavioral areas.

A third specific factor facilitating acceptance of diffusion traits is the idea of *prestige*. This applies equally to the agents of diffusion and to the trait itself. If the person(s) who spread the new trait or urge its acceptance are respected individuals, the trait they represent is likely to be accepted. This is especially the case if such individuals have political or social authority patterns within their group, as in the case of a lineage headman! If the new trait is identified as a prestigious item, it is also likely to be accepted. One wonders about the rather sudden popularity of wine consumption in our own society. Is it because we have finally acquired a taste for this product of the grape or because the drinking of good wine is considered high-class behavior? And, of course, we accept the verdict of wine experts as to which wines are best! One is reminded of the case from one underdeveloped area where ink pens were carried around by everyone because they symbolized the prestige of education—even though few of these individuals could read or write.

Then there are other specific reasons for the rejection of diffused traits. These are reinforced by general factors such as geographic marginality and are in addition to such things as lack of a recognized need, incompatibility, and little or no prestige involvement. Perhaps the major impediment here is *tradition* or *ethnocentricism*. This is somewhat the same for diffusion as it was for origination, but the notion goes a little further. Not only is there the idea that it is wrong to change behaviors that have the sanction of past usage—hence resisting things from within and without—but this as applied to diffusion may be accompanied by feelings that one's own culture is superior to that from which the new traits derive. This may become a formidable psychological barrier to introduced changes.

Then, too, instead of ethnocentricism, *fatalism* often occurs. This is basically a belief in the immutability of present behavior, even if that behavior is perceived of as less than satisfactory.

> ... in nonindustrial societies a very low degree of mastery over nature and social conditions has been achieved. Drought or flood is looked upon as a visitation from gods or evil spirits whom man can propitiate but not control. ... Medical and social services are lacking and people die young. Under such circumstances it is not surprising that people have few illusions about the possibility of improving their lot. A fatalistic outlook, the assumption that whatever happens is the will of God ... is the best adjustment the individual can make to an apparently hopeless situation. (Foster, 1962: 66, 67)

Another specific factor that often leads to rejection of diffused traits is *unforeseen consequences*. A trait may be accepted and then, ultimately, rejected because of the side effects it causes. A classic case comes from rural India where traditional cooking is done over an open dung fire inside the house. This causes acrid smoke to collect and is a prime factor in eye ailments and respiratory diseases. To alleviate this problem, a pottery stove with a chimney was introduced—with dubious success. The smoke may have been a health hazard, but it also served to fumigate the thatch roof of the house against wood-boring ants that can quickly destroy the roof, necessitating costly replacement. Perception of the advantages of the new stove, apparently, were outweighed by the unforeseen consequences associated with its use. So for many reasons, new behavior may be rejected.

The consequences that follow the introduction of a new trait may take a considerable time for their expression, and realization of such long-term results may come too late. Just as one origination may cause others, the acceptance of traits from outside the society may cause profound changes, not always of a valuable nature. An illustrative example of this comes from the Australian aborigines, as reported by Lauriston Sharp. The society in question is the Yir Yoront, who, when first contacted, had no knowledge of metals. By the end of the nineteenth century, European behaviors had begun to spread to them, including a steel axe, which, because of compatibility and recognized superiority, was quickly accepted.

The position occupied by stone axes in the past, however, was very significant. The stone axe was a symbol of masculinity and was acquired by relationships with trading partners in other areas. It could only be borrowed from males (who owned them) by the women and young children. "Thus the axe stood for an important theme in Yir Yoront culture: the superiority and rightful dominance of the male, and the greater value of his concerns and of all things concerned with him." (Sharp, 1952: 20). The introduction of the steel axe considerably altered this situation. First of all, now a man obtained an axe from a mission rather than from his established social contacts; one lost former self-reliance in this regard and became dependent upon missionary definition of "worth" to receive one. Also, women were given axes by missionaries and other whites, which became their own objects of property—upsetting the older mode of male dominance. This also undermined the trade partnerships and the other institutions associated with them, such as initiation and feasting activities.

Among other things, this took some of the excitement away from the dry season fiesta-like tribal gatherings centering around initiations. These had traditionally been the climactic annual occasions for exchanges between trading partners when a man might seek to acquire a whole year's supply of stone axe heads. Now he might find himself prostituting his wife to almost total strangers in return for steel axes or other white man's goods. With trading partnerships weakened, there was less reason to attend the ceremonies and less fun for those who did. (Sharp, 1952: 21)

Even more disruptive is the idea that the new axe was not really so compatible with Yir Yoront culture (in ideas and values) as might first be conceived. Neither enshrined in myth nor associated with the ancestors, the steel axe was difficult for these people to place within a context of traditional behavior. Sharp feels that such upsets to their social and belief systems can only lead to the destruction of all of their culture and eventually, perhaps, to their extinction as a biological group. So, seemingly innocuous changes may have profound consequences.

ACCULTURATION

When anthropologists speak of diffusion they generally assume the processes involved to be multidirectional—traits passing back and forth in a "I-give-to-you-and-you-give-to-me" fashion. They also conceive of it as a more or less sporadic rather than a continuous situation. Sometimes, however, the contacts for diffusion may be relatively permanent, the number of traits diffused rather extensive, and the situation itself a rather one-sided affair with one society donating traits in a very unequal proportion to another. This form of diffusion has been given the special designation of **acculturation.** Acculturation usually accompanies conditions in which some dominant group uses direct force or other pressure to compel a subordinate group to take on patterns from its way of being human. This, then, is a case of rather intensive culture change introduced from the outside. A classic example is the acculturation of American Indians to the life patterns of the national society.

In terms of extremes, there are two outcomes to any extended acculturation situation. If this one-sided process continues long enough, it will result in **assimilation,** the weaker society will lose its cultural (and perhaps biological) distinctiveness and become a part of the dominant society. Many primitive societies at present are in danger of becoming adjuncts of one or another industrial nation. Many American Indians have become "good Americans" with homes in the suburbs and crabgrass! The other alternative is **reaction,** an attempt to retain a sense of original distinctiveness. Because of their subordinate position in the acculturation situation, most purely military reactions are not met with great success. Often, however, people in reaction may employ predominantly supernatural mechanisms. Such attempts are often called *nativistic* or *revitalization movements.* These phenomena were defined by one writer some years ago as "Any conscious, organized attempt on the part of a society's members to revive or perpetuate selected aspects of its culture" (Linton, 1943: 230). One such movement that has been fairly successful—peyotism—was briefly discussed in chapter twenty-one. Other movements appear to have been somewhat less successful in this regard, actually hastening the destruction of older ways of life. With the spread of modern technology to formerly remote areas of the world we may expect an increase in acculturation and its attendant behaviors.

The acceleration of cultural and social change in today's world poses certain problems (even without acculturation) that cut to the core of the anthropological perspective. We have always been concerned with describing and analyzing the patterns of culture of various groups of people and with emphasizing the legitimacy of these ways of being human.

> If a world society is to emerge from the conflict of ethnocentricisms we call nationalism, it can only be on a basis of live and let live, a willingness to recognize the values that are to be found in the most diverse ways of life. Surely, though at times slowly, anthropology has moved toward documenting this position. ... Just as the physical anthropologists have ceaselessly combated the concept of racial superiority, so cultural anthropology has, both explicitly and implicitly in the presentation of its data, documented the essential dignity of all human cultures. (Herskovits, 1964: 242, 243)

In so doing, we have attempted not to disturb those cultural systems under study. With the many changes (both planned and unplanned) now occurring the anthropologist faces a difficult choice. If change becomes inevitable, should we employ our more expert knowledge of the societies in question to make that change as "painless" as possible? Such an attempt, as well as those that selectively introduce improvements in such areas as agriculture and health may be called *applied* anthropology. Anthropologists engaged in such endeavors remain, however, somewhat suspect in the minds of many of their colleagues who (at least intellectually) campaign for the preservation of human diversity. Yet, if the pace of change continues, one suspects that more anthropologists will awaken to a sense of social responsibility and attempt to apply their knowledge and skills to more practical problems.

SUMMARY

1. Sociocultural change occurs in all societies although some are more conservative and traditional in this regard than others. Such changes are encouraged or inhibited by factors of environment, history, and psychology.

2. Innovation is the creation of new traits and their spread within and among societies. Origination is the bringing of something new into existence; it takes the forms of discovery and invention. Diffusion is the spread of the new trait.

3. Various specific factors facilitate origination and diffusion among which are the degree of traditionalism, need, accumulation of cultural traits, compatability, prestige, and unforeseen consequences.

4. Results of diffusion may be assimilation, in which one group, usually subordinate, takes on many traits from another society to the point of losing its original identity; or reaction, in which a society attempts to regain its own identity.

REFERENCES FOR FURTHER READING

There are many useful social science texts on social and cultural change. Not all of them, however, apply to anthropological concerns. One useful text is *Social Change*, by Richard T. LaPiere (1965, McGraw-Hill). A most provocative and entertaining volume that "hits home" for we moderns is *The Dynamics of Change*, by Don Fabun (1967, Prentice-Hall). There is also the small text *Social Change*, second edition, by Wilbert E. Moore (1974, Prentice-Hall); and this publisher also has an entire set of inexpensive paperbacks, the *Modernization of Traditional Societies Series*, which report expertly on various aspects of such phenomena. Three general texts of outstanding importance are *Cultural Dynamics*, by M. J. Herskovits (1964, Knopf); *Anthropology: Cultural Patterns and Processes*, by A. K. Kroeber (1963, Harcourt, Brace & World)—both abridgements of earlier works—and *Innovation: The Basis of Cultural Change*, by H. G. Barnett (1953, McGraw-Hill). As usual, *The World of Man*, by John Honigmann (1959, Harper) has excellent chapters devoted to this topic as does *The Study of Man*, by Ralph Linton (1936, Appleton, Century, Crofts). See also *The Sociology of Invention*, by S. F. Gilfillan (1970, MIT Press). The best general reader from an anthropological perspective is *Beyond the Frontier*, edited by Paul Bohannon and Fred Plog (1967, Natural History Press). A stimulating specific study is by Thomas S. Kuhn, *The Structure of Scientific Revolutions* (1970, University of Chicago Press).

Volumes dealing with change and its results are *Traditional Cultures and the Impact of Technological Change*, by George M. Foster (1962, Harper & Row); *Human Problems in Technological Change*, edited by E. H. Spicer (1965, Wiley); *Introducing Social Change*, by Conrad Arensberg and Arthur Nickoff (1964, Aldine); *A Casebook of Social Change*, edited by Arthur Nickoff (1966, Aldine); *The Springtime of Freedom*, by William McCord (1965, Oxford University Press); and

Applied Anthropology, edited by James Clifton (1970, Houghton-Mifflin). See also *Technological Man*, by Victor C. Ferkiss (1969, New American Library), for a challenging discussion of future change in our own society.

Specific references in the chapter not covered above are Leslie White, "Genius: Its Cause and Incidence," in *The Science of Culture* (1949, Grove Press); H. G. Barnett, "Invention and Cultural Change," in *American Anthropologist* 44 (1942): 14–30; A. L. Kroeber, "Stimulus Diffusion," in *American Anthropologist* 42 (1940): 1–20; Lauriston Sharp, "Steel Axes for Stone-Age Australians," in *Human Organization* 11 (1952): 17–22; and Ralph Linton, "Nativistic Movements," in *American Anthropologist* 45 (1943): 230–40.

GLOSSARY

PART ONE

Adaptation   Adjusting to an environmental situation by specialization or generalization.

Anthropoids   (Anthropoidea) The higher primates, consisting of monkeys, apes and humans.

Aurignacoid   Cover term for those upper Paleolithic tool traditions that display similarity to each other; includes blade tools and artifacts of bone, antler, ivory and horn.

Australopithecine   Forms representing the first stage in human physical evolution.

Biological engineering   A possible future response to genetic problems involving interference by humans in the hereditary process; changing or remaking genetic potential.

Blade tools   Predominant stone tools of the upper Paleolithic period; detached from a prepared core and then trimmed into a great variety of shapes for specialized tasks.

Brachiation theory   Notion that our human forerunners did not separate from the apes until after apes developed a specialization for brachiation.

Catastrophism   The belief that there has been a number of extinctions by cataclysms.

Ceboids   (Ceboidea) The various monkeys of the New World.

Cercopithecoids   (Cercopithecoidea) The various monkeys of the Old World; the closest monkeys (zoologically) to humans.

Civilization   A level of cultural development characterized by an urbanized society, a territorially based state, a symbiotic economy, great advances in scientific knowledge, impressive public works, and, usually, writing.

Classification   An archaeological technique which groups the objects recovered from a site for storage, preservation, and interpretation.

Convergence   The tendency of one group of organisms to develop superficial resemblances to another group of organisms of different ancestry in response to demands of similar environmental situations.

Core tools   Tools manufactured by trimming a lump of stone into the desired shape, converting the core itself into the tool.

Dating   An archaeological technique which may place an artifact or site in time relative to another artifact or site or which may place it absolutely with a chronological date.

Divergence   The tendency of one group of organisms to develop differences from another group of the same ancestry in response to different environmental situations.

Dryopithecus A widespread form of Miocene "ape," from which, possibly, modern apes and humans evolved.

Erectus (Homo erectus) Forms representing the second stage in human physical evolution.

Eugenics A response to genetic problems which attempts to alter the gene frequencies themselves either by encouraging or discouraging human reproduction.

Euthenics A response to genetic problems which creates environments in which defective genes are rendered less disadvantaged.

Evolution The belief that organisms living today have developed over a long and slow process of change during which structures were developed and passed from one variety of organism to another; changes in the frequencies of genotypes and phenotypes over time.

Excavation An archaeological technique which involves digging up the remains at a buried site; done with great care to permit reconstruction of the data recovered.

Extinction The complete dying out of a form of life, or the evolutionary transformation of one species into a different species.

Flake tools Tools manufactured by treating one lump of stone as a source for many tools and making tools out of the flakes struck off from it.

Flaking (knapping) Process of detaching flakes from stone in the manufacture of tools.

Food production Techniques of securing food via plant and animal domestication as opposed to merely collecting wild foods from the environment.

Franco-Cantabrian Tradition The main cave art tradition of Upper Paleolithic times, consisting of painting, engraving, and modeling representations, predominantly of animals.

Gene flow A mechanism of evolution; the interbreeding of organisms of one population with those of another resulting in altered gene frequencies.

General trends in human cultural development Major trends which appear to have generated in the past and may continue to do so in the future, possibly with negative consequences; these include: increasing reliance on culture, expanding utilization of natural resources, declining relative individual knowledge, and increasing efficiency.

Genetic drift A mechanism of evolution which involves a gain or loss in the frequencies of genes due to chance in the reproduction of small populations.

Genetic load The defective and disadvantageous genes possessed by the human species due to an increase in mutation and a decrease in the operation of natural selection.

Genotype The total amount of hereditary potential of an organism; its underlying genetic constitution.

Habilis (Homo habilis) Form living at the same general time as Australopithecines; may possibly be a more advanced type of fossil human.

Handaxe traditions Predominant general purpose core tools of lower Paleolithic period which were manufactured by trimming cores or large flakes on both sides.

Hominoids (Hominoidea) The taxonomic division which includes apes and humans.

Hylobatids (Hylobatidae) The "lesser" apes, including the Gibbon and Siamang.

Incipient cultures Those Mesolithic groups of people who made early experiments in food production.

Interpretation An archaeological technique; going beyond the basic data provided by artifacts and attempting to reconstruct the life ways of the inhabitants of the site.

Irreversibility The inability of an organism to reverse its evolutionary steps and revert to the ancestral form.

Isolation A mechanism of evolution; the segregation of a population due to geographical and/or social circumstances—the more isolation, the greater the possibility of unique gene frequencies.

Jarmo One of the most famous early neolithic farming communities.

Metallurgy Method of making tools and other artifacts by heating metal to a liquified state, pouring the molten material into a mold, and allowing it to harden to the desired shape.

Mosaic evolution Notion that the various physical components of the modern human organism evolved at different rates in response to different environmental evolutionary demands.

Mousteroid Cover term for most of the regionally different tool traditions of the middle Paleolithic period.

Mutation A mechanism of evolution; an accidental alteration in the genetic material of an organism which supplies fresh genetic variation for natural selection.

Natufian culture Near eastern culture about 10,000 B.C. which was close to food production.

Natural selection Mechanism of evolution; as an environment changes, those organisms best suited will survive; survival of the "fittest."

Neanderthal Forms representing the third stage of human physical evolution; thought by some scholars to be an extinct version of Homo sapiens.

Nuclear area A natural habitat containing varieties of plants and animals potentially capable of domestication and where climate favors early human experiments in this direction.

Oldowan tradition Early stone tool tradition consisting mostly of choppers made from river pebbles and flakes manufactured by very simple techniques; mostly general purpose tools.

Phenotype The observable physical characteristics of an organism.

Pongids (Pongidae) The "greater" apes, including the orangutan, gorilla, and chimpanzee.

Pre-brachiation theory Notion that our human forerunners separated from the apes before the apes developed a specialization for brachiation.

Primates The zoological order including the prosimians, monkeys, apes, and humans, whose evolutionary development is mostly associated with life in tree environments.

Prosimians (Prosimii) The lower primates, consisting of tree shrews, lemurs, lorises, and tarsiers.

Race An inbred human population genotypically different from other similarly sized populations; a concept suggesting, perhaps erroneously, that significant human differences exist.

Special creation Belief that the human species was placed on earth by a diety, with the same body and behavior it now possesses.

Sumerians   The first civilization of the Ancient Near East; consisted of a number of city-states.

Taxonomy   A static classifying technique placing phenomena in categories based upon their similarities and differences.

PART TWO

Absolutism   In a political organization the degree to which orders must be followed; based upon coercive power, consensual power, and persuasion.

Acculturation   A special form of diffusion; a rather one-sided situation in which one society donates traits in a very unequal proportion to another, usually weaker, society.

Affinity   In kinship, a nonbiological connection or relationship by marriage.

Allocation   In a political organization, the manner in which one obtains a governmental position of leadership.

Alternative behavior   A situation in which a number of behavioral possibilities exist and in which each is valued and expressed about equally.

Assimilation   A response to acculturation in which one society loses its cultural distinctiveness and becomes part of the other, usually stronger, society.

Association   A form of nonkinship group established in pursuit of some purpose or because of some satisfaction derived by its members; it may be based upon age, sex, or special interest, and may be instrumental or merely expressive.

Band   A political grouping consisting of a number of cooperating families led by a headman; ceremonially characterized by reciprocity.

Calendrical supernatural practices   Rituals that are tied in with a yearly calendar and hence can be predicted in advance.

Caste   In a social stratification system, a hereditary and fixed membership group placement ascribed by birth; usually no movement from one group or rank to another is possible.

Centralization   In a political organization, the existence of a central authority that is acknowledged by the various component groups within a society.

Chief   A political leader who usually occupies a permanent office and has formal, coercive powers (and sometimes supernatural powers as well); often hereditary.

Chiefdom   A political grouping consisting of a number of kinship and residential groups united under a chief and utilizing redistribution in their economic behavior; characterized by some social stratification.

Clan   Either a unilineal descent group tracing back to a fictionalized ancestor (sometimes not human), or people who are unable to prove their actual descent links; often a number of lineages that have created links between themselves.

Class   In a social stratification system, an open group; although membership is initially by birth, final placement is the result of achievement, thus defining the status of the individual more by attributes and behaviors.

Classification   A system of kinship terminology in which different people are classified together under the same linguistic kin term.

Cognatic descent Tracing back to a common ancestor through any sex links so as to (theoretically) include all the possible descendants of a particular ancestor; operation of this principle forms cognatic descent groups.

Communal labor A work situation in which groups of people work together but for individual benefit.

Complex A unit of cultural behavior in which a large group of interrelated traits and patterns have persistency and interdependency as a unit.

Compulsory behavior Behavior required in certain situations in which only one behavioral response is acceptable.

Consanguinity A biological connection or relationship by descent.

Covert culture Behaviors, beliefs, and attitudes that cannot be observed directly but may be inferred.

Critical supernatural practices Rituals that occur in response to some crisis or need, occurring intermittantly as such situations arise.

Cultural relativism The notion that criticism of particular cultural behaviors outside of their integrated contexts is an inadmissable activity.

Culture The learned, integrated and transmitted ideas, activities, and artifacts that are adaptive and that depend upon human social interaction for their existence.

Culture shock The sense of strangeness and alienation one feels as one becomes enmeshed in a foreign society.

Cyclical supernatural practices Rituals that occur in a fairly predictable sequence but that are not tied down to specific dates during the year.

Dependability The frequency with which food gaining activity is successful; an evaluative factor in the comparison of subsistence technology.

Descent kinship groups Groups of relatives united by the operation of various rules of tracing descent back to real or assumed ancestors.

Diffuse-primary sanctions A social control disapproval response of an informal and spontaneous sort with no predictable outcome which is exerted by a community or its representatives; consensus.

Diffuse-secondary sanctions A social control disapproval response of an informal and spontaneous sort with no predictable outcome which is exerted by a person or group on their own behalf; indecision.

Diffusion The process by which originations spread within and among societies.

Discovery The process of origination that involves becoming aware of something that is not previously known or perceived.

Economics The division of labor in a society; the mechanisms for distributing goods and services; the concepts of ownership, property, and inheritance.

Energy The amount of work (measured in calories) a people expend obtaining and raising food; an evaluative factor in the comparison of subsistence technology.

Ethnocentrism   The view that one's own way of life is the only or the best way of behavior.

Ethos   The emotional quality reflected in the major cultural behaviors of a society.

Explicit culture   Behaviors that people are aware of and can talk about and give reasons for; conscious behavior.

Extended family   The familial kinship group consisting of nuclear families linked together by residence rules; furnishes more individuals for labor and other activities than does a single nuclear family.

Extralinguistic communication   Systems or forms of communication which are not themselves language but which depend upon language for their existence, such as writing systems.

Familial kinship groups   Forms of the family brought into existence by marriage and residence rules; may be nuclear or composite.

Focus   A unit of cultural behavior; an area of behavior about which the members of a community show much concern.

Food collection   A system of subsistence technology in which naturally occurring foods are gathered from the environment; includes hunting and gathering, intensive fishing, and foraging.

Food production   A system of subsistence technology in which humans have intervened in nature to promote the development of domesticated plants and animals; includes incipient agriculture, horticulture, plow agriculture, and pastoralism.

Functional prerequisite (cultural imperatives)   The number of things that must be accomplished in any society if it is to survive; things that give culture its adaptive quality.

Headman   A simple type of political leader who has earned the respect, support, and confidence of a group of people; has informal powers.

Ideal culture   Represents what people say they do or say they ought to do; may not really occur in their behavior.

Implicit culture   Behaviors that people are largely unaware of, or, if known, have difficulty finding an explanation for; unconscious behavior.

Incest taboo   A rule prohibiting the mating and marriage of close biological kinsmen.

Individual labor   A work situation in which the individual works by himself for himself.

Innovation   The means by which some new trait comes into existence and spreads within or among societies.

Invention   The process of origination that involves the synthesis or alteration of previously existing traits to create something new.

King   A fairly powerful type of political leader generally found in more complex societies, needed to maintain stability in governmental processes; position usually hereditary.

Language   A series of phonemes arranged into morphemes that are combined in communication to convey meanings to a group or society of people.

Levirate   Custom where a man inherits the wife of his deceased brother.

Lexicostatistics A technique used by linguists in their attempts to date the time of divergence and separation of different languages; based upon retentions of basic vocabulary items.

Lineage The most common descent group in primitive societies; a group of kinsmen who trace themselves back through males or females to a common ancestor.

Magic A set of supernatural techniques by means of which humans can accomplish things beyond their ordinary capabilities; a type of supernaturalism presupposing independent action by humans.

Market exchange The exchange of goods in a market based upon prices; usually not the basic mechanism for securing goods in primitive societies.

Marriage The complex of customs that defines the rights and responsibilities of husbands and wives to each other and to their offspring (as opposed to mating).

Mating Pairing off of men and women on a "sex for the sake of sex" basis (as opposed to marriage responsibilities).

Moiety The division of a society into two unilineal groupings based upon fictionalized or unprovable descent linkings.

Monogamy The marriage of one man to one woman at any one time; single mates.

Morpheme The repeated and distinctive sequences of phonemes that have meaning in a language.

Mythology The body of traditional myths, legends, and folktales of a society or group of people; prose narratives having a supernatural content.

Natural division of labor The division of tasks based upon age and sex differences of the members of a society; skill requirements are secondary.

Naturalism The view that things happen because of the operation of ordinary nonmysterious causes and circumstances.

Nonlinguistic communication Systems or forms of communication which are not themselves language and do not depend upon it for their expression, such as certain body gestures.

Nuclear family The familial kinship group consisting of a man, his wife, and their offspring.

Organized labor A work situation in which individuals work by themselves or in groups for the benefit of other people; they do not participate in all the tasks necessary for survival but depend upon exchange.

Organized-primary sanctions A social control disapproval response where definite recognized procedures exist with predictable outcomes; exerted by a community or its representatives; adjudication.

Organized-secondary sanctions A social control disapproval response where definite recognized procedures exist with predictable outcomes; exerted by a person or group on their own behalf. Negotiation.

Origination The process of bringing a new cultural trait into existence.

Overt culture Behaviors that can be directly observed.

Participant observation An anthropological field work technique in which one participates (up to a point) in the behaviors one is studying in order to enhance one's understanding of them.

Pattern A unit of cultural behavior;

a significantly interrelated series of traits.

Phoneme The distinctive sound possibilities that are utilized and repeated in a given language.

Polygamous family The familial kinship group consisting of nuclear families linked together by plural marriages; furnishes more individuals for labor and other activities than does a single nuclear family.

Polygamy The marriage of an individual to multiple spouses; polygyny where the spouses are female, polyandry where they are male.

Population numbers Number of people that a subsistence technology can support in one area; an evaluative factor in the comparison of subsistence technology.

Preferred behavior A situation in which several behavioral possibilities exist but in which one is valued over others and expressed more frequently.

Prestige economy An economy in which production is mostly for exchange with other producers; an interdependent mode of survival with greater emphasis upon less basic necessities; production mostly for trade.

Priest A type of supernatural practitioner whose "powers" come from indirect contact with the supernatural; he accomplishes no extraordinary things and does not exhibit the unusual behaviors of the Shaman.

Production organization A group of people engaged in the production of some material good; such organizations differ in duration objectives, rewards, and recruitment.

Property The patterns of rights, duties, powers, and other social behaviors granted by societies to individuals or groups with respect to objects or things.

Proxemics The study of the use of space in communication and other human behavior.

Reaction A response to acculturation in which one society attempting to avoid assimilation tries to retain a sense of original distinctiveness, often via nativistic movements.

Real (manifest) culture Actual things or events that exist in the life of a society; ongoing behavior.

Reciprocity An exchange mechanism based upon people acting in a complementary fashion; may be generalized, balanced, or negative; also called gift-giving.

Redistribution An exchange mechanism in which goods move into a center and are realloted from that center; the center may be formal or informal.

Religion Belief in the existence of supernatural beings and the associated practices relating to them; a type of supernaturalism presupposing a dependency relationship between human and god.

Residence rules Regulations as to where newly married individuals should take up residence; basic rules are neolocal (new residence), patrilocal (in area of groom), and matrilocal (in area of bride).

Restricted behaviors Behaviors that are valued and/or expressed only by some members in a given society.

Ritual sanctions The suppression of undesired behaviors by the threat of supernatural means (as in taboos), or by actual human use of such beliefs (as in punishing a witch).

Role The complex of behaviors associated with a status position.

Sapir-Whorf hypothesis The notion that the structure of the language spoken by a group of people shapes the perception of these people since we dissect nature by this particular means; people speaking dissimilar languages then will have different views of reality.

Secret society An association in which the members have (or pretend to have) secret knowledge that nonmembers do not possess; the secret may be membership itself or supernatural power; can be social or antisocial.

Shaman A type of supernatural practitioner whose powers generally come from direct contact with the supernatural; he accomplishes extraordinary things and often exhibits unusual behaviors.

Social group A group of people among whom the possibility for interaction exists, who have a sense of their own identity, and who have some degree of persistence over time; may be primary (more intimate) or secondary (more impersonal.

Social sanction An approval or disapproval response to a mode of behavior by part or all of a society; disapproval responses result in most of the observed forms of social control.

Social stratification A society's hierarchy of ranked groups the levels of which afford their members varying degrees of power, prestige, and social worth.

Sorcery The use of supernatural power in such a manner as to cause harm to one's fellow human beings; generally thought of as a learned technique.

Sororate Custom where a woman inherits the husband of her deceased sister.

Specialization The existence of some person or persons in political organization who have the right to issue orders and administer sanctions.

State A political grouping usually consisting of a large population with legal bases for organization and centralization of political leadership (in primitive societies usually a king); market exchange exists as well as other economic exchange mechanisms; also characterized by a full scale system of social stratification.

Status A social position existing in a human society (e.g., father or chief) that a person comes to occupy (e.g., by ascription or achievement).

Subsistence economy An economy in which production and other behaviors are directly related to the environment and motivated by immediate survival; production chiefly for the use of the producers.

Subsistence technology The tools used to exploit an environment for its food potential and the techniques associated with their use.

Supernaturalism The view that things happen because of the operation of extraordinary and mysterious beings and powers, the existence of which is not susceptible to ordinary kinds of proof.

Surplus The amount of food left over after consumption demands have been met; an evaluative factor in the comparison of subsistence technology.

Technology The tools in the possession of a group of human beings and the techniques associated with their use.

Territorial groups A variety of nonkinship group based upon territorial and geographic proximity; may be a small local group or a larger, maximal group.

Trait The smallest significant unit of cultural behavior; relative to size of topic being considered.

Tribe A political grouping consisting of a number of kinship and residential groupings and integrated by organizations of people that crosscut these groups (e.g., men's clubs and religious groups).

True division of labor The division of tasks based upon skill requirements or certification.

Unilineal descent Tracing descent exclusively through either male or female lines (patrilineal or matrilineal) back to some ancestor; operation of this principle forms unilineal descent groups.

Warfare The organized attack on the members of one social group by those of another based on some clearly understood motivation; it has formal leadership and is sustained until some conclusion is reached.

Witchcraft The use of supernatural power in such a manner as to cause harm to one's fellow human beings; generally thought to be inborn.

AUTHOR INDEX

Aberle, David, 216, 217, 219
Adams, Robert M., *157*
Aldred, Cyril, *172*
Alland, Alexander, Jr., *172*, 182, *185*
Allchin, Bridget and Raymond, *172*
Ardry, Robert, 412, *415*
Arensberg, Conrad, *476*
Asimov, Isaac, 11, *18*, 39
Avi, Virginia, *68*

Balikci, Asen, 240–41, *259*, 344–45, *360*
Balinger, D., *459*
Bandi, Hans-Georg, *139*
Banfield, Edward, *198*
Barnett, H. G., 465, 468, 471, *476*, 477
Barth, Fredrik, 253, *260*, 358, *359*
Bascom, William, 435–36, 442
Basso, Keith, 246, *259*, 329, *335*
Bates, Marston, 17, 176, *186*
Beach, F. A., *310*
Beattie, John, 266, *286*, 382, 383–84, *397*
Benedict, Ruth, 214–15, *219*, 271, *286*
Bennett, John, 216, 217, 219
Berreman, Gerald D., 350, *359*
Bibby, Geoffrey, *119*
Binford, S. R. and Lewis R., 127, *139*, *157*
Birdsell, J. B., *88*
Birdwhistell, Roy, 457, *459*
Bleibtreu, H., *88*
Blumenbach, Johann Friedrich, 175
Bohannan, Paul, 268, 276–77, 279, *286*,
    290–91, *310*, *311*, 338, 339, 366,
    368, *378*, *415*, *476*
Bordaz, Jacques, 117, 118, *119*, *139*
Bordes, Francois, 127, *139*
    94, 97, 102, 180, *185*
Brace, C. Loring, 86, *88*, 89, 91, 92, 93,
Braidwood, Robert J., 146, 149, *157*
Branch, Daniel, 255, *260*
Brose, David, *139*
Brothwell, Don, *119*
Brues, Alice, 181, *186*
Buchler, Ira R., *335*
Burling, Robbins, *459*

Cardozo, Benjamin N., 363
Carniero, Robert, 247, 248, *259*
Carpenter, Clarence, 26, *36*
Carrighar, Sally, 413, 414, *415*

*Numbers in italics indicate citations in
the bibliographical reference sections
which follow each chapter.*

Casagrande, Joseph, *232*
Ceram, C. W., *119*
Chagnon, Napolean, 401–2, 413–14, *415*
Chance, Michael, *36*
Chang, Kwang-Chih, *172*
Chard, Chester S., 122–23, 128, 132,
    137–38, *139*, *172*
Childe, V. Gordon, 152, *157*
Clark, Ella E., 437–39
Clark, Graham, 112, *119*, 123, 132, 137,
    139
Clark, J. Desmond, *139*, *172*
Clark, William, 250, *259*
Cleator, P. E., *459*
Clegg, E. J., *18*
Clifton, James, 477
Cliqnet, Remi, *311*
Cohen, Yehudi, *219*
Cohen, R., *397*
Cole, Sonia, *157*
Collins, John, *219*, 355, *359*, *360*, 379
Commoner, Barry, 192, *197*
Conklin, Harold, 249, *259*
Cooley, Charles H., 314, *335*
Coon, Carleton S., *186*, *259*, *286*
Cooper, John, 340
Cottrell, Leonard, *171*
Creel, H. G., *172*

Dalton, George, *286*
D'Andrade, Roy, *459*
Darwin, Charles, 39–40
Davenport, 279, *286*
Davis, Kingsley, 314–15, *335*
Day, Michael H., *88*
De Cayeax, Andre, *53*
Deetz, James, *119*
Deevy, Edward S., Jr., 189, *198*
DeLumley, Henry, 126, *139*
de Paor, Liam, 114, *119*
DeVore, Irven, 28, *36*, *139*, 238, 239,
    244, *259*
DeVos, George, *359*
Diamond, S., *397*
Dobzhansky, T., 194–95, 196–97, *198*
Dolhinow, Phyllis, *68*, *88*, 89
Douglas, Mary, 385
Downs, James, *88*, 241–43, *259*, 356,
    358, *360*
Dozier, Edward, 334, *335*, *415*
Drucker, Philip, 243, *259*, 275, *286*
Dunn, L. C., 194–95, *198*
Dyson-Hudson, Rada and Neville, 252,
    260

488

489

SUBJECT INDEX

Andaman Islanders, 371
Animal hubandry, 145–46. *See also* Pastoralism
Animalia, 12
Anthropoids, 25–35, 478
Apaches: agriculture, 246; kinship, 329
Apes: description, 29–35; evolution of, 60–61; and humans compared, 62
Archaeology, 104–119; techniques of, 107–18; types of, 104–6
Architecture: public, 151; in urban period, 155–56. *See also* Shelter
Argonauts of the Western Pacific (Malinowski), 272
Art (paleolithic), 133–36
Artifacts: as cultural components, 204; excavation of, 110
Associations, 337–49, 481
Australopithecines, 70–75, 80, 478; and bipedalism, 91–92; tooth size, 93, 94
Avunculate, 306
Azande, 374
Aztecs: technology of, 235–36; warfare, 408

Baboons, 26–29
Bands, 392, 481
Barotse, 426–27
Barter, 277–78; and marriage, 304. *See also* Economics
Basseri, 253
Bear Festival, 430–31
Bedouin: agriculture of, 253, 254; warfare, 410
Biological engineering, 195–97, 478
Bipedalism: advantages of, 66; and hunting, 95; in mosaic evolution, 91–92
Blood: human types, 182; ritual ceremony, 429
Boloki, 283–84
Bones, 180–81
Brachiation: definition, 26; role in evolution, 63–64, 478
Brahmans, 352
Brain size: of human infants, 100; role in evolution, 92–93
Brave New World (Huxley), 195
Bukaua, 340
Bushmen, 137
Bushong, 428
Burial: archaeological sites, 109; paleolithic

Cannibalism: description, 282–83; and disease, 183; in early man, 77–78; paleolithic, 125, 129
Carbon 14 technique, 113–14
Caste, 350–55, 481
Catastrophism, 10, 48, 478
Ceboidea, 25–26

Cercopithecoidea, 26–29
Ceremonies: archaeological sites, 108–9. *See also* Rituals
Cheyenne: initiation, 340–41; leadership, 388
Chief, 386–88, 481
Chiefdoms, 393–94
Chimpanzee, 33–35
China: cultural diffusion from, 469–70; language, 456; marriage in, 304, 306; in urban era, 165
Chordates, 13
Ciexaus, 340
City state, 150
Civilization: definition, 150–51
Clans, 328–29
Classes: and caste, 350–55; Sumerian, 160; taxonomic, 16
Classification: archaeological, 110–12; kinship, 294
Clothing: paleolithic, 133; and technology, 256–58
Communication: extralinguistic, 455–56; of hunters, 99; nonlinguistic, 457–58. *See also* Language
Compadrazzo, 346
Complex (cultural), 213
Conquistadors, 105
Convergence, 47
Copper-Bronze Age, 151. *See also* Urban period
Creation, 10
Cree Indians: social groups, 344; warfare, 408
Cro-Magnon man, 86–87
Culture: and archaeological classification, 111; changes in, 461–70; components of, 204; concept of, 202–3; diffusion of, 469–74; forms of, 210–11; frequency of, 211–12; functional prerequisites for, 216–18; laws of development, 168–70; patterns of, 213; qualities of, 204–8; relativism of, 215–16; role of, in evolution, 93; study of, 221–32
Culture shock, 226
Cuna Indians: marriage customs, 305–6; ownership among, 280
Cuneiform, 153

Daflas, 368
Dance: of bees, 448; antiwitch, 395; and ethos, 214; and initiation, 340, 341; ritual, 430; warfare, 404
Darwinism, 39–40
Dating techniques, 113–16
Death, 215
Dendrochronology, 114
Diffusion, 469–74
Diseases, 182–83

Spinning, 146–47
Spirit Cave site, 143
Steinheim man, 81, 83, 85; handaxe tools, 122
States, 394–95
Stinkards, 352–54
Stone Age: Old (*see* Paleolithic period); Middle (*see* Mesolithic period); New (*see* Neolithic period)
Stratification, 115
Subkingdom, 12–13
Subphylum, 13
Sudra, 352
Suicide, 215
Sumerian culture, 159–64; architecture, 159; education, 161–62; law, 160; religion, 162–63; social classes, 160–61
Supernaturalism, 417–41; and law, 372–75; and leadership, 422–25; and magic, 419–20; and mythology, 435–41; and naturalism, 420–21; practices of, 425–30; reasons for, 421–22; and religion, 417–19; and sorcery, 432–35; and warfare, 408; and witchcraft, 431–32, 433–35
Swanscombe man, 81, 83, 85, 122
Swazi: associations, 341–42; leadership, 390–91
Sweat glands, 96–97
Sythians, 105

Taboo: against incest, 297–99; and law, 372–73
Taos Indians. *See* Pueblo Indians
Tarsiers, 24–25
Taxonomy, 11–17
Technology, 234–58
Tell Ubeidiya site, 122
Temples: Sumerian, 159; urban, 155–56
Terra Amata (France) site, 126
Territory: personal, 457–58; and social groups, 355–59
Teshiktash (Uzbeckistan) site, 129
Tiriki, 342–43
Tiv: exchange customs, 279–80; kinship lineage, 327–28; polygamy, 300
Tiwi, 308–9
Toda, 301, 302
Tools, 121–36; Abbevillean, 124; Acheulean, 124–25, 127; archaeological significance, 116–18; Aurignacoid, 132–33; blade-type, 130–33; dawn-type, 121; effect of, on tooth size, 93–94; evolutionary role, 72–73; flake-type, 117, 122, 124; handaxe tradition, 123, 124–25; Levalloi-

sian, 125, 127; Mousteroid, 127–29; neolithic, 147, 149; pebble-type, 121–23; of Sinanthropus, 78; and technology, 234
Torralba (Spain) site, 126
Traits, 212–13, 468–69
Transportation: in urban period, 152–53; and warfare, 403
Tree shrew, 20–22
Tribes, 392–93
Trobriand Islanders, 272–73
Trukese, 307
Tsimshian, 471
Tupi Namba, 282–83

Ubiad culture, 155
Ulithians: family, 317–18; horticulture, 248
Ur, 163
Urban period, 150–56
Ur-Nammu law code, 161
Uruk culture, 156
Usufruct rights, 282
Utang Na Loob, 270–71

Vaisyas, 352
Vallonet Cave (France) site, 122
Vertebrates, 13–16
Villafranchian period, 70

Wabuwabu, 271–72
Warfare, 150, 399–415; attitudes toward, 215; causes of, 412–14; consequences of, 411–12; definition of, 399–400; functions of, 341, 410–11; motivation for, 406–10; techniques of, 402–6
Warka site, 156
Washo Indians: division of labor among, 266; food gathering, 241–43, 244; social groups, 356, 358
Watanaki, 302–3
Weapons, 402–4
Weaving: neolithic, 146–47; in urban period, 153
Wheel, 152
Witchcraft, 395–96, 431–35
Writing, 153–54
Wurm Glaciation, 81, 82, 83, 86, 136

Yahgan: clothing, 257; initiation, 340
Yako, 330–31
Yanomamo, 401–2, 407, 413–14
Yir Yoront, 473–74
Yoruba, 426
Yurok, 369

Ziggurat, 155–56, 159
Zoological Philosophy (Lamarck), 38
Zulu, 342, 411
Zwai-Chemi site, 144